THE CRITICS' PRIZE PLAYS

THE
Critics' Prize Plays

INTRODUCTION BY

GEORGE JEAN NATHAN

THE WORLD PUBLISHING COMPANY

CLEVELAND AND NEW YORK

PUBLISHED BY *The World Publishing Company*

2231 West 110th Street · Cleveland 2 · Ohio

First Published November 1945

Contents

Introduction

ITS BIRTH INSPIRED by the increasing idiosyncrasies of the annual Pulitzer prize award, the New York Drama Critics' Circle began functioning in 1935. Composed of the critics for the established metropolitan newspapers and magazines, its politely unarticulated but nonetheless clearly discernible purpose was to take over from the anonymous and non-professional committee entrusted with the bestowal of the aforesaid prize the yearly stamp of active, professional, critical approval. Among the critics in these beginning days of the Circle were the following: Percy Hammond of the *Herald Tribune*, who was to be succeeded on his death by Richard Watts, Jr.; Brooks Atkinson of the *Times*; John Mason Brown of the *Post*; Burns Mantle of the *Daily News*; Robert Garland of the *World-Telegram*; Richard Lockridge of the *Sun*; Arthur Pollock of the Brooklyn *Eagle*; Joseph Wood Krutch of the *Nation*; Stark Young of the *New Republic*; Whitney Bolton of the *Morning Telegraph*; Robert Benchley of the *New Yorker*; John Gassner of *Current History*; Gilbert Gabriel of the *American*; John Anderson of the *Journal*; and your present recorder, of the *American Mercury, Vanity Fair, Esquire, Life, Scribner's*, et al.

What directly induced these critics to sponsor an award to that new American play which would seem to the majority of them to be the worthiest of its year was the Pulitzer award given ridiculously for the season of 1934–35 to the sentimental claptrap, *The Old Maid*, which was not only not an original play but a dramatization of another's novel, thus for the second time violating the Pulitzer board's own rules, and which was further and by almost general outside consent utterly worthless from any reputable critical standpoint. And all this in a season that had offered Clifford Odets' *Awake and Sing* and Lillian Hellman's *The Children's Hour*, to say nothing of Robert Sherwood's *The Petrified Forest*, Maxwell Anderson's *Valley Forge* and the like, any of them at their weakest infinitely superior to the exhibit that the Pulitzer committee had seen fit to honor.

But rumbles had preceded the storm. The critics had first begun doubtfully to scratch their heads when, in the season of 1923–24, the Pulitzer prize had been snatched from George Kelly's *The*

Show-Off by Professor Brander Matthews out of the hands of the duly constituted committee of award and had been arbitrarily given by him to his co-member of the Columbia University faculty, Hatcher Hughes, for *Hell-Bent fer Heaven*. They had increased the scratching when, in the succeeding year, the Pulitzer masterminds airily waved aside such plays as *What Price Glory?* and *Desire Under The Elms* and knighted instead something like Sidney Howard's negligible *They Knew What They Wanted*. They had scratched deeper still when subsequently O'Neill's *The Great God Brown* was passed up in favor of the woefully inferior *Craig's Wife*, by George Kelly. They had scratched half their hair out when, in the very next year, the Pulitzer people closed their eyes to plays like *Chicago*, *Broadway* and *Saturday's Children* and pinned their prize on Paul Green's *In Abraham's Bosom*. And when Susan Glaspell's *Alison's House* later on received the award, what was left of the critics' hair was all too little to be finally torn out upon the before-noted award to the Akins-Wharton *The Old Maid*.

It was time to do something.

And the critics did it.

And this is how Eugene O'Neill, who previously had received three of the Pulitzer prizes, viewed their action. "It is a terrible, harrowing experience," O'Neill wrote to the Circle, "for a playwright to be forced to praise critics for anything. There is something morbid and abnormal about it, something destructive to the noble tradition of correct conduct for dramatists. Nevertheless, conscience drives me to reiterate that I think the Critics' Circle award a damned fine idea. Prizes in themselves are neither good nor bad. They have no meaning except that which derives from the recognized authority of the awarders of the prize as judges of true merit. The Critics' Circle possesses that recognized authority, and so I am sure that its awards will deservedly have a significant and growing effect in helping to shape public opinion and in directing the future course of our drama. It is my hope that these yearly awards will direct the attention of the public to the fact that our theatre is now adult and fully capable of standing adult comparison with that of any country in the world today; that it is no longer purely a showshop and an amusement racket, but has grown to be a place where Art may exist."

The Circle's initial award, for the season of 1935–36, was to Maxwell Anderson's *Winterset*, with but three dissenting votes going to Robert Sherwood's *Idiot's Delight*. Dedicating the award, the present recorder, on the ceremonial program over the radio, spoke in part as follows: "There are, as you know, certain other rewards to each year's plays. But for some time now it has seemed to the Circle that they have lost all significance, and what is more important, all probity. They have been so hamstrung by rules and regulations, by by-laws and by-by-laws, that they have come to represent exactly nothing. Whatever anyone may think of the awards made by the Drama Critics' Circle, those awards will at least be forthright and unhedging. The *best* American play of the year: that is and will be the Circle's one and only question. There are and will be no further qualifications; there is and will be no ritualistic hocus-pocus. At least you will know a body of drama critics' undismayed and uncorrupted decision, whether it meets with your approval or whether it does not."

Maxwell Anderson, who previous to the Circle's inauguration had also been the recipient of a Pulitzer prize, accepted the Circle's award with these words:

"Except for the theatre critics of New York no body of men in the country is qualified by training, education and professional experience to render judgment on a season's plays. I am, I assure you seriously, much more interested in that aspect of the ceremony than the fact that the first award goes to *Winterset*. Anybody with the requisite cash can offer a prize for excellence in the theatre, but in order to encourage excellence it is necessary to know it when it appears, and a knowledge of what is excellent is more difficult to obtain than cash. I have never been greatly impressed with the Pulitzer prize for the best play of the year because the final authority for its presentation rests with a committee which is aware only dimly and at second-hand of most of what occurs in the theatres of Broadway. It follows that in so far as the Pulitzer prize has had any influence on our theatre it has been a confusing and misleading influence, an encouragement to mediocrity, a gift passed out to a lucky winner by authorities who possess in this field neither standards nor information. But neither ignorance nor lack of standards can be charged against the Critics' Circle. The critics know very definitely what they are for and why they are for it, and whatever their faults of judgment may be, they *earn* their knowledge of the plays offered during any year by an undeviating attention to what can be seen and heard from the aisle seats of Manhattan playhouses, an attention which amounts on some occasions to sheer martyrdom. I have, in my time, contributed to that martyrdom, and learned by stinging comments in the next day's papers that the boys knew what they were about. I have had both praise and blame in stimulating quantities, and have learned—perhaps unequally—from both."

The Circle's plaque for the season of 1936–37 was given to Mr. Anderson for his *High Tor,* with three dissenting votes going to Paul Green's *Johnny Johnson* and one, that of the present recorder, to Robert Turney's *Daughters of Atreus.* In the season of 1937–38, John Steinbeck's *Of Mice and Men* was honored, with Thornton Wilder's *Our Town* lagging behind in the voting. The following season, 1938–39, brought no award, since the Circle found it could come to no majority decision in the consideration of Lillian Hellman's *The Little Foxes,* Clifford Odets' *Rocket To The Moon,* Robert Sherwood's *Abe Lincoln In Illinois* and William Saroyan's *My Heart's In the Highlands,* the last-named, incidentally, being the choice of the present recorder.

In the season of 1939–40, however, the award again emerged and was given to Saroyan's *The Time Of Your Life,* with Robert Sherwood's *There Shall Be No Night* and Maxwell Anderson's *Key Largo* trailing in the distance. (As if finally taking to heart the Circle's criticism of its awards, the Pulitzer committee followed the Circle's decision and also gave its prize to the Saroyan play. More, it has since followed the Circle in the Circle's decision on two different occasions to make no award.)

Lillian Hellman's *Watch On The Rhine* drew the Circle's prize for the 1940–41 season, with Saroyan's *The Beautiful People* the closest contender—the present recorder's choice, and with Richard Wright's *Native Son* drawing a single vote. The following year, 1941–42, again saw no award, the Circle being unable to attain a majority vote and announcing its withholding of an award with these words: "While the Circle was organized to encourage native playwrights and honor native dramatists, it has also the third obligation of maintaining the standards of the theatre and of dramatic criticism, and it feels it would cause a serious confusion of standards if it merely made a selection from a group of plays none of which seems up to the standards of the previous awards."

But again in the succeeding season, 1942–43, the award was bestowed on Sidney Kingsley's *The Patriots* "for its dignity of material, its thoughtful projection of a great American theme, its vigorous approach to the characters portrayed, and, in spite of certain limitations, its driving final effect on the stage." The losing candidate was Thornton Wilder's *The Skin Of Our Teeth,* which got the Pulitzer prize, just as such defeated candidates in previous years as *Idiot's Delight, Our Town, Abe Lincoln In Illinois* and *There Shall Be No Night* got it, almost in the nature of a consolation prize.

The war began to alter the composition of the Circle in the season of 1942–43. A number of the critics entered the armed services or took up duties in various governmental war branches, and their substitutes proceeded forthwith to occupy their chairs at the Circle's board. In the season of 1943–44, several of the older critics, among them Stark Young and the present recorder, resigned until a future day; and Joseph Wood Krutch privileged himself a sabbatical year in which to work on a life of Samuel Johnson. The reconstituted Circle, including in its membership Lewis Nichols as temporary successor to Brooks Atkinson serving as a war correspondent in China, John Chapman as successor to the retired Burns Mantle, Ward Morehouse in the shoes of Richard Lockridge who had joined the Navy, Howard Barnes as permanent successor to Richard Watts, Jr., who was with the Office of War Information, and Burton Rascoe quickly in and out as temporary occupant of the chair of John Mason Brown, also in the Navy, decided to make no award for the year after vainly arguing the merits of four or five plays, among them Lillian Hellman's *The Searching Wind*, John van Druten's *The Voice Of The Turtle*, James Gow's and Arnaud d'Usseau's *Tomorrow The World* and Edward Chodorov's *Decision*.

For the record, among the critics aside from those already named who have figured in the Circle's ballotings since its inception have been Rosamund Gilder, successor to Edith Isaacs of *Theatre Arts*, Wilella Waldorf who succeeded John Mason Brown on the *Post*, Louis Kronenberger of *PM* and *Time*, Wolcott Gibbs who succeeded Robert Benchley on the *New Yorker*, and George Freedley who followed Whitney Bolton on the *Morning Telegraph*.

II. THE PLAYS

Anderson's *Winterset* was produced by Guthrie McClintic in the Martin Beck Theatre on September 25, 1935, and ran for 179 performances, later returning for an additional 16. Its cast was headed by Richard Bennett, Burgess Meredith and the young Mexican actress, Margo. Serving as the playwright's inspiration was the celebrated case of the State of Massachusetts versus Sacco and Vanzetti. In poetic paraphrase, he tells the story of the son of one such alleged anarchist and his desperate search for evidence that will testify to his father's innocence. The play, its author stated, "is largely in verse and treats a contemporary tragic theme, which makes it more of an experiment than I could wish, for the great masters themselves never tried to make tragic poetry out of the stuff of their own times. To do so is to attempt to establish a new convention, one that may prove impossible of acceptance but to which I was driven by the lively historical sense of our day—a knowledge of period, costume and manners which almost shuts off the writer on historical themes from contemporary comment. Whether or not I have solved the problem in *Winterset* is probably of little moment. But it must be solved if we are to have a great theatre in America. Our theatre has not yet produced anything worthy to endure—and endurance, though it may be a fallible test, is the only test of excellence."

As to the last observation, Mr. Anderson's wholesale pessimism is open to some question. As to his earlier meditations, one may grant him a difficult task at least courageously ventured and, if not altogether satisfactorily achieved, one which at any rate amounts in considerable part to an eloquent and impressive document of hate and defiance, and to a play which in the aggregate was a credit to the Circle's critical judgment.

Mr. Anderson's *High Tor*, which gained him the Circle's accolade a second time, was produced by the same Mr. McClintic in the same Martin Beck Theatre on January 9, 1937, and ran for 171 performances. Its cast was headed, again, by Burgess Meredith and by the imported English actress, Peggy Ashcroft. On this occasion the playwright exercised himself in romantic fantasy and, unusual for him, in comedy both high and low. Contrasting the realistic present day with the legendary romantic past, he succeeded in confecting an exhibit of uneven quality, albeit one that at stray moments managed a lightly pleasant effect. Far beneath the merit of *Winterset* and given at times to a heavily postured colloquialism —and at still other times to a dubious philosophizing—the play nevertheless somehow maneuvered itself into the affections of its audiences, or at least that copious portion of them whose sentimental reaction was of a piece with that of those critics who had vouchsafed it the year's award.

John Steinbeck's *Of Mice and Men* was produced by Sam H. Harris in the Music Box on November 23, 1937, and ran for 207 performances. Its cast contained Wallace Ford, Broderick Crawford, Sam Byrd, John F. Hamilton, Claire Luce, Will Geer and Thomas Findlay, among others. It marked its author's first appearance as a playwright and presented him to a surprised and gratified audience as a dramatist of exceptional character penetration, vibrating dialogue, and general dramaturgical vitality. Few first plays by American authors had produced the impression that this play did; it became the talk of the town overnight. And it was unquestionably its uncommon merit that operated to make doubly disappointing Steinbeck's subsequent effort, *The Moon Is Down*, which, as previously implied, was in its season abruptly dismissed by the Critics' Circle.

William Saroyan's *The Time Of Your Life* was produced by Eddie Dowling in association with the Theatre Guild in the Booth Theatre on October 25, 1939, and ran for 185 performances. Its cast was headed by Mr. Dowling, Julie Haydon, Edward Andrews, Celeste Holm and Gene Kelly. Originally called *The Light Fantastic*, the play proved to be a genuinely fascinating contribution to American drama and, after the delicately beautiful *My Heart's In The Highlands*, established its author as the freshest imagination that had come into our theatre in many years. The theme of the play, which Saroyan originally intended to have spoken before the rise of the curtain, a plan that was properly dismissed as redundant, he stated so: "In the time of your life, live—so that in that good time there shall be no ugliness or death for yourself or for any life your life touches. Seek goodness everywhere and where it is found bring it out of its hiding place and let it be free and unashamed. Place in matter and in flesh the least of the values, for these are the things that hold death and must pass away. . . . In the time of your life, live—so that in that wondrous time you shall not add to the misery and sorrow of the world, but shall smile to the infinite delight and mystery of it."

Lillian Hellman's *Watch On The Rhine* was produced by Herman Shumlin in the Martin Beck Theatre on April 1, 1941, and ran for 378 performances. Its cast was headed by Paul Lukas, George Coulouris, Mady Christians and Lucile Watson. While greatly superior to the other anti-Nazi dramas that had preceded it and while here and there not without the melodramatic drive at which its author is an apt hand, the play seemed to the dissenting critics to be less the plumbing of ideological concepts that its author hoped and intended than a skilful exercise in pure blood and thunder, the latter concealed from the superficial eye in wily dramaturgical bandages and mufflers. But the time was theatrically ripe for its alarms and the majority read stern critical virtues into it where the minority saw only popular and contemporary prehensile qualities. The majority, however, ruled in the case of the public as it did in the case of the Critics' Circle, which gave the play its award by 12 votes to 6 for the next contender, the aforementioned Saroyan's *The Beautiful People*.

Sidney Kingsley's *The Patriots* was produced by the Playwrights' Company in association with Rowland Stebbins in the National Theatre on January 29, 1943, and ran for 157 performances. Its cast was headed by Raymond Edward Johnson as Jefferson, Cecil Humphreys as Washington, and House Jameson as Hamilton. Originally titled *Thomas Jefferson* and for a time tempted to be called *Three Gentlemen Of America*, the drama contrasts the ideas and philosophies of Jefferson and Hamilton in the days of the Democracy's dawn, with the aging Washington hovering over Jefferson as a guardian angel. The Circle's citation accompanying its intelligent award was appropriately phrased, since the play's thoughtful projection of a noble American theme, its vigorous approach to the historical characters and, for all its occasional defects, its final driving stage effect are hardly debatable.

Upon the play's first presentation I observed, as I observe again, that with negligible rant, with gratifying humor, and with a passion brewed from cool intelligence it never descends to mere patriotic strychnine, seldom falters on its dignified course and always, except for its rather cinema-like prologue and some exaggeration in the instance of Hamilton, maintains its inner probity. More, although the play does not forego all the august pokerism which is so generally the portion of historical characters on the stage, it at least gestures very satisfactorily in that direction, which is a credit to its author's extensive research and sound reflective sense. In addition to the Critics' Circle award, the play received the season's prize of the Newspaper Guild and of the Theatre Club, Inc.

GEORGE JEAN NATHAN

Winterset

BY MAXWELL ANDERSON

NOTE

CHARACTERS

Winterset was produced by Guthrie McClintic and opened at
the Martin Beck Theatre in New York on September 25, 1935,
with the following cast of characters:

Trock Estrella	Eduardo Ciannelli
Shadow	Harold Johnsrud
Lucio	Morton L. Stevens
Piny	Fernanda Eliscu
Miriamne	Margo
Garth	Theodore Hecht
Esdras	Anatole Winogradoff
First Girl	Eva Langbord
Second Girl	Ruth Hammond
Hobo	John Philliber
Judge Gaunt	Richard Bennett
Carr	Billy Quinn
Mio	Burgess Meredith
Sailor	St. John Terrell
Radical	Abner Biberman
Policeman	Anthony Blair
Sergeant	Harold Martin
Two Young Men in Serge	Stanley Gould, Walter Holbrook
Two Street Urchins	

Winterset

ACT ONE

SCENE I

SCENE: *The scene is the bank of a river under a bridgehead. A gigantic span starts from the rear of the stage and appears to lift over the heads of the audience and out to the left. At the right rear is a wall of solid supporting masonry. To the left an apartment building abuts against the bridge and forms the left wall of the stage with a dark basement window and a door in the brick wall. To the right, and in the foreground, an outcropping of original rock makes a barricade behind which one may enter through a cleft. To the rear, against the masonry, two sheds have been built by waifs and strays for shelter. The river bank, in the foreground, is black rock worn smooth by years of trampling. There is room for exit and entrance to the left around the apartment house, also around the rock to the right. A single street lamp is seen at the left—and a glimmer of apartment lights in the background beyond. It is an early, dark December morning.*

TWO YOUNG MEN IN SERGE *lean against the masonry, matching bills.* TROCK ESTRELLA *and* SHADOW *come in from the left.*

TROCK

Go back and watch the car.
> (*The* TWO YOUNG MEN *go out.*
> TROCK *walks to the corner and
> looks toward the city.*)
You roost of punks and gulls! Sleep,
   sleep it off,
whatever you had last night, get down
   in warm,
one big ham-fat against another—sleep,
cling, sleep and rot! Rot out your pasty
   guts
with diddling, you had no brain to begin. If you had
there'd be no need for us to sleep on
   iron
who had too much brains for you.

SHADOW

Now look, Trock, look,
what would the warden say to talk like
   that?

TROCK

May they die as I die!
By God, what life they've left me
they shall keep me well! I'll have that
   out of them—
these pismires that walk like men!

SHADOW

Because, look, chief,
it's all against science and penology
for you to get out and begin to cuss
   that way
before your prison vittles are out of
   you. Hell,
you're supposed to leave the pen full
   of high thought,
kind of noble-like, loving toward all
   mankind,
ready to kiss their feet—or whatever
   parts
they stick out toward you. Look at me!

19

TROCK

I see you.
And even you may not live as long as
you think
You think too many things are funny.
Well, laugh.
But it's not so funny.

SHADOW

Come on, Trock, you know me.
Anything you say goes, but give me
leave
to kid a little.

TROCK

Then laugh at somebody else!
It's a lot safer! They've soaked me once
too often
in that vat of poisoned hell they keep
up-state
to soak men in, and I'm rotten inside,
I'm all
one liquid puke inside where I had
lungs
once, like yourself! And now they want
to get me
and stir me in again—and that'd kill
me—
and that's fine for them. But before
that happens to me
a lot of these healthy boys'll know
what it's like
when you try to breathe and have no
place to put air—
they'll learn it from me!

SHADOW

They've got nothing on you, chief.

TROCK

I don't know yet. That's what I'm here
to find out.
If they've got what they might have
it's not a year this time—
no, nor ten. It's screwed down under a
lid.—
I can die quick enough, without help.

SHADOW

You're the skinny kind
that lives forever.

TROCK

He gave me a half a year,
the doc at the gate.

SHADOW

Jesus.

TROCK

Six months I get
and the rest's dirt, six feet.
(LUCIA, *the street-piano man,
comes in right from behind the
rock and goes to the shed
where he keeps his piano.*
PINY, *the apple-woman, follows and stands in the entrance.* LUCIA *speaks to* ES-
TRELLA, *who still stands facing*
SHADOW.)

LUCIA

Morning.
(TROCK *and* SHADOW *go out round
the apartment house without
speaking.*)

PINY

Now what would you call them?

LUCIA

Maybe someting da river washed up.

PINY

Nothing ever washed him—that black
one.

LUCIA

Maybe not, maybe so. More like his pa
and ma raise-a heem in da cellar.
(*He wheels out the piano.*)

PINY

He certainly gave me a turn.
(*She lays a hand on the rock.*)

LUCIA

You don' live-a right, ol' gal. Take
heem easy. Look on da bright-a side.
Never say-a die. Me, every day in
every way I getta be da regular
heller.
(*He starts out.*)

SCENE II

SCENE: *A cellar apartment under the apartment building, floored with cement and roofed with huge boa constrictor pipes that run slantwise from left to right, dwarfing the room. An outside door opens to the left and a door at the right rear leads to the interior of the place. A low squat window to the left. A table at the rear and a few chairs and books make up the furniture.* GARTH, *son of* ESDRAS, *sits alone, holding a violin upside down to inspect a crack at its base. He lays the bow on the floor and runs his fingers over the joint.* MIRIAMNE *enters from the rear, a girl of fifteen.* GARTH *looks up, then down again.*

MIRIAMNE

Garth—

GARTH

The glue lets go. It's the steam, I guess.
It splits the hair on your head.

MIRIAMNE

It can't be mended?

GARTH

I can't mend it.
No doubt there are fellows somewhere
who'd mend it for a dollar—and glad to
    do it.
That is if I had a dollar.—Got a dollar?
No, I thought not.

MIRIAMNE

Garth, you've sat at home here
three days now. You haven't gone out
    at all.
Something frightens you.

GARTH

Yes?

MIRIAMNE

And father's frightened.
He reads without knowing where.
When a shadow falls
across the page he waits for a blow to
    follow
after the shadow. Then in a little while
he puts his book down softly and goes
    out
to see who passed.

GARTH

A bill collector, maybe.
We haven't paid the rent.

MIRIAMNE

No.

GARTH

You're a bright girl, sis.—
You see too much. You run along and
    cook.
Why don't you go to school?

MIRIAMNE

I don't like school.
They whisper behind my back.

GARTH

Yes? About what?

MIRIAMNE

What did the lawyer mean
that wrote to you?

GARTH

    (Rising)
What lawyer?

MIRIAMNE

I found a letter
on the floor of your room. He said,
"Don't get me wrong,
but stay in out of the rain the next few
    days,
just for instance."

GARTH

I thought I burned that letter.

MIRIAMNE

Afterward you did. And then what was
printed
about the Estrella gang—you hid it
from me,
you and father. What is it—about this
murder—?

GARTH

Will you shut up, you fool!

MIRIAMNE

But if you know
why don't you tell them, Garth?
If it's true—what they say—
you knew all the time Romagna wasn't
guilty,
and could have said so—

GARTH

Everybody knew
Romagna wasn't guilty! But they
weren't listening
to evidence in his favor. They didn't
want it.
They don't want it now.

MIRIAMNE

But was that why
they never called on you?—

GARTH

So far as I know
they never'd heard of me—and I can
assure you
I knew nothing about it—

MIRIAMNE

But something's wrong—
and it worries father—

GARTH

What could be wrong?

MIRIAMNE

I don't know.
(A pause.)

GARTH

And I don't know. You're a good kid,
Miriamne,
but you see too many movies. I wasn't
mixed up
in any murder, and I don't mean to be.
If I had a dollar to get my fiddle fixed
and another to hire a hall, by God I'd
fiddle
some of the prodigies back into Sunday
School
where they belong, but I won't get
either, and so
I sit here and bite my nails—but if you
hoped
I had some criminal romantic past
you'll have to look again!

MIRIAMNE

Oh, Garth, forgive me—
But I want you to be so far above such
things
nothing could frighten you. When you
seem to shrink
and be afraid, and you're the brother I
love,
I want to run there and cry, if there's
any question
they care to ask, you'll be quick and
glad to answer,
for there's nothing to conceal!

GARTH

And that's all true—

MIRIAMNE

But then I remember—
how you dim the lights—
and we go early to bed—and speak in
whispers—
and I could think there's a death somewhere behind us—
an evil death—

GARTH

(Hearing a step)
Now for God's sake, be quiet!
(ESDRAS, an old rabbi with a
kindly face, enters from the
outside. He is hurried and
troubled.)

ESDRAS

I wish to speak alone with someone here
if I may have this room. Miriamne—

MIRIAMNE

(*Turning to go*)
Yes, father.
(*The outer door is suddenly
    thrown open.* TROCK *appears.*)

TROCK

(*After a pause*)
You'll excuse me for not knocking.
(SHADOW *follows* TROCK *in.*)
Sometimes it's best to come in quiet.
    Sometimes
it's a good way to go out. Garth's
    home, I see.
He might not have been here if I made
    a point
of knocking at doors.

GARTH

How are you, Trock?

TROCK

I guess
you can see how I am.
(*To* MIRIAMNE)
Stay here. Stay where you are.
We'd like to make your acquaintance.
—If you want the facts
I'm no better than usual, thanks. Not
    enough sun,
my physician tells me. Too much close
    confinement.
A lack of exercise and an overplus
of beans in the diet. You've done well,
    no doubt?

GARTH

I don't know what makes you think so.

TROCK

Who's the family?

GARTH

My father and my sister.

TROCK

Happy to meet you.
Step inside a minute. The boy and I
have something to talk about.

ESDRAS

No, no—he's said nothing—
nothing, sir, nothing!

TROCK

When I say go out, you go—

ESDRAS

(*Pointing to the door*)
Miriamne—

GARTH

Go on out, both of you!

ESDRAS

Oh, sir—I'm old—
old and unhappy—

GARTH

Go on!
(MIRIAMNE *and* ESDRAS *go inside.*)

TROCK

And if you listen
I'll riddle that door!
(SHADOW *shuts the door behind
    them and stands against it.*)
I just got out, you see,
and I pay my first call on you.

GARTH

Maybe you think
I'm not in the same jam you are.

TROCK

That's what I do think.
Who started looking this up?

GARTH

I wish I knew,
and I wish he was in hell! Some
    damned professor
with nothing else to do. If you saw his
    stuff
you know as much as I do.

TROCK

It wasn't you
turning state's evidence?

GARTH

Hell, Trock, use your brain!
The case was closed. They burned
Romagna for it
and that finished it. Why should I
look for trouble
and maybe get burned myself?

TROCK

Boy, I don't know,
but I just thought I'd find out.

GARTH

I'm going straight, Trock.
I can play this thing, and I'm trying
to make a living.
I haven't talked and nobody's talked
to me.
Christ—it's the last thing I'd want!

TROCK

Your old man knows.

GARTH

That's where I got the money that last
time
when you needed it. He had a little
saved up,
but I had to tell him to get it. He's as
safe
as Shadow there.

TROCK

(*Looking at* SHADOW)
There could be people safer
than that son-of-a-bitch.

SHADOW

Who?

TROCK

You'd be safer dead
along with some other gorillas.

SHADOW

It's beginning to look
as if you'd feel safer with everybody
dead,
the whole god-damn world.

TROCK

I would. These Jesus-bitten
professors! Looking up their half-ass
cases!
We've got enough without that.

GARTH

There's no evidence
to reopen the thing.

TROCK

And suppose they called on you
and asked you to testify?

GARTH

Why then I'd tell 'em
that all I know is what I read in the
papers.
And I'd stick to that.

TROCK

How much does your sister know?

GARTH

I'm honest with you, Trock. She read
my name
in the professor's pamphlet, and she
was scared
the way anybody would be. She got
nothing
from me, and anyway she'd go to the
chair
herself before she'd send me there.

TROCK

Like hell.

GARTH

Besides, who wants to go to trial again
except the radicals?—You and I won't
spill
and unless we did there's nothing to
take to court
as far as I know. Let the radicals go on
howling

about getting a dirty deal. They always
howl
and nobody gives a damn. This professor's red—
everybody knows it.

TROCK

You're forgetting the judge.
Where's the damn judge?

GARTH

What judge?

TROCK

Read the morning papers.
It says Judge Gaunt's gone off his nut.
He's got
that damn trial on his mind, and been
going round
proving to everybody he was right all
the time
and the radicals were guilty—stopping
people
in the street to prove it—and now he's
nuts entirely
and nobody knows where he is.

GARTH

Why don't they know?

TROCK

Because he's on the loose somewhere!
They've got
the police of three cities looking for
him.

GARTH

Judge Gaunt?

TROCK

Yes. Judge Gaunt.

SHADOW

Why should that worry you?
He's crazy, ain't he? And even if he
wasn't
he's arguing on your side. You're jittery,
chief.
God, all the judges are looney. You've
got the jitters,

and you'll damn well give yourself
away some time
peeing yourself in public.
    (TROCK *half turns toward* SHADOW
        in anger.)
Don't jump the gun now,
I've got pockets in my clothes, too.
    (*His hand is in his coat pocket.*)

TROCK

All right. Take it easy.
    (*He takes his hand from his
        pocket, and* SHADOW *does the
        same*.)
    (*To* GARTH)
Maybe you're lying to me and maybe
you're not.
Stay at home a few days.

GARTH

Sure thing. Why not?

TROCK

And when I say stay home I mean stay
home.
If I have to go looking for you you'll
stay a long time
wherever I find you.
    (*To* SHADOW)
Come on. We'll get out of here.
    (*To* GARTH)
Be seeing you.
    (SHADOW *and* TROCK *go out. After
        a pause* GARTH *walks over to
        his chair and picks up the vio-
        lin. Then he puts it down and
        goes to the inside door, which
        he opens*.)

GARTH

He's gone.
    (MIRIAMNE *enters*, ESDRAS *behind
        her*.)

MIRIAMNE

    (*Going up to* GARTH)
Let's not stay here.
    (*She puts her hands on his arms*.)
I thought he'd come for something—
horrible.
Is he coming back?

GARTH

I don't know.

MIRIAMNE

Who is he, Garth?

GARTH

He'd kill me if I told you who he is,
that is, if he knew.

MIRIAMNE

Then don't say it—

GARTH

Yes, and I'll say it! I was with a gang
one time
that robbed a pay roll. I saw a murder
done,
and Trock Estrella did it. If that got
out
I'd go to the chair and so would he—
that's why
he was here today—

MIRIAMNE

But that's not true—

ESDRAS

He says it
to frighten you, child.

GARTH

Oh, no I don't! I say it
because I've held it in too long! I'm
damned
if I sit here forever, and look at the
door,
waiting for Trock with his sub-machine
gun, waiting
for police with a warrant!—I say I'm
damned, and I am,
no matter what I do! These piddling
scales
on a violin—first position, third, fifth,
arpeggios in E—and what I'm thinking
is Romagna dead for the murder—dead
while I sat here
dying inside—dead for the thing Trock
did
while I looked on—and I could have
saved him, yes—

but I sat here and let him die instead
of me
because I wanted to live! Well, it's no
life,
and it doesn't matter who I tell, because
I mean to get it over!

MIRIAMNE

Garth, it's not true!

GARTH

I'd take some scum down with me if I
died—
that'd be one good deed—

ESDRAS

Son, son, you're mad—
someone will hear—

GARTH

Then let them hear! I've lived
with ghosts too long, and lied too long.
  God damn you
if you keep me from the truth!—
    (He turns away.)
Oh, God damn the world!
I don't want to die!
    (He throws himself down.)

ESDRAS

I should have known.
I thought you hard and sullen,
Garth, my son. And you were a child,
  and hurt
with a wound that might be healed.
—All men have crimes,
and most of them are hidden, and
  many are heavy
as yours must be to you.
    (GARTH sobs.)
They walk the streets
to buy and sell, but a spreading crim-
son stain
tinges the inner vestments, touches
flesh,
and burns the quick. You're not alone.

GARTH

I'm alone
in this.

ESDRAS

Yes, if you hold with the world that only
those who die suddenly should be revenged.
But those whose hearts are cancered, drop by drop
in small ways, little by little, till they've borne
all they can bear, and die—these deaths will go
unpunished now as always. When we're young
we have faith in what is seen, but when we're old
we know that what is seen is traced in air
and built on water. There's no guilt under heaven,
just as there's no heaven, till men believe it—
no earth, till men have seen it, and have a word
to say this is the earth.

GARTH

Well, I say there's an earth,
and I say I'm guilty on it, guilty as hell.

ESDRAS

Yet till it's known you bear no guilt at all—
unless you wish. The days go by like film,
like a long written scroll, a figured veil
unrolling out of darkness into fire
and utterly consumed. And on this veil,
running in sounds and symbols of men's minds
reflected back, - life flickers and is shadow
going toward flame. Only what men can see
exists in that shadow. Why must you rise and cry out:
That was I, there in the ravelled tapestry,
there, in that pistol flash, when the man was killed.
I was there, and was one, and am bloodstained!
Let the wind

and fire take that hour to ashes out of time
and out of mind! This thing that men call justice,
this blind snake that strikes men down in the dark,
mindless with fury, keep your hand back from it,
pass by in silence—let it be forgotten, forgotten!—
Oh, my son, my son—have pity!

MIRIAMNE

But if it was true
and someone died—then it was more than shadow—
and it doesn't blow away—

GARTH

Well, it was true.

ESDRAS

Say it if you must. If you have heart to die,
say it, and let them take what's left—there was little
to keep, even before—

GARTH

Oh, I'm a coward—
I always was. I'll be quiet and live. I'll live
even if I have to crawl. I know.
(*He gets up and goes into the inner room.*)

MIRIAMNE

Is it better
to tell a lie and live?

ESDRAS

Yes, child. It's better.

MIRIAMNE

But if I had to do it—
I think I'd die.

ESDRAS

Yes, child. Because you're young.

<table>
<tr><td>

MIRIAMNE

Is that the only reason?
</td><td>

ESDRAS

The only reason.
</td></tr>
</table>

SCENE III

SCENE: *Under the bridge, evening of the same day. When the curtain rises* MIRIAMNE *is sitting alone on the ledge at the rear of the apartment house. A spray of light falls on her from a street lamp above. She shivers a little in her thin coat, but sits still as if heedless of the weather. Through the rocks on the other side a* TRAMP *comes down to the river bank, hunting a place to sleep. He goes softly to the apple-woman's hut and looks in, then turns away, evidently not daring to preëmpt it. He looks at* MIRIAMNE *doubtfully. The door of the street-piano man is shut. The vagabond passes it and picks carefully among some rags and shavings to the right.* MIRIAMNE *looks up and sees him but makes no sign. She looks down again, and the man curls himself up in a makeshift bed in the corner, pulling a piece of sacking over his shoulders.* TWO GIRLS *come in from round the apartment house.*

1ST GIRL

Honest, I never heard of anything so romantic. Because you never liked him.

2ND GIRL

I certainly never did.

1ST GIRL

You've got to tell me how it happened. You've got to.

2ND GIRL

I couldn't. As long as I live I couldn't. Honest, it was terrible. It was terrible.

1ST GIRL

What was so terrible?

2ND GIRL

The way it happened.

1ST GIRL

Oh, please—not to a soul, never.

2ND GIRL

Well, you know how I hated him because he had such a big mouth. So he reached over and grabbed me, and I began all falling to pieces inside, the way you do—and I said, "Oh, no you don't mister," and started screaming and kicked a hole through the windshield and lost a shoe, and he let go and was cursing and growling because he borrowed the car and didn't have money to pay for the windshield, and he started to cry, and I got so sorry for him I let him, and now he wants to marry me.

1ST GIRL

Honest, I never heard of anything so romantic!

(*She sees the sleeping* TRAMP.)

My God, what you won't see!

(*They give the* TRAMP *a wide berth, and go out right. The* TRAMP *sits up looking about him.* JUDGE GAUNT, *an elderly, quiet man, well dressed but in clothes that have seen some weather, comes in uncertainly from the left. He holds a small clipping in his hand and goes up to the Hobo.*)

GAUNT

(*Tentatively*)

Your pardon, sir. Your pardon, but perhaps you can tell me the name of this street.

HOBO

Huh?

GAUNT

The name of this street?

HOBO

This ain't no street.

GAUNT

There, where the street lamps are.

HOBO

That's the alley.

GAUNT

Thank you. It has a name, no doubt?

HOBO

That's the alley.

GAUNT

I see. I won't trouble you. You wonder why I ask, I daresay.—I'm a stranger.— Why do you look at me?
(*He steps back.*)
I—I'm not the man you think. You've mistaken me, sir.

HOBO

Huh?

JUDGE

Perhaps misled by a resemblance. But you're mistaken—I had an errand in this city. It's only by accident that I'm here—

HOBO

(*Muttering*)
You go to hell.

JUDGE

(*Going nearer to him, bending over him*)
Yet why should I deceive you? Before God, I held the proofs in my hands. I hold them still. I tell you the defense was cunning beyond belief, and un-scrupulous in its use of propaganda— they gagged at nothing—not even—
(*He rises.*)
No, no—I'm sorry—this will hardly in-

terest you. I'm sorry. I have an errand.
(*He looks toward the street.* ES-DRAS *enters from the basement and goes to* MIRIAMNE. *The* JUDGE *steps back into the shadows.*)

ESDRAS

Come in, my daughter. You'll be cold here.

MIRIAMNE

After a while.

ESDRAS

You'll be cold. There's a storm coming.

MIRIAMNE

I didn't want him to see me crying. That was all.

ESDRAS

I know.

MIRIAMNE

I'll come soon.
(ESDRAS *turns reluctantly and goes out the way he came.* MIRI-AMNE *rises to go in, pausing to dry her eyes.* MIO *and* CARR, *road boys of seventeen or so, come round the apartment house. The* JUDGE *has disap-peared.*)

CARR

Thought you said you were never com-ing east again.

MIO

Yeah, but—I heard something changed my mind.

CARR

Same old business?

MIO

Yes. Just as soon not talk about it.

CARR

Where did you go from Portland?

MIO

Fishing—I went fishing. God's truth.

CARR

Right after I left?

MIO

Fell in with a fisherman's family on the coast and went after the beautiful mackerel fish that swim in the beautiful sea. Family of Greeks—Aristides Marinos was his lovely name. He sang while he fished. Made the pea-green Pacific ring with his bastard Greek chanties. Then I went to Hollywood High School for a while.

CARR

I'll bet that's a seat of learning.

MIO

It's the hind end of all wisdom. They kicked me out after a time.

CARR

For cause?

MIO

Because I had no permanent address, you see. That means nobody's paying school taxes for you, so out you go.
(*To* MIRIAMNE)
What's the matter, kid?

MIRIAMNE

Nothing.
(*She looks up at him, and they pause for a moment.*)
Nothing.

MIO

I'm sorry.

MIRIAMNE

It's all right.
(*She withdraws her eyes from his and goes out past him. He turns and looks after her.*)

CARR

Control your chivalry.

MIO

A pretty kid.

CARR

A baby.

MIO

Wait for me.

CARR

Be a long wait?
(MIO *steps swifty out after* MIRIAMNE, *then returns.*)
Yeah?

MIO

She's gone.

CARR

Think of that.

MIO

No, but I mean—vanished. Presto—into nothing—prodigioso.

CARR

Damn good thing, if you ask me. The homely ones are bad enough, but the lookers are fatal.

MIO

You exaggerate, Carr.

CARR

I doubt it.

MIO

Well, let her go. This river bank's loaded with typhus rats, too. Might as well die one death as another.

CARR

They say chronic alcoholism is nice but expensive. You can always starve to death.

MIO

ns more likely.
(*Lowering his voice*)
how, I found Professor Hobhouse's
ussion of the Romagna case. I think
has something. It occurred to me I
ght follow it up by doing a little
uthing on my own account.

CARR

es?

MIO

I have done a little. And it leads me to
somewhere in that tenement house that
backs up against the bridge. That's how
I happen to be here.

CARR

They'll never let you get anywhere
with it, Mio. I told you that before.

MIO

I know you did.

CARR

The State can't afford to admit it was
wrong, you see. Not when there's been
that much of a row kicked up over it.
So for all practical purposes the State
was right and your father robbed the
pay roll.

MIO

There's still such a thing as evidence.

CARR

It's something you can buy. In fact, at
the moment I don't think of anything
you can't buy, including life, honor,
virtue, glory, public office, conjugal affection and all kinds of justice, from
the traffic court to the immortal nine.
Go out and make yourself a pot of
money and you can buy all the justice
you want. Convictions obtained, convictions averted. Lowest rates in years.

MIO

I know all that.

CARR

Sure.

MIO

This thing didn't happen to you.
They've left you your name
and whatever place you can take. For
my heritage
they've left me one thing only, and
that's to be
my father's voice crying up out of the
earth
and quicklime where they stuck him.
Electrocution
doesn't kill, you know. They eviscerate
them
with a turn of the knife in the dissect-
ing room.
The blood spurts out. The man was
alive. Then into
the lime pit, leave no trace. Make it
short shrift
and chemical dissolution. That's what
they thought
of the man that was my father. Then
my mother—
I tell you these county burials are swift
and cheap and run for profit! Out of
the house
and into the ground, you wife of a
dead dog. Wait,
here's some Romagna spawn left.
Something crawls here—
something they called a son. Why
couldn't he die
along with his mother? Well, ease him
out of town,
ease him out, boys, and see you're not
too gentle.
He might come back. And, by their
own living Jesus,
I will go back, and hang the carrion
around their necks that made it!
Maybe I can sleep then.
Or even live.

CARR

You have to try it?

MIO

Yes.
Yes. It won't let me alone. I've tried to
live

MIO

Not always. I tried it. After the second day I walked thirty miles to Niagara Falls and made a tour of the plant to get the sample of shredded wheat biscuit on the way out.

CARR

Last time I saw you you couldn't think of anything you wanted to do except curse God and pass out. Still feeling low?

MIO

Not much different.
(*He turns away, then comes back.*)
Talk about the lost generation, I'm the only one fits that title. When the State executes your father, and your mother dies of grief, and you know damn well he was innocent, and the authorities of your home town politely inform you they'd consider it a favor if you lived somewhere else—that cuts you off from the world—with a meat-axe.

CARR

They asked you to move?

MIO

It came to that.

CARR

God, that was white of them.

MIO

It probably gave them a headache just to see me after all that agitation. They knew as well as I did my father never staged a holdup. Anyway, I've got a new interest in life now.

CARR

Yes—I saw her.

MIO

I don't mean the skirt.—No, I got wind of something, out west, some college professor investigating the trial and turning up new evidence. Couldn't find anything he'd written out there, so I

beat it east and
island just in time
ing up in the publ
ter. I know now w
have been doing s.
started. They've bee
their reading in the
room. Man, what a
stank, too, but a hobo
ten because his shoes ar

CARR

Tennyson.

MIO

Right. Jeez, I'm glad we met
Never knew anybody else th
track me through the driven
Victorian literature.

CARR

Now you're cribbing from some
forgotten criticism of Ben Jonson's
man plagiarisms.

MIO

Where did you get your education
sap?

CARR

Not in the public library, sap. My father kept a news-stand.

MIO

Well, you're right again.
(*There is a faint rumble of thunder.*)
What's that? Winter thunder?

CARR

Or Mister God, beating on His little tocsin. Maybe announcing the advent of a new social order.

MIO

Or maybe it's going to rain coffee and doughnuts.

CARR

Or maybe it's going to rain.

Seer

Any
dis
he
mi
sl

and forget it—but I was birthmarked
with hot iron
into the entrails. I've got to find out
who did it
and make them see it till it scalds their
eyes
and make them admit it till their
tongues are blistered
with saying how black they lied!
(HERMAN, *a gawky shoe salesman,
enters from the left.*)

HERMAN

Hello. Did you see a couple of girls go
this way?

CARR

Couple of girls? Did we see a couple
of girls?

MIO

No.

CARR

No. No girls.
(HERMAN *hesitates, then goes out
right.* LUCIA *comes in from the
left, trundling his piano.* PINY
follows him, weeping.)

PINY

They've got no right to do it—

LUCIA

All right, hell what, no matter, I got to
put him away, I got to put him away,
that's what the hell!
(TWO STREET URCHINS *follow him
in.*)

PINY

They want everybody on the relief rolls
and nobody making a living?

LUCIA

The cops, they do what the big boss
says. The big boss, that's the mayor,
he says he heard it once too often, the
sextette—

PINY

They want graft, that's all. It's a new
way to get graft—

LUCIA

Oh, no, no, no! He's a good man, the
mayor. He's just don't care for music,
that's all.

PINY

Why shouldn't you make a living on
the street? The National Biscuit Company ropes off Eighth Avenue—and
does the mayor do anything? No, the
police hit you over the head if you try
to go through!

LUCIA

You got the big dough, you get the
pull, fine. No big dough, no pull, what
the hell, get off the city property! Tomorrow I start cooking chestnuts . . .
(*He strokes the piano fondly. The*
TWO GIRLS *and* HERMAN *come
back from the right.*)
She's a good little machine, this baby.
Cost plenty—and two new records I
only played twice. See, this one.
(*He starts turning the crank, talking while he plays.*)
Two weeks since they play this one in
a picture house.
(A SAILOR *wanders in from the
left. One of the* STREET UR-
CHINS *begins suddenly to dance
a wild rumba, the others
watch.*)
Good boy—see, it's a lulu—it itches in
the feet!
(HERMAN, *standing with his girl,
tosses the boy a penny. He
bows and goes on dancing;
the other* URCHIN *joins him.
The* SAILOR *tosses a coin.*)

SAILOR

Go it, Cuba! Go it!
(LUCIA *turns the crank, beaming.*)

2ND GIRL

Oh, Herman!
(*She throws her arms around* HER-
MAN *and they dance.*)

1ST URCHIN
Hey, pipe the professionals!

1ST GIRL
Do your glide, Shirley. Do your glide!

LUCIA
Maybe we can't play in front, maybe we can play behind!
> (*The* HOBO *gets up from his nest and comes over to watch. A* YOUNG RADICAL *wanders in.*)

Maybe you don't know, folks! Tonight we play good-bye to the piano! Good-bye forever! No more piano on the streets! No more music! No more money for the music-man! Last time, folks! Good-bye to the piano—good-bye forever!
> (MIRIAMNE *comes out the rear door of the apartment and stands watching. The* SAILOR *goes over to the* 1ST GIRL *and they dance together.*)

Maybe you don't know, folks! Tomorrow will be sad as hell, tonight we dance! Tomorrow no more Verdi, no more rumba, no more good time! Tonight we play good-bye to the piano, good-bye forever!
> (*The* RADICAL *edges up to* MIRIAMNE *and asks her to dance. She shakes her head and he goes to* PINY *who dances with him. The* HOBO *begins to do a few lonely curvets on the side above.*)

Hoy! Hoy! Pick 'em up and take 'em around! Use the head, use the feet! Last time forever!
> (*He begins to sing to the air.*)

MIO
Wait for me, will you?

CARR
Now's your chance.
> (MIO *goes over to* MIRIAMNE *and holds out a hand, smiling. She stands for a moment uncertain, then dances with him.* ESDRAS *comes out to watch.* JUDGE

> GAUNT *comes in from the left. There is a rumble of thunder.*)

LUCIA
Hoy! Hoy! Maybe it rains tonight, maybe it snows tomorrow! Tonight we dance good-bye.
> (*He sings the air lustily. A* POLICE- MAN *comes in from the left and looks on.* TWO OR THREE PEDES- TRIANS *follow him.*)

POLICEMAN
Hey you!
> (LUCIA *goes on singing.*)

Hey, you!

LUCIA
(*Still playing*)
What you want?

POLICEMAN
Sign off!

LUCIA
What you mean? I get off the street!

POLICEMAN
Sign off!

LUCIA
(*Still playing*)
What you mean?
> (*The* POLICEMAN *walks over to him.* LUCIA *stops playing and the* DANCERS *pause.*)

POLICEMAN
Cut it.

LUCIA
Is this a street?

POLICEMAN
I say cut it out.
> (*The* HOBO *goes back to his nest and sits in it, watching.*)

LUCIA
It's the last time. We dance good-bye to the piano.

POLICEMAN

You'll dance good-bye to something else if I catch you cranking that thing again.

LUCIA

All right.

PINY

I'll bet you don't say that to the National Biscuit Company!

POLICEMAN

Lady, you've been selling apples on my beat for some time now, and I said nothing about it—

PINY

Selling apples is allowed—

POLICEMAN

You watch yourself—
(*He takes a short walk around the place and comes upon the* HOBO.)
What are you doing here?
(*The* HOBO *opens his mouth, points to it, and shakes his head.*)
Oh, you are, are you?
(*He comes back to Lucia.*)
So you trundle your so-called musical instrument to wherever you keep it, and don't let me hear it again.
(*The* RADICAL *leaps on the base of the rock at right. The* 1ST GIRL *turns away from the* SAILOR *toward the* 2ND GIRL *and* HERMAN.)

SAILOR

Hey, captain, what's the matter with the music?

POLICEMAN

Not a thing, admiral.

SAILOR

Well, we had a little party going here—

POLICEMAN

I'll say you did.

2ND GIRL

Please, officer, we want to dance.

POLICEMAN

Go ahead. Dance.

2ND GIRL

But we want music!

POLICEMAN

(*Turning to go*)
Sorry. Can't help you.

RADICAL

And there you see it, the perfect example of capitalistic oppression! In a land where music should be free as air and the arts should be encouraged, a uniformed minion of the rich, a guardian myrmidon of the Park Avenue pleasure hunters, steps in and puts a limit on the innocent enjoyments of the poor! We don't go to theatres! Why not? We can't afford it! We don't go to night clubs, where women dance naked and the music drips from saxophones and leaks out of Rudy Vallee—we can't afford that either!—But we might at least dance on the river bank to the strains of a barrel organ—!
(*GARTH comes out of the apartment and listens.*)

POLICEMAN

It's against the law!

RADICAL

What law? I challenge you to tell me what law of God or man—what ordinance—is violated by this spontaneous diversion? None! I say none! An official whim of the masters who should be our servants!—

POLICEMAN

Get down! Get down and shut up!

RADICAL

By what law, by what ordinance do you order me to be quiet?

POLICEMAN

Speaking without a flag. You know it.

RADICAL

(*Pulling out a small American flag*)

There's my flag! There's the flag of this United States which used to guarantee the rights of man—the rights of man now violated by every third statute of the commonweal—

POLICEMAN

Don't try to pull tricks on me! I've seen you before! You're not making any speech, and you're climbing down—

JUDGE GAUNT

(*Who has come quietly forward*)

One moment, officer. There is some difference of opinion even on the bench as to the elasticity of police power when applied in minor emergencies to preserve civil order. But the weight of authority would certainly favor the defendant in any equitable court, and he would be upheld in his demand to be heard.

POLICEMAN

Who are you?

JUDGE GAUNT

Sir, I am not accustomed to answer that question.

POLICEMAN

I don't know you.

GAUNT

I am a judge of some standing, not in your city but in another with similar statutes. You are aware, of course, that the bill of rights is not to be set aside lightly by the officers of any municipality—

POLICEMAN

(*Looking over* GAUNT's *somewhat bedraggled costume*)

Maybe they understand you better in the town you come from, but I don't get your drift.—

(*To the* RADICAL)

I don't want any trouble, but if you ask for it you'll get plenty. Get down!

RADICAL

I'm not asking for trouble, but I'm staying right here.

(*The* POLICEMAN *moves toward him.*)

GAUNT

(*Taking the policeman's arm, but shaken off roughly*)

I ask this for yourself, truly, not for the dignity of the law nor the maintenance of precedent. Be gentle with them when their threats are childish—be tolerant while you can—for your least harsh word will return on you in the night—return in a storm of cries!—

(*He takes the policeman's arm again.*)

Whatever they may have said or done, let them disperse in peace! It is better that they go softly, lest when they are dead you see their eyes pleading, and their outstretched hands touch you, fingering cold on your heart!—I have been harsher than you. I have sent men down that long corridor into blinding light and blind darkness!

(*He suddenly draws himself erect and speaks defiantly.*)

And it was well that I did so! I have been an upright judge! They are all liars! Liars!

POLICEMAN

(*Shaking* GAUNT *off so that he falls*)

Why, you fool, you're crazy!

GAUNT

Yes, and there are liars on the force! They came to me with their shifty lies!

(*He catches at the policeman, who pushes him away with his foot.*)

POLICEMAN

You think I've got nothing better to do than listen to a crazy fool?

1ST GIRL

Shame, shame!

POLICEMAN

What have I got to be ashamed of? And what's going on here, anyway? Where in hell did you all come from?

RADICAL

Tread on him! That's right! Tread down the poor and the innocent!
(*There is a protesting murmur in the crowd.*)

SAILOR

(*Moving in a little*)
Say, big boy, you don't have to step on the guy.

POLICEMAN

(*Facing them, stepping back*)
What's the matter with you? I haven't stepped on anybody!

MIO

(*At the right, across from the* POLICEMAN)
Listen now, fellows, give the badge a chance.
He's doing his job, what he gets paid to do,
the same as any of you. They're all picked men,
these metropolitan police, hand picked for loyalty and a fine up-standing pair of shoulders on their legs—it's not so easy
to represent the law. Think what he does
for all of us, stamping out crime!
Do you want to be robbed and murdered in your beds?

SAILOR

What's eating you?

RADICAL

He must be a capitalist.

MIO

They pluck them fresh
from Ireland, and a paucity of head-piece
is a prime prerequisite. You from Ireland, buddy?

POLICEMAN

(*Surly*)
Where are you from?

MIO

Buddy, I tell you flat
I wish I was from Ireland, and could boast
some Tammany connections. There's only one drawback
about working on the force. It infects the brain,
it eats the cerebrum. There've been cases known,
fine specimens of manhood, too, where autopsies,
conducted in approved scientific fashion,
revealed conditions quite incredible
in policemen's upper layers. In some, a trace,
in others, when they've swung a stick too long,
there was nothing there!—but nothing! Oh, my friends,
this fine athletic figure of a man
that stands so grim before us, what will they find
when they saw his skull for the last inspection?
I fear me a little puffball dust will blow away
rejoining earth, our mother—and this same dust,
this smoke, this ash on the wind, will represent
all he had left to think with!

HOBO

Hooray!
(*The* POLICEMAN *turns on his heel and looks hard at the* HOBO, *who slinks away.*)

POLICEMAN

Oh, yeah?

MIO

My theme
gives ears to the deaf and voice to the
     dumb! But now
forgive me if I say you were most un-
     kind
in troubling the officer. He's a simple
     man
of simple tastes, and easily confused
when faced with complex issues. He
     may reflect
on returning home, that is, so far as he
is capable of reflection, and conclude
that he was kidded out of his uniform
     pants,
and in his fury when this dawns on
     him
may smack his wife down!

POLICEMAN

That'll be about enough from you, too,
professor!

MIO

May I say that I think you have managed this whole situation rather badly,
from the beginning?—

POLICEMAN

You may not!
     (TROCK slips in from the back-
          ground. The TWO YOUNG MEN
          IN SERGE come with him.)

MIO

Oh, but your pardon, sir! It's apparent
to the least competent among us that
you should have gone about your task
more subtly—the glove of velvet, the
hand of iron, and all that sort of thing—

POLICEMAN

Shut that hole in your face!

MIO

Sir, for that remark I shall be satisfied
with nothing less than an unconditional
apology! I have an old score to settle

with policemen, brother, because
they're fools and fat-heads, and you're
one of the most fatuous fat-heads that
ever walked his feet flat collecting
graft! Tell that to your sergeant back in
the booby-hatch.

POLICEMAN

Oh, you want an apology, do you?
You'll get an apology out of the other
side of your mouth!
     (He steps toward MIO. CARR sud-
          denly stands in his path.)
Get out of my way!
     (He pauses and looks round him;
          the crowd looks less and less
          friendly. He lays a hand on his
          gun and backs to a position
          where there is nobody behind
          him.)
Get out of here, all of you! Get out!
What are you trying to do—start a riot?

MIO

There now, that's better! That's in the
best police tradition. Incite a riot yourself and then accuse the crowd.

POLICEMAN

It won't be pleasant if I decide to let
somebody have it! Get out!
     (The onlookers begin to melt
          away. The SAILOR goes out left
          with the GIRLS and HERMAN.
          CARR and MIO go out right,
          CARR whistling "The Star
          Spangled Banner." The HOBO
          follows them. The RADICAL
          walks past with his head in the
          air. PINY and LUCIA leave the
          piano where it stands and slip
          away to the left. At the end
          the POLICEMAN is left standing
          in the center, the JUDGE near
          him. ESDRAS stands in the door-
          way. MIRIAMNE is left sitting
          half in shadows and unseen by
          ESDRAS.)

JUDGE GAUNT

     (To the POLICEMAN)
Yes, but should a man die, should it be

necessary that one man die for the good of many, make not yourself the instrument of death, lest you sleep to wake sobbing! Nay, it avails nothing that you are the law—this delicate ganglion that is the brain, it will not bear these things—!

(*The* POLICEMAN *gives the* JUDGE *the once-over, shrugs, decides to leave him there and starts out left.* GARTH *goes to his father—a fine sleet begins to fall through the street lights.* TROCK *is still visible.*)

GARTH

Get him in here, quick.

ESDRAS

Who, son?

GARTH

The Judge, damn him!

ESDRAS

Is it Judge Gaunt?

GARTH

Who did you think it was? He's crazy as a bedbug and telling the world. Get him inside!

(*He looks round.*)

ESDRAS

(*Going up to* GAUNT)
Will you come in, sir?

GAUNT

You will understand, sir. We old men know how softly we must proceed with these things.

ESDRAS

Yes, surely, sir.

GAUNT

It was always my practice—always. They will tell you that of me where I am known. Yet even I am not free of regret—even I. Would you believe it?

ESDRAS

I believe we are none of us free of regret.

GAUNT

None of us? I would it were true. I would I thought it were true.

ESDRAS

Shall we go in, sir? This is sleet that's falling.

GAUNT

Yes. Let us go in.

(ESDRAS, GAUNT *and* GARTH *enter the basement and shut the door.* TROCK *goes out with his men. After a pause* MIO *comes back from the right, alone. He stands at a little distance from* MIRIAMNE.)

MIO

Looks like rain.
(*She is silent.*)
You live around here?
(*She nods gravely.*)
I guess
you thought I meant it—about waiting here to meet me.
(*She nods again.*)
I'd forgotten about it till I got that winter
across the face. You'd better go inside.
I'm not your kind. I'm nobody's kind but my own.
I'm waiting for this to blow over.
(*She rises.*)
I lied. I meant it—
I meant it when I said it—but there's too much black
whirling inside me—for any girl to know.
So go on in. You're somebody's angel child
and they're waiting for you.

MIRIAMNE

Yes. I'll go.
(*She turns.*)

MIO

And tell them
when you get inside where it's warm,
and you love each other,
and mother comes to kiss her darling,
    tell them
to hang on to it while they can, be-
    lieve while they can
it's a warm safe world, and Jesus finds
    his lambs
and carries them in his bosom.—I've
    seen some lambs
that Jesus missed. If they ever want
    the truth
tell them that nothing's guaranteed in
    this climate
except it gets cold in winter, nor on this
    earth
except you die sometime.
        (*He turns away.*)

MIRIAMNE

I have no mother.
And my people are Jews.

MIO

Then you know something about it.

MIRIAMNE

Yes.

MIO

Do you have enough to eat?

MIRIAMNE

Not always.

MIO

What do you believe in?

MIRIAMNE

Nothing.

MIO

Why?

MIRIAMNE

How can one?

MIO

It's easy if you're a fool. You see the
    words
in books. Honor, it says there, chivalry,
    freedom,
heroism, enduring love—and these
are words on paper. It's something to
    have them there.
You'll get them nowhere else.

MIRIAMNE

What hurts you?

MIO

Just that.
You'll get them nowhere else.

MIRIAMNE

Why should you want them?

MIO

I'm alone, that's why. You see those
    lights,
along the river, cutting across the
    rain—?
those are the hearths of Brooklyn, and
    up this way
the love-nests of Manhattan—they turn
    their points
like knives against me—outcast of the
    world,
snake in the streets.—I don't want a
    hand-out.
I sleep and eat.

MIRIAMNE

Do you want me to go with you?

MIO

Where?

MIRIAMNE

Where you go.
        (*A pause. He goes nearer to her.*)

MIO

Why, you god-damned little fool—
what made you say that?

MIRIAMNE

I don't know.

MIO

If you have a home
stay in it. I ask for nothing. I've
schooled myself
to ask for nothing, and take what I can
get,
and get along. If I fell for you, that's
my look-out,
and I'll starve it down.

MIRIAMNE

Wherever you go, I'd go.

MIO

What do you know about loving?
How could you know?
Have you ever had a man?

MIRIAMNE

(*After a slight pause*)
No. But I know.
Tell me your name.

MIO

Mio. What's yours?

MIRIAMNE

Miriamne.

MIO

There's no such name.

MIRIAMNE

But there's no such name as Mio!
M.I.O. It's no name.

MIO

It's for Bartolomeo.

MIRIAMNE

My mother's name was Miriam,
so they called me Miriamne.

MIO

Meaning little Miriam?

MIRIAMNE

Yes.

MIO

So now little Miriamne will go in
and take up quietly where she dropped
them all
her small housewifely cares.—When I
first saw you,
not a half-hour ago, I heard myself
saying,
this is the face that launches ships for
me—
and if I owned a dream—yes, half a
dream—
we'd share it. But I have no dream.
This earth
came tumbling down from chaos, fire
and rock,
and bred up worms, blind worms that
sting each other
here in the dark. These blind worms
of the earth
took out my father—and killed him,
and set a sign
on me—the heir of the serpent—and he
was a man
such as men might be if the gods were
men—
but they killed him—
as they'll kill all others like him
till the sun cools down on the stabler
molecules,
yes, till men spin their tent-worm webs
to the stars
and what they think is done, even in
the thinking,
and they are the gods, and immortal,
and constellations
turn for them all like mill wheels—still
as they are
they will be, worms and blind. Enduring love,
oh gods and worms, what mockery!—
And yet
I have blood enough in my veins. It
goes like music,
singing, because you're here. My body
turns
as if you were the sun, and warm. This
men called love
in happier times, before the Freudians
taught us
to blame it on the glands. Only go in

before you breathe too much of my
  atmosphere
and catch death from me.

MIRIAMNE

I will take my hands
and weave them to a little house, and
  there
you shall keep a dream—

MIO

God knows I could use a dream
and even a house.

MIRIAMNE

You're laughing at me, Mio!

MIO

The worms are laughing.
I tell you there's death about me
and you're a child! And I'm alone and
  half mad
with hate and longing. I shall let you
  love me
and love you in return, and then, why
  then
God knows what happens!

MIRIAMNE

Something most unpleasant?

MIO

Love in a box car—love among the
  children.
I've seen too much of it. Are we to live
in this same house you make with
  your two hands
mystically, out of air?

MIRIAMNE

No roof, no mortgage!
Well, I shall marry a baker out in Flat-
  bush,
it gives hot bread in the morning! Oh,
  Mio, Mio,
in all the unwanted places and waste
  lands
that roll up into the darkness out of sun
and into sun out of dark, there should
  be one empty
for you and me.

MIO

No.

MIRIAMNE

Then go now and leave me.
I'm only a girl you saw in the tene-
  ments,
and there's been nothing said.

MIO

Miriamne.
  (*She takes a step toward him.*)

MIRIAMNE

Yes.
  (*He kisses her lips lightly.*)

MIO

Why, girl, the transfiguration on the
  mount
was nothing to your face. It lights from
  within—
a white chalice holding fire, a flower
  in flame,
this is your face.

MIRIAMNE

And you shall drink the flame
and never lessen it. And round your
  head
the aureole shall burn that burns there
  now,
forever. This I can give you. And so
  forever
the Freudians are wrong.

MIO

They're well-forgotten
at any rate.

MIRIAMNE

Why did you speak to me
when you first saw me?

MIO

I knew then.

MIRIAMNE

And I came back
because I must see you again. And we
  danced together

and my heart hurt me. Never, never, never,
though they should bind me down and tear out my eyes,
would I ever hurt you now. Take me with you, Mio,
let them look for us, whoever there is to look,
but we'll be away.
(MIO *turns away toward the tenement.*)

MIO

When I was four years old
we climbed through an iron gate, my mother and I,
to see my father in prison. He stood in the death-cell
and put his hand through the bars and said, My Mio,
I have only this to leave you, that I love you,
and will love you after I die. Love me then, Mio,
when this hard thing comes on you, that you must live
a man despised for your father. That night the guards,
walking in flood-lights brighter than high noon,
led him between them with his trousers slit
and a shaven head for the cathodes. This sleet and rain
that I feel cold here on my face and hands
will find him under thirteen years of clay
in prison ground. Lie still and rest, my father,
for I have not forgotten. When I forget
may I lie blind as you. No other love,
time passing, nor the spaced light-years of suns
shall blur your voice, or tempt me from the path
that clears your name—
till I have these rats in my grip
or sleep deep where you sleep.
(*To* MIRIAMNE)
I have no house,

nor home, nor love of life, nor fear of death,
nor care for what I eat, or who I sleep with,
or what color of calcimine the Government
will wash itself this year or next to lure
the sheep and feed the wolves. Love somewhere else,
and get your children in some other image
more acceptable to the State! This face of mine
is stamped for sewage!
(*She steps back, surmising.*)

MIRIAMNE

Mio—

MIO

My road is cut
in rock, and leads to one end. If I hurt you, I'm sorry.
One gets over hurts.

MIRIAMNE

What was his name—
your father's name?

MIO

Bartolomeo Romagna.
I'm not ashamed of it.

MIRIAMNE

Why are you here?

MIO

For the reason
I've never had a home. Because I'm a cry
out of a shallow grave, and all roads are mine
that might revenge him!

MIRIAMNE

But Mio—why here—why here?

MIO

I can't tell you that.

MIRIAMNE

No—but—there's someone
lives here—lives not far—and you mean
   to see him—
you mean to ask him—
   (*She pauses.*)

MIO

Who told you that?

MIRIAMNE

His name
is Garth—Garth Esdras—

MIO

   (*After a pause, coming nearer*)
Who are you, then? You seem
to know a good deal about me.—Were
   you sent
to say this?

MIRIAMNE

You said there was death about you!
   Yes,
but nearer than you think! Let it be as
   it is—
let it all be as it is, never see this place
nor think of it—forget the streets you
   came
when you're away and safe! Go before
   you're seen
or spoken to!

MIO

Will you tell me why?

MIRIAMNE

As I love you
I can't tell you—and I can never see
   you—

MIO

I walk where I please—

MIRIAMNE

Do you think it's easy for me
to send you away?
   (*She steps back as if to go.*)

MIO

Where will I find you then
if I should want to see you?

MIRIAMNE

Never—I tell you
I'd bring you death! Even now. Listen!
   (SHADOW *and* TROCK *enter be-*
   tween the bridge and the tene-
   ment house.) MIRIAMNE *pulls*
   MIO *back into the shadow of*
   the rock to avoid being seen.)

TROCK

Why, fine.

SHADOW

You watch it now—just for the record,
   Trock—
you're going to thank me for staying
   away from it
and keeping you out. I've seen men get
   that way,
thinking they had to plug a couple of
   guys
and then a few more to cover it up,
   and then
maybe a dozen more. You can't own all
and territory adjacent, and you can't
slough all the witnesses, because every
   man
you put away has friends—

TROCK

I said all right.
I said fine.

SHADOW

They're going to find this judge,
and if they find him dead it's just too
   bad,
and I don't want to know anything
   about it—
and you don't either.

TROCK

You all through?

SHADOW

Why sure.

TROCK

All right.
We're through too, you know.

SHADOW

Yeah?
(*He becomes wary.*)

TROCK

Yeah, we're through.

SHADOW

I've heard that said before, and afterwards
somebody died.
(TROCK *is silent.*)
Is that what you mean?

TROCK

You can go.
I don't want to see you.

SHADOW

Sure, I'll go.
Maybe you won't mind if I just find out
what you've got on you. Before I turn
my back
I'd like to know.
(*Silently and expertly he touches*
TROCK'S *pockets, extracting a*
gun.)
Not that I'd distrust you,
but you know how it is.
(*He pockets the gun.*)
So long, Trock.

TROCK

So long.

SHADOW

I won't talk.
You can be sure of that.

TROCK

I know you won't.
(SHADOW *turns and goes out right,*
past the rock and along the
bank. As he goes the TWO
YOUNG MEN IN BLUE SERGE
enter from the left and walk

slowly after SHADOW. *They*
look toward TROCK *as they en-*
ter and he motions with his
thumb in the direction taken
by SHADOW. *They follow*
SHADOW *out without haste.*
TROCK *watches them disappear,*
then slips out the way he
came. MIO *comes a step for-*
ward, looking after the two
men. Two or three shots are
heard, then silence. MIO *starts*
to run after SHADOW.)

MIRIAMNE

Mio!

MIO

What do you know about this?

MIRIAMNE

The other way,
Mio—quick!
(CARR *slips in from the right, in*
haste.)

CARR

Look, somebody's just been shot.
He fell in the river. The guys that did
the shooting
ran up the bank.

MIO

Come on.
(MIO *and* CARR *run out right.*
MIRIAMNE *watches uncertainly,*
then slowly turns and walks to
the rear door of the tenement.
She stands there a moment,
looking after Mio, then goes in,
closing the door. CARR *and* MIO
return.)

CARR

There's a rip tide past the point. You'd
never find him.

MIO

No.

CARR

You know a man really ought to carry insurance living around here.—God, it's easy, putting a fellow away. I never saw it done before.

MIO

(*Looking at the place where Miriamne stood*)
They have it all worked out.

CARR

What are you doing now?

MIO

I have a little business to transact in this neighborhood.

CARR

You'd better forget it.

MIO

No.

CARR

Need any help?

MIO

Well, if I did I'd ask you first. But I don't see how it would do any good. So you keep out of it and take care of yourself.

CARR

So long, then.

MIO

So long, Carr.

CARR

(*Looking down-stream*)
He was drifting face up. Must be half-way to the island the way the tide runs.
(*He shivers.*)
God, it's cold here. Well—
(*He goes out to the left.* MIO *sits on the edge of the rock.* LUCIA *comes stealthily back from between the bridge and the tenement, goes to the street-piano and wheels it away.* PINY *comes in. They take a look at Mio, but say nothing.* LUCIA *goes into his shelter and* PINY *into hers.* MIO *rises, looks up at the tenement, and goes out to the left.*)

ACT TWO

SCENE: *The basement as in Scene 2 of Act One. The same evening.* ESDRAS *sits at the table reading,* MIRIAMNE *is seated at the left, listening and intent. The door of the inner room is half open and* GARTH's *violin is heard. He is playing the theme from the third movement of Beethoven's Archduke Trio.* ESDRAS *looks up.*

ESDRAS

I remember when I came to the end
of all the Talmud said, and the com-
    mentaries,
then I was fifty years old—and it was
    time
to ask what I had learned. I asked this
    question
and gave myself the answer. In all the
    Talmud

there was nothing to find but the names
    of things,
set down that we might call them by
    those names
and walk without fear among things
    known. Since then
I have had twenty years to read on and
    on
and end with Ecclesiastes. Names of
    names,

evanid days, evanid nights and days
and words that shift their meaning.
  Space is time,
that which was is now—the men of tomorrow
live, and this is their yesterday. All
  things
that were and are and will be, have
  their being
then and now and to come. If this
  means little
when you are young, remember it. It
  will return
to mean more when you are old.

MIRIAMNE

I'm sorry—I
was listening for something.

ESDRAS

It doesn't matter.
It's a useless wisdom. It's all I have,
but useless. It may be there is no time,
but we grow old. Do you know his
  name?

MIRIAMNE

Whose name?

ESDRAS

Why, when we're young and listen for
  a step
the step should have a name—
      (MIRIAMNE, *not hearing, rises and*
      goes to the window. GARTH *en-*
      ters from within, carrying his
      violin and carefully closing the
      door.)

GARTH

      (*As* ESDRAS *looks at him*)
Asleep.

ESDRAS

He may
sleep on through the whole night—then
  in the morning
we can let them know.

GARTH

We'd be wiser to say nothing—
let him find his own way back.

ESDRAS

How did he come here?

GARTH

He's not too crazy for that. If he wakes
  again
we'll keep him quiet and shift him off
  tomorrow.
Somebody'd pick him up.

ESDRAS

How have I come
to this sunken end of a street, at a life's
  end—?

GARTH

It was cheaper here—not to be tran-
  scendental—
So—we say nothing—?

ESDRAS

Nothing.

MIRIAMNE

Garth, there's no place
in this whole city—not one—
where you wouldn't be safer
than here—tonight—or tomorrow.

GARTH

      (*Bitterly*)
Well, that may be.
What of it?

MIRIAMNE

If you slipped away and took
a place somewhere where Trock
  couldn't find you—

GARTH

Yes—
using what for money? and why do
  you think
I've sat here so far—because I love my
  home
so much? No, but if I stepped round
  the corner
it'd be my last corner and my last step.

MIRIAMNE

And yet—
if you're here—they'll find you here—
Trock will come again—
and there's worse to follow—

GARTH

Do you want to get me killed?

MIRIAMNE

No.

GARTH

There's no way out of it. We'll wait
and take what they send us.

ESDRAS

Hush! You'll wake him.

GARTH

I've done it.
I hear him stirring now.
(*They wait quietly.* JUDGE GAUNT
opens the door and enters.)

GAUNT

(*In the doorway*)
I beg your pardon—
no, no, be seated—keep your place—I've
made
your evening difficult enough, I fear;
and I must thank you doubly for your
kindness,
for I've been ill—I know it.

ESDRAS

You're better, sir?

GAUNT

Quite recovered, thank you. Able, I
hope,
to manage nicely now. You'll be re-
warded
for your hospitality—though at this moment
(*He smiles.*)
I'm low in funds.
(*He inspects his billfold.*)
Sir, my embarrassment
is great indeed—and more than mone-
tary,

for I must own my recollection's vague
of how I came here—how we came together—
and what we may have said. My name
is Gaunt,
Judge Gaunt, a name long known in
the criminal courts,
and not unhonored there.

ESDRAS

My name is Esdras—
and this is Garth, my son. And
Miriamne,
the daughter of my old age.

GAUNT

I'm glad to meet you.
Esdras. Garth Esdras.
(*He passes a hand over his eyes.*)
It's not a usual name.
Of late it's been connected with a
case—
a case I knew. But this is hardly the
man.
Though it's not a usual name.
(*They are silent.*)
Sir, how I came here,
as I have said, I don't well know. Such
things
are sometimes not quite accident.

ESDRAS

We found you
outside our door and brought you in.

GAUNT

The brain
can be overworked, and weary, even
when the man
would swear to his good health. Sir,
on my word
I don't know why I came here, nor
how, nor when,
nor what would explain it. Shall we say
the machine
begins to wear? I felt no twinge of it.—
You will image how much more than
galling
I feel it, to ask my way home—and
where I am—
but I do ask you that.

ESDRAS

This is New York City—
or part of it.

GAUNT

Not the best part, I presume?
(*He smiles grimly.*)
No, not the best.

ESDRAS

Not typical, no.

GAUNT

And you—
(*To* GARTH)
you are Garth Esdras?

GARTH

That's my name.

GAUNT

Well, sir.
(*To* ESDRAS)
I shall lie under the deepest obligation
if you will set an old man on his path,
for I lack the homing instinct, if the truth
were known. North, east and south
mean nothing to me
here in this room.

ESDRAS

I can put you in your way.

GARTH

Only you'd be wiser to wait a while—
if I'm any judge.—

GAUNT

It happens I'm the judge—
(*With stiff humor*)
in more ways than one. You'll forgive
me if I say
I find this place and my predicament
somewhat distasteful.
(*He looks round him.*)

GARTH

I don't doubt you do;
but you're better off here.

GAUNT

Nor will you find it wise
to cross my word as lightly as you seem
inclined to do. You've seen me ill and
shaken—
and you presume on that.

GARTH

Have it your way.

GAUNT

Doubtless what information is required
we'll find nearby.

ESDRAS

Yes, sir—the terminal,—
if you could walk so far.

GAUNT

I've done some walking—
to look at my shoes.
(*He looks down, then puts out a
hand to steady himself.*)
That—that was why I came—
never mind—it was there—and it's gone.
(*To* GARTH)
Professor Hobhouse—
that's the name—he wrote some trash
about you
and printed it in a broadside.
—Since I'm here I can tell you
it's a pure fabrication—lacking facts
and legal import. Senseless and impu-
dent,
written with bias—with malicious intent
to undermine the public confidence
in justice and the courts. I knew it
then—
all he brings out about this testimony
you might have given. It's true I could
have called you,
but the case was clear—Romagna was
known guilty,
and there was nothing to add. If I've
endured
some hours of torture over their attacks
upon my probity—and in this torture
have wandered from my place, wandered perhaps
in mind and body—and found my way
to face you—

why, yes, it is so—I know it—I beg of
    you
say nothing. It's not easy to give up
a fair name after a full half century
of service to a state. It may well rock
the surest reason. Therefore I ask of you
say nothing of this visit.

GARTH

I'll say nothing.

ESDRAS

Nor any of us.

GAUNT

Why, no—for you'd lose, too.
You'd have nothing to gain.

ESDRAS

Indeed we know it.

GAUNT

I'll remember you kindly. When I've
returned, there may be some mystery
made of where I was—we'll leave it a
mystery?

GARTH

Anything you say.

GAUNT

Why, now I go with much more peace
of mind—if I can call you friends.

ESDRAS

We shall be grateful
for silence on your part, Your Honor.

GAUNT

Sir—
if there were any just end to be served
by speaking out, I'd speak! There is
    none. No—
bear that in mind!

ESDRAS

We will, Your Honor.

GAUNT

Then—
I'm in some haste. If you can be my
    guide,
we'll set out now.

ESDRAS

Yes, surely.
>   (*There is a knock at the door. The
>   four look at each other with
>   some apprehension.* MIRIAMNE
>   *rises.*)

I'll answer it.

MIRIAMNE

Yes.
>   (*She goes into the inner room and
>   closes the door.* ESDRAS *goes to
>   the outer door. The knock is
>   repeated. He opens the door.*
>   MIO *is there.*)

ESDRAS

Yes, sir.

MIO

May I come in?

ESDRAS

Will you state your business, sir?
It's late—and I'm not at liberty—

MIO

Why, I might say
that I was trying to earn my tuition
    fees by peddling magazines. I could
    say that,
or collecting old newspapers—paying
    cash—
highest rates—no questions asked—
>   (*He looks round sharply.*)

GARTH

We've nothing to sell.
What do you want?

MIO

Your pardon, gentlemen.
My business is not of an ordinary kind,
and I felt the need of this slight intro-
    duction
while I might get my bearings. Your
    name is Esdras,
or they told me so outside.

GARTH

What do you want?

MIO

Is that the name?

GARTH

Yes.

MIO

I'll be quick and brief.
I'm the son of a man who died many
    years ago
for a pay roll robbery in New England.
    You
should be Garth Esdras, by what I've
    heard. You have
some knowledge of the crime, if one
    can believe
what he reads in the public prints, and
    it might be
that your testimony, if given, would
    clear my father
of any share in the murder. You may
    not care
whether he was guilty or not. You may
    not know.
But I do care—and care deeply, and
    I've come
to ask you face to face.

GARTH

To ask me what?

MIO

What do you know of it?

ESDRAS

This man Romagna,
did he have a son?

MIO

Yes, sir, this man Romagna,
as you choose to call him, had a son,
    and I
am that son, and proud.

ESDRAS

Forgive me.

MIO

Had you known him,
and heard him speak, you'd know why
    I'm proud, and why
he was no malefactor.

ESDRAS

I quite believe you.
If my son can help he will. But at this
    moment,
as I told you—could you, I wonder, come
    tomorrow,
at your own hour?

MIO

Yes.

ESDRAS

By coincidence
we too of late have had this thing in
    mind—
there have been comments printed, and
    much discussion
which we could hardly avoid.

MIO

Could you tell me then
in a word?—What you know—
is it for him or against him?—
that's all I need.

ESDRAS

My son knows nothing.

GARTH

No.
The picture-papers lash themselves to
    a fury
over any rumor—make them up when
    they're short
of bedroom slops.—This is what hap-
    pened. I
had known a few members of a gang
    one time
up there—and after the murder they
    picked me up
because I looked like someone that was
    seen
in what they called the murder car.
    They held me
a little while, but they couldn't identify
    me
for the most excellent reason I wasn't
    there
when the thing occurred. A dozen years
    later now
a professor comes across this, and sees
    red

and asks why I wasn't called on as a
witness
and yips so loud they syndicate his picture
in all the rotos. That's all I know about
it.
I wish I could tell you more.

ESDRAS

Let me say too
that I have read some words your
father said,
and you were a son fortunate in your
father,
whatever the verdict of the world.

MIO

There are few
who think so, but it's true, and I thank
you. Then—
that's the whole story?

GARTH

All I know of it.

MIO

They cover their tracks well, the inner
ring
that distributes murder. I came three
thousand miles
to this dead end.

ESDRAS

If he was innocent
and you know him so, believe it, and
let the others
believe as they like.

MIO

Will you tell me how a man's
to live, and face his life, if he can't believe
that truth's like a fire,
and will burn through and be seen
though it takes all the years there are?
While I stand up and have breath in
my lungs
I shall be one flame of that fire;
it's all the life I have.

ESDRAS

Then you must live so.
One must live as he can.

MIO

It's the only way
of life my father left me.

ESDRAS

Yes? Yet it's true
the ground we walk on is impacted
down
and hard with blood and bones of those
who died
unjustly. There's not one title to land
or life,
even your own, but was built on rape
and murder,
back a few years. It would take a fire
indeed
to burn out all this error.

MIO

Then let it burn down,
all of it!

ESDRAS

We ask a great deal of the world
at first—then less—and then less.
We ask for truth
and justice. But this truth's a thing unknown
in the lightest, smallest matter—and as
for justice,
who has once seen it done? You loved
your father,
and I could have loved him, for every
word he spoke
in his trial was sweet and tolerant, but
the weight
of what men are and have, rests heavy
on
the graves of those who lost. They'll
not rise again,
and their causes lie there with them.

GAUNT

If you mean to say
that Bartolomeo Romagna was innocent,
you are wrong. He was guilty.
There may have been injustice
from time to time, by regrettable
chance, in our courts,
but not in that case, I assure you.

MIO

Oh, you assure me!
You lie in your scrag teeth, whoever
you are!
My father was murdered!

GAUNT

Romagna was found guilty
by all due process of law, and given
his chance
to prove his innocence.

MIO

What chance? When a court
panders to mob hysterics, and the jury
comes in loaded to soak an anarchist
and a foreigner, it may be due process
of law
but it's also murder!

GAUNT

He should have thought of that
before he spilled blood.

MIO

He?

GAUNT

Sir, I know too well
that he was guilty.

MIO

Who are you? How do you know?
I've searched the records through, the
trial and what
came after, and in all that million
words
I found not one unbiased argument
to fix the crime on him.

GAUNT

And you yourself,
were you unprejudiced?

MIO

Who are you?

ESDRAS

Sir,
this gentleman is here, as you are here,
to ask my son, as you have asked, what
ground

there might be for this talk of new evidence
in your father's case. We gave him the
same answer
we've given you.

MIO

I'm sorry. I'd supposed
his cause forgotten except by myself.
There's still
a defense committee then?

GAUNT

There may be. I
am not connnected with it.

ESDRAS

He is my guest,
and asks to remain unknown.

MIO

(After a pause, looking at GAUNT)
The judge at the trial
was younger, but he had your face.
Can't be
that you're the man?—Yes—Yes.—The
jury charge—
I sat there as a child and heard your
voice,
and watched that Brahminical mouth.
I knew even then
you meant no good to him. And now
you're here
to winnow out truth and justice—the
fountain-head
of the lies that slew him! Are you Judge
Gaunt?

GAUNT

I am.

MIO

Then tell me what damnation to what
inferno
would fit the toad that sat in robes and
lied
when he gave the charge, and knew he
lied! Judge that,
and then go to your place in that hell!

GAUNT

I know and have known
what bitterness can rise against a court

when it must say, putting aside all weakness,
that a man's to die. I can forgive you that,
for you are your father's son, and you think of him
as a son thinks of his father. Certain laws
seem cruel in their operation; it's necessary
that we be cruel to uphold them. This cruelty
is kindness to those I serve.

MIO

I don't doubt that.
I know who it is you serve.

GAUNT

Would I have chosen
to rack myself with other men's despairs,
stop my ears, harden my heart, and listen only
to the voice of law and light, if I had hoped
some private gain for serving? In all my years
on the bench of a long-established commonwealth
not once has my decision been in question
save in this case. Not once before or since.
For hope of heaven or place on earth, or power
or gold, no man has had my voice, nor will
while I still keep the trust that's laid on me
to sentence and define.

MIO

Then why are you here?

GAUNT

My record's clean. I've kept it so. But suppose
with the best intent, among the myriad tongues
that come to testify, I had missed my way

and followed a perjured tale to a lethal end
till a man was forsworn to death?
Could I rest or sleep
while there was doubt of this,
even while there was question in a layman's mind?
For always, night and day,
there lies on my brain like a weight, the admonition:
see truly, let nothing sway you; among all functions
there's but one godlike, to judge. Then see to it
you judge as a god would judge, with clarity,
with truth, with what mercy is found consonant
with order and law. Without law men are beasts,
and it's a judge's task to lift and hold them
above themselves. Let a judge be once mistaken
or step aside for a friend, and a gap is made
in the dykes that hold back anarchy and chaos,
and leave men bond but free.

MIO

Then the gap's been made,
and you made it.

GAUNT

I feared that too. May you be a judge
sometime, and know in what fear,
through what nights long
in fear, I scanned and verified and compared
the transcripts of the trial.

MIO

Without prejudice,
no doubt. It was never in your mind to prove
that you'd been right.

GAUNT

And conscious of that, too—
that that might be my purpose—watchful of that,

and jealous as his own lawyer of the
    rights
that should hedge the defendant!
And still I found no error,
shook not one staple of the bolts that
    linked
the doer to the deed! Still following on
from step to step, I watched all mod-
    ern comment,
and saw it centered finally on one fact—
Garth Esdras was not called. This is
    Garth Esdras,
and you have heard him. Would his
    deposition
have justified a new trial?

MIO

No. It would not.

GAUNT

And there I come, myself. If the man
    were still
in his cell, and waiting, I'd have no
    faint excuse
for another hearing.

MIO

I've told you that I read
the trial from beginning to end. Every
    word you spoke
was balanced carefully to keep the
    letter
of the law and still convict—convict, by
    Christ,
if it tore the seven veils! You stand here
    now
running cascades of casuistry, to prove
to yourself and me that no judge of
    rank and breeding
could burn a man out of hate! But
    that's what you did
under all your varnish!

GAUNT

I've sought for evidence,
and you have sought. Have you found
    it? Can you cite
one fresh word in defense?

MIO

The trial itself

was shot full of legerdemain, prear-
    ranged to lead
the jury astray—

GAUNT

Could you prove that?

MIO

Yes!

GAUNT

And if
the jury were led astray, remember it's
the jury, by our Anglo-Saxon custom,
that finds for guilt or innocence. The
    judge
is powerless in that matter.

MIO

Not you! Your charge
misled the jury more than the evidence,
accepted every biased meaning, dis-
    tilled
the poison for them!

GAUNT

But if that were so
I'd be the first, I swear it, to step down
among all men, and hold out both my
    hands
for manacles—yes, publish it in the
    streets,
that all I've held most sacred was de-
    filed
by my own act. A judge's brain be-
    comes
a delicate instrument to weigh men's
    lives
for good and ill—too delicate to bear
much tampering. If he should push
    aside
the weights and throw the beam, and
    say, this once
the man is guilty, and I will have it so
though his mouth cry out from the
    ground,
and all the world
revoke my word, he'd have a short way
    to go
to madness. I think you'd find him in
    the squares,
stopping the passers-by with argu-
    ments,—

see, I was right, the man was guilty
there—
this was brought in against him, this—
and this—
and I was left no choice! It's no light
thing
when a long life's been dedicate to one
end
to wrench the mind awry!

MIO

By your own thesis
you should be mad, and no doubt you
are.

GAUNT

But my madness
is only this—that I would fain look back
on a life well spent—without one stain
—one breath
of stain to flaw the glass—not in men's
minds
nor in my own. I take my God as witness
I meant to earn that clearness, and believe
that I have earned it. Yet my name is
clouded
with the blackest, fiercest scandal of
our age
that's touched a judge. What I can do
to wipe
that smutch from my fame I will. I
think you know
how deeply I've been hated, for no
cause
that I can find there. Can it not be—
and I ask this
quite honestly—that the great injustice
lies
on your side and not mine? Time and
time again
men have come before me perfect in
their lives,
loved by all who knew them, loved at
home,
gentle, not vicious, yet caught so ripe
red-handed
in some dark violence there was no de-
nying
where the onus lay.

MIO

That was not so with my father!

GAUNT

And yet it seemed so to me. To other
men
who sat in judgment on him. Can you
be sure—
I ask this in humility—that you,
who were touched closest by the tragedy,
may not have lost perspective—may
have brooded
day and night on one theme—till your
eyes are tranced
and show you one side only?

MIO

I see well enough.

GAUNT

And would that not be part of the mal-
ady—
to look quite steadily at the drift of
things
but see there what you wish—not what
is there—
not what another man to whom the
story
was fresh would say is there?

MIO

You think I'm crazy.
Is that what you meant to say?

GAUNT

I've seen it happen
with the best and wisest men. I but ask
the question.
I can't speak for you. Is it not true
wherever
you walk, through the little town where
you knew him well,
or flying from it, inland or by the sea,
still walking at your side, and sleeping
only
when you too sleep, a shadow not your
own
follows, pleading and holding out its
hands
to be delivered from shame?

MIO

How you know that
by God I don't know.

GAUNT

Because one spectre haunted you and
me—
and haunts you still, but for me it's laid
to rest
now that my mind is satisfied. He died
justly and not by error.
(*A pause.*)

MIO

(*Stepping forward*)
Do you care to know
you've come so near to death it's mir-
acle
that pulse still beats in your splotchy
throat?
Do you know
there's murder in me?

GAUNT

There was murder in your sire,
and it's to be expected! I say he died
justly, and he deserved it!

MIO

Yes, you'd like too well
to have me kill you! That would prove
your case
and clear your name, and dip my father's name
in stench forever! You'll not get that
from me!
Go home and die in bed, get it under
cover,
your lux-et-lex putrefaction of the right
thing,
you man that walks like a god!

GAUNT

Have I made you angry
by coming too near the truth?

MIO

This sets him up,
this venomous slug, this sets him up in
a gown,
deciding who's to walk above the earth
and who's to lie beneath! And giving
reasons!
The cobra giving reasons; I'm a god,
by Buddha, holy and worshipful my
fang,

and can I sink it in!
(*He pauses, turns as if to go, then
sits.*)
This is no good.
This won't help much.
(*The* JUDGE *and* ESDRAS *look at
each other.*)

GAUNT

We should be going.

ESDRAS

Yes.
(*They prepare to go.*)
I'll lend you my coat.

GAUNT

(*Looking at it with distaste*)
No, keep it. A little rain
shouldn't matter to me.

ESDRAS

It freezes as it falls,
and you've a long way to go.

GAUNT

I'll manage, thank you.
(GAUNT *and* ESDRAS *go out,* ESDRAS
obsequious, closing the door.)

GARTH

(*Looking at* MIO's *back*)
Well?

MIO

(*Not moving*)
Let me sit here a moment.
(GARTH *shrugs his shoulders and
goes toward the inner door.*
MIRIAMNE *opens it and comes
out.* GARTH *looks at her, then
at Mio, then lays his fingers on
his lips. She nods.* GARTH *goes
out.* MIRIAMNE *sits and watches*
MIO. *After a little he turns and
sees her.*)

MIO

How did you come here?

MIRIAMNE

I live here.

MIO

Here?

MIRIAMNE

My name is Esdras. Garth
is my brother. The walls are thin.
I heard what was said.

MIO

(*Stirring wearily*)
I'm going. This is no place for me.

MIRIAMNE

What place
would be better?

MIO

None. Only it's better to go.
Just to go.
(*She comes over to him, puts her
arm round him and kisses his
forehead.*)

MIRIAMNE

Mio.

MIO

What do you want?
Your kisses burn me—and your arms.
  Don't offer
what I'm never to have! I can have
  nothing. They say
they'll cross the void sometime to the
  other planets
and men will breathe in that air.
Well, I could breathe there,
but not here now. Not on this ball of
  mud.
I don't want it.

MIRIAMNE

They can take away so little
with all their words. For you're a king
  among them.
I heard you, and loved your voice.

MIO

I thought I'd fallen
so low there was no further, and now
  a pit

opens beneath. It was bad enough that
  he
should have died innocent, but if he
  were guilty—
then what's my life—what have I left to
  do—?
The son of a felon—and what they spat
  on me
was earned—and I'm drenched with the
  stuff.
Here on my hands
and cheeks, their spittle hanging! I
  liked my hands
because they were like his. I tell you
  I've lived
by his inocence, lived to see it flash
and blind them all—

MIRIAMNE

Never believe them, Mio,
never.
(*She looks toward the inner door.*)

MIO

But it was truth I wanted, truth—
not the lies you'd tell yourself, or tell
  a woman,
or a woman tells you! The judge with
  his cobra mouth
may have spat truth—and I may be
  mad! For me—
your hands are too clean to touch me.
  I'm to have
the scraps from hotel kitchens—and instead of love
those mottled bodies that hitch themselves through alleys
to sell for dimes or nickels. Go, keep
  yourself chaste
for the baker bridegroom—baker and
  son of a baker,
let him get his baker's dozen on you!

MIRIAMNE

No—
say once you love me—say it once; I'll
  never
ask to hear it twice, nor for any kindness,
and you shall take all I have!
(GARTH *opens the inner door and
  comes out.*)

GARTH

I interrupt
a love scene, I believe. We can do without
your adolescent mawkishness.
      (*To* MIRIAMNE)
You're a child.
You'll both remember that.

MIRIAMNE

I've said nothing to harm you—
and will say nothing.

GARTH

You're my sister, though,
and I take a certain interest in you.
   Where
have you two met?

MIRIAMNE

We danced together.

GARTH

Then
the dance is over, I think.

MIRIAMNE

I've always loved you
and tried to help you, Garth. And
   you've been kind.
Don't spoil it now.

GARTH

Spoil it how?

MIRIAMNE

Because I love him.
I didn't know it would happen. We
   danced together.
And the world's all changed. I see you
   through a mist,
and our father, too. If you brought this
   to nothing
I'd want to die.

GARTH

      (*To* MIO)
You'd better go.

MIO

Yes, I know.
      (*He rises. There is a trembling
      knock at the door.* MIRIAMNE
      goes to it. The HOBO *is there
      shivering.*)

HOBO

Miss, could I sleep under the pipes tonight, miss?
Could I, please?

MIRIAMNE

I think—not tonight.

HOBO

There won't be any more nights—
if I don't get warm, miss.

MIRIAMNE

Come in.
      (*The* HOBO *comes in, looks round
      deprecatingly, then goes to a
      corner beneath a huge heating
      pipe, which he crawls under as
      if he'd been there before.*)

HOBO

Yes, miss, thank you.

GARTH

Must we put up with that?

MIRIAMNE

Father let him sleep there—
last winter.

GARTH

Yes, God, yes.

MIO

Well, good night.

MIRIAMNE

Where will you go?

MIO

Yes, where? As if it mattered.

GARTH

Oh, sleep here, too.
We'll have a row of you under the
pipes.

MIO

No, thanks.

MIRIAMNE

Mio, I've saved a little money. It's only
some pennies, but you must take it.
(*She shakes some coins out of a
box into her hand.*)

MIO

No, thanks.

MIRIAMNE

And I love you.
You've never said you love me.

MIO

Why wouldn't I love you
when you're clean and sweet,
and I've seen nothing sweet or clean
this last ten years? I love you. I leave
you that
for what good it may do you. It's none
to me.

MIRIAMNE

Then kiss me.

MIO

(*Looking at* GARTH)
With that scowling over us? No.
When it rains, some spring
on the planet Mercury, where the
spring comes often,
I'll meet you there, let's say. We'll wait
for that.
It may be some time till then.
(*The outside door opens and* ES-
DRAS *enters with* JUDGE GAUNT,
then, after a slight interval,
TROCK *follows.* TROCK *surveys
the interior and its occupants
one by one, carefully.*)

TROCK

I wouldn't want to cause you incon-
venience,
any of you, and especially the Judge.
I think you know that. You've all got
things to do—
trains to catch, and so on. But trains
can wait.
Hell, nearly anything can wait, you'll
find,
only I can't. I'm the only one that can't
because I've got no time. Who's all this
here?
Who's that?
(*He points to the* HOBO.)

ESDRAS

He's a poor half-wit, sir,
that sometimes sleeps there.

TROCK

Come out. I say come out,
whoever you are.
(*The* HOBO *stirs and looks up.*)
Yes, I mean you. Come out.
(*The* HOBO *emerges.*)
What's your name?

HOBO

They mostly call me Oke.

TROCK

What do you know?

HOBO

No, sir.

TROCK

Where are you from?

HOBO

I got a piece of bread.
(*He brings it out, trembling.*)

TROCK

Get back in there!
(*The* HOBO *crawls back into his
corner.*)
Maybe you want to know why I'm doing this.
Well, I've been robbed, that's why—
robbed five or six times;
the police can't find a thing—so I'm out
for myself—

if you want to know.
(*To* MIO)
Who are you?

MIO

Oh, I'm a half-wit,
came in here by mistake. The difference is
I've got no piece of bread.

TROCK

What's your name?

MIO

My name?
Theophrastus Such. That's respectable.
You'll find it all the way from here to
the coast
on the best police blotters.
Only the truth is we're a little touched
in the head,
Oke and me. You'd better ask somebody else.

TROCK

Who is he?

ESDRAS

His name's Romagna. He's the son.

TROCK

Then what's he doing here? You said
you were on the level.

GARTH

He just walked in. On account of the
stuff in the papers. We didn't ask him.

TROCK

God, we are a gathering. Now if we
had Shadow we'd be all here, huh?
Only I guess we won't see Shadow. No,
that's too much to ask.

MIO

Who's Shadow?

TROCK

Now you're putting questions. Shadow
was just nobody, you see. He blew
away. It might happen to anyone.

(*He looks at* GARTH.)
Yes, anyone at all.

MIO

Why do you keep your hand in your
pocket, friend?

TROCK

Because I'm cold, punk. Because I've
been outside and it's cold as the tomb
of Christ.
(*To* GARTH)
Listen, there's a car waiting at the
street to take the Judge home. We'll
take him to the car.

GARTH

That's not necessary.

ESDRAS

No.

TROCK

I say it is, see? You wouldn't want to
let the Judge walk, would you? The
Judge is going to ride where he's going,
with a couple of chauffeurs, and everything done in style. Don't you worry
about the Judge. He'll be taken care
of. For good.

GARTH

I want no hand in it.

TROCK

Anything happens to me happens to
you too, musician.

GARTH

I know that.

TROCK

Keep your mouth out of it then. And
you'd better keep the punk here tonight, just for luck.
(*He turns toward the door. There
is a brilliant lightning flash
through the windows, followed
slowly by dying thunder.*
TROCK *opens the door. The rain
begins to pour in sheets.*)

Jesus, somebody tipped it over again!
        (*A cough racks him.*)
Wait till it's over. It takes ten days off
me every time I step into it.
        (*He closes the door.*)
Sit down and wait.
                (*Lightning flashes again. The
                thunder is fainter.* ESDRAS,
                GARTH *and the* JUDGE *sit down.*)

GAUNT

We were born too early. Even you who
        are young
are not of the elect. In a hundred years
man will put his finger on life itself,
        and then
he will live as long as he likes. For you
        and me
we shall die soon—one day, one year
        more or less,
when or where, it's no matter. It's what
        we call
an indeterminate sentence. I'm hungry.
        (GARTH *looks at* MIRIAMNE.)

MIRIAMNE

There was nothing left
tonight.

HOBO

I've got a piece of bread.
        (*He breaks his bread in two and
        hands half to the* JUDGE.)

GAUNT

I thank you, sir.
        (*He eats.*)
This is not good bread.
        (*He rises.*)
Sir, I am used
to other company. Not better, perhaps,
but their clothes were different. These
are what it's the fashion to call the un-
derprivileged.

TROCK

Oh, hell!
        (*He turns toward the door.*)

MIO

        (*To* TROCK)
It would seem that you and the Judge
know each other.

TROCK

        (TROCK *faces him.*)
I've been around.

MIO

Maybe you've met before.

TROCK

Maybe we have.

MIO

Will you tell me where?

TROCK

How long do you want to live?

MIO

How long? Oh, I've got big ideas about
that.

TROCK

I thought so. Well, so far I've got nothing against you but your name, see?
You keep it that way.
        (*He opens the door. The rain still
        falls in torrents. He closes the
        door. As he turns from it, it
        opens again, and* SHADOW,
        *white, bloodstained and drip-
        ping, stands in the doorway.*
        GARTH *rises.* TROCK *turns.*)

GAUNT

        (*To the* HOBO)
Yet if one were careful of his health,
ate sparingly, drank not at all, used
himself wisely, it might be that even an
old man could live to touch immortal-
ity. They may come on the secret
sooner than we dare hope. You see? It
does no harm to try.

TROCK

        (*Backing away from* SHADOW)
By God, he's out of his grave!

SHADOW

        (*Leaning against the doorway,
        holding a gun in his hands*)
Keep your hands where they belong,
        Trock.
You know me.

TROCK

Don't! Don't! I had nothing to do with it!
(*He backs to the opposite wall.*)

SHADOW

You said the doctor gave you six months to live—well, I don't give you that much. That's what you had, six months, and so you start bumping off your friends to make sure of your damn six months. I got it from you. I know where I got it.
Because I wouldn't give it to the Judge. So he wouldn't talk.

TROCK

Honest to God—

SHADOW

What God?
The one that let you put three holes in me
when I was your friend? Well, He let me get up again and walk till I could find you. That's as far as I get, but I got there, by God! And I can hear you even if I can't see!
(*He takes a staggering step forward.*)
A man needs blood
to keep going.—I got this far.—And now I can't see!
It runs out too fast—too fast—
when you've got three slugs
clean through you.
Show me where he is, you fools! He's here!
I got here!
(*He drops the gun.*)
Help me! Help me! Oh, God! Oh, God!
I'm going to die! Where does a man lie down?
I want to lie down!
(MIRIAMNE *starts toward* Shadow. GARTH *and* ESDRAS *help him into the next room,* MIRIAMNE *following.* TROCK *squats in his corner, breathing hard, looking at the door.* MIO *stands, watching* TROCK. GARTH *returns, wiping his hand with a*

handkerchief. MIO *picks up and pockets the gun.* MIRIAMNE *comes back and leans against the door jamb.*)

GAUNT

You will hear it said that an old man makes a good judge, being calm, clear-eyed, without passion. But this is not true. Only the young love truth and justice. The old are savage, wary, violent, swayed by maniac desires, cynical of friendship or love, open to bribery and the temptations of lust, corrupt and dastardly to the heart. I know these old men. What have they left to believe, what have they left to lose? Whorers of daughters, lickers of girls' shoes, contrivers of nastiness in the night, purveyors of perversion, worshippers of possession! Death is the only radical. He comes late, but he comes at last to put away the old men and give the young their places. It was time.
(*He leers.*)
Here's one I heard yesterday:
Marmaduke behind the barn
got his sister in a fix;
he says damn instead of darn;
ain't he cute? He's only six!

HOBO

He, he, he!

GAUNT

And the hoot-owl hoots all night,
and the cuckoo cooks all day,
and what with a minimum grace of God
we pass the time away.

HOBO

He, he, he—I got ya!
(*He makes a sign with his thumb.*)

GAUNT
(*Sings*)
And he led her all around
and he laid her on the ground
and he ruffled up the feathers of her cuckoo's nest!

HOBO

Ho, ho, ho!

GAUNT

I am not taken with the way you laugh. You should cultivate restraint.
(ESDRAS *reënters.*)

TROCK

Shut the door.

ESDRAS

He won't come back again.

TROCK

I want the door shut! He was dead, I tell you!
(ESDRAS *closes the door.*)
And Romagna was dead, too, once! Can't they keep a man under ground?

MIO

No. No more! They don't stay under ground any more, and they don't stay under water! Why did you have him killed?

TROCK

Stay away from me! I know you!

MIO

Who am I, then?

TROCK

I know you, damn you! Your name's Romagna!

MIO

Yes! And Romagna was dead, too, and Shadow was dead, but the time's come when you can't keep them down, these dead men! They won't stay down! They come in with their heads shot off and their entrails dragging! Hundreds of them! One by one—all you ever had killed! Watch the door! See!—It moves!

TROCK

(*Looking, fascinated, at the door*)
Let me out of here!
(*He tries to rise.*)

MIO

(*The gun in his hand*)
Oh, no! You'll sit there and wait for them! One by one they'll come through that door, pulling their heads out of the gunny-sacks where you tied them—glauming over you with their rotten hands! They'll see without eyes and crawl over you—Shadow and the paymaster and all the rest of them—putrescent bones without eyes! Now! Look! Look! For I'm first among them!

TROCK

I've done for better men than you! And I'll do for you!

GAUNT

(*Rapping on the table*)
Order, gentlemen, order! The witness will remember that a certain decorum is essential in the court-room!

MIO

By God, he'll answer me!

GAUNT

(*Thundering*)
Silence! Silence! Let me remind you of courtesy toward the witness! What case is this you try?

MIO

The case of the state against Bartolomeo Romagna for the murder of the paymaster!

GAUNT

Sir, that was disposed of long ago!

MIO

Never disposed of, never, not while I live!

GAUNT

Then we'll have done with it now! I deny the appeal! I have denied the appeal before and I do so again!

HOBO

He, he!—He thinks he's in the moving pictures!
(*A flash of lightning.*)

GAUNT

Who set that flash! Bailiff, clear the court! This is not Flemington, gentlemen! We are not conducting this case to make a journalistic holiday!

(*The thunder rumbles faintly.* GARTH *opens the outside door and faces a solid wall of rain.*)

Stop that man! He's one of the defendants!

(GARTH *closes the door.*)

MIO

Then put him on the stand!

GARTH

What do you think you're doing?

MIO

Have you any objection?

GAUNT

The objection is not sustained. We will hear the new evidence. Call your witness.

MIO

Garth Esdras!

GAUNT

He will take the stand!

GARTH

If you want me to say what I said before I'll say it!

MIO

Call Trock Estrella then!

GAUNT

Trock Estrella to the stand!

TROCK

No, by God!

MIO

Call Shadow, then! He'll talk! You thought he was dead, but he'll get up again and talk!

TROCK

(*Screaming*)

What do you want of me?

MIO

You killed the paymaster! You!

TROCK

You lie! It was Shadow killed him!

MIO

And now I know! Now I know!

GAUNT

Again I remind you of courtesy toward the witness!

MIO

I know them now!
Let me remind you of courtesy toward the dead!
He says that Shadow killed him! If Shadow were here
he'd say it was Trock! There were three men involved
in the new version of the crime for which
my father died! Shadow and Trock Estrella
as principals in the murder—Garth as witness!—
Why are they here together?—and you
—the Judge—
why are you here? Why, because you were all afraid
and you drew together out of that fear to arrange
a story you could tell! And Trock killed Shadow
and meant to kill the Judge out of that same fear—
to keep them quiet! This is the thing I've hunted
over the earth to find out, and I'd be blind
indeed if I missed it now!
(*To* GAUNT)
You heard what he said:
It was Shadow killed him! Now let the night conspire
with the sperm of hell! It's plain beyond denial

even to this fox of justice—and all his
  words
are curses on the wind! You lied! You
  lied!
You knew this too!

GAUNT

(*Low*)
Let me go. Let me go!

MIO

Then why
did you let my father die?

GAUNT

Suppose it known,
but there are things a judge must not
  believe
though they should head and fester
  underneath
and press in on his brain. Justice once
  rendered
in a clear burst of anger, righteously,
upon a very common laborer,
confessed an anarchist, the verdict
  found
and the precise machinery of law
invoked to know him guilty—think
  what furor
would rock the state if the court then
  flatly said
all this was lies—must be reversed? It's
  better,
as any judge can tell you, in such cases,
holding the common good to be worth
  more
than small injustice, to let the record
  stand,
let one man die. For justice, in the
  main,
is governed by opinion. Communities
will have what they will have, and it's
  quite as well,
after all, to be rid of anarchists. Our
  rights
as citizens can be maintained as rights
only while we are held to be the peers
of those who live about us. A vendor
  of fish
is not protected as a man might be
who kept a market. I own I've sometimes wished

this was not so, but it is. The man you
  defend
was unfortunate—and his misfortune
  bore
almost as heavily on me.—I'm broken—
broken across. You're much too young
  to know
how bitter it is when a worn connec-
  tion chars
and you can't remember—can't remember.
  (*He steps forward.*)
You
will not repeat this? It will go no further?

MIO

No.
No further than the moon takes the
  tides—no further
than the news went when he died—
when you found him guilty
and they flashed that round the earth.
  Wherever men
still breathe and think, and know
  what's done to them
by the powers above, they'll know.
  That's all I ask.
That'll be enough.
  (TROCK *has risen and looks darkly*
  at MIO.)

GAUNT

Thank you. For I've said some things
a judge should never say.

TROCK

Go right on talking.
Both of you. It won't get far, I guess.

MIO

Oh, you'll see to that?

TROCK

I'll see to it. Me and some others.
Maybe I lost my grip there just for a
  minute.
That's all right.

MIO

Then see to it! Let it rain!
What can you do to me now when the
  night's on fire

with this thing I know? Now I could
almost wish
there was a god somewhere—I could
almost think
there was a god—and he somehow
brought me here
and set you down before me here in
the rain
where I could wring this out of you!
For it's said,
and I've heard it, and I'm free! He was
as I thought him,
true and noble and upright, even when
he went
to a death contrived because he was as
he was
and not your kind! Let it rain! Let the
night speak fire
and the city go out with the tide, for
he was a man
and I know you now, and I have my
day!
>   (*There is a heavy knock at the
>   outside door.* MIRIAMNE *opens
>   it, at a glance from* GARTH. *The*
>   POLICEMAN *is there in oil-
>   skins.*)

POLICEMAN

Evening.
>   (*He steps in, followed by a* SER-
>   GEANT, *similarly dressed.*)

We're looking for someone
might be here. Seen an old man around
acting a little off?
>   (*To* ESDRAS)

You know the one
I mean. You saw him out there. Jeez!
You've got a funny crowd here!
>   (*He looks round. The* HOBO
>   *shrinks into his corner.*)

That's the one I saw.
What do you think?

SERGEANT

That's him. You mean to say
you didn't know him by his pictures?
>   (*He goes to* GAUNT)

Come on, old man.
You're going home.

GAUNT

Yes, sir. I've lost my way.
I think I've lost my way.

SERGEANT

I'll say you have.
About three hudred miles. Now don't
you worry.
We'll get you back.

GAUNT

I'm a person of some rank
in my own city.

SERGEANT

We know that. One look at you
and we'd know that.

GAUNT

Yes, sir.

POLICEMAN

If it isn't Trock!
Trock Estrella. How are you, Trock?

TROCK

Pretty good,
Thanks.

POLICEMAN

Got out yesterday again, I hear?

TROCK

That's right.

SERGEANT

Hi'ye, Trock?

TROCK

O.K.

SERGEANT

You know we got orders
to watch you pretty close. Be good
now, baby,
or back you go. Don't try to pull anything,
not in my district.

TROCK

No, sir.

SERGEANT

No bumping off.
If you want my advice quit carrying a
gun.
Try earning your living for once.

TROCK

Yeah.

SERGEANT

That's an idea.
Because if we find any stiffs on the
    river bank
we'll know who to look for.

MIO

Then look in the other room!
I accuse that man of murder! Trock
    Estrella!
He's a murderer!

POLICEMAN

Hello. I remember you.

SERGEANT

Well, what murder?

MIO

It was Trock Estrella
that robbed the pay roll thirteen years
    ago
and did the killing my father died for!
    You know
the Romagna case! Romagna was inno-
    cent,
and Trock Estrella guilty!

SERGEANT

(*Disgusted*)
Oh, what the hell!
That's old stuff—the Romagna case.

POLICEMAN

Hey, Sarge!
    (*The* SERGEANT *and* POLICEMAN
        come closer together.)
The boy's a professional kidder. He
    took me over
about half an hour ago. He kids the
    police
and then ducks out!

SERGEANT

Oh, yeah?

MIO

I'm not kidding now.
You'll find a dead man there in the next
    room
and Estrella killed him!

SERGEANT

Thirteen years ago?
And nobody smelled him yet?

MIO

(*Pointing*)
I accuse this man
of two murders! He killed the pay-
    master long ago
and had Shadow killed tonight. Look,
    look for yourself!
He's there all right!

POLICEMAN

Look boy. You stood out there
and put the booby sign on the dumb
    police
because they're fresh out of Ireland.
    Don't try it twice.

SERGEANT

(*To* GARTH)
Any corpses here?

GARTH

Not that I know of.

SERGEANT

I thought so.
    (MIO *looks at* MIRIAMNE.)
    (*To* MIO)
Think up a better one.

MIO

Have I got to drag him
out here where you can see him?
    (*He goes toward the inner door.*)
Can't you scent a murder
when it's under your nose? Look in!

MIRIAMNE

No, no—there's no one—there's no one
    there!

SERGEANT

(*Looking at* MIRIAMNE)
Take a look inside.

POLICEMAN

Yes, sir.
    (*He goes into the inside room.
        The* SERGEANT *goes up to the
        door. The* POLICEMAN *returns.*)

He's kidding, Sarge. If there's a cada-
ver
in here I don't see it.

MIO

You're blind then!
(*He goes into the room, the* SER-
GEANT *following him.*)

SERGEANT

What do you mean?
(*He comes out,* MIO *following
him.*)
When you make a charge of murder
it's better to have
the corpus delicti, son. You're the kind
puts in
fire alarms to see the engine!

MIO

By God, he was there!
He went in there to die.

SERGEANT

I'll bet he did.
And I'm Haile Selassie's aunt! What's
your name?

MIO

Romagna.
(*To* GARTH)
What have you done with him?

GARTH

I don't know what you mean.

SERGEANT

(*To* GARTH)
What's he talking about?

GARTH

I wish I could tell you.
I don't know.

SERGEANT

He must have seen something.

POLICEMAN

He's got
the Romagna case on the brain. You
watch yourself,
chump, or you'll get run in.

MIO

Then they're in it together!
All of them!
(*To* MIRIAMNE)
Yes, and you!

GARTH

He's nuts, I say.

MIRIAMNE

(*Gently*)
You have dreamed something—isn't it
true?
You've dreamed—
But truly, there was no one—
(MIO *looks at her comprehend-
ingly.*)

MIO

You want me to say it.
(*He pauses.*)
Yes, by God, I was dreaming.

SERGEANT

(*To* POLICEMAN)
I guess you're right.
We'd better be going. Haven't you got
a coat?

GAUNT

No, sir.

SERGEANT

I guess I'll have to lend you mine.
(*He puts his oilskins on* GAUNT.)
Come on, now. It's getting late.
(GAUNT, *the* POLICEMAN *and the*
SERGEANT *go out.*)

TROCK

They're welcome to him.
His fuse is damp. Where is that walking fool
with the three slugs in him?

ESDRAS

He fell in the hall beyond
and we left him there.

TROCK

That's lucky for some of us. Is he out
this time
or is he still butting around?

ESDRAS

He's dead.

TROCK

That's perfect.
       (*To* MIO)
Don't try using your firearms, amigo
    baby,
the Sarge is outside.
       (*He turns to go.*)
Better ship that carrion
back in the river! The one that walks
    when he's dead;
maybe he'll walk the distance for you.

GARTH

Coming back?

TROCK

Well, if I come back,
you'll see me. If I don't, you won't. Let
    the punk
go as far as he likes. Turn him loose
    and let him go.
And may you all rot in hell.
       (*He pulls his coat around him and
        goes to the left.* MIRIAMNE
        *climbs up to look out a win-
        dow.*)

MIRIAMNE

He's climbing up to the street,
along the bridgehead.
       (*She turns.*)
Quick, Mio! It's safe now! Quick!

GARTH

Let him do as he likes.

MIRIAMNE

What do you mean? Garth! He means
    to kill him!
You know that!

GARTH

I've no doubt Master Romagna
can run his own campaign.

MIRIAMNE

But he'll be killed!

MIO

Why did you lie about Shadow?
       (*There is a pause.* GARTH *shrugs,
        walks across the room, and
        sits.*)
You were one of the gang!

GARTH

I can take a death if I have to! Go tell
    your story,
only watch your step, for I warn you,
    Trock's out gunning
and you may not walk very far. Oh, I
    could defend it
but it's hardly worth while.
If they get Trock they get me too.
Go tell them. You owe me nothing.

ESDRAS

This Trock you saw,
no one defends him. He's earned his
    death so often
there's nobody to regret it. But his
    crime,
his same crime that has dogged you,
    dogged us down
from what little we had, to live here
    among the drains,
where the waterbugs break out like a
    scrofula
on what we eat—and if there's lower to
    go
we'll go there when you've told your
    story. And more
that I haven't heart to speak—

MIO

       (*To* GARTH)
My father died
in your place. And you could have
    saved him!
You were one of the gang!

GARTH

Why, there you are.
You certainly owe me nothing.

MIRIAMNE

       (*Moaning*)
I want to die.
I want to go away.

MIO

Yes, and you lied!
And trapped me into it!

MIRIAMNE

But Mio, he's my brother.
I couldn't give them my brother.

MIO

No. You couldn't.
You were quite right. The gods were
    damned ironic
tonight, and they've worked it out.

ESDRAS

What will be changed
if it comes to trial again? More blood
    poured out
to a mythical justice, but your father
    lying still
where he lies now.

MIO

The bright, ironical gods!
What fun they have in heaven! When
    a man prays hard
for any gift, they give it, and then one
    more
to boot that makes it useless.
    (*To* MIRIAMNE)
You might have picked
some other stranger to dance with!

MIRIAMNE

I know.

MIO

Or chosen
some other evening to sit outside in the
    rain.

But no, it had to be this. All my life
    long
I've wanted only one thing, to say to
    the world
and prove it: the man you killed was
    clean and true
and full of love as the twelve-year-old
    that stood
and taught in the temple. I can say
    that now
and give my proofs—and now you stick
    a girl's face
between me and the rites I've sworn
    the dead
shall have of me! You ask too much!
    Your brother
can take his chance! He was ready
    enough to let
an innocent man take certainty for him
to pay for the years he's had. That
    parts us, then,
but we're parted anyway, by the same
    dark wind
that blew us together. I shall say what
    I have to say.
    (*He steps back.*)
And I'm not welcome here.

MIRIAMNE

But don't go now! You've stayed
too long! He'll be waiting!

MIO

Well, is this any safer?
Let the winds blow, the four winds of
    the world,
and take us to the four winds.
    (*The three are silent before him.
    He turns and goes out.*)

ACT THREE

SCENE: *The river bank outside the tenement, a little before the close of the previous act. The rain still falls through the street lamps. The* TWO NATTY YOUNG MEN IN SERGE AND GRAY *are leaning against the masonry in a ray of light, concentrating on a game of chance. Each holds in his hand a packet of ten or fifteen crisp bills. They compare the numbers on the top notes and immediately a bill changes hands. This goes on with varying fortune until the tide begins to run toward the* 1ST GUNMAN, *who has accumulated nearly the whole supply. They play on in complete silence, evidently not wishing to make any noise. Occasionally they raise their heads slightly to look carefully about. Luck begins to favor the* 2ND GUNMAN, *and the notes come his way. Neither evinces the slightest interest in how the game goes. They merely play on, bored, half-absorbed. There is a slight noise at the tenement door. They put the bills away and watch.* TROCK *comes out, pulls the door shut and comes over to them. He says a few words too low to be heard, and without changing expression the* YOUNG MEN *saunter toward the right.* TROCK *goes out to the left, and the* 2ND PLAYER, *catching that out of the corner of his eye, lingers in a glimmer of light to go on with the game. The* 1ST, *with an eye on the tenement door, begins to play without ado, and the bills again shift back and forth, then concentrate in the hands of the* 1ST GUNMAN. *The* 2ND *shrugs his shoulders, searches his pockets, finds one bill, and playing with it begins to win heavily. They hear the door opening, and putting the notes away, slip out in front of the rock.* MIO *emerges, closes the door, looks round him and walks to the left. Near the corner of the tenement he pauses, reaches out his hand to try the rain, looks up toward the street, and stands uncertainly a moment. He returns and leans against the tenement wall.* MIRIAMNE *comes out.* MIO *continues to look off into space as if unaware of her. She looks away.*

MIO

This rather takes one off his high horse. —What I mean, tough weather for a hegira. You see, this is my sleeping suit, and if I get it wet—basta!

MIRIAMNE

If you could only hide here.

MIO

Hide?

MIRIAMNE

Lucia would take you in. The street-piano man.

MIO

At the moment, I'm afflicted with claustrophobia. I prefer to die in the open, seeking air.

MIRIAMNE

But you could stay there till daylight.

MIO

You're concerned about me.

MIRIAMNE

Shall I ask him?

MIO

No. On the other hand there's a certain reason in your concern. I looked up the street and our old friend Trock hunches patiently under the warehouse eaves.

MIRIAMNE

I was sure of that.

MIO

And here I am, a young man on a cold night, waiting the end of the rain. Being

read my lesson by a boy, a blind boy
—you know the one I mean. Knee-deep
in the salt-marsh, Miriamne, bitten
from within, fought.

MIRIAMNE

Wouldn't it be better if you came back
in the house?

MIO

You forget my claustrophobia.

MIRIAMNE

Let me walk with you, then. Please. If
I stay beside you he wouldn't dare.

MIO

And then again he might.—We don't
speak the same language, Miriamne.

MIRIAMNE

I betrayed you. Forgive me.

MIO

I wish I knew this region. There's
probably a path along the bank.

MIRIAMNE

Yes. Shadow went that way.

MIO

That's true, too. So here I am, a young
man on a wet night, and blind in my
weather eye. Stay and talk to me.

MIRIAMNE

If it happens—it's my fault.

MIO

Not at all, sweet. You warned me to
keep away. But I would have it. Now
I have to find a way out. It's like a
chess game. If you think long enough
there's always a way out.—For one or
the other.—I wonder why white always
wins and black always loses in the
problems. White to move and mate in
three moves. But what if white were to
lose—ah, what then? Why, in that case,
obviously black would be white and
white would be black.—As it often is.
—As we often are.—Might makes white.
Losers turn black. Do you think I'd
have time to draw a gun?

MIRIAMNE

No.

MIO

I'm a fair shot. Also I'm fair game.
  (*The door of the tenement opens
  and* GARTH *comes out to look
  about quickly. Seeing only* MIO
  and MIRIAMNE *he goes in and
  comes out again almost immediately carrying one end of a
  door on which a body lies
  covered with a cloth. The*
  HOBO *carries the other end.
  They go out to the right with
  their burden.*)
This is the burial of Shadow, then;
feet first he dips, and leaves the haunts
    of men.
Let us make mourn for Shadow, wetly
    lying,
in elegiac stanzas and sweet crying.
Be gentle with him, little cold waves
    and fishes;
nibble him not, respect his skin and
    tissues—

MIRIAMNE

Must you say such things?

MIO

My dear, some requiem is fitting over
the dead, even for Shadow. But the last
rhyme was bad.

Whittle him not, respect his dying
    wishes.

That's better. And then to conclude:

His aromatic virtues, slowly rising
will circumnamb the isle, beyond dis-
    guising.
He clung to life beyond the wont of
    men.
Time and his silence drink us all.
    Amen.

How I hate these identicals. The
French allow them, but the French
have no principles anyway. You know,
Miriamne, there's really nothing mys-
terious about human life. It's purely
mechanical, like an electric appliance.

Stop the engine that runs the generator
and the current's broken. When we
think the brain gives off a small electric
discharge—quite measurable, and constant within limits. But that's not what
makes your hair stand up when frightened.

MIRIAMNE

I think it's a mystery.

MIO

Human life? We'll have to wear veils
if we're to keep it a mystery much
longer. Now if Shadow and I were
made up into sausages we'd probably
make very good sausages.

MIRIAMNE

Don't—

MIO

I'm sorry. I speak from a high place,
far off, long ago, looking down. The
cortège returns.
        (GARTH *and the* HOBO *return,
        carrying the door, the cloth ly-
        ing loosely over it.*)
I hope you placed an obol in his mouth
to pay the ferryman? Even among the
Greeks a little money was prerequisite
to Elysium.
        (GARTH *and the* HOBO *go inside,
        silent.*)
No? It's grim to think of Shadow
lingering among lesser shades on the
hither side. For lack of a small gratuity.
        (ESDRAS *comes out the open door
        and closes it behind him.*)

ESDRAS

You must wait here, Mio, or go inside.
  I know
you don't trust me, and I haven't
  earned your trust.
You're young enough to seek truth—
and there is no truth;
and I know that—
but I shall call the police and see that
  you
get safely off.

MIO

It's a little late for that.

ESDRAS

I shall try.

MIO

And your terms? For I daresay you
make terms?

ESDRAS

No.

MIO

Then let me remind you what will happen.
The police will ask some questions.
When they're answered
they'll ask more, and before they're
  done with it
your son will be implicated.

ESDRAS

Must he be?

MIO

I shall not keep quiet.
    (*A pause.*)

ESDRAS

Still, I'll go.

MIO

I don't ask help, remember. I make no
  truce.
He's not on my conscience, and I'm not
  on yours.

ESDRAS

But you
could make it easier, so easily.
He's my only son. Let him live.

MIO

His chance of survival's
better than mine, I'd say.

ESDRAS

I'll go.

MIO

I don't urge it.

ESDRAS

No. I put my son's life in your hands.
When you're gone,
that may come to your mind.

MIO

Don't count on it.

ESDRAS

Oh,
I count on nothing.
(*He turns to go.* MIRIAMNE *runs
over to him and silently kisses
his hands.*)
Not mine, not mine, my daughter!
They're guilty hands.
(*He goes out left.* GARTH's *violin
is heard within.*)

MIO

There was a war in heaven
once, all the angels on one side, and all
the devils on the other, and since that
time
disputes have raged among the learned,
concerning
whether the demons won, or the angels.
Maybe
the angels won, after all.

MIRIAMNE

And again, perhaps
there are no demons or angels.

MIO

Oh, there are none.
But I could love your father.

MIRIAMNE

I love him. You see,
he's afraid because he's old. The less
one has
to lose the more he's afraid.

MIO

Suppose one had
only a short stub end of life, or held
a flashlight with the batteries run down
till the bulb was dim, and knew that
he could live
while the glow lasted. Or suppose one
knew
that while he stood in a little shelter
of time
under a bridgehead, say, he could live,
and then,
from then on, nothing. Then to lie and
turn

with the earth and sun, and regard
them not in the least
when the bulb was extinguished or he
stepped beyond
his circle into the cold? How would he
live
that last dim quarter-hour, before he
went,
minus all recollection, to grow in grass
between cobblestones?

MIRIAMNE

Let me put my arms round you, Mio.
Then if anything comes, it's for me,
too.
(*She puts both arms round him.*)

MIO

Only suppose
this circle's charmed! To be safe until
he steps
from this lighted space into dark! Time
pauses here
and high eternity grows in one quarter-
hour
in which to live.

MIRIAMNE

Let me see if anyone's there—
there in the shadows.
(*She looks toward the right.*)

MIO

It might blast our eternity—
blow it to bits. No, don't go. This is
forever,
here where we stand. And I ask you,
Miriamne,
how does one spend a forever?

MIRIAMNE

You're frightened?

MIO

Yes.
So much that time stands still.

MIRIAMNE

Why didn't I speak—
tell them—when the officers were here?
I failed you
in that one moment!

MIO

His life for mine? Oh, no.
I wouldn't want it, and you couldn't
give it.
And if I should go on living we're cut
apart
by that brother of yours.

MIRIAMNE

Are we?

MIO

Well, think about it.
A body lies between us, buried in quicklime.
Your allegiance is on the other side of
that grave
and not to me.

MIRIAMNE

No, Mio! Mio, I love you!

MIO

I love you, too, but in case my life
went on
beyond that barrier of dark—then Garth
would run his risk of dying.

MIRIAMNE

He's punished, Mio.
His life's been torment to him. Let him
go,
for my sake, Mio.

MIO

I wish I could. I wish
I'd never seen him—or you. I've steeped
too long
in this thing. It's in my teeth and
bones. I can't
let go or forget. And I'll not add my
lie
to the lies that cumber his ground. We
live our days
in a storm of lies that drifts the truth
too deep
for a path or shovel; but I've set my
foot on a truth
for once, and I'll trail it down!
(*A silence.* MIRIAMNE *looks out to
the right.*)

MIRIAMNE

There's someone there—
I heard—
(CARR *comes in from the right.*)

MIO

It's Carr.

CARR

That's right. No doubt about it.
Excuse me.

MIO

Glad to see you. This is Miriamne.
Carr's a friend of mine.

CARR

You're better employed
than when I saw you last.

MIO

Bow to the gentleman,
Miriamne. That's meant for you.

MIRIAMNE

Thank you, I'm sure.
Should I leave you, Mio? You want to
talk?

MIO

Oh, no,
we've done our talking.

MIRIAMNE

But—

CARR

I'm the one's out of place—
I wandered back because I got worried about you,
that's the truth.—Oh—those two fellows
with the hats
down this way, you know, the ones
that ran
after we heard the shooting—they're
back again,
lingering or malingering down the
bank,
revisiting the crime, I guess. They may
mean well.

MIO

I'll try to avoid them.

CARR

I didn't care
for the way they looked at me.—No luck, I suppose,
with that case history? The investigation
you had on hand?

MIO

I can't say. By the way,
the stiff that fell in the water and we saw swirling
down the eddy, he came trudging up, later on,
long enough to tell his name. His name was Shadow,
but he's back in the water now. It's all in an evening.
These things happen here.

CARR

Good God!

MIO

I know.
I wouldn't believe it if you told it.

CARR

But—
the man was alive?

MIO

Oh, not for long! He's dunked
for good this time. That's all that's happened.

CARR

Well,
if you don't need me—

MIRIAMNE

You had a message to send—
have you forgotten—?

MIO

I?—Yes, I had a message—
but I won't send it—not now.

MIRIAMNE

Then I will—!

MIO

No.
Let it go the way it is! It's all arranged
another way. You've been a good scout, Carr,
the best I ever knew on the road.

CARR

That sounds
like making your will.

MIO

Not yet, but when I do
I've thought of something to leave you.
It's the view
of Mt. Rainier from the Seattle jail,
snow over cloud. And the rusty chain in my pocket
from a pair of handcuffs my father wore. That's all
the wordly goods I'm seized of.

CARR

Look, Mio—hell—
if you're in trouble—

MIO

I'm not. Not at all. I have
a genius that attends me where I go,
and guards me now. I'm fine.

CARR

Well, that's good news.
He'll have his work cut out.

MIO

Oh, he's a genius.

CARR

I'll see you then.
I'll be at the Grand Street place. I'm lucky tonight,
and I can pay. I could even pay for two.

MIO

Thanks, I may take you up.

CARR

Good night.

MIO

Right, Carr.

CARR
(*To* MIRIAMNE)
Good night.

MIRIAMNE
(*After a pause*)
Good night.
(CARR *goes out to the left.*)
Why did you do that? He's your genius,
   Mio,
and you let him go.

MIO
I couldn't help it.

MIRIAMNE
Call him.
Run after him and call him!

MIO
I tried to say it
and it strangled in my throat. I might
   have known
you'd win in the end.

MIRIAMNE
Is it for me?

MIO
For you?
It stuck in my throat, that's all I know.

MIRIAMNE
Oh, Mio,
I never asked for that! I only hoped
Garth could go clear.

MIO
Well, now he will.

MIRIAMNE
But you—
It was your chance!

MIO
I've lost
my taste for revenge if it falls on you.
   Oh, God,
deliver me from the body of this death
I've dragged behind me all these years!
   Miriamne!
Miriamne!

MIRIAMNE
Yes!

MIO
Miriamne, if you love me
teach me a treason to what I am, and
   have been,
till I learn to live like a man! I think
   I'm waking
from a long trauma of hate and fear
   and death
that's hemmed me from my birth—and
   glimpse a life
to be lived in hope—but it's young in
   me yet, I can't
get free, or forgive! But teach me how
   to live
and forget to hate!

MIRIAMNE
He would have forgiven.

MIO
He?

MIRIAMNE
Your father.
   (*A pause.*)

MIO
(*Another pause.*)
You'll think it strange, but I've never
remembered that.

MIRIAMNE
How can I help you?

MIO
You have.

MIRIAMNE
If I were a little older—if I knew
the things to say! I can only put out
   my hands
and give you back the faith you bring
   to me
by being what you are. Because to me
you are all hope and beauty and bright-
   ness drawn
across what's black and mean!

MIO

He'd have forgiven—
Then there's no more to say—I've
  groped long enough
through this everglades of old revenges
  —here
the road ends.—Miriamne, Miriamne,
the iron I wore so long—it's eaten
  through
and fallen from me. Let me have your
  arms.
They'll say we're children—Well—the
  world's made up
of children.

MIRIAMNE

Yes.

MIO

But it's too late for me.

MIRIAMNE

No.
    (*She goes into his arms, and they
        kiss for the first time.*)
Then we'll meet again?

MIO

Yes.

MIRIAMNE

Where?

MIO

I'll write—
or send Carr to you.

MIRIAMNE

You won't forget?

MIO

Forget?
Whatever streets I walk, you'll walk
  them, too,
from now on, and whatever roof or
  stars
I have to house me, you shall share my
  roof
and stars and morning, I shall not forget.

MIRIAMNE

God keep you!

MIO

And keep you. And this to remember!
If I should die, Miriamne, this half-
  hour
is our eternity. I came here seeking
light in darkness, running from the
  dawn,
and stumbled on a morning.
    (*One of the* YOUNG MEN IN SERGE
        *strolls in casually from the
        right, looks up and down with-
        out expression, then, seem-
        ingly having forgotten some-
        thing, retraces his steps and
        goes out.* ESDRAS *comes in
        slowly from the left. He has
        lost his hat, and his face is
        bleeding from a slight cut on
        the temple. He stands abjectly
        near the tenement.*)

MIRIAMNE

Father—what is it?
    (*She goes towards* ESDRAS.)

ESDRAS

Let me alone.
    (*He goes nearer to* MIO.)
He wouldn't let me pass.
The street's so icy up along the bridge
I had to crawl on my knees—he kicked
  me back
three times—and then he held me there
  —I swear
what I could do I did! I swear to you
I'd save you if I could.

MIO

What makes you think
that I need saving?

ESDRAS

Child, save yourself if you can!
He's waiting for you.

MIO

Well, we knew that before.

ESDRAS

He won't wait much longer. He'll come
  here—
he told me so. Those damned six
  months of his—

he wants them all—and you're to die—
you'd spread
his guilt—I had to listen to it—

MIO

Wait—
　　(*He walks forward and looks cas-
　　ually to the right, then returns.*)
There must be some way up through
the house and out
across the roof—

ESDRAS

He's watching that. But come in—
and let me look.—

MIO

I'll stay here, thanks. Once in
and I'm a rat in a deadfall—I'll stay
here—
look for me if you don't mind.

ESDRAS

Then watch for me—
I'll be on the roof—
　　(*He goes in hurriedly.*)

MIO

　　(*Looking up*)
Now all you silent powers
that make the sleet and dark, and never
yet
have spoken, give us a sign, let the
throw be ours
this once, on this longest night, when
the winter sets
his foot on the threshold leading up to
spring
and enters with remembered cold—let
fall
some mercy with the rain. We are two
lovers
here in your night, and we wish to live.

MIRIAMNE

Oh, Mio—
if you pray that way, nothing good will
come!
You're bitter, Mio.

MIO

How many floors has this building?

MIRIAMNE

Five or six. It's not as high as the
bridge.

MIO

No, I thought not. How many pome-
granate seeds
did you eat, Persephone?

MIRIAMNE

Oh, darling, darling,
if you die, don't die alone.

MIO

I'm afraid I'm damned
to hell, and you're not damned at all.
　Good God,
how long he takes to climb!

MIRIAMNE

The stairs are steep.
　　(*A slight pause.*)

MIO

I'll follow him.

MIRIAMNE

He's there—at the window—now.
He waves you to go back, not to go in.
Mio, see, that path between the rocks—
they're not watching that—they're out
　at the river—
I can see them there—they can't watch
　both—
it leads to a street above.

MIO

I'll try it, then.
Kiss me. You'll hear. But if you never
hear—
then I'm the king of hell, Persephone,
and I'll expect you.

MIRIAMNE

Oh, lover, keep safe.

MIO

Good-bye.
　　(*He slips out quickly between the
　　rocks. There is a quick ma-
　　chine gun rat-tat. The violin*

stops. MIRIAMNE *runs toward the path.* MIO *comes back slowly, a hand pressed under his heart.*)
It seems you were mistaken.

MIRIAMNE

Oh, God, forgive me!
(*She puts an arm round him. He sinks to his knees.*)
Where is it, Mio? Let me help you in!
Quick, quick,
let me help you!

MIO

I hadn't thought to choose—this—ground—
but it will do.
(*He slips down.*)

MIRIAMNE

Oh, God, forgive me!

MIO

Yes?
The king of hell was not forgiven then,
Dis is his name, and Hades is his home—
and he goes alone—

MIRIAMNE

Why does he bleed so? Mio, if you go
I shall go with you.

MIO

It's better to stay alive.
I wanted to stay alive—because of you—
I leave you that—and what he said to me dying:
I love you, and will love you after I die.
Tomorrow, I shall still love you, as I've loved
the stars I'll never see, and all the mornings
that might have been yours and mine.
Oh, Miriamne,
you taught me this.

MIRIAMNE

If only I'd never seen you
then you could live—

MIO

That's blasphemy—Oh, God,
there might have been some easier way of it.
You didn't want me to die, did you, Miriamne—?
You didn't send me away—?

MIRIAMNE

Oh, never, never—

MIO

Forgive me—kiss me—I've got blood on your lips—
I'm sorry—it doesn't matter—I'm sorry—
(ESDRAS *and* GARTH *come out.*)

MIRIAMNE

Mio—
I'd have gone to die myself—you must hear this, Mio,
I'd have died to help you—you must listen, sweet,
you must hear it—
(*She rises.*)
I can die, too, see! You! There!
You in the shadows!—You killed him to silence him!
(*She walks toward the path.*)
But I'm not silenced! All that he knew I know,
and I'll tell it tonight; Tonight—
tell it and scream it
through all the streets—that Trock's a murderer
and he hired you for this murder!
Your work's not done—
and you won't live long! Do you hear?
You're murderers, and I know who you are!
(*The machine gun speaks again. She sinks to her knees.* GARTH *runs to her.*)

GARTH

You little fool!
(*He tries to lift her.*)

MIRIAMNE

Don't touch me!
(*She crawls toward* MIO.)
Look, Mio! They kill me, too. Oh, you can believe me

now, Mio. You can believe I wouldn't
  hurt you,
because I'm dying! Why doesn't he answer me?
Oh, now he'll never know!
  (*She sinks down, her hand over
  her mouth, choking.* GARTH
  *kneels beside her, then rises,
  shuddering. The* HOBO *comes
  out.* LUCIA *and* PINY *look out.*)

ESDRAS

It lacked only this.

GARTH

Yes.
  (ESDRAS *bends over* MIRIAMNE,
  then rises slowly.)
Why was the bastard born? Why did
he come here?

ESDRAS

Miriamne—Miriamne—yes, and Mio,
one breath shall call you now—forgive
  us both—
forgive the ancient evil of the earth
that brought you here—

GARTH

Why must she be a fool?

ESDRAS

Well, they were wiser than you and I.
  To die
when you are young and untouched,
  that's beggary
to a miser of years, but the devils
  locked in synod
shake and are daunted when men set
  their lives
at hazard for the heart's love, and lose.
  And these,

who were yet children, will weigh more
  than all
a city's elders when the experiment
is reckoned up in the end. Oh, Miriamne,
and Mio—Mio, my son—know this
  where you lie,
this is the glory of earth-born men and
  women,
not to cringe, never to yield, but standing,
take defeat implacable and defiant,
die unsubmitting. I wish that I'd died
  so,
long ago; before you're old you'll wish
that you had died as they have. On this
  star,
in this hard star-adventure, knowing
  not
what the fires mean to right and left,
  nor whether
a meaning was intended or presumed,
man can stand up, and look out blind,
  and say:
in all these turning lights I find no clue,
only a masterless night, and in my
  blood
no certain answer, yet is my mind my
  own,
yet is my heart a cry toward something
  dim
in distance, which is higher than I am
and makes me emperor of the endless
  dark
even in seeking! What odds and ends
  of life
men may live otherwise, let them live,
  and then
go out, as I shall go, and you. Our part
is only to bury them. Come, take her
  up.
They must not lie here.
  (LUCIA *and* PINY *come near to
  help.* ESDRAS *and* GARTH *stoop
  to carry* MIRIAMNE.)

High Tor

BY MAXWELL ANDERSON

NOTE

CHARACTERS

Guthrie McClinic presented Maxwell Anderson's HIGH TOR for the first time on any stage in the Hanna Theater, Cleveland, Ohio, Wednesday night, December 30, 1936, with this cast:

THE INDIAN	*Harry Irvine*
VAN VAN DORN	*Burgess Meredith*
JUDITH	*Mab Maynard*
ART. J. BIGGS	*Harold Moffet*
JUDGE SKIMMERHORN	*Thomas W. Ross*
LISE	*Peggy Ashcroft*
CAPTAIN ASHER	*Byron McGrath*
PIETER	*John Philliber*
A SAILOR	*William Casamo*
DE WITT	*Charles D. Brown*
DOPE	*Leslie Gorall*
ELKUS	*Hume Cronyn*
BUDDY	*John Drew Colt*
PATSY	*Charles Forrester*
A. B. SKIMMERHORN	*John M. Kline*
BUDGE	*Jackson Halliday*

DUTCH CREW OF THE *Onrust*

High Tor

ACT ONE

SCENE I

SCENE: *A section of the broad flat trap-rock summit of High Tor, from which one looks out into sky and from which one might look down a sheer quarter mile to the Tappan Zee below. A cluster of hexagonal pillared rocks masks the view to the left and a wind-tortured small hemlock wedges into the rock floor at the right. Light from the setting sun pours in from the left, and an ancient* INDIAN, *wearing an old greatcoat thrown round him like a blanket, stands in the rays from a cleft, making his prayer to the sunset.*

THE INDIAN

I make my prayer to you, the falling fire,
bearing in mind the whisper in my ears
from the great spirit, talking on the wind,
whispering that a young race, in its morning,
should pray to the rising sun, but a race that's old
and dying, should invoke the dying flame
eaten and gulfed by the shark-toothed mountain-west,
a god that dies to live. As we have died,
my race of the red faces and old ways,
and as we hope to rise, I give you thanks
for light, for the coming summer that will warm
my snake's blood, cold and crawling; for the rain
that fed the ripe May apples in the woods
in secret for me; for the waterfall
where the trout climb and pause under my hand,
taken in silence; for quiet on the hills
where the loud races dare not walk for fear

lest they be lost, where their blind hunters pass
peering with caps and guns, but see no game,
and curse as they go down, while the raccoon waits,
the woodchuck stands erect to catch the wind,
the partridge steps so lightly over leaves
the listening fox hears nothing, the possum hangs
head down, looking through his hands, and takes no breath,
the gray squirrel turns to stone against the rock,
watching the owl, the rabbit holds his ears
steady above the trembling of his heart
and the crow mocks down the shell-bark. I am fed
and sheltered on this mountain where their hands
are helpless. But I am old as my race is old;
my eyes hunt day and night along the ground
the grave where I shall lie; my ears have heard
dead women calling upward from the earth,

87

mother and wife and child: "You are
   welcome here;
you are no longer welcome where you
   walk,
but here you are most welcome." I
   shall go,
and lie and sleep, and I shall give you
   thanks,
O God that dies, that my last night is
   dark
and long, for I am tired, but yet I ask
one summer more, that I may be warm
   again,
and watch the nestlings grown upon
   the crag,
and hear the wild geese honking south
   by night,
if this may be, but if it may not be
then is my prayer, that when I lie to
   sleep
I may lie long, sleep soundly, hear no
   step,
hear only through the earth your step
   in spring,
O God of the dying fire!
      (van dorn *and* judith *come in*
      from the right.)

VAN DORN

Evening, John.

THE INDIAN

Evening.

VAN DORN

Had any luck so far?

THE INDIAN

Yes. Plenty of luck.

VAN DORN

Found it?

THE INDIAN

Yes.

VAN DORN

O.K., John, let me know.
Let me know in time.

THE INDIAN

I will. Good night.

VAN DORN

Good night.
      (*The* INDIAN *slips away through*
      the rocks to the left.)

JUDITH

Who is it, Van?

VAN

Just an Indian.

JUDITH

Are there Indians?
I didn't know there were any Indians
left.

VAN

Well, there's one. There's not much left
of him, and he's the last around here.

JUDITH

He's hunting for something?
You asked him if he'd found it.

VAN

Um—yes, you see,
he's looking for a place to make his
   grave,
and he's kind of captious about it—
   folks get that way
along toward the end, wanting their
   bones done up
in some particular fashion. Maybe because
that's all you've got to leave about that
   time
and you want it the way you want it.

JUDITH

Did he tell you this?

VAN

We've got an understanding. When he
   feels it
coming over him he's going to die
he'll let me know, and I'll go dig him in
so the crows and foxes can't get at him.
   See,
he's all alone in the world. We fixed
   this up
a couple of years ago.

JUDITH

But you couldn't Van,
without a permit. A burial permit.

VAN

Oh,
I guess you could. This getting old and
dying
and crawling into the ground, that was
invented
back before medical examiners
and taxes and all that. The old boy's
clean.
He'll go right back to dirt.

JUDITH

But, Van, you can't!
People can't die that way!

VAN

I guess they can.
What the hell good's being wrapped in
cellophane?
You don't keep anyway.

JUDITH

You're impossible
to live with! Why do you say such
things? If I
should die—you'd get a pine box!—

VAN

If you should die
the old boy that drives the sun around
up there,
he'd unhitch, and put the cattle out
to grass, and give it up. He'd plumb
lose interest
if you should die. Maybe I would myself,
I don't say. Maybe I would.—Fetch out
that supper.
We want to see what we eat.

JUDITH
        (Opening a lunch box)
It's dinner, Van,
not supper.

VAN

That's what I said. Fetch out that dinner.

When it gets a little darker what's
black's pepper
and what's green's parsley; still you
can't be sure.
It might be ants.

JUDITH

Just the same we'll quarrel.
We'll always quarrel.

VAN

Oh, no. We've both got sense.
What's the sense fighting?
        (He looks at a paper that was
        round the lunch.)

JUDITH

And you shouldn't read at table.

VAN

I never do. The Nanuet bank's been
robbed.
My God, there's not enough money in
Nanuet
to buy their gas for a get-away. One
night
pap and me sat in on a poker game
in Nanuet and took twenty-seven dollars
out of town. Next day they couldn't do
business.
The place was clean.

JUDITH

There were troopers at the train
tonight, and sirens going through Haverstraw,
but the robbers got away.

VAN

They took twenty-five thousand.
How'd twenty-five thousand get to
Nanuet?
It's against nature.

JUDITH

It didn't stay there long.

VAN

No—I understand that.
But just to have it there in passing,
just

to look at, just to fool the customers,
how do they do it?

JUDITH

Maybe it wasn't real.

VAN

Federal money, that's it. Some of the
    stuff
Jim Farley prints in Washington with
    the stamps
to pay you for voting straight. Only
    now you see it
and now you don't.

JUDITH

They say it buys as much
as if you earned it.

VAN

Bad for the stomach, though,
to live on humble pie.

JUDITH

I'd rather work.

VAN

Well, as I said, don't work if you don't
    feel like it.
Any time you want to move up in the
    hills
and sleep with me, it's a bargain.

JUDITH

Van!

VAN

Why not?
We'll get married if that's what you
    mean.

JUDITH

You haven't any job. And you make
    it sound
like animals.

VAN

I'm fond of animals.

JUDITH

You shoot them all the time.

VAN

Well, I get hungry.
Any man's liable to get hungry.

JUDITH

Van, I want to talk to you seriously.

VAN

Can't be done.
Listen, things get serious enough
without setting out to do it.

JUDITH

Van, this spring
you had three weeks' work, laying dry
    wall.
You could have had more, but you
    didn't take it.
You're an expert mason—

VAN

I'm good at everything.

JUDITH

But you work three weeks in the year—

VAN

That's all I need—

JUDITH

And all the rest of the year you hunt
    or fish
or sleep, or God knows what—

VAN

Ain't it the truth?

JUDITH

Last fall I came looking for you once,
    and you
were gone—gone to Port Jervis hunting
    —deer,
you said on the postcard—

VAN

Sure, I was hunting deer—
didn't I bring you half a venison?

JUDITH

But not a word to me till I got the
    postcard
ten days later—

VAN

Didn't have a minute—

JUDITH

Then last winter there's a note nailed
  to a tree
and you're in Virginia, down in the
  Dismal Swamp
tracking bear. Now, for God's sake,
  Van,
it's no way to live.

VAN

Jeez, it's a lot of fun.

JUDITH

Maybe for you.

VAN

You want me to take that job.

JUDITH

Why don't you, Van?

VAN

Porter in a hotel, lugging up satchels,
opening windows, maybe you get a
  dime.
I'd choke to death.

JUDITH

I'd see you every day.

VAN

Yeah, I could see you on the mezza-
  nine,
taking dictation from the drummer
  boys,
all about how they can't get home. You
  can stand it,
a woman stands that stuff, but if you're
  a man
I say it chokes you.

JUDITH

We can't live in your cabin
and have no money, like the Jackson
  Whites
over at Suffern.

VAN

Hell, you don't need money.
Pap worked that out. All you need's a
  place to sleep
and something to eat. I've never seen
  the time
I couldn't find a meal on the mountain
  here,
rainbow trout, jugged hare, something
  in season
right around the zodiac.

JUDITH

You didn't like
the Chevrolet factory, either?

VAN

  (*Walking toward the cliff edge*)
Look at it, Judy.
That's the Chevrolet factory, four miles
  down,
and straight across, that's Sing Sing.
  Right from here
you can't tell one from another; get inside,
and what's the difference? You're in
  there, and you work,
and they've got you. If you're in the
  factory
you buy a car, and then you put in
  your time
to pay for the goddam thing. If you get
  in a hurry
and steal a car, they put you in Sing
  Sing first,
and then you work out your time. They
  graduate
from one to the other, back and forth,
  those guys,
paying for cars both ways. But I was
  smart.
I parked at a polis station and rung
  the bell
and took to the woods. Not for your
  Uncle Dudley.
They plugged the dice.

JUDITH

But one has to have a car.

VAN

Honest to God now, Judy, what's the
   hurry?
Where in hell are we going?

JUDITH

If a man works hard,
and has ability, as you have, Van,
he takes a place among them, saves his
   money,
works right out of the ruck and gets
   above
where he's safe and secure.

VAN

I wouldn't bet on it much.

JUDITH

But it's true.

VAN

All right, suppose it's true. Suppose
a man saves money all his life, and
   works
like hell about forty years, still he can
   say:
good-bye, I'm going. I'm on easy street
from now on. What's he do?

JUDITH

Takes a vacation.

VAN

Goes fishing, maybe? I'm on vacation
   now.
Why should I work for forty years to
   earn
time off when I've got it?

JUDITH

It's not always easy,
you know it's not. There was that time
   last winter
when I helped you out.

VAN

Why, sure, you helped me out.
Why wouldn't you? But if you didn't
   help me
I'd get along.

JUDITH

Yes, you would. I know you would.
But you don't even seem to want
   money. You won't take it
when they bring it to you.

VAN

When did they bring me any?

JUDITH

And what if there was a child?

VAN

Why he'd be fine—
the less they have the better they like
   it.—Oh,
you mean the trap-rock company, wanting to buy
High Tor? They offered seven hundred
   dollars—
and they offered pap ten thousand before he died,
and he wouldn't sell.

JUDITH

He wouldn't?

VAN

They want to chew
the back right off this mountain, the
   way they did
across the clove there. Leave the old
   palisades
sticking up here like billboards, nothing
   left
but a false front facing the river. Not
   for pap,
and not for me. I like this place.

JUDITH

But, Van Van Dorn!
Ten thousand dollars!

VAN

Well, it's Federal money.
Damn stuff evaporates. Put it in a sock
along with moth balls, and come back
   next year,
and there's nothing left but the smell.
   Look, Judy, it's

a quarter mile straight down to the
Tappan Zee
from here.—You can see fifteen miles of
river
north and south. I grew up looking at
it.
Hudson came up that river just about
three hundred years ago, and lost a
ship
here in the Zee. They say the crew
climbed up
this Tor to keep a lookout for the fleet
that never came. Maybe the Indians
got them.
Anyway on dark nights before a storm,
they say you sometimes see them.

JUDITH

Have you seen them?

VAN

The Dutchman? Maybe I have. You
can't be sure.
It's pretty wild around here when it
storms.
That's when I like it best. But look at
it now.
There was a Jaeger here from Switzerland
last year. He took one squint at this
and said
they could keep their Alps, for all him.
Look at the willows
along the far breakwater.

JUDITH

It's beautiful.

VAN

Every night I come back here like the
Indian
to get a fill of it. Seven hundred dollars
and tear it down? Hell, no.
  (BIGGS and SKIMMERHORN come in
  from the right, a bit bedraggled, and wiping their brows.
  SKIMMERHORN carries a brief-
  case. It is growing darker.)

BIGGS

Hey listen, Mac, any houses round
here?

VAN

Guess you're off the beat, buddy; never
heard of any houses on the mountain.

SKIMMERHORN

Come on, Art; we're doing well if we're
down at the road before dark.

BIGGS

Look, Mac, maybe you can help us out.
You familiar with this region, at all?

VAN

I've been around here some.

BIGGS

Well, we're all afternoon hunting a
cabin that's somewhere along the ridge.
Ever hear of it?

VAN

Anybody live in it?

BIGGS

Fellow named Van Dorn.

VAN

Oh, yes, sure.

BIGGS

You know where it is?

VAN

Sure. You climb down the face of the
cliff here and keep left along the ledge
about a hundred yards, then you turn
sharp left through a cleft up the ridge.
Follow the trail about half a mile and
there you are.

SKIMMERHORN

Down the face of the cliff?

VAN

Down through the rocks there, then
turn left—

SKIMMERHORN

A monkey couldn't go down there,
hanging on with four hands and a tail!

VAN

Well, you can always walk along back toward Little Tor, and cut down from there through the gulch. There's a slough at the bottom of the ravine, but if you get through that you can see the cabin up on the sidehill. About four miles that way.

SKIMMERHORN

Yeah, we'll set right out. I always did want to get lost up here and spend a night in the hills.

VAN

Oh, you'll get lost, all right.

BIGGS

Any snakes?

VAN

No, you might see a copperhead, or a timber rattler.

SKIMMERHORN

Coming back down?

BIGGS

Yeah, we'd better go down. Thanks.

VAN

Don't mention it.
    (BIGGS and SKIMMERHORN go out
      to the right.)

JUDITH

But they were looking for you?

VAN

Yeah.

JUDITH

Why didn't you tell them?

VAN

What?

JUDITH

Who you were!

VAN

They didn't ask about that.

JUDITH

But out of common courtesy!

VAN

Well, you see, I know who they are.

JUDITH

Who are they?

VAN

Art J. Biggs, Junior, and Skimmerhorn, Judge Skimmerhorn.

JUDITH

But why not talk to them?

VAN

Oh, we communicate by mail. I've got a dozen letters stacked up from the firm:
Skimmerhorn, Skimmerhorn, Biggs and Skimmerhorn,
and maybe two or three Skimmerhorns I left out
printed across the top. They're realtors, whatever that is, and they own the trap-rock company,
and one of the Skimmerhorns, he's probate judge,
and goes around condemning property when they want to make a rake-off.
    Take a letter:
Dear Skimmerhorn—

JUDITH

But they're the trap-rock men!

VAN

That's what I said.

JUDITH

I'll call them!

VAN

Oh, no; oh, no!
I've got nothing to say to those two buzzards
except I hope they break their fat-back necks
on their own trap-rock.

JUDITH

You take a lot for granted.

VAN

Do I?

JUDITH

You think, because I said I loved you once,
that's the end; I'm finished.

VAN

Oh, far from it.

JUDITH

Oh, yes—you think because a girl's been kissed
she stays kissed, and after that the man does her thinking for her.

VAN

Hell, it's all I can do
to handle my own thinking.

JUDITH

If we're married
I'll have to live the way you want to live.
You prefer being a pauper!

VAN

Get it straight!
I don't take money nor orders, and I live
as I damn well please.

JUDITH

But we'd live like paupers!
and you could have a fortune!

VAN

Seven hundred dollars?

JUDITH

You could get more!

VAN

I don't mean to sell at all.

JUDITH

You see; it's your place, and your thinking! You decide,
but I'd have to stand it with you!

VAN

What do you want?

JUDITH

Something to start on; and now, you see, we could have it,
only you won't!

VAN

I can't, Judy, that's the truth.
I just can't.

JUDITH

They'll get it anyway.
They've worked right up to where your land begins,
and they won't stop for you. They'll just condemn it
and take it.

VAN

They'll be in trouble.

JUDITH

You can't make trouble
for companies. They have a dozen lawyers
and ride right over you. I've worked for them.
It's never any use.

VAN

Well, I won't sell.

JUDITH

We'll call it off then.

VAN

What?

JUDITH

Between you and me.

VAN

Only you don't mean it.

JUDITH

I know I do, though.
You haven't thought about it, and so you think
I couldn't do it. But it's better now than later.

VAN

You don't know what it means to me
if you can say it.

JUDITH

It means as much to me,
but I look ahead a little.

VAN

What do you see?

JUDITH

Two people growing old
and having children, running wild in
    the woods
with nothing.

VAN

There's no better place to run.
But I've been counting on you. More
    than you know.
More than—Judy, this is the kind of
    night
we've been in love most.

JUDITH

Yes, we could be in love,
but that's not everything.

VAN

Well, just about.
What else do we get?

JUDITH

I think I'd better go.
It's getting dark.

VAN

You could find your way by the beacon.

JUDITH

I'd better go.
        (BIGGS *and* SKIMMERHORN *come
        back from the right.*)

BIGGS

Listen, Mac, would you do something
    for us?

VAN

I don't know.

BIGGS

Could you take a paper round to Van
Dorn and leave it with him?

VAN

A summons?

BIGGS

A sort of notice.

VAN

Yeah, a notice to appear. No, I couldn't.

BIGGS

It's worth a dollar to me.

VAN

I'd be cheating you.

SKIMMERHORN

Make it two dollars.

VAN

You'd be throwing away money.

SKIMMERHORN

Never mind that part of it. Will you
do it?

VAN

You'll take a running jump over the
edge of the cliff and think things over on
the way down before I serve any papers for you.

BIGGS

What's the matter with us?

VAN

Might be hoof and mouth disease, for
all I know. You certainly brought an
awful stench up here with you.

SKIMMERHORN

Not much on manners, these natives.

VAN

My rule in life is keep away from
skunks.

BIGGS

You'll get the tar kicked out of you one of these days.

VAN

Make it today.

JUDITH

If you gentlemen care to know, this is Mr. Van Dorn.

BIGGS

Say, are you Van Dorn?

VAN

Sure I am.

BIGGS

(*Extending a hand*)
Oh, in that case, forget it—you're the fellow we want to see!—Boy, we apologize—
(*He uncovers.*)
and to the lady, too! Listen, I don't know what to say but you've got us all wrong. We want to buy this place!

VAN

You like the view, I suppose?

BIGGS

Certainly is a view.

VAN

You wouldn't spoil it, of course? You wouldn't move in with a million dollars worth of machinery and cut the guts out of the mountain, would you?

SKIMMERHORN

We always leave the front—the part you see from the river.

VAN

But you take down all the law allows.

SKIMMERHORN

Well, we're in business.

VAN

Not with me.

JUDITH

Do you mind if I ask how much you're offering?

BIGGS

We said seven hundred, but I'll make it a thousand right here and now.

SKIMMERHORN

As a matter of fact, we'll make it two thousand.

BIGGS

Yeah, all right. Two thousand for the hundred and seven acres.

JUDITH

But you offered Mr. Van Dorn's father ten thousand before he died.

SKIMMERHORN

His father had a clear title, right down from the original Dutch patroon to the original Van Dorn. But unfortunately the present Mr. Van Dorn has a somewhat clouded claim to the acreage.

VAN

My father's title was clear, and he left it to me.

SKIMMERHORN

The truth is he should have employed a lawyer when he drew his will, because the instrument, as recorded, is faulty in many respects. It was brought before me in my capacity as probate judge at Ledentown.

VAN

And in your capacity as second vice-president of the trap-rock company you shot it full of holes.

SKIMMERHORN

Sir, I keep my duties entirely separate.

VAN

Sure, but when your left hand takes money your right hand finds out about it. And when there's too much to carry

away in both hands you use a basket.
You're also vice-president of the power
company, and you stole right-of-ways
clear across the county north and
south—

SKIMMERHORN

We paid for every foot of land—

VAN

Yes, at your own price.

BIGGS

Let's not get in an argument, Mr. Van
Dorn, because the fact that your father's will was improperly drawn means
he died intestate and the land goes to
his heirs. Now we've found twenty-
seven Van Dorns living at Blauvelt, all
claiming relationship and all willing to
sign away their rights for a consideration.

VAN

The best you can do you'll need my
name in your little paper, and you
won't have it.

SKIMMERHORN

To put it straight, you'll take three
thousand dollars, and I'll hold the will
valid.

VAN

Oh, it's three thousand, now?

BIGGS

You'll say that's crooked, but it's not.
It's perfectly legal—and it's what you
get.

VAN

I'm still waiting to hear what you do
about my signature.

SKIMMERHORN

It's quite possible you'll be held incompetent by the court and a guardian
appointed.

VAN

Me, incompetent.

SKIMMERHORN

But I've got the validation in my
pocket, naming you executor, if you'll
sell.

BIGGS

And by God, anybody that won't take
money when it's offered to him is incompetent! And you'll take it now or
not at all! I don't go mountain-climbing every day with a blank check in my
pocket!
(A pause.)
Come on: It's bad enough sliding down
that trail by daylight.

VAN

Well, I wouldn't want to make you
nervous,
a couple of eminent respectables
like you two—but a dog won't bite a
Dutchman—
maybe you've heard that—and the reason is
a Dutchman's poison when he don't
like you. Now,
I'm Dutch and I don't like you.

SKIMMERHORN

That's a threat?

VAN

Not at all. Only don't try to eat me
or you'll curl up. I'm poison to a
hound-dog,
and you're both sons-of-bitches.

BIGGS

Come on.
(The daylight is now gone. The
airplane beacon lights the
scene from the right.)

VAN

What's more
there's something funny about this
mountain-top.
It draws fire. Every storm on the Tappan Zee
climbs up here and wraps itself around
High Tor, and blazes away at what
you've got,

airplane beacon, steam-shovels, anything
newfangled. It smashed the beacon
twice. It blew
the fuses on your shovel and killed a
man
only last week. I've got a premonition
something might happen to you.

BIGGS

God, he's crazy.

SKIMMERHORN

Yeah, let him talk.
    (*There is a sudden rumbling roar
    of falling rock.*)

BIGGS

What's that?

VAN

That's nothing much.
That's just a section of the cliff come
down
across the trail. I've been expecting it
this last two years. You'd better go
down this way.

BIGGS

This way?

VAN

Yeah.

BIGGS

No, thanks.

VAN

Just as you say.
But there's something definitely hostile
here
toward you two pirates. Don't try that
trail in the dark.
Not if you want to be buried in your
vaults
in Mount Repose. Your grieving families
might have to move two thousand tons
of rock
to locate your remains. You think High
Tor's
just so much raw material, but you're
wrong.

A lot of stubborn men have died up
here
and some of them don't sleep well.
They come back
and push things round, these dark
nights. Don't blame me
if anything falls on you.

SKIMMERHORN

Oh, what the hell!
Let's get out of here.
    (*Another long rumble of falling
    rock.*)

VAN

Another rock-fall.
Once they start there's likely to be
more.
Something hanging round in the dark
up here
doesn't like you boys. Not only me.
Better go down this way.

BIGGS

Thanks.
    (BIGGS *and* SKIMMERHORN *go out
    to the right.*)

JUDITH

What do you mean?

VAN

I don't know.

JUDITH

They'll say you threatened them.
Good-bye, Van.

VAN

You'll be up tomorrow?

JUDITH

No.
    (*She steps down into a cleft.*)

VAN

You'd better let me see you down.

JUDITH

Oh, no.
I can climb. Stay here and guard your
rock—
you think so much of it.

VAN

When will I see you?

JUDITH

Never.
We'll forget about it. You had a choice
and you chose High Tor. You're in love
with your mountain.
Well, keep your mountain.

VAN

All right.

JUDITH

Good night.

VAN

Good night.
(*She disappears down the rocks.*
VAN *sits in the shadow, looking into darkness. After a moment a barely perceptible* FIG-
URE *enters from the gloom at
the right and crosses the stage
toward the rocks at the left.*

*At the foot of the climb he
pauses and his face is caught
in the light of the beacon. He
is seen to be young or middle-
aged, bearded, and wearing
the costume of a Dutch sailor
of the sixteen hundreds. He
climbs the rocks, and* ANOTHER
SAILOR, *a small cask strapped
to his shoulders, follows.* THREE
MORE *cross the stage similarly,
then the* CAPTAIN *and* HIS WIFE
*pause, like the others, in the
light of the beacon. The* CAP-
TAIN *is like his men, only
younger perhaps;* HIS WIFE *is a
tiny figure, with a delicate girl-
ish face looking out from under
the Dutch bonnet. They too
pass up the rocks, and are followed by a rolling* SILENUS *in
the same garments. As they
vanish* VAN *rises, looking after
them.*)
Uh—huh—going to rain.

SCENE II

SCENE: *The curtain goes up on complete darkness enfolding the summit of the
Tor. There is a long cumbrous rolling, as of a ball going down a bowling alley,
a flash of white light, a crackling as of falling pins and a mutter dying into
echo along the hills. The flash reveals the outline of the Tor, black against the
sky, and on it the figures of the* DUTCH CREW. *Again the roll, the flash, the
break and the dying away. The beam of the airplane beacon steals into the
scene sufficiently to suggest the bowlers, some of them standing, some sitting
about the keg, the* CAPTAIN'S WIFE *a little apart from the rest. Beyond the
peak is a moving floor, the upper side of blown cloud.*

THE CAPTAIN'S WIFE

I'm weary of it, Martin! When you
drink
there should be one on guard to watch
the river
lest the ship come, and pass, and we
must haunt
the dark another year!

THE CAPTAIN

To humor her,
Pieter, old son, climb down and post
the Zee,
and mind you keep good lookout.

PIETER

Ships, aye, ships—
when the ball's rolling and there's gin
in hand
I go to post. My luck!

THE CAPTAIN

When you shipped with me
you signed the voyage.

PIETER

Is this sea or land?
I'm no foot soldier!

THE CAPTAIN

March!

PIETER

Aye, aye. I'm going.
(PIETER *detaches himself from
the group and goes down the
rocks.*)

THE CAPTAIN

Are you content?

THE CAPTAIN'S WIFE

When the *Half Moon* returns
and we have boarded her, and the
wind scuds fair
into the east—yes, when we see the
wharves
of Texel town across the Zuyder Zee,
with faces waiting for us, hands and
cries
to welcome our returning, then perhaps
I shall be content.

A SAILOR

Now God, for Texel town.

ANOTHER SOLDIER

(*Rising*)
I'll drink no more.

DE WITT

(*The Silenus*)
Drink up, lads, and forget.
It's a long way to the Texel. Drink your
drink
and play your play.

THE CAPTAIN

Drink up and play it out.

THE CAPTAIN'S WIFE

Have you forgotten how the cobbled
street
comes down by cranks and turns upon
the quay,
where the *Onrust* set sail? The traders'
doors
under the blowing signs, bright colors
hung
to catch unwary eyes? The bakers'
ovens

and the long, hot brown loaves? The
red-coal fires
and silver under candles? There your
wives
wait for you, their sharp roofs in Amsterdam
cut on a rainy sky.

THE CAPTAIN

Be quiet, Lise.
You were so much in love you must
come with me;
you were so young that I was patient
with you,
but now day long, night long you carp
and quarrel,
a carping wife.

LISE

We stay so long—so long;
Asher, at first the days were years, but
now
the years are days; the ship that set us
down
to watch this river palisade becomes
alike with supper-stories round a hearth
when we were children. Was there this
ship at all,
was there a sailor-city, Amsterdam,
where the salt water washed the shallow piers
and the wind went out to sea? Will the
ship return,
and shall I then see the Netherlands
once more,
with sabots clattering homeward from
the school
on winter evenings?

ASHER

Aye, there was a ship,
and we wait here for her, but she's long
away,
somewhere up-river.

LISE

And how you drink and drink,
distill your liquor on the mountain-top
and bowl against the light. But when
you break it
these new strange men come build it
up again;

and giant shovels spade the mountain
  down,
and when you break them still the new
  strange men
rig them afresh and turn them on the
  rock,
eating the pillared stone. We must go
  back.
There's no safety here.

A SAILOR

We must go back.

ASHER

These muttering fools!

LISE

Oh, Asher, I'm afraid!
For one thing I have known, and never
  told
lest it be true, lest you be frightened,
  too,
lest we be woven of shadow! As the
  years
have gone, each year a century, they
  seem
less real, and all the boundaries of
  time,
our days and nights and hours, merge
  and are one,
escaping me. Then sometimes in a
  morning
when all the crew come down the
  rocks together,
holding my breath, I see you in the
  light,
and back of you the gray rock bright
  and hard,
seen through figures of air! And you,
  and you,
and you were but cloud-drift walking,
  pierced by the light,
translucent in the sun.

DE WITT

Now damn the woman!

LISE

Love, love, before our blood
be shadow only, in a dark fairyland
so far from home, we must go back, go
  back

where earth is earth, and we may live
  again
and one day be one day!

ASHER

Why, then, I knew it,
and I have known it, now that you
  know it, too.
But the old Amsterdam of our fare-
  wells
lies in another world. The land and sea
about us on this dark side of the earth
is thick with demons, heavy with enchantment,
cutting us off from home.

LISE

Is it enchantment?
Yes, it may be. At home there were
  tulips growing
along my bordered path, but here the
  flowers
are strange to me, not one I knew, no
  trace
of any flower I knew; no, seedlings set
upon a darkened, alien outer rim
of sea, blown here as we were blown,
  enchanted,
drunken and blind with sorcery.

ASHER

And yet
what we're to have we shall have here.
  Years past
the demons of this air palsied our
  hands,
fixed us upon one pinnacle of time,
and on this pinnacle of stone, and all
the world we knew slid backward to
  the gulf,
stranding us here like seaweed on the
  shingle,
remembering the sea. In Texel town
new houses have gone up, after new
  fashions;
the children of the children of our
  days,
lying awake to think of what has been,
reach doubtfully beyond the clouds of
  years
back to our sailing out of Texel. Men

are like the gods, work miracles, have
power
to pierce the walls with music. Their
beacon light
destroys us. You have seen us in the
sun,
wraithlike, half-effaced, the print we
make
upon the air thin tracery, permeable,
a web of wind. They have changed us.
We may take
the fire-balls of the lightning in our
hands
and bowl them down the level floor of
cloud
to wreck the beacon, yet there was a
time
when these were death to touch. The
life we keep
is motionless as the center of a storm,
yet while we can we keep it; while we
can
snuff out to darkness their bright
sweeping light,
melt down the harness of the slow machines
that hew the mountain from us. When
it goes
we shall go too. They leave us this
place, High Tor,
and we shall have no other. You learn
it last.
A long while now we've known.

A SAILOR

Aye, aye, a long while.

ASHER

Come, we'll go down.
(*The* CAPTAIN *and his* MEN *go
out, leaving only* DE WITT *with*
LISE.)

LISE

That's why they drink.

DE WITT

It's enough to drive a sailor-man to
drink, by the great jib boom, marooned
somewhere on the hinder parts of the
earth and degenerating hourly to the
status of a flying Dutchman, half-spook

and half God-knows-what. Maps and
charts we have, compass and sextant,
but the ships these days are bewitched
like ourselves, spanking up and down
the Mauritius with sails struck, against
wind and tide, and on fire from below.
Drink? Why wouldn't we drink? A
pewter flagon of Hollands gin puts
manhood into the remnants and gives a
sailor courage to look out on these
fanciful new devils that ride sea, land
and air on a puff of blue smoke.
They're all witches and mermaids,
these new-world devils, dancing
around on bubbles, speaking a language God never heard, and nothing
human about them except when they
fall they break like the rest of us.

LISE

If I had known. It's not too late. The
sun
still rises in the east and lays a course
toward the old streets and days. These
are my hands
as when I was a child. Some great
magician,
binding a half-world in his wiles, has
laid
a spell here. We must break it and go
home.
I see this clearly.

DE WITT

Lise, little heart, the devils are too
much for us. God knows it's a hard
thing to say, and I'd help you if I
could help myself, but all hell wouldn't
know where we are nor where we
ought to go. The very points of the
compass grow doubtful these latter
years, partly because I'm none too
sober and partly because the great
master devil sits on top of the world
stirring up north and south with a long
spoon to confuse poor mariners. I've
seen him at it, a horned bull three
times the size of Dundenberg and with
more cloven feet than the nine beasts
in Revelations. Very clearly I saw him,
too, as clear as you see the east and a
path across the waters.

LISE

Are we to wait till all the color steals
from flower and cloud, before our eyes;
  till a wind
out of the morning from the Tappan
  Zee
lifts us, we are so light, for all our crying,
and takes us down the valleys toward
  the west,
and all we are becomes a voiceless cry
heard on the wind?

DE WITT

We'll see the time, if they continue to
work on us, when we'll be apparent in
a strong light only by the gin contained
in our interior piping. The odor itself,
along with that of church-warden tobacco, should be sufficient to convince
a magistrate of our existence.—You
tremble, little Lise, and you weep, but
look now, there's a remedy I've had in
mind. Fall in love with one of them.
Fall in love with one of these same
strange new-world magicians. I shall
choose me out one of their female mer-
maid witches, and set my heart on her,
and become a man again. And for
God's sake let her love me strongly
and hold on, lest I go down the brook
like a spring freshlet in the next
pounding rain.

LISE

I gave my love long ago, and it's no
  help.
I love enough.

DE WITT

Aye, but he's in a worse case than you
are, the Captain. Saving his captaincy,
there's not enough belief in him to
produce half a tear in a passion of sobbing. You'll make me weep, little one,
and what tears I have I shall need, lest
my protestation turns out to be a dry
rain.

LISE

Aye, we were warned before we came
  away
against the cabalistic words and signs
of those who dwell along these unknown waters;
never to watch them dance nor hear
  them sing
nor draw their imprecations—lest their
  powers
weave a weird medicine throughout
  the air,
chilling the blood, transfixing body and
  mind
and we be chained invisibly, our eyes
  darkened,
our wrists and breasts pulseless, an-
  chored in time,
like birds blown back in a wind. But
  we have listened,
and we are stricken through with light
  and sound,
empty as autumn leaves, empty as
  prayers
that drift in a godless heaven. Mean-
  ingless,
picked clean of meaning, stripped of
  bone and will,
the chrysalids of locusts staring here
at one another.

DE WITT

If it's true it's enough to make a man
weep for himself, Lise, and for all lost
mariners, wherever they are, and for us
more than any, here on these spell-
bound rocks, drawing up water from
time past—the well growing deeper,
and the water lower, till there be none.
  (*He turns away to go down the
    path.*)

SCENE III

SCENE: *Another section of the Tor, in darkness save for the airplane beacon. A large steam shovel reaches in from an adjacent excavation and hangs over the rock, the control cables dangling.* VAN *is alone on the stage looking at the machinery. He reaches up, catches a cable, and swings the shovel a little.* BIGGS *and* SKIMMERHORN *enter from the right.*

BIGGS

Hey, what are you doing with that shovel?

VAN

Did you know you're trespassing? Also when a man owns land he owns the air above it and the rock below. That means this damn shovel of yours is also trespassing.

BIGGS

Oh, it's Van Dorn. We'll have that moved tomorrow, Mr. Van Dorn. Somebody's made a miscue and left it hanging over the line.

SKIMMERHORN

By the way, that trail's gone out completely, Mr. Van Dorn; there's a fifty foot sheer drop there now, where it was. Now we've got to get off, if you can think of any way to manage it.

VAN

I'm not worrying about it. Spend the night. No charge.

SKIMMERHORN

The truth is I have to be in court early tomorrow, and a man needs his sleep.

VAN

Afraid you'd doze off on the bench and somebody else might take a trick? Oh, you'd wake up before they got far with anything. The Skimmerhorns are automatic that way.

BIGGS

You don't know any other trail down?

VAN

I showed you the one I knew, and you both turned green looking at it. What am I supposed to do now? Pin wings on you?
(*He goes out to the right.*)

SKIMMERHORN

I think I'll swear out a warrant for that squirt. He's too independent by half.

BIGGS

On what ground?

SKIMMERHORN

He threatened us, didn't he?

BIGGS

And where'll that get us?

SKIMMERHORN

He might be easier to talk to in jail.

BIGGS

That's true.

SKIMMERHORN
(*Sitting on a rock*)
This is a hell of a mess.

BIGGS

You're explaining to me?

SKIMMERHORN

What did we ever come up here for?

BIGGS

Twenty-two thousand dollars.

SKIMMERHORN

Will we get it?

BIGGS

It'll look all right on the books.

SKIMMERHORN

It's not good enough, though.

BIGGS

What are you grousing about?

SKIMMERHORN

Because I want my dinner, damn it! And because I'm tired of taking forty per cent and giving you sixty on all the side bets! I want half!

BIGGS

You're damn sight more likely to get your dinner. You're overpaid already.

SKIMMERHORN

The will's perfectly good. I could find holes in it, but I've probated plenty much the same.

BIGGS

What of it?

SKIMMERHORN

A judge has some conscience, you know. When he sets a precedent he likes to stick to it.

BIGGS

I never knew your conscience to operate except on a cash basis. You want half.

SKIMMERHORN

Yes, I want half.

BIGGS

Well, you don't get it. Any other judge I put in there'd work for nothing but the salary and glad of the job. You take a forty per cent cut and howl for more. The woods are full of shyster lawyers looking for probate judgeships and I'll slip one in at Ledentown next election.

SKIMMERHORN

Oh, no, you won't, Art; oh, no, you won't. You wouldn't do that to an old friend like me; because if you did, think what I'd do to an old friend like you.

BIGGS

Well, maybe I wouldn't. Not if you're reasonable. Look, what's the difference between forty per cent and fifty per cent? Practically nothing!

SKIMMERHORN

Then why don't you give it to me?

BIGGS

Because, try and get it!—

SKIMMERHORN

Damn it, I'm hungry.—I ought to telephone my wife, too.

BIGGS

Why don't you?

SKIMMERHORN

Maybe it's fun for you—nothing to eat, no place to sleep, cold as hell, black as Tophet and a storm coming up! Only I'm not used to it!

BIGGS

You're pulling down forty per cent of twenty-two thousand dollars for the night's work. I say it's worth it.

SKIMMERHORN

Think we could slide down one of those cables?

BIGGS

Maybe you could, Humpty-Dumpty, but not me.

SKIMMERHORN

I'm going to look at it.
(*He goes out left,* BIGGS *following. After a moment* THREE MEN *climb in through the rocks at the right, one of them carrying*

a small zipper satchel. They throw themselves down wearily on the rock. They are, in brief, the Nanuet bank robbers, ELKUS, DOPE *and* BUDDY.)

DOPE

God, I got no wind.
(*A siren is heard faintly, far down on the road.*)

ELKUS

Sons a' bitches a' troopers.

DOPE

What'd you want to wreck the car for?

ELKUS

Want to get caught with the stuff on you?

BUDDY

We'll get four hundred years for this.

ELKUS

Shut up!

DOPE

You didn't need to wreck the car, though.

ELKUS

Didn't you hear the trooper slam on the brakes when he went by? You'd be wearing bracelets right now if I hadn't dumped the old crate over the embankment! The way it is he thinks he's following us, and he'll blow that fire alarm all the way to Bear Mountain Bridge. Only hope he meets something solid head-on at ninety miles an hour.

DOPE

What I want to know is where we go from here.

ELKUS

Down the other side and pick up a car.
(*The siren is heard receding.*)

BUDDY

We'll get four hundred years for this.

ELKUS

What do you think you are, a chorus? Go on back to St. Thomas's and sing it to the priest. You're about as much help as a flat tire

BUDDY

I never wanted to be in it. I was only lookout—you're both witness to that.

ELKUS

What good do you think that does you, you poor fish? Brace up and take it like a man. There's twenty-five thousand in that bag and some of it's yours.

DOPE

How do you know it's twenty-five thousand?

ELKUS

It's the Orangeburg pay roll.
(BUDDY *looks off left.*)

BUDDY

Before God, it's Judge Skimmerhorn!

ELKUS

What? Where?

BUDDY

There. Coming round the rocks. Judge Skimmerhorn of Ledentown.

ELKUS

Does he know you?

BUDDY

Sure, he knows me.

ELKUS

We're out climbing, see? Hikers, see? On a picnic.
(*They stand.* ELKUS *holds the satchel behind him casually.* BIGGS *and* SKIMMERHORN *come in.*)

BIGGS

Hello.

ELKUS

How are you?

BIGGS

Out walking?

ELKUS

That's right. Climbed up on a bet.

SKIMMERHORN

Isn't that Buddy?

BUDDY

Yes, sir. Evening, Judge.

SKIMMERHORN

You're a long way from home.

BUDDY

Yes, sir.

BIGGS

Think you could show us a way down? We're stuck up here.

BUDDY

There's a patch down the cliff. Yes, sir.

SKIMMERHORN

No, thanks. I saw that one. Going to camp here?

ELKUS

Might as well. Sure.

SKIMMERHORN

Bring anything to eat?

ELKUS

Matter of fact, we didn't.
(*He sets the satchel down behind the rock, unobtrusively.*)

SKIMMERHORN

Not a thing?

ELKUS

Not a thing.

SKIMMERHORN

That's funny. Camping with nothing to eat.

ELKUS

Yeah, it is kinda funny.

DOPE

We ate before we started.
(*He smiles cunningly.*)

ELKUS

That's right. The Dope's right for once. We ate before we started.

SKIMMERHORN

Wish I had.

BUDDY

You—you staying up here tonight, sir?

SKIMMERHORN

Seems that way. We came up looking for somebody.

ELKUS

Looking for somebody?

SKIMMERHORN

That's what I said.

ELKUS

Who was it?

BIGGS

That's our business.

ELKUS

I see.

SKIMMERHORN

(*Coming near the three*)
Listen, Buddy, you're young and ambitious. Would you do something for me if you got well paid?

BUDDY

I guess so, Judge.

SKIMMERHORN

(*Sitting on the rock and incidentally over the satchel*)
We're done in, traipsing around the rocks. Would you climb down the Tor and get to Haverstraw and telephone my wife I can't come home?

BUDDY

I guess so, wouldn't I, Elkus?

ELKUS

Up to you.

SKIMMERHORN

And while you're there will you buy a
dozen sandwiches and some beer?

BUDDY

Yes, sir.

SKIMMERHORN

There's another thing you could do.
Call up the state troopers for me, and
tell them I'm here and I want them to
come up and make an arrest.

BUDDY

You—want to arrest somebody?

SKIMMERHORN

You get it. What do you say?

BUDDY

I—I guess so. Is it all right, Elkus?

DOPE

Oh—no. Oh—no.

ELKUS

Sure it's O.K. Why not?

BUDDY

It'd take about five hours—to get down
and back.

SKIMMERHORN

Damn it—I'll starve to death.

DOPE

What do you want to make an arrest
for?

BIGGS

That's our business.

BUDDY

All right. I'll go.

SKIMMERHORN

Here's five dollars for you. And another when you get back. And make it
fast, will you?

BUDDY

Yes, sir.
(*He starts out right.*)

ELKUS

Just a minute, Bud.
(ELKUS *and* DOPE *follow* BUDDY
out to converse with him.)

BIGGS

You might have made it two dozen
sandwiches.

SKIMMERHORN

I guess I will.
(*He starts to rise, places his hand
on the satchel, and jumps.*)
Christ, what's that?
(*He kicks the satchel, then flips it
up into the rocks.*)

BIGGS

Yeah?

SKIMMERHORN

I thought it was a snake. Somebody's
mouldy luggage. People are always
throwing truck around.
(*He calls*)
Say, for God's sake, get started, will
you?

BUDDY

(*Outside*)
Yes, sir. Right away.
(ELKUS *and* DOPE *return.*)

ELKUS

I guess we'll all go.
(*He looks nonchalantly where the
satchel was.*)

SKIMMERHORN

Fine. Will you make it two dozen
sandwiches?

ELKUS

What the hell's going on here?

SKIMMERHORN

We're hungry, that's all.

ELKUS

Are you two finnegling with us? Because if you are—!

BIGGS

What are you looking for?

ELKUS

Nothing. Who said I was looking for anything?

DOPE

Hey, Elkus! They got the troopers up here!
(DE WITT's *broad Dutch hat appears above the rocks in the rear, looking, for the moment, remarkably like that of a state trooper.* ELKUS *and* DOPE *freeze, looking at it.*)

ELKUS

(*Drawing a gun*)
Why, you fat pimps!
(DE WITT *disappears.*)

DOPE

Beat it, you fool!
(ELKUS *and* DOPE *scatter out to right.*)

BIGGS

(*Looking at the rocks*)
What was all that about?

SKIMMERHORN

I hope they bring those sandwiches.
(*He also stares toward the rear.*)

BIGGS

Sandwiches? They're not bringing sandwiches for anybody, those two.
(*He calls*)
Hey! Hey, you! Anybody there?—What did he mean by troopers?

SKIMMERHORN

Want to take a look?

BIGGS

I'm plenty unhappy, right where I am.
(SKIMMERHORN *climbs up on the rocks.*)

SKIMMERHORN

Wish to God I did see a **trooper.**

BIGGS

Nobody there?

SKIMMERHORN

Not a thing. Hey! Hey, you!
(*A silence.*)
Nope. Nobody.

BIGGS

Looks to me as if we just missed being stuck up by a couple of lunatics.

SKIMMERHORN

If I can't eat I'm going to sleep.

BIGGS

Maybe you've never tried adjusting yourself to igneous limestone.

SKIMMERHORN

I'm about to try it now.

BIGGS

You have my sympathy.
(SKIMMERHORN *stretches out on the rock, takes off his coat for a pillow and lies down.*)

SKIMMERHORN

Thanks.

BIGGS

Beautiful shape you have. A lot of slop tied up with a piece of string.

SKIMMERHORN

(*Sitting up*)
God it's cold. Listen, we could use one coat for a pillow and put the other one over us.

BIGGS

What other one?

SKIMMERHORN

Yours.

BIGGS

A proposition, huh?

SKIMMERHORN

You going to sit up all night?

BIGGS

In some ways it might be preferable.

SKIMMERHORN

You can't prop yourself on end forever,
like a duck on a rock.

BIGGS

Pull yourself together, then. You stick
out behind like a bump on a duck. All
right. Move over.

SKIMMERHORN

Your coat's bigger than mine.
(*They pull* BIGG's *coat around
them and lie down.*)

BIGGS

Just a couple of perfect forty-nines.
Where the hell am I supposed to put
my hip bone?

SKIMMERHORN

You juggle your own hip bones.
(DE WITT *appears on the rocks at
the rear, looking down.*)

BIGGS

If you snore, you probate judge, I'll
have you disbarred.

SKIMMERHORN

Go to sleep.

BIGGS

Wish I thought I could. On bed rock.
Wake me early, mother dear.

SKIMMERHORN

Shut up.
(DE WITT *meanwhile has opened
the satchel and now brings it
down into the light to examine
the contents. He sits down,
takes out five packets of bills,
shakes the satchel, then begins
to go through the inner pockets. He finds a roll of pennies,*

*which he breaks open into his
hands.*)

DE WITT

Copper pieces, by the great jib boom,
enough to purchase a new wig, if a
man ever got back to a place where
money was useful to him. A counting-
house full of them wouldn't buy a ship
from one of these semi-demi-demi-
semi-devils, so that's no good.
(*Two snores rise in concert from*
BIGGS *and* SKIMERHORN. DE
WITT *goes over to them, dropping the money.*)
What kind of demi-semi-devil do you
think you are, with four legs and two
faces, both looking the same direction?
Jesu Maria, it's a kind of centaur, as
big one way as another, no arms, and
feet the size of dishpans.

BIGGS

What's that?

DE WITT

(*Backing away*)
It's the rear end that talks, evidently,
the front being fast asleep in the manner of a figure-head.

BIGGS

Who's there? Did somebody speak?

DE WITT

None too clear in the back thinker, I
should say, which would be a natural
result of lugging two sets of brains,
fore and aft. I'd incline to communicate with the front end, but if necessary
I'll converse with the posterior.

BIGGS

(*Sitting up, looking at* DE WITT)
Skimmerhorn!

SKIMMERHORN

What's the matter?

BIGGS

I'm damned if I know.

SKIMMERHORN

Go to sleep, then.

BIGGS

Do you believe in apparitions?

SKIMMERHORN

No.

BIGGS

Well, there's a figure of fun sitting talking to me, right out of a masquerade ball.

SKIMMERHORN

You been drinking?

BIGGS

What would I find to drink?

DE WITT

If the forecastle wakes now I shall play both ends against the middle, like a marine auctioneer. I want to buy a boat.

BIGGS

You've come to the wrong shop, sailor. I'm in the real-estate business, and it's a long mile down to sea level.

(SKIMMERHORN *sits up suddenly.*)

DE WITT

You have no boats?

BIGGS

No boats.

SKIMMERHORN

What in the hell?—

BIGGS

I told you I'm damned if I know.

DE WITT

And the front end has no boats?

BIGGS

You're the front end, see. He wants to know if you've got boats.

SKIMMERHORN

No, stranger, no boats.

DE WITT

Ah.

(*He shakes his head mournfully, turns him about and goes to the right, still muttering.*)

The great plague on them, the lying, two-headed fairies out of a witch's placket. What chance has an honest man against a two-faced double-tongued beast, telling the same tale—

(*He disappears through the rocks.*)

BIGGS

Did you see what I saw?

SKIMMERHORN

Not if you saw what I saw. What I saw wasn't possible.—Did you fake that thing?

BIGGS

Fake it? I saw it.

SKIMMERHORN

Oh, no—! Nobody saw that—what I saw. I didn't either. I've got a family to support. They aren't going to put me away anywhere.

BIGGS

Whatever it was, it left a calling card. Looks as if he ate his lunch here, supposing a thing like that eats lunch. Maybe he left some for us.

SKIMMERHORN

I don't want any of that.

BIGGS

(*Rising and turning the packages over with his foot.*)

There's something in it.

SKIMMERHORN

Help yourself.

BIGGS
(*Opening a package, tossing the cover away.*)
You know what this is?

SKIMMERHORN
Probably a sheaf of contracts with the devil, all ready to sign.

BIGGS
No, it's money.

SKIMMERHORN
Money!
(*He leaps to his feet.*)

BIGGS
Fives and tens.
(*He opens another package.* SKIMMERHORN *does the same.*)

SKIMMERHORN
Well, bless the poor little Dutchman's heart—after all we said about him, too!

BIGGS
Think he left it?

SKIMMERHORN
It wasn't there before.

BIGGS
No.

SKIMMERHORN
Were you born with a caul, or anything?

BIGGS
Always before I had to work for it, or steal it. Never till tonight have I been waked up by a little man in a big hat, fetching it to me in packages.

SKIMMERHORN
Are you asleep?

BIGGS
I probably am, asleep and dreaming.

SKIMMERHORN
If you're dreaming, you're dreaming that I found money.

BIGGS
Oh, you found it now?

SKIMMERHORN
Fifty-fifty.

BIGGS
Wait a minute. You know what money this is?

SKIMMERHORN
No.
(BIGGS *picks up a discarded envelope.*)

BIGGS
It came out of the Nanuet bank.
(SKIMMERHORN *takes the envelope from him.*)

SKIMMERHORN
If that little guy's a bank robber he's certainly careless with the proceeds.

BIGGS
That's where it came from.

SKIMMERHORN
In that case we ought to give it back. For the reward.

BIGGS
No reward offered yet.

SKIMMERHORN
Maybe we ought to give it back anyway.

BIGGS
Think so?

SKIMMERHORN
Might be marked bills.

BIGGS
No, it's not. I was talking with the president of the bank on the 'phone.

Made up for a pay roll. No marks on any of it.

SKIMMERHORN

It ought to be returned, though.

BIGGS

Sure, it should. Question is, will it be?

SKIMMERHORN

I think so, don't you?

BIGGS

I'm inclined to think so. Bank robbing's away out of my line.

SKIMMERHORN

Mine, too, as a matter of fact. The president of the bank's a friend of yours?

BIGGS

Yes, he is, in a way. Oh, he's gypped me a couple of times, same as you would.

SKIMMERHORN

He wouldn't lose anything.

BIGGS

Oh, no, he's insured.

SKIMMERHORN

Has it occurred to you the little Dutchman that was here might not mean any good to us?

BIGGS

Did you see a little Dutchman?

SKIMMERHORN

I thought I did, there for a minute.

BIGGS

I don't believe that any more.

SKIMMERHORN

Certainly doesn't sound very likely.

BIGGS

We'd better count it. Man never ought to carry money around without knowing how much it is.

SKIMMERHORN

Yeah, let's count it. It said twenty-five thousand in the paper.

BIGGS

You know, nobody in the world would ever know who had it?

SKIMMERHORN

No, they wouldn't.

BIGGS

What do you say?

SKIMMERHORN

I say fifty-fifty.

BIGGS

Damn you, Skimmerhorn, if I hadn't been in business with you for twenty years I'd say you were a crook!

SKIMMERHORN

If I wasn't a crook after twenty years with you I'd be slow in the head and hard of hearing!

BIGGS

What's fifty per cent of twenty-five thousand? Twelve thousand five hundred? And what's forty per cent? Ten thousand! Are you going to hold up the deal for two thousand five hundred?

SKIMMERHORN

I certainly am.

BIGGS

All right, take it. Fifty-fifty on this one deal.

SKIMMERHORN

And on the Van Dorn deal, too.

BIGGS

Why, you fat louse—
    (VAN DORN *comes in from the
        right out of the shadows.*)

VAN

Sorry to bother you gentlemen, but—

BIGGS

(*As they stuff the bills into their
pockets*)
Where the hell did you come from?

VAN

Why, you're not friends of mine, but
there's a storm blowing in and it occurred to me I might show you where
you could keep dry under a ledge.

BIGGS

Thanks. Much obliged.

VAN

Want me to go with you?

BIGGS

No, thanks.—Let's get a little nearer the
light.

SKIMMERHORN

Good idea.
(BIGGS *and* SKIMMERHORN *go out
right.* VAN *looks after them,
then picks up one of the discarded envelopes and studies
it. He sits.* LISE *comes up the
rocks in the rear and stands
looking out to the river, shad-
ing her eyes from the beacon.*)

LISE

You who have watched this river in the
past
till your hope turned bitterness, pity
me now,
my hope gone, but no power to keep
my eyes
from the mocking water. The hills
come down like sand,
and the long barges bear them off to
town,
to what strange market in what strange
town,
devouring mountains? but never, in all
days,
never, though I should watch here
without rest,
will any ship come downward with the
tide

flying the flag we knew.
(VAN *rises.* LISE *draws back an instant, then comes down a step
toward him.*)
Do you hear my voice?

VAN

Yes, lady.

LISE

Do you see me in the light,
as I see you?

VAN

Yes.

LISE

You are one of those
the earth bears now, the quick, fierce
wizard men
who plow the mountains down with
steel, and set new mountains in their
sky. You've come to drive
machines through the white rock's
heart.

VAN

Not I. I haven't.
I hate them all like poison.

LISE

You're against them—
the great machines?

VAN

I'd like to smash the lot,
and the men that own them.

LISE

Oh, if there were a friend
among so many enemies! I wish
I knew how to make you friend. But
now my voice
shrinks back in me, reluctant, a cold
thing,
fearing the void between us.—I have
seen you.
I know you. You are kind.

VAN

How do you know?

LISE

When I have been most lonely in the
    spring,
the spring rain beating with my heart,
    I made
a wild flower garden; none of these I
    knew,
for none I knew are here, flowers of
    the woods,
little and lovely, nameless. One there
    was
like a pink moccasin, another low
with blotted leaves, wolf-toothed, and
    many more
rooted among the fern. I saw you then
come on this garden, secret as the tears
wept for lost days, and drew my breath
    in dread
that you should laugh and trample it.
    You smiled
and then went on. But when I came
    again
there was a new flower growing with
    the rest,
one I'd not seen. You brought and
    placed it there
only for love of gardens, ignorant
    whose
the garden you enriched. What was
    this flower?

VAN

Wild orchid. It was your garden?

LISE

Yes. You know
the names of all the flowers?

VAN

Yes.

LISE

But then
you'd teach them to me?

VAN

Yes.

LISE

Teach me the names.
What is the tall three-petaled one that's
    black
almost, the red's so dark?

VAN

That's trillium.
Speaking of flowers, tell me your name.

LISE

It's Lise,
or used to be.

VAN

Not now?

LISE

I'm weary of it,
and all things that I've been. You have
    a lover?
She'll be angry?

VAN

She's angry now. She's off
and gone. She won't come back.

LISE

Love me a little,
enough to save me from the dark. But
    if
you cannot give me love, find me a
    way!
The seas lie black between your harbor
    town
and mine, but your ships are quick. If
    I might see
the corner where the three streets come
    to an end
on sundial windows, there, a child by
    a fire—
no, but it's gone!

VAN

I've seen you on the hills
moving with shadows. But you're not
    shadow.

LISE

No.
Could one live and be shadow?

VAN

Take my hand.

LISE

I dare not.

VAN

Come, let me see your garden.

LISE

No.
I dare not. It is your race that thins
    our blood
and gathers round, besieging us with
    charms
to stay the feet of years. But I know
    you kind.—
Love me a little. Never put out your
    hand
to touch me, lest some magic in your
    blood
reach me, and I be nothing. What I am
I know not, under these spells, if I be
    cloud
or dust. Nor whether you dream of me,
    or I
make you of light and sound. Between
    this stone
and the near constellations of the stars
I go and come, doubting now whence
    I come
or when I go. Cling to me. Keep me
    still.
Be gentle. You were gentle with the
    orchid.—
Take my hand now.

VAN

You're cold.

LISE

Yes.

VAN

Here on the Tor
the sun beats down like murder all day
    long
and the wind comes up like murder in
    the night.
I'm cold myself.

LISE

How have I slipped so far
from the things you have? I'm puzzled
    here and lost.
Is it so different for you? Keep my
    hand

and tell me. In these new times are all
    men shadow?
All men lost?

VAN

Sometimes I stand here at night
and look out over the river when a fog
covers the lights. Then if it's dark
    enough
and I can't see my hands or where the
    rock
leaves off against the cloud, and I'm
    alone,
then, well I'm damned if I know who
    I am,
staring out into that black. Maybe I'm
    cloud
and maybe I'm dust. I might be old
    as time.
I'd like to think I knew. A man gets
    that way
standing staring at darkness.

LISE

Then—you do know.
It's better now.—Somewhere along a
    verge
where your life dips in dusk and my
    gray days
lift to the light a moment, we walk
    there
and our eyes meet.—Look, when the
    wizards come
to tear the mountain down, I'll have no
    place.
I'll be gone then.

VAN

Child, they won't get our mountain!
Not if I have to shoot them as they
    come
they won't get our mountain! The
    mountain's mine,
and you're to make your garden where
    you like;
their feet won't step across it! All their
    world's
made up of fat men doing tricks with
    laws
to manage tides and root up hills. The
    hills
can afford to laugh at them! A race of
    grubs
bred down from men!

LISE

Is it the light I feel
come flooding back in me? Light or
    their charms
broken here, seeing your face?

VAN

Your hands are warm.

LISE

I'm not cold now! for an instant I'm
    not cold,
seeing your face. This is your wiz-
    ardry.
Let me stand here and see you.

ELKUS

(*Outside*)
Somewhere around here it was. Over
toward the crane.

DOPE

(*Outside*)
What'd you go and put down the
satchel for?

ELKUS

(*Outside*)
How did I know he'd sit on top of it?
    (VAN *and* LISE *slip out through
    the rocks at the rear.* ELKUS
    and DOPE *come in furtively
    from the right.*)

DOPE

That's where. Under that rock.

ELKUS

Keep your eye peeled. They're probably beating the woods for us.

DOPE

What's that?
    (*He picks up an envelope.*)

ELKUS

They got it.

DOPE

God damn the rotten business! Now we
will get four hundred years.

ELKUS

Now you're saying it—

DOPE

What are we going to do?

ELKUS

I'm going to send Buddy back with
sandwiches to see if the Judge got the
money. If he did we'll stick him up.

DOPE

Hey, how about the troopers?

ELKUS

If that was troopers I'm Admiral
Dewey. Troopers would a' used the
artillery. Come on.

DOPE

O.K. Some pennies here.

ELKUS

To hell with 'em.
    (DOPE *flings the pennies to the left
    along the ledge.*)

DOPE

Get going.
    (ELKUS *and* DOPE *go out right.*
    BIGGS *and* SKIMMERHORN *come
    in along the ledge.*)

BIGGS

Now it's raining money. I got the price
of a morning paper square in the eye.

SKIMMERHORN

I've got two thousand five hundred in
a breast pocket, five thousand in a side
pocket, and five thousand in the bill-
fold.
    (*He slaps his rear.*)
How do I look?

BIGGS

No different. Just a lot of slop tied up
with string. I've got five thousand in
each side pocket and two thousand
five hundred in the back. How do I
look?

SKIMMERHORN

You? All you need now's a pair of wings.

BIGGS

Wish I could find the little guy with the big heart that gave us the money. Maybe he'd help us down off this devil's belfry.

SKIMMERHORN

How about that shovel? Any possibility of making it pick us up and set us down below there?

BIGGS

Well—if anybody was running it, sure. If it swung us over on that dump we could slide the rest of the way. You might wear out that last five thousand of yours, the five thousand that's bringing up the rear there.

SKIMMERHORN

When do they come to work in the morning?

BIGGS

They won't come to work tomorrow. They can't do any more till we buy this land.

SKIMMERHORN

That's fine. That's just dandy.

BIGGS

Nice idea though. Somebody might come along that could run the engine.

SKIMMERHORN

You don't think that boy's coming back with the sandwiches?

BIGGS

No, I don't.

SKIMMERHORN

The way I feel inside I may never live to spend the money.

BIGGS

Who you going to leave it to?

SKIMMERHORN

Yeah?

Oh, all right. Nothing personal.
(*They sit facing the audience. The* CAPTAIN *and* HIS CREW, *including* DE WITT, *seep in through the rocks about them and stand quietly looking on.*)
There was something in that—what you said about needing a pair of wings.

SKIMMERHORN

I should say that wings was the last thing likely to grow on you. You might grow horns, or a cloven hoof, or a tail, but wings, no. Not unless somebody slipped up behind you and bashed you over the head.

BIGGS

You know, you'd murder me for what I've got in my pockets?

SKIMMERHORN

You thought of it first. Who am I going to leave it to, you said.

BIGGS

Just the same I wouldn't feel right if you were standing behind me with a rock in your hand.
(*The* CREW *move in a little.*)

SKIMMERHORN

You wouldn't?

BIGGS

No. At the moment I wouldn't like to think anybody was creeping up behind me.
(*He stiffens.*)
And by God there is somebody behind me.

SKIMMERHORN

(*Without turning*)
What makes you think so?

BIGGS

(*Running a hand over his hair*)
I just feel it. Turn around, will you?
Take a look.

SKIMMERHORN

(*Shivering*)
I will not.—Now you've got me worried.—Or else I'm getting light-headed for lack of food.
(BIGGS *ducks suddenly, as if from an imaginary blow.* SKIMMERHORN *dodges in sympathy, and with their heads drawn in like turtles they creep forward on hands and knees.*)

BIGGS

See anything?

SKIMMERHORN

There's nothing there, you ass! What are you dodging? Want to scare me to death? Go on, turn around and face it like a man!

BIGGS

Now!

SKIMMERHORN

Now!
(*They whirl in concert, on their knees, facing the* CREW. *They look at each other.*)

BIGGS

You're crazy!

SKIMMERHORN

I certainly am. And so are you.

BIGGS

That isn't there at all. There's nothing there.

SKIMMERHORN

All right, you go up and hit it. I'll stay right here, and you go punch it in the nose.
(BIGGS *stands up.*)

BIGGS

Uh—how do you do?—Maybe you—wanted to give us something, huh?
(*To* DE WITT)
Uh—I see you brought your friends with you.—If you want the money back you can have it, you know. We don't want the money.
(*He sticks a hand in his pocket.*)
How much was it now?
(*The* CREW *look at each other gravely, tapping their foreheads.* SKIMMERHORN *rises.*)
Anything we could do, you know, we'd be glad to do. We're just trying to get down off here.

SKIMMERHORN

You know what it is, Art; it's a moving picture company. And have they got the laugh on us? Thinking they're real. It's all right, boys, we're onto you.

BIGGS

Is that so? Say, I guess that's so. Was that moving picture money you gave us, you fellows? We thought that was real. Ha ha! That's a good one. I guess you must have thought we were pretty funny, backing up that way and jumping around. You had us scared stiff!
(*The* CREW *shake their heads at each other.*)

SKIMMERHORN

Come on, now, you aren't bluffing us at all. We've seen the pictures work over at Suffern. We were right out on location there with actors and producers and everything. Some of those girls didn't care whether they wore clothes or not. You're probably used to that where you come from, but I certainly got a kick out of pictures. Fifty chorus girls changing clothes in the bushes over there.
(*A silence.* DE WITT *goes over to the* CAPTAIN *and whispers in his ear.*)

ASHER

Lay a hand to it.
(DE WITT *catches hold of the dangling cable.*)

DE WITT

Lay a hand to it, lads. Heave.
(*The* CREW *catch the rope and haul on it, sailor-fashion. The shovel begins to descend.*)

THE CREW

(*Pulling down*)
Heave! Heave! Heave! Heave!
Coming a blow, coming a blow;
Sea runs black; glass runs low;
Heave! Heave!
Yardarm dips; foam's like snow!
Heave!
(*The shovel touches ground.*)

BIGGS

Say, that's an act if I ever saw one.
What kind of picture you putting on?
(*The* CAPTAIN *points to the interior of the shovel, looking at* BIGGS *and* SKIMMERHORN.)
What's up, anyway? Want us to go aboard? You know, we were just saying if somebody could run that thing we might get across to the dump and slide down out of here. Think you could swing it across there?
(*The* SAILORS *maneuver behind the two, edging them into the machine.*)
You might haul us up there and not be able to get us down, you know. It's mighty friendly of you to try it, but you'll have your work cut out. Sure, I'll get in. I'll try anything once.
(*He steps in,* SKIMMERHORN *follows reluctantly. The* CAPTAIN *and* DE WITT *guard their retreat. The* SAILORS *catch hold of the cable.*)
Take it easy, now.

THE CREW

Hoist! Hoist! Hoist! Hoist!
Tar on a rope's end, man on a yard.
Wind through an eye-bolt, points on a card;
Hoist! Hoist!
Weevil in the biscuit, rats in the lard,
Hoist!
(*They hand the two up as far as*

seems necessary, and swing the crane out over the abyss. Then they stop to contemplate their handiwork.)

BIGGS

I'll tell you what—if you catch that line over there some of you can hold back while the rest pull and that'll swing it around.—If that don't work you'd better pull it down again and we'll just wait till morning.
(*The* CREW *continue to stare silently.*)

SKIMMERHORN

I'm getting sick at my stomach, boys; you better make it snappy. It gives me the megrims to look down this way.
(*He draws his feet up suddenly.*)

BIGGS

Hey, don't rock the boat, you fool! It's a thousand miles straight down!

SKIMMERHORN

I'm going to be sick.

BIGGS

You better take us down, fellows. It's no good. You can't make it.

DE WITT

How about a game of bowls?
(*The* CAPTAIN *nods.*)

PIETER

Aye, a game of bowls.
(*Led by the* CAPTAIN, *the* CREW *begin to file out.*)

BIGGS

Hey, you wouldn't leave us up here, would you? Hey, listen! You! You can have that money back, you know! We don't want the money! What in the name of time?—Listen, what did we ever do to you?—A joke's a joke, after all, but this thing might let go any minute! What's more you're responsi-

ble if anything happens to us! There's such a thing as laws in this country!
(*But they have all gone.*)

SKIMMERHORN

I'm sick.

BIGGS

You'll be sicker before you're out of this mess.—What do you think they meant by that?

SKIMMERHORN

I don't know.—Quit kicking me, will you? I'm sick.

BIGGS

Well, keep it to yourself.

SKIMMERHORN

I wish I thought I could.

BIGGS

Help, somebody! Help! We're stuck up here!

SKIMMERHORN

What good's that going to do?

BIGGS

You don't think they'll leave us here, do you?

SKIMMERHORN

I don't know. I don't care. I wish I was dead!—Say, keep away from me, will you? What are you trying to do, pick my pocket?

BIGGS

Pick your pocket, you fish? All I ask is keep your feet out of my face.

SKIMMERHORN

Well, where in hell's my bill-fold?

BIGGS

How do I know? Do you think I took it?

SKIMMERHORN

Come on, now. Where is it?
(*He searches his clothes frantically.*)

BIGGS

You're probably sitting on it.—You are sitting on it. There it is.

SKIMMERHORN

(*Finding it*)
Jeez, I might have lost it.

BIGGS

Now you'd better count it. Just to make sure it's good.

SKIMMERHORN

I think I will.
(*He begins to count the bills.*)
It's good money, Art. Look at it.

BIGGS

Not a bad idea, either.
(*He takes out money and counts it. There is a flash, a long roll and a crash of thunder. Then another and another.*)
Isn't that coming pretty close?

SKIMMERHORN

What?

BIGGS

The lightning, you fool! Put your money away before you get it wet. You know what I think?

SKIMMERHORN

No.

BIGGS

There's something up there taking pot shots at us.

SKIMMERHORN

There's one thing about money you find. You don't have to pay income tax on it.

BIGGS

That's true.
(*There is a terrific flash, a crash, and the stage is in darkness.*)
That one got the beacon!
(*Another flash runs right down the crane.*)
Good God, will you quit that? That's close enough!—Say, do you know any prayers?

SKIMMERHORN

I know one.

BIGGS

Say it, will you?

SKIMMERHORN

Matthew, Mark, Luke and John,
Bless the bed that I lie on.

BIGGS

That's not much good, that one.

SKIMMERHORN

It's the only one I know.—Hey, catch it—hey!

BIGGS

What?
(*The lightning is now an almost perpetual illumination, the thunder a constant roll.*)

SKIMMERHORN

I dropped fourteen ten dollar bills!

BIGGS

Do you know we're going to die here?

SKIMMERHORN

We're going to what?

BIGGS

Will you quit counting money? We're going to be killed! We're going to die right here in our own steam shovel!

SKIMMERHORN

Oh, no. I can't die now. I'm not ready to die!

BIGGS

I wish you'd put up your money, then, and pray!

SKIMMERHORN

I don't know how to pray.
(*A crash.*)

BIGGS

(*On his knees*)
Oh, God, I never did this before, and I don't know how, but keep me safe here and I'll be a better man! I'll put candles on the altar, yes, I'll get that Spring Valley church fixed up, the one that's falling down! I can do a lot for you if you'll let me live! Oh, God—
(*A crash.*)

SKIMMERHORN

(*On his knees, his hands full of money*)
Oh, God, you wouldn't do a thing like that, hang us up in our own steam shovel, wet through, and then strike us with lightning! Oh, God, you've been kind to us tonight, and given us things we never expected to get so easy; don't spoil it now!—God damn it, there goes another batch of bills!
(*He snatches at the falling money, and is hauled back by* BIGGS.)
I don't know how to pray! What makes you think there's anybody up there, anyway?
(*Another crash.*)

BIGGS

Say the one you know then, for God's sake—say it!

SKIMMERHORN

Matthew, Mark, Luke and John,
Bless the bed that I lie on!

BIGGS

Matthew, Mark, Luke and John,
Bless the bed—Oh, God, I've got an old mother dependent on me; please let

me live! Why don't you tell him you'll give the money back?

SKIMMERHORN

Because I won't! And you won't, either!
(*A crash.*)

BIGGS

Now you've done it! Can't you keep anything to yourself? There's such a thing as being politic, even when you're talking to God Almighty!
(*Thunder again.*)

ACT TWO

SCENE I

SCENE: *The Tor and the steam shovel as before, only five or six hours later. It's still pitch dark, and* BIGGS *and* SKIMMERHORN *are still in the shovel. They are, however, fast asleep in much the same postures they took formerly on the ground. Under the shovel sits* DE WITT, *picking up and smoothing on his knee a few bills which he has found blowing loose on the rock. The beacon light flashes into the scene.*

DE WITT

There comes on the light again, too, the sweeping light that withers a body's entrails. No sooner out than lit again.—
(*Two snores rise from the sleeping pair.*)
Aye, take your ease and rest, you detachable Doppelgangers, swollen with lies, protected by the fiends, impervious to lightning, shedding rain like ducks—and why wouldn't you shed rain? your complexions being pure grease and your insides blubber? You can sleep, you can rest. You of the two-bottoms. You make nothing of the lightning playing up and down your backbones, or turning in on cold iron, but a poor sailor out of Holland, what rest has he?—
(*He smoothes a bill.*)
These will be tokens and signs, these will, useful in magic, potent to ward off evil or put a curse on your enemies. Devil's work or not, I shall carry them on me, and make myself a match for these fulminating latter-day spirits.
(*He pouches the bills.*)
I'm hanged if it's not noticeable at once, a sort of Dutch courage infused into the joints and tissues from the mere pocketing up of their infernal numbered papers.
(*He takes out a bill and looks at it.*)
That's sorcery, that's witchcraft, that's black art for you—that's a trick after the old one's heart; why, this stuff would make a man out of a cocked hat and a pair of crutches!
(*He slaps his chest.*)
Now I shall face destiny and take it like a pinch of snuff! Which reminds me I could use a pinch of snuff.
(*He takes out his snuffbox.*)
Snuff? When have I reached for snuff? It would seem to me I haven't gone after snuff in something like two hundred years!
(*He ladles into both nostrils and sneezes violently.*)
Aha, DeWitt! You're a man, DeWitt! A man and a devil! And what shall we wish for now that we have wishing papers in the pockets of our pantaloons? What but a woman, one of these new female furies of theirs, wearing pants like a man, and with nothing to indicate her sex but the general conformation!
(*He draws out bills.*)
Let my woman appear, god of the numbered papers, and let her wear

what she likes, so long as a man can
make out how she's made. Let her appear within this next three minutes, for
God knows how long this mood will
last in an old man!
     (*He takes another pinch of snuff.*)
Aha! Destiny, present occasions!
     (BUDDY *enters carrying beer and*
     sandwiches.)

BUDDY

Hello.

DE WITT

What answer would a man make to
that now? That's a strange greeting.

BUDDY

Seen a couple of old fat men around
anywhere?

DE WITT

Boy, I have seen nothing else all night.

BUDDY

Where are they?

DE WITT

You wish to find a couple of old fat
men?

BUDDY

That's right.

DE WITT

I begin to doubt the supernal powers
of these new angel-demons. Here he
stands in their presence and asks very
foolishly if old DeWitt has seen them.

BUDDY

What's foolish about that?

DE WITT

A very cheap, witless little cabin boy
unless all signs fail. One who carries
packages and lives very badly by the
day on half a skilling. A cabin boy.

BUDDY

What's the matter with you?

DE WITT

What do you carry in the bag?

BUDDY

That's my business.

DE WITT

He has a business then. He is not perhaps so witless as he appears.

BUDDY

Are you going to tell me where those
two are or do you want me to blow
your brains out?

DE WITT

Is my carcass so thin you think to puff
my brains out with a breath? Look,
'prentice devil, I am one of you. I bear
your signs and symbols. Here you see
your own countersign, a cabalistic device of extreme rarity and force. What
have you in the bag?

BUDDY

Nothing but sandwiches. What do you
mean, you're one of us?

DE WITT
     (*Waving a sheaf of bills*)
You should recognize the insignium.

BUDDY

Where'd you get it?

DE WITT

It blew away from these same two fat
men, 'prentice devil, but now I have it,
and it's mine and I obtain power over
you. Let me see these sandwiches.

BUDDY

It blew away from the fat men, huh?
All right, that's what I want to know.
It's mine, see? Hand it over.

DE WITT

You reveal yourself a very young and tender 'prentice.

BUDDY

Hand it over or I'll fill you full of holes.
(*He sets down his packages and draws a gun, but* DE WITT *is beforehand with two flintlock pistols.*)

DE WITT

You will drop your child's armory on the ground, cabin boy, or I shall pull both triggers at once and blast you halfway to the water.
(BUDDY *drops the gun.*)
I tell you I am now a great devil and violent. When I wish merely I have my way.
(BUDDY *suddenly takes to his heels.* DE WITT *pulls the triggers one after another; the hammers click but there is no explosion.*)
Why, this new world is not so bad. I am left in possession of the field.
(*He picks up the automatic and the bag and retreats to his rock.*)
They fight with the weapons of children. Why, this new world begins to be mine, to do as I please with. Whatever kind of witch a sandwich may be come out and let me interrogate you.
(*He takes out sandwiches.*)
If it be the food eaten by witches and wizards so much the better, for I am now a wizard myself, and by the great jib boom I haven't tasted food in God knows when.
(*He eats.*)
A sweet and excellent morsel, very strong with garlic and salami, medicinal for the veins and bladder.
(*He looks at his pistols.*)
A little glazed powder in the priming now, and these two will speak with more authority if it becomes necessary to defend my position.
(*He opens his powder horn and renews the priming.*)
We have seen the time, these blunder-busses and myself, when we could defend a crow's nest against a whole crew in mutiny.
(*He pushes away the beer bottles with his foot.*)
I will eat your rations, cabin boy out of the new age, and I will master you all, men and maids, now that my strength comes back, but I will not drink your drink. As Pastor Van Dorf observed very wisely before we sailed; you may eat the food of the savages, said he, when you have voyaged to the new lands overseas; you may share their rations, you may even make up to their females after the fashion of sailors when the flesh is weak, but drink none of their drink, said he, lest it prove to be Circe's liquor and turn you all to hogs.
(*He eats.*)
Now I have small inclination to be a hog, but a man I will be, and a very good man, too, of the fieriest model.
(*He hears* JUDITH's *step.*)
Take care now, take care! I'm an armed man and a man of blood!
(JUDITH *enters.*)

JUDITH

(*At some distance*)
I beg your pardon, sir—

DE WITT

A woman, by the great tropical cross, a salvage woman, come in answer to my unspoken desires.
(*He rises.*)
Your humblest servant, lady salvage; don't run away, please. I'm a poor lost little man, wouldn't hurt a fly.

JUDITH

Who are you?

DE WITT

I'm a poor bosun, ma'am, but grown, God knows how, to something of a person this last quarter hour.

JUDITH

Are you lost?

DE WITT

Completely adrift, ma'am, on my own mountain.

JUDITH

I don't think I've seen you before.

DE WITT

That may be, though I'm by way of being one of the earliest inhabitants, not counting Indians and Patagonians.

JUDITH

You live on the mountain?

DE WITT

I maintain a residence here, though the situation eludes me at the moment.

JUDITH

Then you are acquainted with Van— Van Dorn?

DE WITT

I have seen him about.

JUDITH

Have you seen him tonight? I want to find him.

DE WITT

A mere blind, I should say, a maidenly defense, not to be too forthright; but sent by the talisman she is.

JUDITH

You have seen him?

DE WITT

God help him, I have, and in none too sanctified an attitude, saving your ladyship, for the lad was obviously a bit taken with the captain's wife, and she a married woman of some years' standing, young though she appear.

JUDITH

Where was he?
(She takes a step nearer to him.)

DE WITT

I was never one to break in on a budding romance, sweetheart, and out of sheer delicacy I looked the other way.

JUDITH

No, but where was he, please? I can show you the path.

DE WITT

If you hunt out a very pretty little mistress in a bonnet somewhat behind the fashion, and look under the bonnet, you may chance to find him there.

JUDITH

Who are you?

DE WITT

Alpheus DeWitt, your most humble, bosun in the King's navy.

JUDITH

Forgive me—I shall look elsewhere—

DE WITT

Oh, but I assure you the lad's head over ears, ma'am, and loathe you'd be to interrupt him. Now a pretty lass like yourself should have no trouble replacing one sailor man with another in these stirring times. They come and go like a run of salmon.

JUDITH

Thank you.

DE WITT

I am myself a notionable lad. Salt tears have been wept for me by one and another.

JUDITH

No doubt.

DE WITT

I'm a blunt man, but constant and of considerable substance on my own wharf. Could you find it in your heart to love me?

JUDITH

I'm sorry, no.

DE WITT

To save a sad and desperate man from such a death as the lines of frost on a window? This is a kindly face, this of mine, and a kindly heart under a worn jerkin. These are real tears on my cheeks, too, and I weep them for you, lady.

JUDITH

I've never seen you till this moment.

DE WITT

Yet you could save me from their sorcery, with one touch of your hand. I waited here for you, and you came.

JUDITH

You're horrible. Your face is horrible!

DE WITT

Is it, truly?

JUDITH

Ancient and terrible and horrible!— Tell me where he is. I must know.

DE WITT

I don't know where he is.—You will think better of it. You need only pity me a little at first, or even laugh at me —so you do it kindly—

JUDITH

I'm in no mood for laughing, though you're ridiculous enough in that get-up.

DE WITT

It's not the latest, I know. And I'm a sad and broken man, lady, lost here among the lesser known peaks on the west side of the world, and looking only for a hand to help me.

JUDITH

I don't think you're lost at all.

DE WITT

Yes, lady, quite lost.—Nevertheless they run from me! You should have seen the lad run when I snapped my pistols at him.

JUDITH

(*Stepping back*)

I should think he would.—Isn't there someone coming there now?

(*She points to the right.* DE WITT *faces about, reaching for his pistols.* JUDITH *slips away left.*)

DE WITT

If there be, watch what soldierly stand old DeWitt makes in defense of a lady! Come out, children of the new Satan, show yourselves in the light!

(ELKUS *and* DOPE *appear at right.*)

ELKUS

Stick 'em up, bo!

(*They train automatics on him.*)

DE WITT

More toys! Stand back, you cheap new devils!

ELKUS

Keep your hands down or I'll let you have it!

DE WITT

Watch now how a man holds off the fiends.

(*He lifts his pistols.*)

ELKUS

Give it to him!

(*They fire a fusillade at* DE WITT, *who stands unmoved.*)

DE WITT

Firecrackers! You think me a devil like yourselves, to be exorcised with firecrackers?

ELKUS

Give it to him again!

(*They fire once more.*)

DE WITT

Look, you puny devils, I'm a patient man, but in one moment I shall blow you both into the Tappan Zee!

ELKUS

(*Stepping up and pouring bullets into him*)
Too bad about you!
(*To* DOPE)
Take the money off him.

DOPE

There's something funny about this guy! I can see right through him!

ELKUS

No wonder. He's full of holes as a tennis racket.

DOPE

No, by God, I can see through him! Look!
(*They step back together.*)

ELKUS

What kind of a thing are you?

DE WITT

I'm not a man to be daunted by loud noises and firecrackers, Beelzebub! Go seek your place with the new father of hell before I send you there! Wizards!

ELKUS

Where's the money?

DE WITT

I have a talisman and I ate a sandwich, devils!

DOPE

Look, he's a moving picture! He's a regular church window! Look!

DE WITT

Disperse or I fire!

ELKUS

Keep out of the way of that sawed-off shotgun!

(DOPE *suddenly runs in and shoots* DE WITT *through the head, then retreats.*)

DE WITT

I warn you I begin to be annoyed!

DOPE

It's no use, chief. I blew his brains out, and he's standing right there!

BIGGS

(*Looking over the side of the shovel*)
It's a war.

ELKUS

Who said that?

DOPE

Damned if I know.

ELKUS

Beat it.

DOPE

Yeah, beat it. Let the money hang. I'm for Canada.

ELKUS

You said it.
(*They turn tail. As they are going* DE WITT *fires his pistols in the air.*)

DE WITT

Now am I master of the world of things,
a buccaneer, a devil and a rake!
Women love mastery, and they ran from me;
they ran, these minor devils, ran from De Witt!
Look where they go there, sweetheart!
(*He turns.*)
God, she's gone!
Lady! New-world lady! Are you lost?
(*He follows her.*)
Look now, I've dispersed them, brats and wizards,

spawn out of hell, they ran! I'm master
here,
I'm master of the world! Look, lady!
(*He goes out left.*)

SKIMMERHORN

Are you awake?

BIGGS

I hope not. I hope this is a nightmare
and I wake up at home in bed.

SKIMMERHORN

How did we get here?

BIGGS

It must have been something we ate.

SKIMMERHORN

I didn't eat anything.

BIGGS

There's a bag of sandwiches down
there on the ground.

SKIMMERHORN

That's a pleasant thought.

BIGGS

Look for yourself.

SKIMMERHORN

You're right. It's a bag of sandwiches.

BIGGS

Didn't we send somebody for sandwiches and beer, away back there before all this started?

SKIMMERHORN

I don't know. I'm all wet, and I'm stuck
to the shovel.

BIGGS

You do seem to be kind of going to
pieces. What's the matter with your
toupee?

SKIMMERHORN

The glue must have melted.
(*He takes off his wig.*)
Now I'll catch cold.

BIGGS

If any of your constituency sees you in
that condition you're out of office for
good.

SKIMMERHORN

I don't even care if I fall out. I feel
terrible.

BIGGS

Might be more comfortable for me if
you did fall out.
(*He shifts his weight.*)

SKIMMERHORN

Sit down! Quit rocking the boat!

BIGGS

I've got a cramp. Ouch!

SKIMMERHORN

Don't shove me!
(*He pushes* BIGGS.)

BIGGS

(*Pushing back*)
You want to pitch me overboard?

SKIMMERHORN

Hey! You know I might have gone out?

BIGGS

What do you care?

SKIMMERHORN

I'll show you what I care!
(*They lock in a deadly struggle
on the verge.*)

BIGGS

Wait, Skimmer, look now! If one of us
goes down the other goes too. Look at
the drop. You don't want to splash on
those rocks and I don't either.

SKIMMERHORN

Let go then.

BIGGS

I'll let go when you do. I'll count three
and we'll both let go.

SKIMMERHORN

All right.

BIGGS

One—two—three.
(*They let go and catch the ropes over the swinging basket.*)
That's better. Now take it easy, buddy. You woke up feeling like poison this morning. After this you count ten when you get an impulse to push anybody.

SKIMMERHORN

Same to you.

BIGGS

Fine.
(*They sit down cautiously.*)

SKIMMERHORN

How in hell did those sandwiches get there?

BIGGS

How in the hell did we get here?

SKIMMERHORN

You haven't got a fishing hook on you, have you?

BIGGS

No, I haven't.
(*They sit gloomily looking at the sandwiches.* LISE *and* VAN *come in from the left.*)

VAN

Nothing in all the woods
is silent as the owl; you see his shadow
but never hear his wings. The partridge now,
every time he takes off he creaks and cranks
like an old Ford. You never heard such a fuss;
but he's quiet on the ground.

LISE

And is there a squirrel
that flies, bird-fashion?

VAN

Well, there's a flying squirrel,
but he's more the glider type. No engine, see,
but he'll do thirty yards. He's on the way
to be a bat if he's not careful.

LISE

How?

VAN

He'll leave off tail and put on wing until
he's mostly wing. No doubt the bat was once
some kind of flying mouse.

LISE

Some men have wings.
I've seen them overhead.

VAN

That's all put on.
They've no more wings than a goat.
When they come down.

LISE

I've hoped that it was true that men had wings.

VAN

Why?

LISE

Oh, they've lived so long, and tried so hard,
and it all comes to nothing.

VAN

Having wings,
would that be something?

LISE

Yes, it seems so. And yet
a bird has wings.

VAN

And he gets nowhere.

LISE

Yes.
Nothing but just to be a bird, and fly,
and then come down. Always the thing
    itself
is less than when the seed of it in
    thought
came to a flower within, but such a
    flower
as never grows in gardens.

BIGGS

Eh—Van Dorn!

VAN

(*Looking up*)
What are you doing on the roost, you
    birds?
Building a nest?

BIGGS

We can't get down.

VAN

I'd say
it ought to be just as easy to get down
as it was to get up there.

SKIMMERHORN

Will you help us out?

VAN

You look all right to me. What happened to you?

BIGGS

Everything.

VAN

How did you get there?

BIGGS

God,
it's a long story.

VAN

You've been there all night?

BIGGS

Yes, all night.

VAN

I wouldn't want to spoil it.
It's too good to be true. You see those
    two,
Lise, there in the scoop?

LISE

They're pitiful.
Shouldn't you help them?

VAN

No. Since time began
there haven't been two fat-guts that
    deserved
a hoisting like those two. In their own
    machine—
that makes it perfect.

LISE

What have they done?

VAN

They've been
themselves, that's all. Two thieves, a
    probate judge
and a manipulator, hand and glove
to thieve what they can get. They've
    got High Tor
among other things, and mean to carve
    it down,
at three cents a square yard.

LISE

These poor old men?

VAN

Yes, these poor old men.

LISE

Let them hang there then!

VAN

They'll hang there for all me.
    (LISE *and* VAN *turn to go.*)

SKIMMERHORN

I'll tell you what,
Van Dorn, I'll let you have that valida-
    tion
if you'll help me down.

VAN

That means I'd own the land?

SKIMMERHORN

Yes, you'd own it.

VAN

Only you'd cancel it,
once you got down.

SKIMMERHORN

To tell the truth I couldn't,
not if you had the paper.

VAN

Toss it over;
I'd like to see it.
(SKIMMERHORN *gets out an en-*
velope and throws it to VAN.)

BIGGS

You're a simple judge!
Now the land's his.

VAN

There's a bond goes with this,
a bond signed by the court. Oh, I
looked it up.
I've read that much law.

SKIMMERHORN

Yes, I'll keep the bond
till we're on your level.

VAN

Then I'd advise you both
to make yourself a nest with two-three
sticks,
like a couple of crows, and settle down
to see
what you can hatch—or maybe lay an
egg—
you'll have plenty of time.

BIGGS

Come now, Van Dorn,
we're in a bad way. It drops off
straight down
a thousand feet here, and Judge Skimmerhorn

has vertigo. Why, just to save a life,
out of common humanity, lean on that
cable
and pull us in.

VAN

This one?
(*He pulls. The shovel dips.*)

BIGGS

Oh, no, no! God,
do you want to dump us out!

VAN

You said to pull it.

BIGGS

Not that one! This! Pull up on that
again!
We're sliding!

VAN

Sure.
(*He rights the shovel.*)
Now you know how it feels
when you kick out the props from
under men
and slide 'em on the relief rolls. Ever
think
how that might feel?

BIGGS

You don't know what we've both
been through, Van Dorn. Rained on
and struck by lightning,
no dinner; we're half-crazy; we've had
nightmares,
funny people in hats; that's how we
got here,
one of those nightmares!

VAN

You sound disconnected.
Maybe you've lost your minds; still I'm
not melting
down in my shoes with compunction.
The fact is
he's clinging to the bond, Judge Skimmerhorn;
he's not too sunk for that. Now here's
my bargain:

You're hanging onto life by one steel
cable,
but that's much safer than the spider
web
most men have to trust to. Toss me the
bond,
Judge Skimmerhorn, or I'll give this
line a yank
and you won't even hang.

SKIMMERHORN

You wouldn't do it.

VAN

Oh, wouldn't I? For a two-cent lollipop
I'd pull the chain right now!

SKIMMERHORN

You wouldn't do it!

VAN

Hang on, then! Just for a taste, how's
the incline now?
A little steep?
        (*He pulls the line. The shovel tips
        as before.*)

BIGGS

Pull it up! Take the God damn bond!—
throw it to him!

SKIMMERHORN

I will not!

VAN

Try this then.
        (*He tips the shovel further.*)

BIGGS

Give him his bond! I'm slipping!

SKIMMERHORN

I will not!

BIGGS

I say you will! What's good the money
to you if you're bologny?

SKIMMERHORN

What money?

BIGGS

You know what money!

SKIMMERHORN

Straighten it up.

VAN

Do I get the bond?

SKIMMERHORN

Hell, yes!
        (VAN *restores their equilibrium.*)
You get the bond if you agree to accept
five thousand for your claim.
        (*He brings out a paper.*)

VAN

Don't stall with me!
I'll never have a chance like this again,
and it's hard to resist!

SKIMMERHORN

I'm offering you five thousand!
Five thousand! Cash!

VAN

        (*Leaping to the rope*)
Keep it!

BIGGS

Give him his bond!
        (*He wrenches the paper from
        SKIMMERHORN and sails it to
        VAN.*)
And now you've got it how's five thou-
sand sound?
You settle for it?

VAN

Bid against them, Lise. It's a game.
What would you say, Lise?
They offer me five thousand.

LISE

Pieces of silver?

VAN

Pieces of silver.

LISE

(*Smiling*)
But I'll give you more!
Only five thousand for this crag at
    dawn
shedding its husk of cloud to face a
    sunrise
over the silver bay? For silver haze
wrapping the crag at noon, before a
    storm
cascading silver levin? For winter rains
that run in silver down the black rock's
    face
under a gray-sedge sky? For loneliness
here on this crag? I offer you nine
    thousand!
To be paid in silver!

VAN

You hear? I've got nine thousand;
what am I offered?

BIGGS

Make it ten thousand—
and let us down in the bargain!

VAN

Yes? Ten thousand?
A mountain for ten thousand? Hear
    them, Lise,
In their despair they lift it by a grand!
Should it go for ten?

SKIMMERHORN

We'll never get it back—
but that's all right.

VAN

Yes, Lise?

LISE

Will they pay
no more then for the piling of this
    stone,
set in its tall hexagonals by fire
before men were? Searching a hundred
    kingdoms
men will not find a site for lodge or
    tower
more kingly! A hundred thousand, sir,
    in silver,
this is my offer!

VAN

Come now, meet it boys—
I have a hundred thousand!

BIGGS

She's a fraud!
She's no dealer; she's a ringer, primed
to put the price up! What do you mean
    by silver?
She won't pay silver!

VAN

Coinage of the moon,
but it's current here!

SKIMMERHORN

Ten thousand, cash, and that's
the last. Five thousand out of my
    pocket, see,
and five from Biggs!
      (*He pulls out a bundle of bills.*
      BIGGS *does the same.*)
Take a good look at cash,
see how that operates!
      (*He tosses down the roll.* BIGGS
      follows suit.)

VAN

You go well-heeled
when you go mountain-climbing. Is it
    real?

SKIMMERHORN

Well, look it over. Count it.
      (VAN *takes up one packet, then
      another.*)

VAN

Where did it come from?

SKIMMERHORN

Where would you think?

VAN

I'll say I got a shock.
      (*He studies the bills again.*)
I don't want your money.

BIGGS

What's wrong with it?

VAN

Didn't I tell you I had a hundred thousand?
Take the stuff back. We reckon in
    moonlight here!
Put up your mitts!
    (*He tosses the bundles back.*)

BIGGS

It's yours if you want it.

VAN

No,
oh, no, I thank you. It's no sale.
    What's more
I never meant to sell. The auctioneer's
about to take a walk.

BIGGS

Well, look, we're sitting
right where we were.

VAN

You sit there for your health,
and think it over.

SKIMMERHORN

You won't do that, Van Dorn,
just leave us here.

VAN

Watch me, if you don't think so.
    (*He gives an arm to* LISE.)
Let me tell you about those babes in
    the wood,
did I say they were thieves?
    (*They start out.*)

BIGGS

Make it fifteen!

VAN

Go to sleep.

SKIMMERHORN

Well, twenty! and let us down!

VAN

Sweet dreams.

SKIMMERHORN

We'll run you out of the state, Van
Dorn!

VAN

You'll have to get down first!

SKIMMERHORN

Is he going away
and leave us sitting?

BIGGS

Looks like it.
    (VAN *and* LISE *move off.*)

SKIMMERHORN

Say, Van Dorn,
will you pitch us up a sandwich?

VAN

Sure; they're soggy,
lying out in the rain.
    (*He returns and tosses sandwiches
        to them.*)

BIGGS

Thanks.

VAN

Don't mention it.
    (*He goes out right with Lise.*
        BIGGS *and* SKIMMERHORN *un-
        wrap sandwiches.*)

SKIMMERHORN

He got away with that bond.

BIGGS

Yeah.

SKIMMERHORN

Looks as if we wouldn't make anything
on Van Dorn.

BIGGS

That's what it looks like.

SKIMMERHORN

Christ.

BIGGS

Well, we've still got the windfall.

SKIMMERHORN

Yeah, we've got that.

BIGGS

And here he comes again.

SKIMMERHORN

Who?

BIGGS

Our mascot, little rabbit's foot, little good-luck token, little knee-high with the big heart.
(DE WITT *comes in from the left, looks at the place where the sandwiches were and then at the two in the shovel. He mutters.*)

DE WITT

Magic again! More devil's work! And the woman
gone, slipped round a turn, and the scent was cold
for an old dog like me. By the mizzen yards,
it's wearing to the temper of a man
even if he's not choleric!—And those two,
those buzzards of evil omen, brooding there
on how they'll cut the mountain like a pie
and sell it off in slices!
(*He looks at his pistols.*)
One apiece.
It should be just enough, and it's a wonder
I never thought of it.

(*He lifts his pistols, the two drop their sandwiches into the void, and cower down; he clicks the hammers.*)
Damp again! Well, boys,
we'll fix that.
(*He sits down to freshen the priming.*)
They'll brood over us no more,
those two sea-lions. Damn the rain and mist;
it penetrates the priming! Damn the flint,
and damn the spring! A brace of fine horse-pistols,
that's what the Jew said back in Amsterdam;
it takes a horse to cock 'em. Now then, damn you,
blow 'em off their perch!
(*As he rises his eye catches something out on the Zee. He stands transfixed for a moment, watching.*)
It can't be there!
It's there! It's gone! I saw it! Captain Asher!
Captain! Captain! Captain! Captain Asher!
(BIGGS *and* SKIMMERHORN *have ducked down again.* DE WITT *rushes out to the right, firing his pistols in the air in his excitement.* BIGGS *sits up, then* SKIMMERHORN.)

SKIMMERHORN

Am I hurt? Do you see blood anywhere?

BIGGS

It seems there was nothing there.
(*They contemplate the place where* DE WITT *stood.*)

SCENE II

Scene: *Another part of the Tor.* Lise *is sitting high up on a ledge, looking out over the Zee.* Van *stands near her, looking at her as she speaks. She has his old felt hat in her lap and has woven a wreath of dandelions around the brim. The beacon light strikes athwart her face.*

LISE
But nobody likes this flower?

VAN
I like it now.
I used to think it was a weed, but now,
well, it's a flower now.

LISE
The dandelion.
Where will you find another prodigal
so merry or so golden or so wasteful,
pouring out treasure down the sides of
    hills
and cupping it in valleys?

VAN
Buttercups
and touch-me-nots. The touch-me-not's
    a shoe,
a tiny golden shoe, with a hair-spring
    latchet
for bees to loosen.

LISE
When did you part from Judith?

VAN
Judith?

LISE
When did she go away?

VAN
Last evening.
But it seems longer.

LISE
Why?

VAN
Why, a lot's happened.—
It's almost morning.

LISE
How do you know?
    (*He steps up to the ledge.*)

VAN
See that star,
that heavy red star back in the west?
    When that
goes down, then look for the morning
    star across
Long Island Sound, and after that the
    lights
dim down in the gray.

LISE
You loved her, very much?

VAN
Yes.

LISE
I loved someone too. I love him still.

VAN
No, you're mine now.
    (*He sits beside her.*)

LISE
See the great gulf that lies
between the heavy red star down the
    west
and the star that comes with morning?
    It's a long way.
There's that much lies between us.

VAN
Not for me.

LISE
Even for you.—You're weary?

VAN

Well, the truth is
I sometimes sleep at night.

LISE

Put your head down.
I'll hold you.
    (*He lays his head on her knees
    and stretches out.*)
Now I'll wish that I could sing
and make you sleep. Somehow they're
   all forgotten,
the old songs. Over and over when the
   birds
begin at morning I try hard to catch
one tune of theirs. There's one that
   seems to say:
    Merrily, merrily, chirr, chirr,
    Lueté, lueté, stee—
    Merrily, merrily, chirr, lueté,
    Chirr, lueté, stee.
That's only what it says; for what it
   sings
you'll have to ask the bird.

VAN

I know it, though.
That's the song sparrow.

LISE

Have I come so near?

VAN

Say it again.

LISE

I can't. May I ask you something?

VAN

Yes.

LISE

There's so much that's changed now
   men can fly .
and hear each other across seas, must
   men
still die—do they die still?

VAN

Oh, yes, they die.
Why do you ask?

LISE

Because I'm still so young,
and yet I can't remember all the years
there must have been.—In a long night
   sometimes
I try to count them, but they blow in
   clouds
across the sky, the dancing firefly years,
incredible numbers.—Tell me how old
   you are
before you go to sleep.

VAN

Lying here now
there's not much logic in arithemtic.
Five, or six, maybe. Five or six thousand, maybe.
But when I'm awake I'm twenty-three.

LISE

No more?

VAN

No more.

LISE

Tell me why it is I am as I am
and not like you?

VAN

I don't know, Lise.

LISE

But tell me.
Have I been enchanted here? I've seen
the trap-rock men, there in the shovel,
   seeming
so stupid and so pitiful. Could these
use charms and rites to hold wrecked
   mariners
forever in a deep cataleptic spell
high on a mountain-fringe?

VAN

The trap-rock men?
They're no more wizards than I am.
   They buy
and sell, and when they've had their
   fill of dust
they die like the rest of us.

LISE

But they laid spells
about us?

VAN

There are no wizards and no spells.
Just men and women and money and
the earth
the way it always was. The trap-rock
men
don't know you're here.

LISE

It's not sorcery then. If I had died
and left my bones here on the mountain-top
but had no memory of it, and lived on
in dreams, it might be as it is. As
children
sure we were told of living after death,
but there were angels there, and onyx
stone
paving an angel city, and they sang
eternally, no darkness and no sun,
nothing of earth. Now can it be men
die
and carry thence no memory of death,
only this curious lightness of the hands,
only this curious darkness of the mind,
only to be still changeless with the
winters
passing; not gray, not lined, not
stricken down,
but stamped forever on the moving air,
an echo and an image? Restless still
with the old hungers, drifting among
men,
till one by one forgotten, fading out
like an old writing, undecipherable,
we lose our hold and go? Could it be
true?
Could this be how men die?

VAN

(Half asleep)
It may be, Lise.
I love you when you speak.

LISE

And I love you.
But I am dead, and all the crew is
dead;

all of the Onrust crew—and we have
clung
beyond our place and time, on into a
world
unreal as sleep, unreal as this your
sleep
that comes upon you now. Oh, you
were cruel
to love me and to tell me I am dead
and lie here warm and living! When
you wake
we shall be parted—you will have a
world
but I'll have none! There's a chill falls
on me,
the night-dew gathering, or my mind's
death chill—
knowing at last I know.—You haven't
heard.
You told me this in a half-dream.
You've been kind.
You never thought to hurt me. Are you
asleep?

VAN

I think I was.

LISE

Sleep, sleep. There was once a song,
if only I could call back air and words,
about a king who watched a goblet rising
and falling in the sea. It came to land
and on the rim the king's name was in-
scribed
with a date many years before. Oh,
many years,
a hundred or three hundred. Then he
knew
that all his life was lived in an old
time,
swept out, given to the waters. What
remained
was but this goblet swimming in the
sea,
touching his dust by chance.—But he's
asleep.
And very well he might be with dull
stories
out of old songs.—Sleep, sweet; let me
have
your head here on my knees, only this
night,

and your brown hair round my finger.
> (*A girl's shadowy figure comes in
> from the right, walking lightly,
> pauses, as if at seeing them,
> and turns to go, the face still
> unrevealed.*)

Are you Judith?

JUDITH
Yes.

LISE
The lad's asleep, but when he wakes
you'll have him back.

JUDITH
Do you dispose of him
just as you please?

LISE
No. It's not what I please.
It's what will happen.

JUDITH
I don't know who you are.

LISE
I'm but a friend of his. You left him
  bitter
going away so lightly. I was bitter—
and so we tried to play at being lovers,
but it won't do. He'll wake, and he'll
  be yours,
all as it was. Only if I may hold him
while he lies here asleep, it helps a
  little
and I'll be happier.

JUDITH
You'll keep him then
after he wakes.

LISE
No.

JUDITH
Then why are you crying?

LISE
Am I crying?
Well, they're not for him, nor you,
  these tears;

something so far away, so long ago,
so hopeless, so fallen, so lost, so deep
  in dust
the names wash from the urns, summons my tears,
not love or longing. Only when you
  have him,
love him a little better for your sake,
for your sake only, knowing how bitterly
I cried, for times past and things done.

JUDITH
You're strange—
the dress you wear's strange, too.—
Who are you then?
I'm—afraid of you!

LISE
Afraid of tears
and a voice out of long ago? It's all I
  have.

JUDITH
No—no—I'm not afraid. Only for him.
I've done my crying, too.—Shall I come
  back?

LISE
Don't wake him now. Come back at
  dawn. You'll find him
here alone.
> (TWO *or* THREE SAILORS *appear on
> the rocks at the rear, looking
> out over the Zee.*)

PIETER
Look for yourself.

A SAILOR
Aye.

PIETER
Do you make her out?

THE SAILOR
She's the square top-yards.

ANOTHER SAILOR
Now, God, if it were she!

PIETER

It's the brigantine! The *Onrust* from up-river tacking this way!

ASHER

(*Outside*)

Lise! Lise! Lise!
(*The* CAPTAIN *comes in at the rear with* DE WITT.)
Lise, the ship's on the river! Quick, there's haste!
She must catch the tide down-stream!

LISE

Hush! Hush! You'll wake him!

ASHER

But look across the Zee! The *Onrust's* in and waiting for us!

LISE

But you say it, Asher,
only to comfort me. There is no ship,
nor are we caught in spells here, or enchanted,
but spectres of an old time. The life we live
is but a lingering, a clinging on,
our dust remembering. There is no ship,
only a phantom haunting down the Zee
as we still haunt the heights.

ASHER

Look! The *Onrust!*
Look, Lise!

LISE

Yes, I see it.

ASHER

Will you come?

LISE

Why should I stay? Why should I go? For go
or stay we're phantoms still.

ASHER

But will you come?
Who is this lad?

LISE

Her lad. But he was hurt
and fell asleep.
(VAN *wakes and lifts his head.*)

ASHER

Come quickly!

LISE

Yes, for his sake
it's better I should go.

VAN

Where must you go?
(*She rises.*)

LISE

The *Onrust's* on the river
and we must catch the tide.

VAN

Would you leave me now?

LISE

Yes, I must leave you.

VAN

You'll go back with him?

LISE

Yes.

VAN

And was nothing meant of all we said?

LISE

What could we mean, we two? Your hurt's quite cured
and mine's past curing.

VAN

Let me go with you then.

LISE

I should have told you if I'd only known
how we stood at the tangent of two worlds
that touched an instant like two wings of storm

drawn out of night; touched and flew
off, and, falling,
fall now asunder through a wide abyss,
not to touch again.
(*She steps back among the
rocks.*)

VAN

Let them go if they like!
What do I care about worlds? Any
world you have
I'll make it mine!

LISE

You told me in your sleep.
There is no witchcraft. Men are as
they were;
we're parted now.

VAN

Give me your hand again!
They dare not take you from me, dare
not touch you
no matter who they are, or where they
come from—
they have no hold on us!

LISE

If I could stay!
If I could stay with you. And tend my
garden
only a little longer!

VAN

Put out your hand!

LISE

There were too many, many, many
years.

VAN

I'll be alone here—

LISE

No, not alone. When you must walk
the air,
as all must walk it sometime, with a
tread
that stirs no leaf, and breathe here with
a breath
that blows impalpable through smoke
or cloud,

when you are as I am, a bending wind
along the grain, think of me sometimes
then
and how I clung to earth. The earth
you have
seems now so hard and firm, with all
its colors
sharp for the eye, as a taste's sharp to
the tongue,
you'll hardly credit how its outlines
blur
and wear out as you wear. Play now
with fire
while fire will burn, bend down the
bough and eat
before the fruit falls. For there comes a
time
when the great sun-lit pattern of the
earth
shakes like an image under water,
darkens,
dims, and the clearest voices that we
knew
are sunken bells, dead sullen under
sea,
receding. Look in her eyes.
(VAN *looks at* JUDITH.)

ASHER

Come!

LISE

See, the dawn
points with one purple finger at a star
to put it out. When it has quite gone
out
then we'll be gone.
(VAN *looks at the dawn, then
turns back toward* LISE.)

VAN

Lise! Lise!
(*But even as he speaks* LISE *and
the* CREW *have disappeared.*)

LISE

(*Unseen*)
This is your age, your dawn, your life
to live.
The morning light strikes through us,
and the wind

that follows after rain tugs at our
      sails—
and so we go.

DE WITT
   (*Still half-seen*)
And welcome you are to the age, too,
an age of witches and sandwiches, an
age of paper, an age of paper money
and paper men, so that a poor Dutch
wraith's more man
than the thickest of you!
   (*He steps back and vanishes. It is
      now dawn.*)

VAN
She never said good-bye.

JUDITH
There is a ship.

VAN
Yes?

JUDITH
Tiny, with black, square sails;
low and small.

VAN
   (*Still looking after* LISE)
She'll be a phantom too
like all the rest. The canvas casts no
      shadow;
the light sifts through the spars. A
      moonlight rig
no doubt they call it.

JUDITH
I think I hear their voices
as they go down the crag.

VAN
But you won't see them.
No matter what you hear.

THE SAILORS
   (*A wisp of chantey in the dis-
      tance*)
Coming a blow, coming a blow,
sea runs black, glass runs low.

VAN
Just voices down the wind.
Why, then they were all mist, a fog
      that hangs
along the crevices of hills, a kind
of memory of things you read in books,
things you thought you'd forgotten.
      She was here,
and she was real, but she was cloud,
      and gone,
and the hill's barren of her.

JUDITH
There are no ghosts.

VAN
I know—but these were ghosts or I'm a
      ghost,
and all of us. God knows where we
      leave off
and ghosts begin. God knows where
      ghosts leave off
and we begin.

JUDITH
You were in love with her.

VAN
She leaves the mountain barren now
      she's gone.
And she was beautiful.

JUDITH
I came to tell you
that I was wrong—I mean about the
      land—
what you have here is better than one
      buys
down in the towns. But since I come
      too late
I'll say it and then go.—Your way was
      best.
I think it always would be.—So, good
      night, Van—
or, rather, it's good morning.

VAN
Yes, it's morning.—
Is it too late?

JUDITH

Oh, Van, I think it is.
It was for Lise you were calling, not
for Judith. I can't say I blame you
much,
because she is more beautiful. And yet
you love her, and not me. You'll say
they're ghosts
and won't come back. Perhaps. I'm not
so certain
about the way of ghosts. She may
come back.
And you still love her.

VAN

There's no ship at all.
It faded in the dawn. And all the mists
that hung about the Tor, look how
they lift,
pouring downstream with the wind.
Whatever it was,
was said, or came between us, it's all
gone
now it's daylight again.

JUDITH

I came to say
if only I could keep you, you should
keep
the Tor, or what you wished. I'm sorry
I went.
I'm sorry this has happened. But it has.
And so—

VAN

Should I keep the Tor?

JUDITH

Yes, if you like.

VAN

God knows they haven't left me much
of it.
Look, where the new road winds along
the ledge.
Look at the jagged cut the quarries
make
down to the south, and there's a boy
scout trail
running along the ridge Mount Ivy
way,
where they try out their hatchets.

There's the light,
and steps cut into stone the linesmen
blew
for better climbing. The crusher underneath
dumps road rock into barges all day
long
and sometimes half the night. The
West Shore tunnel
belches its trains above the dead la-
goons
that line the brickyards. Their damned
shovel hangs
across my line, ready to gouge the peak
we're standing on. Maybe I'm ghost
myself
trying to hold an age back with my
hands;
maybe we're all the same, these ghosts
of Dutchmen
and one poor superannuated Indian
and one last hunter, clinging to his
land
because he's always had it. Like a
wasp
that tries to build a nest above your
door—
and when you brush it down he builds
again,
then when you brush it down he builds
again—
but after a while you get him.

JUDITH

Then you'll sell?

VAN

I guess if you were with me then we'd
sell
for what we could, and move out far-
ther west
where a man's land's his own. But if
I'm here
alone, I'll play the solitary wasp
and sting them till they get me.

JUDITH

If it's your way
then it's your way.

VAN

I'll sell it if you'll stay.
Won't you stay with me, Judith?

JUDITH

I think I'd always hear you calling Lise while I was standing by. I took a wrong turning once, when I left you and went down the hill, and now it may not ever be the same.
(*She turns.*)

ACT THREE

SCENE: *The shovel still hangs over the verge, and* BIGGS *and* SKIMMERHORN *still occupy it. The rising sun sends level rays across the rock, lighting their intent faces as they stare downward.* BIGGS *has torn a handkerchief into strips and tied them together into a string. He appears to be fishing for something which lies below the ledge, out of view of the audience. Over and over he tries his cast.*

SKIMMERHORN

Little to the left.

BIGGS

You don't say?

SKIMMERHORN

Little to the right.

BIGGS

Put it to a tune and sing it, why don't you?

SKIMMERHORN

There! Almost!

BIGGS

I don't need any umpire.

SKIMMERHORN

Let me try it.

BIGGS

Oh, no. You always were a butterfingers.
(*The string tightens.*)
By Golly!

SKIMMERHORN

It's on!

BIGGS

You're explaining to me?
(*He pulls up. A bottle of beer emerges from below.*)

SKIMMERHORN

Fifty per cent!

BIGGS

What?
(*He pauses, the bottle in air.*)

SKIMMERHORN

You tore up my handkerchief! Fifty per cent. That's the natural division between capital and labor.

BIGGS

Oh, now I'm labor and you're capital.
(*He pulls up carefully.*)

SKIMMERHORN

Fifty per cent!

BIGGS

I get the first pull at it. That's all I ask.
(*The string parts, and the bottle descends silently into the void.*)
That's that.

SKIMMERHORN

You should 'a let me handle it.

BIGGS

Yeah. No doubt.

SKIMMERHORN

Am I thirsty?

BIGGS

Wait till the sun gets up a little. We'll be pan-fried in this thing.

SKIMMERHORN

Look!
(*He points down the rocks.*)

BIGGS

If it's more of those little people I give up.

SKIMMERHORN

It's a trooper.

BIGGS

What do you know? Up early for a trooper, too. Listen, about that stuff in our pockets?

SKIMMERHORN

Yeah?

BIGGS

Do we say anything about it?

SKIMMERHORN

Do you?

BIGGS

Do you?

SKIMMERHORN

No.

BIGGS

Neither do I, then.

SKIMMERHORN

Beautiful morning.

BIGGS

I always say it's worth while being up early just to catch the sunrise.
(*A* TROOPER *climbs in followed by* SKIMMERHORN SENIOR.)

THE TROOPER

Hello!

BIGGS

Hello, Patsy.

PATSY

Say, you boys had the wives worried down in Ledentown. Been looking for you all night. There they are, Mr. Skimmerhorn.

SKIMMERHORN, SR.

(*Winded*)
Good God!
(*He sits, a hand to his heart.*)
And I climbed up here. We thought you were under that rock slide.

SKIMMERHORN

I guess you're disappointed.

SENIOR

The next time you two go on a bat and spend a night up a tree you can stay there and sober up.

SKIMMERHORN

We haven't been drinking.

SENIOR

(*Pointing to a bottle*)
What's that?

SKIMMERHORN

Beer. But we didn't have a **drop to** drink. I'd certainly appreciate a swallow of that now.

PATSY

(*Tossing up bottle*)
Here you are. Hair of the dog that bit you.

BIGGS

We're not drunk. We're dry. We didn't have a drop to drink nor a bite to eat.

PATSY

All right. All right. Only the ground's covered with beer and sandwiches.

BIGGS

You tell 'em how it was, Skimmer.

SKIMMERHORN

You tell 'em.

BIGGS

Well, you see, the whole thing's pretty complicated.

PATSY

I know. I've been through it. You wake up in the morning and you can't believe it yourself.

BIGGS

I don't mean that. I'm sober as a judge.

PATSY

Yeah, what judge?
        (*He hauls at a cable.*)
Can you lend me a hand with this, A.B.?

SENIOR

Give me a minute.
        (*The shovel tips.*)

BIGGS

Hey, not that one! The other one!

PATSY

Sorry. Not much of a mechanic.

BIGGS

Straighten it up again.
        (*Patsy does so.*)

SKIMMERHORN

Are we never getting off this? My legs are paralyzed sitting here.

BIGGS

So are mine.

PATSY

        (*Hauling down*)
It's too much for me alone.

SKIMMERHORN

Got your wind yet, A.B.?

SENIOR

I don't know whether I want you down yet. You had your good time, now you can put in a few minutes paying for it.

SKIMMERHORN

Oh, we had a good time, did we?

SENIOR

What were you doing? You came up here to buy Van Dorn's property; you're gone all night, and the whole damn town's up all night hunting for you! And we find you up in a steam shovel enjoying a hang-over!

PATSY

And now I know what a hang-over looks like.

BIGGS

I tell you we didn't even have a drink of water!

SENIOR

I believe that!

BIGGS

And we're thirsty! Have you got an opener?

PATSY

No, I haven't.

SENIOR

Before you open anything tell me what you were doing last night. Did you see Van Dorn?

SKIMMERHORN

Sure we saw him.

SENIOR

Well, what did he say?

SKIMMERHORN

He said no.

SENIOR

And I suppose that took all night?

SKIMMERHORN

We had an argument.

SENIOR

And then he chased you up the crane, I suppose?

SKIMMERHORN

No.

SENIOR

Well, how did you get up there?

SKIMMERHORN

We were hauled up.

SENIOR

All right. Who hauled you up?

SKIMMERHORN

You tell him, Art.

BIGGS

Oh, no. You tell him.

SKIMMERHORN

As a matter of fact, I don't think it happened.

SENIOR

You're there, aren't you?

SKIMMERHORN

Yes, we're here.

SENIOR

Well, if you weren't drunk how did you get there?

SKIMMERHORN

Well, you see, first we tried to negotiate with Van Dorn.

SENIOR

And he wouldn't take the money?

SKIMMERHORN

That's right.

SENIOR

Did you tell him he didn't really own the land? Till the will was validated?

SKIMMERHORN

Yes, we told him that.

SENIOR

And he still wouldn't talk business?

SKIMMERHORN

He's stubborn. Stubborn as a mule.

SENIOR

Did you tell him you could take the land away from him?

SKIMMERHORN

Oh, yes.

SENIOR

And you offered him the twenty-five thousand?

BIGGS

We offered him a fair price.

SENIOR

You were authorized to say twenty-five thousand.

BIGGS

We didn't quite get to that. We offered ten.

SKIMMERHORN

You see, we thought we'd save the company some money.

SENIOR

I'll bet you did. You thought you'd make a little on the side, and I'd never know.

SKIMMERHORN

Oh, no.

BIGGS

Oh, no.

SENIOR

All right, you offered ten and he wouldn't take it. Then what happened?

SKIMMERHORN

Well, we couldn't get down because of the slide, so some sailors offered to let us down in this thing.

SENIOR

Sailors—up here?

SKIMMERHORN

Little men, in big hats.

BIGGS

Might have been a moving picture company.

SENIOR

Yeah? Any elephants? Or snakes?

SKIMMERHORN

We're trying to tell you the truth!

PATSY

Certainly sounds like delirium tremens, boys.

SENIOR

Never mind, you were hauled up by pink elephants, and then what?

SKIMMERHORN

Van Dorn came along and started to dump us down the cliff.

SENIOR

What's Van Dorn look like? Kind of an octopus, with long feelers?

SKIMMERHORN

Are you going to let us down out of this basket?

SENIOR

No. Not till you come across with what's been going on.

SKIMMERHORN

All right. I'll talk when I'm down.

SENIOR

Can a grown man get pie-eyed on beer?

PATSY

Must have been something stronger.
(VAN DORN *comes in from the right.*)

SENIOR

Who are you?

VAN

Oh, I'm nobody. I just own the property.

SENIOR

What property?

VAN

This.

SENIOR

Are you Van Dorn?

VAN

I am.

SENIOR

I'm A. B. Skimmerhorn, Mr. Van Dorn, president of Igneous Trap-rock, and I'm glad to meet you.
(*He puts out a hand.*)

VAN

(*Ignoring the hand*)
Are these friends of yours?

SENIOR

One's a nephew and one's a partner. Why?

VAN

Because any friend of theirs is no friend of mine.
(JUDITH *and* THE INDIAN *enter at the rear. She is leading him.*)

PATSY

Who do you think you're talking to?

VAN

A. B. Skimmerhorn, of Skimmerhorn, Skimmerhorn, Biggs and Skimmerhorn, small-time crooks and petty thieving done. Cheap.

SENIOR

Now, to be frank, there may have been some misunderstanding, Mr. Van Dorn. Those two were hardly in condition to negotiate. But I can offer you a fair price for your land, and if you don't take it we may have to push you a little, because we want this acreage and we intend to have it.

SKIMMERHORN

He's got the validation papers.

SENIOR

You gave him the validation papers?

BIGGS

We had to. He started to trip the machine.

SENIOR

That puts us in a sweet mess, that does. Will you take twenty-five thousand?

VAN

No.

SENIOR

Will you take fifty thousand?

VAN

No.

SENIOR

Then we go home, and the machinery can rust here. That's the best I can do.

VAN

Fine. Let it rust.

JUDITH

Van?

VAN

Yes, Judith.

JUDITH

There's someone here to see you.

VAN

You want to see me, John?

THE INDIAN

But I can wait. I have time enough.

VAN

I'll be right with you.

JUDITH

I had to bring him, Van, because he said his eyes were bad. He couldn't see the way.

VAN

Thanks, Judith.

SENIOR

Look, Van Dorn, you know the saying, every man has his price. I've heard it said
God has his price, if you'll go high enough.
Set a figure.

VAN

I'm not thinking of prices.
I won't want to sell. Hell, fifty thousand's
too much money for me.

SENIOR

We'll give you less.

VAN

I don't want less or more. It's not a matter of money.

SENIOR

Will you take a partnership in the company?

VAN

No.

SENIOR

Good God, what do you want?

VAN

I want to have it back the way it was
before you came here. And I won't get
    that. I know
What kind of fool I look to all of you,
all but old John there. But I'll be a
    fool
along with John, and keep my own,
    before
I let you have an inch. John, fifty thou-
    sand
or this old hill-top. Is it worth keeping?

THE INDIAN

No.

VAN

No?

THE INDIAN

It's gone already. Not worth keeping.

VAN

I thought you'd say it was. I counted
    on you
to be my friend in that.

THE INDIAN

It's an old question,
one I heard often talked of round the
    fire
when the hills and I were younger.
    Then as now
the young braves were for keeping
    what was ours
whatever it cost in blood. And they did
    try,
but when they'd paid their blood, and
    still must sell,
the price was always less than what it
    was
before their blood was paid.

VAN

Well, that may be.

THE INDIAN

I wish now I had listened when they
    spoke
their prophecies, the sachems of the
    tents;
they were wiser than I knew. Wisest of
    all,
Iachim, had his camp here on this Tor
before the railroad came. I saw him
    stand
and look out toward the west, toward
    the sun dying,
and say, "Our god is now the setting
    sun,
and we must follow it. For other races,
out of the east, will live here in their
    time,
one following another. Each will build
its cities, and its monuments to gods
we dare not worship. Some will come
    with ships,
and some with wings, and each will
    desecrate
the altars of the people overthrown,
but none will live forever. Each will
    live
its little time, and fly before the feet
of those who follow after." Let them
    come in
despoiling, for a time is but a time
and these will not endure. This little
    hill,
let them have the little hill, and find
    your peace
beyond, for there's no hill worth a
    man's peace
while he may live and find it. But they
    fought it out
and died, and sleep here.

SENIOR

Why, this is a wise Indian.
A little pessimistic about the aims
of civilization, but wise anyway.
What do you say, Van Dorn?

THE INDIAN

You too will go
like gnats on the wind. An evening and
    a day,
but still you have your day. Build mon-
    uments

and worship at your temples. But you
  too
will go.

SENIOR

You're on my side, so I don't mind,
but you have a damned uncomfortable
  way
of speaking. I'm a Republican myself,
but I don't go that far! What do you
  say, Van Dorn?
Can we do business?

VAN

Judith?

JUDITH

I'm out of it.
It's your decision. I'd say keep it
  though
if you want to keep it.

VAN

I'll sell it. Fifty thousand.
On one condition. There's a burying
  ground
I want to keep.

SENIOR

Sure. That can be arranged.
It's settled, then. Come down to Ledentown
tomorrow and get your money.

VAN

Yes, I'll come.

SENIOR

Why three cheers, boys. We're out of
  the woods. Take hold,
Van Dorn, and swing these topers off
  the limb.
Then they can sign the pledge.
  (A TROOPER appears with ELKUS
  and DOPE.)

BUDGE (The Trooper.)

Help me keep an eye on these two,
will you, Patsy? I've got a confession
out of them on the Nanuet bank robbery, and they say the money's up
here.

PATSY

Up here? Whereabouts?

BUDGE

They left it in a satchel.

PATSY

There's the satchel, all right.
  (He examines it.)
Empty.

BUDGE

Looks like a stall, you guys. You buried
it.

ELKUS

Didn't keep a cent, officer. Somebody up
here got it.

BUDGE

Well, who?

ELKUS

Last time I saw it one of those birds
sat down on it.
  (He points to BIGGS and SKIMMER-
  HORN.)

PATSY

You know who they are? That's Judge
Skimmerhorn of the Probate Court, and
Arthur Biggs of the Trap-rock Com-
pany.

ELKUS

Well, one of them sat down on it.

BUDGE

Why didn't he pick it up?

ELKUS

I don't know whether he saw it.

DOPE

And then there was a little guy in a
big hat that had some of it.

PATSY

Yeah? Who?

BUDGE

That's right. Buddy said something about a little guy in a big hat.

PATSY

You think he got away with it?

ELKUS

He had some of it, and we haven't got a cent.

BUDGE

So now we have to look for a little guy in a big hat. Any other description?

ELKUS

Short and fat, had two sawed-off shotguns, and wore knee-pants.

DOPE

And you could see right through him.
(BUDGE *is writing in a notebook.*)

PATSY

What?

DOPE

You could see right through him.

BUDGE

I'm beginning to think I can see right through you.

PATSY

Check on that. Elkus, you saw him. Could you see through him?

ELKUS

Certainly was a funny-looking guy. Looked as if you could see right through him.

BUDGE

You expect me to send that out over the country: "Look for a short, fat man with a big hat and two sawed-off shotguns. Dangerous. You can see right through him."?

PATSY

They buried the money, Budge. Or else they're screwy.

ELKUS

I thought I was screwy. You couldn't hurt him with a gun.

BUDGE

What do you mean?

DOPE

We bored him full of holes and he wouldn't even sit down.

BUDGE

You mean he kept on running?

DOPE

Running? He just stood there and let us shoot him. Like shooting through a window.

BUDGE

Must have been wearing a vest.

DOPE

I shot him through the head! Two feet away! And it just made him mad!

PATSY

Take 'em away, Budge. They're nuts.

ELKUS

But he had the money! Buddy saw him with the money!

PATSY

They're all three nuts.

BUDGE

I never heard a line like that before.

PATSY

Who lives around here?

VAN

I guess I'm the only one that lives near-by.

PATSY

Did you hear any shooting last night?

VAN

Plenty of it.

PATSY

Did you take a look round?

VAN

Yes, I did.

PATSY

Did you see a little guy in a big hat?

VAN

Six or seven of them.

BUDGE

What!

VAN

Six or seven of them.

BUDGE

I suppose you could see right through them?

VAN

Once in a while.

BUDGE

I'm going to quit writing this down. There's enough here to get me fired already.

PATSY

If you saw six or seven where did they go?

VAN

Down the river.

PATSY

In a car?

VAN

In a ship.

PATSY

Sounds like a motor-boat gang. Well, that's something. They went down the river.

VAN

But I can tell you where there's thirty dollars of the money.

BUDGE

Where?

VAN

On the ledge there below the shovel.
(BUDGE *and* PATSY *step over to look.*)

BUDGE

There it is. Three ten dollar bills. How did it get there?

VAN

I don't know. I just happened to see it.

BUDGE

Did you try to get it?

VAN

No. I thought it probably belonged to the gentlemen up there in the scoop.

PATSY

Did one of you drop some money, Judge?

SKIMMERHORN

I don't think so. Not me.

BIGGS

Not me.

PATSY

Did either of you see a little man in a big hat?
(*The two look at each other.*)

SKIMMERHORN

Why, yes, we did.
(PATSY *and* BUDGE *look at each other.*)

BUDGE

Well, if they say so he must have been here.

PATSY

What was he doing?

SKIMMERHORN

He was fighting with those two.
(*He points to* ELKUS *and* DOPE.)

BIGGS

A regular war.

PATSY

Say, listen to that.

BUDGE

Do you know if he took anything out
of the satchel?

SKIMMERHORN

Yes, I think he did. He had the satchel.

BUDGE

Now we're getting somewhere.

PATSY

You don't know where he went?

SKIMMERHORN

No.

PATSY

If you saw anything else that might
give us a clue—?

SKIMMERHORN

No, not a thing.

PATSY

It beats me.

VAN

Want me to suggest a question?

PATSY

What?

VAN

Ask the Judge if he gained any weight
during the night.

PATSY

What's the matter with you?

VAN

Looks to me like he picked up a good
deal.

PATSY

I'll think up my own questions, thanks.
Might as well trundle the yeggs back
to jail, Budge. Whoever got the stuff
it's gone.

BUDGE

That's what it looks like.

VAN

Aren't you going to help the Judge
down before you go?

BIGGS

Oh, don't bother. We'll get down.

SKIMMERHORN

No hurry. We're all right. You take
care of your prisoners.

PATSY

Might as well lend a hand while we're
here.

BIGGS

Run along, boys. We're all right. Don't
worry about us.

PATSY

(*To* BUDGE)
Want to wait a minute?

BUDGE

Well, I'm due back, if they can make
it themselves.

BIGGS

Sure.

VAN

Oh, don't leave those poor fellows up
on that crane! They've been there all
night!

SKIMMERHORN

We're fine. You run along.

BUDGE

Well, take a drag on the rope, Patsy. I'll wait.
(PATSY *and* VAN *haul the shovel down.*)

SKIMMERHORN

No need to go to all this trouble.

PATSY

No trouble at all.

VAN

A pleasure. Why you were asking me all night to get you out of this.
(*The shovel touches ground. The two sit still.*)

PATSY

What's the matter?

SKIMMERHORN

Guess my legs are asleep.

BIGGS

Mine too.

PATSY

I'll help you up.
(*They are pulled to their feet, staggering. Their pockets are very obvious.*)

BUDGE

How about it? O.K.?

PATSY

All set. Say, you are loaded down. Carried plenty of lunch, I guess?

BIGGS

Oh, we brought plenty.

VAN

(*Tapping* BIGGS' *pocket*)
I told you they gained weight. Something in the air up here.

ELKUS

Couldn't be money, could it?

BIGGS

As a matter of fact, some of it is. We were carrying cash to pay Van Dorn for his farm.

PATSY

Cash?

BIGGS

Yeah, cash.

PATSY

How much?

BIGGS

Just what we were authorized to pay. Twenty-five thousand.

VAN

Funny thing, too. It's got the Orangebury pay roll stamp on it.

BIGGS

Well, hardly.

PATSY

What makes you think so?

VAN

I saw it. They offered me ten thousand.

PATSY

Just for the record, I'd better look at it, Judge.

SKIMMERHORN

I wouldn't if I were you. I'm hardly under suspicion of bank robbery.

PATSY

I'll take a look at it.
(*He holds out a hand.* BIGGS *passes him a package.*)

SENIOR

I don't get this at all.

PATSY

It's got the Orangeburg stamp on it, all right.

SKIMMERHORN

Must be some mistake. They must have got the money mixed at the bank.

PATSY

Sure. Well, if that's all we can easy check on that.

VAN

Sure. You'd better check on it.

SKIMMERHORN

Are you under the impression that we robbed the bank?

VAN

You explain it. I can't.

SENIOR

You say you drew the money to pay Van Dorn?

SKIMMERHORN

That's right, A.B.

SENIOR

And it's got the Orangeburg label on it?

SKIMMERHORN

That's what they say.

SENIOR

I'll have something to say to the bank about that.

SKIMMERHORN

Oh, I'll take care of it. Just a clerical error.

PATSY

I'm afraid I'll have to take the money, though. Oh, you'll get your own money back, but if this is the Orangeburg money—

BIGGS

Sure, take it.
(*They unload.*)

PATSY

And I guess I really ought to put you both under arrest.

BIGGS

What? Under arrest?

PATSY

Wouldn't you say so, Budge?

BUDGE

Don't see any way out of it. Doesn't mean anything. Just an examination.

SKIMMERHORN

I'd like to keep it out of the papers, if possible, of course. An examination might be very embarrassing—you see, I have political enemies.

BIGGS

Always ready to think the worst of a man, and print it, too.

PATSY

Still, I guess we'll have to have an examination. Just for the record.

SKIMMERHORN

You know who we are, of course?

PATSY

Yes, sir.

SKIMMERHORN

I won't submit to an examination! It's preposterous!

PATSY

I don't see how we can get out of it, though. Because we had a robbery, and here's the money, and we've got to explain it somehow.

SKIMMERHORN

I won't submit to it!

PATSY

You got an extra pair of handcuffs there, Budge?

BUDGE

Yeah,

SKIMMERHORN

All right. I'll go.

BIGGS

Sure. We'll go. And we'll make a lot of people sorry!

PATSY

Go on ahead, Budge.
(BUDGE *starts out with his prisoners.*)

DOPE

But how about the little guy with the big hat? How about him?

BUDGE

I'll tell you about him. It's entirely possible there wasn't any little guy in a big hat.

DOPE

But we all saw him!

BUDGE

Oh, no, you didn't see him. You saw right through him. And the reason was he wasn't there.
(BUDGE, ELKUS *and* DOPE *go out.*)

BIGGS

You don't think we made that up, about the man in the big hat?

PATSY

Well, you have to admit it doesn't sound exactly plausible.
(PATSY, BIGGS *and* SKIMMERHORN *go out.*)

SENIOR

(*As he goes*)
It shakes a man's faith in evidence.
(*To* VAN)
See you tomorrow.

VAN

I'll be there.
(SKIMMERHORN SENIOR *goes out.*)
So now—I've sold the Tor.

THE INDIAN

Yes, but it's better.

VAN

Better than living on a grudge, I guess. It might come down to that.

THE INDIAN

There's wilder land,
and there are higher mountains, in the west.

VAN

Out Port Jervis way.

THE INDIAN

Perhaps. You'll find them.

JUDITH

He came to tell you, Van—this is his death-day.
I'll go now.

VAN

All right, John.

THE INDIAN

Could I keep it?
The hand I held? It's a new thing, being blind,
when you've had an Indian's eyes.
(JUDITH *returns and gives him her hand again.*)

JUDITH

I'll stay a while.

THE INDIAN

When I had lost the path
halfway along the ridge, there at my feet
I heard a woman crying. We came on together, for she led me. There'll be time
for crying later. Take her west with you.
She'll forget the mountain.

VAN

Will you come?

JUDITH

I'd remember Lise!

VAN

Was there a Lise?
I think she was my dream of you and
   me
and how you left the mountain barren
   once
when you were gone. She was my
   dream of you
and how you left the Tor. Say you'll
   come with me.

JUDITH

Yes.

THE INDIAN

It's a long day's work to dig a grave
in stony ground. But you're young and
   have good shoulders.
It should be done tonight.

VAN

I'll have it done
even if you don't need it. Tell me the
   place.

THE INDIAN

There's still an Indian burying ground
   that lies
behind the northern slope. Beneath it
   runs
a line of square brown stones the white
   men used
to mark their dead. Below still, in a
   ring,
are seven graves, a woman and six
   men,
the Indians killed and laid there. In the
   freshet,
after the rain last night, the leaf-mould
   washed,
and the seven looked uncovered at the
   sky,
white skeletons with flintlocks by their
   sides,
and on the woman's hand a heavy ring
made out of gold. I laid them in again.

VAN

Seven graves—a woman and six men—
Maybe they'll rest now.

THE INDIAN

Dig them in deeper, then.
They're covered only lightly.

VAN

I'll dig them deeper.

THE INDIAN

But you must make my grave with my
   own people,
higher, beneath the ledge, and dig it
   straight,
and narrow. And you must place me in
   the fashion
used by the Indians, sitting at a game,
not fallen, not asleep. And set beside
   me
water and food. If this is strange to
   you,
think only I'm an Indian with strange
   ways,
but I shall need them.

VAN

Don't worry. You shall have it
just the way you want it.

THE INDIAN

Shall we go?

VAN

One last look at the rock? It's not too
   late
to hold out on the bargain. Think of
   the gouge
they'll make across these hills.

JUDITH

If it's for me
you sell, we'll have enough without
   it, Van.
We'll have each other.

VAN

Oh, but you were right.
When they wash over you, you either
   swim
or drown. We won't be here.

THE INDIAN

And there's one comfort.
I heard the wise Iachim, looking down
when the railroad cut was fresh, and
the bleeding earth
offended us. There is nothing made, he
said,
and will be nothing made by these new
men,
high tower, or cut, or buildings by a
lake
that will not make good ruins.

JUDITH

Ruins? This?

THE INDIAN

Why, when the race is gone, or looks
aside
only a little while, the white stone
darkens,
the wounds close, and the roofs fall,
and the walls
give way to rains. Nothing is made by
men
but makes, in the end, good ruins.

VAN

Well, that's something.
But I can hardly wait.

Of Mice and Men

BY JOHN STEINBECK

CHARACTERS

This play was first presented by Sam H. Harris at the Music Box Theatre on the evening of November 23, 1937, with the following cast:

GEORGE	*Wallace Ford*
LENNIE	*Broderick Crawford*
CANDY	*John F. Hamilton*
THE BOSS	*Thomas Findlay*
CURLEY	*Sam Byrd*
CURLEY'S WIFE	*Claire Luce*
SLIM	*Will Geer*
CARLSON	*Charles Slattery*
WHIT	*Walter Baldwin*
CROOKS	*Leigh Whipper*

SYNOPSIS OF SCENES

ACT ONE

SCENE I: A sandy bank of the Salinas River.
Thursday night.
SCENE II: The interior of a bunkhouse.
Late Friday morning.

ACT TWO

SCENE I: The same as Act I, Scene II.
About seven-thirty Friday evening.
SCENE II: The room of the stable buck, a lean-to.
Ten o'clock Saturday evening.

ACT THREE

SCENE I: One end of a great barn.
Mid-afternoon, Sunday.
SCENE II: Same as Act I, Scene I.
Sunday night.

TIME: The present.

PLACE: An agricultural valley in Northern California.

Of Mice and Men

ACT ONE

SCENE I

Thursday night.
A sandy bank of the Salinas River sheltered with willows—one giant sycamore right, upstage.
The stage is covered with dry leaves. The feeling of the stage is sheltered and quiet.
Stage is lit by a setting sun.

Curtain rises on an empty stage. A sparrow is singing. There is a distant sound of ranch dogs barking aimlessly and one clear quail call. The quail call turns to a warning call and there is a beat of the flock's wings. Two figures are seen entering the stage in single file, with GEORGE, *the short man, coming in ahead of* LENNIE. *Both men are carrying blanket rolls. They approach the water. The small man throws down his blanket roll, the large man follows and then falls down and drinks from the river, snorting as he drinks.*

GEORGE (*irritably*). Lennie, for God's sake, don't drink so much. (*Leans over and shakes* LENNIE.) Lennie, you hear me! You gonna be sick like you was last night.

LENNIE (*dips his whole head under, hat and all. As he sits upon the bank, his hat drips down the back*). That's good. You drink some, George. You drink some too.

GEORGE (*kneeling and dipping his finger in the water*). I ain't sure it's good water. Looks kinda scummy to me.

LENNIE (*imitates, dipping his finger also*). Look at them wrinkles in the water, George. Look what I done.

GEORGE (*drinking from his cupped palm*). Tastes all right. Don't seem to be runnin' much, though. Lennie, you oughtn' to drink water when it ain't running. (*Hopelessly*) You'd drink water out of a gutter if you was thirsty. (*He throws a scoop of water into his face and rubs it around with his hand, pushes himself back and embraces his knees.* LENNIE, *after watching him, imitates him in every detail.*)

GEORGE (*beginning tiredly and growing angry as he speaks*). God damn it, we could just as well of rode clear to the ranch. That bus driver didn't know what he was talkin' about. "Just a little stretch down the highway," he says. "Just a little stretch"—damn near four miles. I bet he didn't want to stop at the ranch gate. . . . I bet he's too damn lazy to pull up. Wonder he ain't too lazy to stop at Soledad at all! (*Mumbling*) Just a little stretch down the road.

LENNIE (*timidly*). George?

GEORGE. Yeh . . . what you want?

167

LENNIE. Where we goin', George?

GEORGE (*jerks down his hat furiously*). So you forgot that already, did you? So I got to tell you again! Jeez, you're a crazy bastard!

LENNIE (*softly*). I forgot. I tried not to forget, honest to God, I did!

GEORGE. Okay, okay, I'll tell you again. (*With sarcasm*) I ain't got nothin' to do. Might just as well spen' all my time tellin' you things. You forgit 'em and I tell you again.

LENNIE (*continuing on from his last speech*). I tried and tried, but it didn't do no good. I remember about the rabbits, George!

GEORGE. The hell with the rabbits! You can't remember nothing but them rabbits. You remember settin' in that gutter on Howard Street and watchin' that blackboard?

LENNIE (*delightedly*). Oh, sure! I remember that . . . but . . . wha'd we do then? I remember some girls come by, and you says—

GEORGE. The hell with what I says! You remember about us goin' in Murray and Ready's and they give us work cards and bus tickets?

LENNIE (*confidently*). Oh, sure, George . . . I remember that now. (*Puts his hand into his side coat-pocket; his confidence vanishes. Very gently*) . . . George?

GEORGE. Huh?

LENNIE (*staring at the ground in despair*). I ain't got mine. I musta lost it.

GEORGE. You never had none. I got both of 'em here. Think I'd let you carry your own work card?

LENNIE (*with tremendous relief*). I thought I put it in my side pocket. (*Puts his hand in his pocket again.*)

GEORGE (*looking sharply at him; and as he looks,* LENNIE *brings his hand out of his pocket*). Wha'd you take out of that pocket?

LENNIE (*cleverly*). Ain't a thing in my pocket.

GEORGE. I know there ain't. You got it in your hand now. What you got in your hand?

LENNIE. I ain't got nothing! George! honest!

GEORGE. Come on, give it here!

LENNIE (*holds his closed hand away from* GEORGE). It's on'y a mouse!

GEORGE. A mouse? A live mouse?

LENNIE. No . . . just a dead mouse. (*Worriedly*) I didn't kill it. Honest. I found it. I found it dead.

GEORGE. Give it here!

LENNIE. Leave me have it, George.

GEORGE (*sternly*). Give it here! (LENNIE *reluctantly gives him the mouse.*) What do you want of a dead mouse, anyway?

LENNIE (*in a propositional tone*). I was petting it with my thumb while we walked along.

GEORGE. Well, you ain't pettin' no mice while you walk with me. Now let's see if you can remember where we're going. (GEORGE *throws it across the water into the brush.*)

LENNIE (*looks startled and then in embarrassment hides his face against his knees*). I forgot again.

GEORGE. Jesus Christ! (*Resignedly*) Well, look, we are gonna work on a ranch like the one we come from up north.

LENNIE. Up north?

GEORGE. In Weed!

LENNIE. Oh, sure I remember—in Weed.

GEORGE (*still with exaggerated patience*). That ranch we're goin' to is right down there about a quarter mile. We're gonna go in and see the boss.

LENNIE (*repeats as a lesson*). And see the boss!

GEORGE. Now, look! I'll give him the work tickets, but you ain't gonna say a word. You're just gonna stand there and not say nothing.

LENNIE. Not say nothing!

GEORGE. If he finds out what a crazy bastard you are, we won't get no job. But if he sees you work before he hears you talk, we're set. You got that?

LENNIE. Sure, George . . . sure. I got that.

GEORGE. Okay. Now when we go in to see the boss, what you gonna do?

LENNIE (*concentrating*). I . . . I . . . I ain't gonna say nothing . . . jus' gonna stand there.

GEORGE (*greatly relieved*). Good boy, that's swell! Now say that over two or three times so you sure won't forget it.

LENNIE (*drones softly under his breath*). I ain't gonna say nothing . . . I ain't gonna say nothing. . . . (*Trails off into a whisper.*)

GEORGE. And you ain't gonna do no bad things like you done in Weed neither.

LENNIE (*puzzled*). Like I done in Weed?

GEORGE. So you forgot that too, did you?

LENNIE (*triumphantly*). They run us out of Weed!

GEORGE (*disgusted*). Run us out, hell! We run! They was lookin' for us, but they didn't catch us.

LENNIE (*happily*). I didn't forget that, you bet.

GEORGE (*lies back on the sand, crosses his hands under his head. And again* LENNIE *imitates him*). God, you're a lot of trouble! I could get along so easy and nice, if I didn't have you on my tail. I could live so easy!

LENNIE (*hopefully*). We gonna work on a ranch, George.

GEORGE. All right, you got that. But we're gonna sleep here tonight, because . . . I want to. I want to sleep out. (*The light is going fast, dropping into evening. A little wind whirls into the clearing and blows leaves. A dog howls in the distance.*)

LENNIE. Why ain't we goin' on to the ranch to get some supper? They got supper at the ranch.

GEORGE. No reason at all. I just like it here. Tomorrow we'll be goin' to work. I seen thrashing machines on the way down; that means we'll be buckin' grain bags. Bustin' a gut liftin' up them bags. Tonight I'm gonna lay right here an' look up! Tonight there ain't a grain bag or a boss in the world. Tonight, the drinks is on the . . . house. Nice house we got here, Lennie.

LENNIE (*gets up on his knees and looks down at* GEORGE, *plaintively*). Ain't we gonna have no supper?

GEORGE. Sure we are. You gather up

some dead willow sticks. I got three cans of beans in my bindle. I'll open 'em up while you get a fire ready. We'll eat 'em cold.

LENNIE (*companionably*). I like beans with ketchup.

GEORGE. Well, we ain't got no ketchup. You go get wood, and don't you fool around none. Be dark before long. (LENNIE *lumbers to his feet and disappears into the brush.* GEORGE *gets out the bean cans, opens two of them, suddenly turns his head and listens. A little sound of splashing comes from the direction that* LENNIE *has taken.* GEORGE *looks after him; shakes his head.* LENNIE *comes back carrying a few small willow sticks in his hand.*) All right, give me that mouse.

LENNIE (*with elaborate pantomime of innocence*). What, George? I ain't got no mouse.

GEORGE (*holding out his hand*). Come on! Give it to me! You ain't puttin' nothing over. (LENNIE *hesitates, backs away, turns and looks as if he were going to run. Coldly*) You gonna give me that mouse or do I have to take a sock at you?

LENNIE. Give you what, George?

GEORGE. You know goddamn well, what! I want that mouse!

LENNIE (*almost in tears*). I don't know why I can't keep it. It ain't nobody's mouse. I didn' steal it! I found it layin' right beside the road. (GEORGE *snaps his fingers sharply, and* LENNIE *lays the mouse in his hand.*) I wasn't doin' nothing bad with it. Just stroking it. That ain't bad.

GEORGE (*stands up and throws the mouse as far as he can into the brush, then he steps to the pool, and washes his hands*). You crazy fool! Thought you could get away with it, didn't you? Don't you think I could see your feet

was wet where you went in the water to get it? (LENNIE *whimpers like a puppy.*) Blubbering like a baby. Jesus Christ, a big guy like you! (LENNIE *tries to control himself, but his lips quiver and his face works with an effort.* GEORGE *puts his hand on* LENNIE's *shoulder for a moment.*) Aw, Lennie, I ain't takin' it away just for meanness. That mouse ain't fresh. Besides, you broke it pettin' it. You get a mouse that's fresh and I'll let you keep it a little while.

LENNIE. I don't know where there is no other mouse. I remember a lady used to give 'em to me. Ever' one she got she used to give it to me, but that lady ain't here no more.

GEORGE. Lady, huh! . . . Give me them sticks there. . . . Don't even remember who that lady was. That was your own Aunt Clara. She stopped givin' 'em to you. You always killed 'em.

LENNIE (*sadly and apologetically*). They was so little. I'd pet 'em and pretty soon they bit my fingers and then I pinched their head a little bit and then they was dead . . . because they was so little. I wish we'd get the rabbits pretty soon, George. They ain't so little.

GEORGE. The hell with the rabbits! Come on, let's eat! (*The light has continued to go out of the scene so that when* GEORGE *lights the fire, it is the major light on the stage.* GEORGE *hands one of the open cans of beans to* LENNIE.) There's enough beans for four men.

LENNIE (*sitting on the other side of the fire, speaks patiently*). I like 'em with ketchup.

GEORGE (*explodes*). Well, we ain't got any. Whatever we ain't got, that's what you want. God Almighty, if I was alone, I could live so easy. I could go get a job of work and no trouble. No mess . . . and when the end of the month come, I could take my fifty bucks and go into town and get whatever I want. Why, I could stay in a cat-house all night. I could eat any place I want. Order any damn thing.

LENNIE (*plaintively, but softly*). I didn't want no ketchup.

GEORGE (*continuing violently*). I could do that every damn month. Get a gallon of whiskey or set in a pool room and play cards or shoot pool. (LENNIE *gets up to his knees and looks over the fire, with frightened face.*) And what have I got? (*Disgustedly*) I got *you.* You can't keep a job and you lose me every job I get!

LENNIE (*in terror*). I don't mean nothing, George.

GEORGE. Just keep me shovin' all over the country all the time. And that ain't the worst—you get in trouble. You do bad things and I got to get you out. It ain't bad people that raises hell. It's dumb ones. (*He shouts*) You crazy son-of-a-bitch, you keep me in hot water all the time. (LENNIE *is trying to stop* GEORGE's *flow of words with his hands. Sarcastically*) You just wanta feel that girl's dress. Just wanta pet it like it was a mouse. Well, how the hell'd she know you just wanta feel her dress? How'd she know you'd just hold onto it like it was a mouse?

LENNIE (*in a panic*). I didn't mean to, George!

GEORGE. Sure you didn't mean to. You didn't mean for her to yell bloody hell, either. You didn't mean for us to hide in the irrigation ditch all day with guys out lookin' for us with guns. Alla time it's something you didn't mean. God damn it, I wish I could put you in a cage with a million mice and let them pet *you.* (GEORGE's *anger leaves him suddenly. For the first time he seems to see the expression of terror on* LENNIE's *face. He looks down ashamedly at the fire, and maneuvers some beans*

onto the blade of his pocket-knife and puts them into his mouth.)

LENNIE (*after a pause*). George! (GEORGE *purposely does not answer him.*) George?

GEORGE. What do you want?

LENNIE. I was only foolin', George. I don't want no ketchup. I wouldn't eat no ketchup if it was right here beside me.

GEORGE (*with a sullenness of shame*). If they was some here you could have it. And if I had a thousand bucks I'd buy ya a bunch of flowers.

LENNIE. I wouldn't eat no ketchup, George. I'd leave it all for you. You could cover your beans so deep with it, and I wouldn't touch none of it.

GEORGE (*refusing to give in from his sullenness, refusing to look at* LENNIE). When I think of the swell time I could have without you, I go nuts. I never git no peace!

LENNIE. You want I should go away and leave you alone?

GEORGE. Where the hell could you go?

LENNIE. Well, I could . . . I could go off in the hills there. Some place I could find a cave.

GEORGE. Yeah, how'd ya eat? You ain't got sense enough to find nothing to eat.

LENNIE. I'd find things. I don't need no nice food with ketchup. I'd lay out in the sun and nobody would hurt me. And if I found a mouse—why, I could keep it. Wouldn't nobody take it away from me.

GEORGE (*at last he looks up*). I been mean, ain't I?

LENNIE (*presses his triumph*). If you don't want me, I can go right in them hills, and find a cave. I can go away any time.

GEORGE. No. Look! I was just foolin' ya. 'Course I want you to stay with me. Trouble with mice is you always kill 'em. (*He pauses.*) Tell you what I'll do, Lennie. First chance I get I'll find you a pup. Maybe you wouldn't kill it. That would be better than mice. You could pet it harder.

LENNIE (*still avoiding being drawn in*). If you don't want me, you only gotta say so. I'll go right up on them hills and live by myself. And I won't get no mice stole from me.

GEORGE. I want you to stay with me. Jesus Christ, somebody'd shoot you for a coyote if you was by yourself. Stay with me. Your Aunt Clara wouldn't like your runnin' off by yourself, even if she is dead.

LENNIE. George?

GEORGE. Huh?

LENNIE (*craftily*). Tell me—like you done before.

GEORGE. Tell you what?

LENNIE. About the rabbits.

GEORGE (*near to anger again*). You ain't gonna put nothing over on me!

LENNIE (*pleading*). Come on, George . . . tell me please! Like you done before.

GEORGE. You get a kick out of that, don't you? All right, I'll tell you. And then we'll lay out our beds and eat our dinner.

LENNIE. Go on, George.
(*Unrolls his bed and lies on his side, supporting his head on one hand.* GEORGE *lays out his bed and sits cross-legged on it.* GEORGE *repeats the next speech rhythmically, as though he had said it many times before.*)

GEORGE. Guys like us that work on ranches is the loneliest guys in the world. They ain't got no family. They don't belong no place. They come to a ranch and work up a stake and then they go in to town and blow their stake. And then the first thing you know they're poundin' their tail on some other ranch. They ain't got nothin' to look ahead to.

LENNIE (*delightedly*). That's it, that's it! Now tell how it is with us.

GEORGE (*still almost chanting*). With us it ain't like that. We got a future. We got somebody to talk to that gives a damn about us. We don't have to sit in no barroom blowin' in our jack, just because we got no place else to go. If them other guys gets in jail, they can rot for all anybody gives a damn.

LENNIE (*Who cannot restrain himself any longer. Bursts into speech*). But not us! And why? Because . . . because I got you to look after me . . . and you got me to look after you . . . and that's why! (*He laughs.*) Go on, George!

GEORGE. You got it by heart. You can do it yourself.

LENNIE. No, no. I forget some of the stuff. Tell about how it's gonna be.

GEORGE. Some other time.

LENNIE. No, tell how it's gonna be!

GEORGE. Okay. Some day we're gonna get the jack together and we're gonna have a little house, and a couple of acres and a cow and some pigs and . . .

LENNIE (*shouting*). And live off the fat of the land! And have rabbits. Go on, George! Tell about what we're gonna have in the garden. And about the rabbits in the cages. Tell about the rain in the winter . . . and about the stove and how thick the cream is on the milk, you can hardly cut it. Tell about that, George!

GEORGE. Why don't you do it yourself —you know all of it!

LENNIE. It ain't the same if I tell it. Go on now. How I get to tend the rabbits.

GEORGE (*resignedly*). Well, we'll have a big vegetable patch and a rabbit hutch and chickens. And when it rains in the winter we'll just say to hell with goin' to work. We'll build up a fire in the stove, and set around it and listen to the rain comin' down on the roof— Nuts! (*Begins to eat with his knife.*) I ain't got time for no more. (*He falls to eating.* LENNIE *imitates him, spilling a few beans from his mouth with every bite.* GEORGE, *gesturing with his knife*) What you gonna say tomorrow when the boss asks you questions?

LENNIE (*stops chewing in the middle of a bite, swallows painfully. His face contorts with thought*). I . . . I ain't gonna say a word.

GEORGE. Good boy. That's fine. Say, maybe you're gittin' better. I bet I can let you tend the rabbits . . . specially if you remember as good as that!

LENNIE (*choking with pride*). I can remember, by God!

GEORGE (*as though remembering something, points his knife at* LENNIE's *chest*). Lennie, I want you to look around here. Think you can remember this place? The ranch is 'bout a quarter mile up that way. Just follow the river and you can get here.

LENNIE (*looking around carefully*). Sure, I can remember here. Didn't I remember 'bout not gonna say a word?

GEORGE. 'Course you did. Well, look,

Lennie, if you just happen to get in trouble, I want you to come right here and hide in the brush.

LENNIE (*slowly*). Hide in the brush.

GEORGE. Hide in the brush until I come for you. Think you can remember that?

LENNIE. Sure I can, George. Hide in the brush till you come for me!

GEORGE. But you ain't gonna get in no trouble. Because if you do I won't let you tend the rabbits.

LENNIE. I won't get in no trouble. I ain't gonna say a word.

GEORGE. You got it. Anyways, I hope so. (GEORGE *stretches out on his blankets. The light dies slowly out of the fire until only the faces of the two men can be seen.* GEORGE *is still eating from his can of beans.*) It's gonna be nice sleeping here. Lookin' up . . . and the leaves . . . Don't build up no more fire. We'll let her die. Jesus, you feel free when you ain't got a job—if you ain't hungry.
(*They sit silently for a few moments. A night owl is heard far off. From across the river there comes the sound of a coyote howl and on the heels of the howl all the dogs in the country start to bark.*)

LENNIE (*from almost complete darkness*). George?

GEORGE. What do you want?

LENNIE. Let's have different color rabbits, George.

GEORGE. Sure. Red rabbits and blue rabbits and green rabbits. Millions of 'em!

LENNIE. Furry ones, George. Like I seen at the fair in Sacramento.

GEORGE. Sure. Furry ones.

LENNIE. 'Cause I can jus' as well go away, George, and live in a cave.

GEORGE (*amiably*). Aw, shut up.

LENNIE (*after a long pause*). George?

GEORGE. What is it?

LENNIE. I'm shutting up, George. (*A coyote howls again.*)

SCENE II

Late Friday morning.
The interior of a bunkhouse.
Walls, white-washed board and bat. Floors unpainted.
There is a heavy square table with upended boxes around it used for chairs.
Over each bunk there is a box nailed to the wall which serves as two shelves on which are the private possessions of the working men.
On top of each bunk there is a large noisy alarm clock ticking madly.
The sun is streaking through the windows. NOTE: *Articles in the boxes on wall are soap, talcum powder, razors, pulp magazines, medicine bottles, combs, and from nails on the sides of the boxes a few neckties.*
There is a hanging light from the ceiling over the table, with a round dim reflector on it.

The curtain rises on an empty stage. Only the ticking of the many alarm clocks is heard.

CANDY, GEORGE *and* LENNIE *are first seen passing the open windows of the bunkhouse.*

CANDY. This is the bunkhouse here. Door's around this side. (*The latch on the door rises and* CANDY *enters, a stoop-shouldered old man. He is dressed in blue jeans and a denim coat. He carries a big push broom in his left hand. His right hand is gone at the wrist. He grasps things with his right arm between arm and side. He walks into the room followed by* GEORGE *and* LENNIE. *Conversationally*) The boss was expecting you last night. He was sore as hell when you wasn't here to go out this morning. (*Points with his handless arm.*) You can have them two beds there.

GEORGE. I'll take the top one . . . I don't want you falling down on me. (*Steps over to the bunk and throws his blankets down. He looks into the nearly empty box shelf over it, then picks up a small yellow can.*) Say, what the hell's this?

CANDY. I don' know.

GEORGE. Says "positively kills lice, roaches and other scourges." What the hell kinda beds you givin' us, anyway? We don't want no pants rabbits.

CANDY (*shifts his broom, holding it between his elbow and his side, takes the can in his left hand and studies the label carefully*). Tell you what . . . last guy that had this bed was a blacksmith. Helluva nice fellow. Clean a guy as you'd want to meet. Used to wash his hands even *after* he et.

GEORGE (*with gathering anger*). Then how come he got pillow-pigeons?

(LENNIE *puts his blankets on his bunk and sits down, watching* GEORGE *with his mouth slightly open.*)

CANDY. Tell you what. This here blacksmith, name of Whitey, was the kinda guy that would put that stuff around even if there wasn't no bugs. Tell you what he used to do. He'd peel *his* boiled potatoes and take out every little spot before he et it, and if there was a red splotch on an egg, he'd scrape it off. Finally quit about the food. That's the kind of guy Whitey was. Clean. Used to dress up Sundays even when he wasn't goin' no place. Put on a necktie even, and then set in the bunkhouse.

GEORGE (*skeptically*). I ain't so sure. What da' ya say he quit for?

CANDY (*puts the can in his pocket, rubs his bristly white whiskers with his knuckles*). Why . . . he just quit the way a guy will. Says it was the food. Didn't give no other reason. Just says "give me my time" one night, the way any guy would.

(GEORGE *lifts his bed tick and looks underneath, leans over and inspects the sacking carefully.* LENNIE *does the same with his bed.*)

GEORGE (*half satisfied*). Well, if there's any grey-backs in this bed, you're gonna hear from me! (*He unrolls his blankets and puts his razor and bar of soap and comb and bottle of pills, his liniment and leather wristband in the box.*)

CANDY. I guess the boss'll be out here in a minute to write your name in. He sure was burned when you wasn't here this morning. Come right in when we was eatin' breakfast and says, "Where the hell's them new men?" He give the stable buck hell, too. Stable buck's a nigger.

GEORGE. Nigger, huh!

CANDY. Yeah. (*Continues*) Nice fellow too. Got a crooked back where a horse kicked him. Boss gives him hell when he's mad. But the stable buck don't give a damn about that.

GEORGE. What kinda guy is the boss?

CANDY. Well, he's a pretty nice fella for a boss. Gets mad sometimes. But he's pretty nice. Tell you what. Know what he done Christmas? Brung a gallon of whiskey right in here and says, "Drink hearty, boys, Christmas comes but once a year!"

GEORGE. The hell he did! A whole gallon?

CANDY. Yes, sir. Jesus, we had fun! They let the nigger come in that night. Well, sir, a little skinner name Smitty took after the nigger. Done pretty good too. The guys wouldn't let him use his feet so the nigger got him. If he could a used his feet Smitty says he would have killed the nigger. The guys says on account the nigger got a crooked back Smitty can't use his feet. (*He smiles in reverie at the memory.*)

GEORGE. Boss the owner?

CANDY. Naw! Superintendent. Big land company. . . . Yes, sir, that night . . . he come right in here with a whole gallon . . . he set right over there and says, "Drink hearty, boys," . . . he says. . . . (*The door opens. Enter the* BOSS. *He is a stocky man, dressed in blue jean trousers, flannel shirt, a black un-buttoned vest and a black coat. He wears a soiled brown Stetson hat, a pair of high-heeled boots and spurs. Ordinarily he puts his thumbs in his belt.* CANDY, *shuffling towards the door, rubbing his whiskers with his knuckles as he goes*) Them guys just come. (CANDY *exits and shuts the door behind him.*)

BOSS. I wrote Murray and Ready I wanted two men this morning. You got your work slips?

GEORGE (*digs in his pockets, produces two slips, and hands them to the* BOSS). Here they are.

BOSS (*reading the slips*). Well, I see it

wasn't Murray and Ready's fault. It says right here on the slip, you was to be here for work this morning.

GEORGE. Bus driver give us a bum steer. We had to walk ten miles. That bus driver says we was here when we wasn't. We couldn't thumb no rides. (GEORGE *scowls meaningly at* LENNIE *and* LENNIE *nods to show that he understands.*)

BOSS. Well, I had to send out the grain teams short two buckers. It won't do any good to go out now until after dinner. You'd get lost. (*Pulls out his time book, opens it to where a pencil is stuck between the leaves. Licks his pencil carefully.*) What's your name?

GEORGE. George Milton.

BOSS. George Milton. (*Writing*) And what's yours?

GEORGE. His name's Lennie Small.

BOSS. Lennie Small. (*Writing*) Le's see, this is the twentieth. Noon the twentieth. . . . (*Makes positive mark. Closes the book and puts it in his pocket.*) Where you boys been workin'?

GEORGE. Up around Weed.

BOSS (*to* LENNIE). You too?

GEORGE. Yeah. Him too.

BOSS (*to* LENNIE). Say, you're a big fellow, ain't you?

GEORGE. Yeah, he can work like hell, too.

BOSS. He ain't much of a talker, though, is he?

GEORGE. No, he ain't. But he's a hell of a good worker. Strong as a bull.

LENNIE (*smiling*). I'm strong as a bull. (GEORGE *scowls at him and* LENNIE

drops his head in shame at having forgotten.)

BOSS (*sharply*). You are, huh? What can you do?

GEORGE. He can do anything.

BOSS (*addressing* LENNIE.) What can you do?

(LENNIE, *looking at* GEORGE, *gives a high nervous chuckle.*)

GEORGE (*quickly*). Anything you tell him. He's a good skinner. He can wrestle grain bags, drive a cultivator. He can do anything. Just give him a try.

BOSS (*turning to* GEORGE). Then why don't you let *him* answer? (LENNIE *laughs.*) What's he laughing about?

GEORGE. He laughs when he gets excited.

BOSS. Yeah?

GEORGE (*loudly*). But he's a goddamn good worker. I ain't saying he's bright, because he ain't. But he can put up a four hundred pound bale.

BOSS (*hooking his thumbs in his belt*). Say, what you sellin'?

GEORGE. Huh?

BOSS. I said what stake you got in this guy? You takin' his pay away from him?

GEORGE. No. Of course I ain't!

BOSS. Well, I never seen one guy take so much trouble for another guy. I just like to know what your percentage is.

GEORGE. He's my . . . cousin. I told his ole lady I'd take care of him. He got kicked in the head by a horse when he was a kid. He's all right. . . . Just ain't bright. But he can do anything you tell him.

BOSS (*turning half away*). Well, God knows he don't need no brains to buck barley bags. (*He turns back.*) But don't you try to put nothing over, Milton. I got my eye on you. Why'd you quit in Weed?

GEORGE (*promptly*). Job was done.

BOSS. What kind of job?

GEORGE. Why . . . we was diggin' a cesspool.

BOSS (*after a pause*). All right. But don't try to put nothing over 'cause you can't get away with nothing. I seen wise guys before. Go out with the grain teams after dinner. They're out pickin' up barley with the thrashin' machines. Go out with Slim's team.

GEORGE. Slim?

BOSS. Yeah. Big, tall skinner. You'll see him at dinner. (*Up to this time the* BOSS *has been full of business. He has been calm and suspicious. In the following lines he relaxes, but gradually, as though he wanted to talk but felt always the burden of his position. He turns toward the door, but hesitates and allows a little warmth into his manner.*) Been on the road long?

GEORGE (*obviously on guard*). We was three days in 'Frisco lookin' at the boards.

BOSS (*with heavy jocularity*). Didn't go to no night clubs, I 'spose?

GEORGE (*stiffly*). We was lookin' for a job.

BOSS (*attempting to be friendly*). That's a great town if you got a little jack, 'Frisco.

GEORGE (*refusing to be drawn in*). We didn't have no jack for nothing like that.

BOSS (*realizes there is no contact to establish; grows rigid with his position again*). Go out with the grain teams after dinner. When my hands work hard they get pie and when they loaf they bounce down the road on their can. You ask anybody about me. (*He turns and walks out of bunkhouse.*)

GEORGE (*turns to* LENNIE). So you wasn't gonna say a word! You was gonna leave your big flapper shut. I was gonna do the talkin'. . . . You goddamn near lost us the job!

LENNIE (*stares hopelessly at his hands*). I forgot.

GEORGE. You forgot. You always forget. Now, he's got his eye on us. Now, we gotta be careful and not make no slips. You keep your big flapper shut after this.

LENNIE. He talked like a kinda nice guy towards the last.

GEORGE (*angrily*). He's the boss, ain't he? Well, he's the boss first an' a nice guy afterwards. Don't you have nothin' to do with no boss, except do your work and draw your pay. You can't never tell whether you're talkin' to the nice guy or the boss. Just keep your goddamn mouth shut. Then you're all right.

LENNIE. George?

GEORGE. What you want now?

LENNIE. I wasn't kicked in the head with no horse, was I, George?

GEORGE. Be a damn good thing if you was. Save everybody a hell of a lot of trouble!

LENNIE (*flattered*). You says I was your cousin.

GEORGE. Well, that was a goddamn lie. And I'm glad it was. Why, if I was a relative of yours—(*He stops and listens, then steps to the front door, and looks out.*) Say, what the hell you doin', listenin'?

CANDY (*comes slowly into the room. By a rope, he leads an ancient drag-footed, blind sheep dog. Guides it from running into a table leg, with the rope. Sits down on a box, and presses the hind quarters of the old dog down*). Naw . . . I wasn't listenin'. . . . I was just standin' in the shade a minute, scratchin' my dog. I jest now finished swamping out the washhouse.

GEORGE. You was pokin' your big nose into our business! I don't like nosey guys.

CANDY (*looks uneasily from GEORGE to LENNIE and then back*). I jest come there . . . I didn't hear nothing you guys was sayin'. I ain't interested in nothing you was sayin'. A guy on a ranch don't never listen. Nor he don't ast no questions.

GEORGE (*slightly mollified*). Damn right he don't! Not if the guy wants to stay workin' long. (*His manner changes.*) That's a helluva ole dog.

CANDY. Yeah. I had him ever since he was a pup. God, he was a good sheep dog, when he was young. (*Rubs his cheek with his knuckles.*) How'd you like the boss?

GEORGE. Pretty good! Seemed all right.

CANDY. He's a nice fella. You got ta take him right, of course. He's runnin' this ranch. He don't take no nonsense.

GEORGE. What time do we eat? Eleven-thirty?
(*CURLEY enters. He is dressed in working clothes. He wears brown high-heeled boots and has a glove on his left hand.*)

CURLEY. Seen my ole man?

CANDY. He was here just a minute ago, Curley. Went over to the cookhouse, I think.

CURLEY. I'll try to catch him. (*Looking over at the new men, measuring them. Unconsciously bends his elbow and closes his hand and goes into a slight crouch. He walks gingerly close to LENNIE.*) You the new guys my ole man was waitin' for?

GEORGE. Yeah. We just come in.

CURLEY. How's it come you wasn't here this morning?

GEORGE. Got off the bus too soon.

CURLEY (*again addressing LENNIE*). My ole man got to get the grain out. Ever bucked barley?

GEORGE (*quickly*). Hell, yes. Done a lot of it.

CURLEY. I mean him. (*To LENNIE.*) Ever bucked barley?

GEORGE. Sure he has.

CURLEY (*irritatedly*). Let the big guy talk!

GEORGE. 'Spose he don't want ta talk?

CURLEY (*pugnaciously*). By Christ, he's gotta talk when he's spoke to. What the hell you shovin' into this for?

GEORGE (*stands up and speaks coldly*). Him and me travel together.

CURLEY. Oh, so it's that way?

GEORGE (*tense and motionless*). What way?

CURLEY (*letting the subject drop*). And you won't let the big guy talk? Is that it?

GEORGE. He can talk if he wants to tell you anything. (*He nods slightly to* LENNIE.)

LENNIE (*in a frightened voice*). We just come in.

CURLEY. Well, next time you answer when you're spoke to, then.

GEORGE. He didn't do nothing to you.

CURLEY (*measuring him*). You drawin' cards this hand?

GEORGE (*quietly*). I might.

CURLEY (*stares at him for a moment, his threat moving to the future*). I'll see you get a chance to ante, anyway. (*He walks out of the room.*)

GEORGE (*after he has made his exit*). Say, what the hell's he got on his shoulder? Lennie didn't say nothing to him.

CANDY (*looks cautiously at the door*). That's the boss's son. Curley's pretty handy. He done quite a bit in the ring. The guys say he's pretty handy.

GEORGE. Well, let 'im be handy. He don't have to take after Lennie. Lennie didn't do nothing to him.

CANDY (*considering*). Well . . . tell you what, Curley's like a lot a little guys. He hates big guys. He's alla time pickin' scraps with big guys. Kinda like he's mad at 'em because *he* ain't a big guy. You seen little guys like that, ain't you—always scrappy?

GEORGE. Sure, I seen plenty tough little guys. But this here Curley better not make no mistakes about Lennie. Lennie ain't handy, see, but this Curley punk's gonna get hurt if he messes around with Lennie.

CANDY (*skeptically*). Well, Curley's pretty handy. You know, it never did seem right to me. 'Spose Curley jumps a big guy and licks him. Everybody says what a game guy Curley is. Well, 'spose he jumps 'im and gits licked, everybody says the big guy oughta pick somebody his own size. Seems like Curley ain't givin' nobody a chance.

GEORGE (*watching the door*). Well, he better watch out for Lennie. Lennie ain't no fighter. But Lennie's strong and quick and Lennie don't know no rules. (*Walks to the square table, and sits down on one of the boxes. Picks up scattered cards and pulls them together and shuffles them.*)

CANDY. Don't tell Curley I said none of this. He'd slough me! He jus' don't give a damn. Won't ever get canned because his ole man's the boss!

GEORGE (*cuts the cards. Turns over and looks at each one as he throws it down*). This guy Curley sounds like a son-of-a-bitch to me! I don't like mean little guys!

CANDY. Seems to me like he's worse lately. He got married a couple of weeks ago. Wife lives over in the boss's house. Seems like Curley's worse'n ever since he got married. Like he's settin' on a ant-hill an' a big red ant come up an' nipped 'im on the turnip. Just feels so goddamn miserable he'll strike at anything that moves. I'm kinda sorry for 'im.

GEORGE. Maybe he's showin' off for his wife.

CANDY. You seen that glove on his left hand?

GEORGE. Sure I seen it!

CANDY. Well, that glove's full of vaseline.

GEORGE. Vaseline? What the hell for?

CANDY. Curley says he's keepin' that hand soft for his wife.

GEORGE. That's a dirty kind of a thing to tell around.

CANDY. I ain't quite so sure. I seen such funny things a guy will do to try to be nice. I ain't sure. But you jus' wait till you see Curley's wife!

GEORGE (*begins to lay out a solitaire hand, speaks casually*). Is she purty?

CANDY. Yeah. Purty, but—

GEORGE (*studying his cards*). But what?

CANDY. Well, she got the eye.

GEORGE (*still playing at his solitaire hand*). Yeah? Married two weeks an' got the eye? Maybe that's why Curley's pants is fulla ants.

CANDY. Yes, sir, I seen her give Slim the eye. Slim's a jerk-line skinner. Hell of a nice fella. Well, I seen her give Slim the eye. Curley never seen it. And I seen her give a skinner named Carlson the eye.

GEORGE (*pretending a very mild interest*). Looks like we was gonna have fun!

CANDY (*stands up*). Know what I think? (*Waits for an answer.* GEORGE *doesn't answer.*) Well, I think Curley's married himself a tart.

GEORGE (*casually*). He ain't the first. Black queen on a red king. Yes, sir . . . there's plenty done that!

CANDY (*moves towards the door, leading his dog out with him*). I got to be settin' out the wash basins for the guys. The teams'll be in before long. You guys gonna buck barley?

GEORGE. Yeah.

CANDY. You won't tell Curley nothing I said?

GEORGE. Hell, no!

CANDY (*just before he goes out the door, he turns back*). Well, you look her over, mister. You see if she ain't a tart! (*He exits.*)

GEORGE (*continuing to play out his solitaire. He turns to* LENNIE). Look, Lennie, this here ain't no set-up. You gonna have trouble with that Curley guy. I seen that kind before. You know what he's doin'. He's kinda feelin' you out. He figures he's got you scared. And he's gonna take a sock at you, first chance he gets.

LENNIE (*frightened*). I don't want no trouble. Don't let him sock me, George!

GEORGE. I hate them kind of bastards. I seen plenty of 'em. Like the ole guys says: "Curley don't take no chances. He always figures to win." (*Thinks for a moment.*) If he tangles with you, Lennie, we're goin' get the can. Don't make no mistake about that. He's the boss's kid. Look, you try to keep away from him, will you? Don't never speak to him. If he comes in here you move clear to the other side of the room. Will you remember that, Lennie?

LENNIE (*mourning*). I don't want no trouble. I never done nothing to him!

GEORGE. Well, that won't do you no good, if Curley wants to set himself up for a fighter. Just don't have nothing to do with him. Will you remember?

LENNIE. Sure, George . . . I ain't gonna say a word.
(*Sounds of the teams coming in from the fields, jingling of harness, croak of heavy laden axles, men talking to and cussing the horses. Crack of a whip and from a distance a voice calling.*)

SLIM'S VOICE. Stable buck! Hey! Stable buck!

GEORGE. Here come the guys. Just don't say nothing.

LENNIE (*timidly*). You ain't mad, George?

GEORGE. I ain't mad at you. I'm mad at this here Curley bastard! I wanted we should get a little stake together. Maybe a hundred dollars. You keep away from Curley.

LENNIE. Sure I will. I won't say a word.

GEORGE (*hesitating*). Don't let 'im pull you in—but—if the son-of-a-bitch socks you—let him have it!

LENNIE. Let him have what, George?

GEORGE. Never mind. . . . Look, if you get in any kind of trouble, you remember what I told you to do.

LENNIE. If I get in any trouble, you ain't gonna let me tend the rabbits?

GEORGE. That's not what I mean. You remember where we slept last night. Down by the river?

LENNIE. Oh, sure I remember. I go there and hide in the brush until you come for me.

GEORGE. That's it. Hide till I come for you. Don't let nobody see you. Hide in the brush by the river. Now say that over.

LENNIE. Hide in the brush by the river. Down in the brush by the river.

GEORGE. If you get in trouble.

LENNIE. If I get in trouble.
(*A brake screeches outside and a call: "Stable buck, oh, stable buck!" "Where the hell's that goddamn nigger?" Suddenly* CURLEY'S WIFE *is standing in the door. Full, heavily rouged lips. Wide-spaced, made-up eyes, her fingernails are bright red, her hair hangs in little rolled clusters like sausages. She wears a cotton house dress and red mules, on the insteps of which are little bouquets of red ostrich feathers.* GEORGE *and* LENNIE *look up at her.*)

CURLEY'S WIFE. I'm lookin' for Curley!

GEORGE (*looks away from her*). He was in here a minute ago but he went along.

CURLEY'S WIFE (*puts her hands behind her back and leans against the door frame so that her body is thrown forward*). You're the new fellas that just come, ain't you?

GEORGE (*sullenly*). Yeah.

CURLEY'S WIFE (*bridles a little and inspects her fingernails*). Sometimes Curley's in here.

GEORGE (*brusquely*). Well, he ain't now!

CURLEY'S WIFE (*playfully*). Well, if he ain't, I guess I'd better look some place else.
(LENNIE *watches her, fascinated.*)

GEORGE. If I see Curley I'll pass the word you was lookin' for him.

CURLEY'S WIFE. Nobody can't blame a person for lookin'.

GEORGE. That depends what she's lookin' for.

CURLEY'S WIFE (*a little weary, dropping her coquetry*). I'm jus' lookin' for somebody to talk to. Don't you never jus' want to talk to somebody?

SLIM (*offstage*). Okay! Put that lead pair in the north stalls.

CURLEY'S WIFE (*to* SLIM, *offstage*). Hi, Slim!

SLIM (*voice offstage*). Hello.

CURLEY'S WIFE. I—I'm tryin' to find Curley.

SLIM'S VOICE (*offstage*). Well, you ain't tryin' very hard. I seen him goin' in your house.

CURLEY'S WIFE (*turning back toward* GEORGE *and* LENNIE). I gotta be goin'! (*She exits hurriedly.*)

GEORGE (*looking around at* LENNIE). Jesus, what a tramp! So, that's what Curley picks for a wife. God Almighty, did you smell that stink she's got on? I can still smell her. Don't have to see *her* to know she's around.

LENNIE. She's purty!

GEORGE. Yeah. And she's sure hidin' it. Curley got his work ahead of him.

LENNIE (*still staring at the doorway where she was*). Gosh, she's purty!

GEORGE (*turning furiously at him*). Listen to me, you crazy bastard. Don't you even look at that bitch. I don't care what she says or what she does. I seen 'em poison before, but I ain't never seen no piece of jail bait worse than her. Don't you even smell near her!

LENNIE. I never smelled, George!

GEORGE. No, you never. But when she was standin' there showin' her legs, you wasn't lookin' the other way neither!

LENNIE. I never meant no bad things, George. Honest I never.

GEORGE. Well, you keep away from her. You let Curley take the rap. He let himself in for it. (*Disgustedly*) Glove full of vaseline. I bet he's eatin' raw eggs and writin' to patent-medicine houses.

LENNIE (*cries out*). I don't like this place. This ain't no good place. I don't like this place!

GEORGE. Listen—I don't like it here no better than you do. But we gotta keep it till we get a stake. We're flat. We gotta get a stake. (*Goes back to the table, thoughtfully.*) If we can get just a few dollars in the poke we'll shove off and go up to the American River and pan gold. Guy can make a couple dollars a day there.

LENNIE (*eagerly*). Let's go, George. Let's get out of here. It's mean here.

GEORGE (*shortly*). I tell you we gotta stay a little while. We gotta get a stake. (*The sounds of running water and rattle of basins are heard.*) Shut up now, the guys'll be comin' in! (*Pensively*) Maybe we ought to wash up. . . . But hell, we ain't done nothin' to get dirty.

SLIM (*enters. He is a tall, dark man in blue jeans and a short denim jacket. He carries a crushed Stetson hat under his arm and combs his long dark damp hair straight back. He stands and moves with a kind of majesty. He finishes combing his hair. Smoothes out his crushed hat, creases it in the middle and puts it on. In a gentle voice*). It's brighter'n a bitch outside. Can't hardly see nothing in here. You the new guys?

GEORGE. Just come.

SLIM. Goin' to buck barley?

GEORGE. That's what the boss says.

SLIM. Hope you get on my team.

GEORGE. Boss said we'd go with a jerk-line skinner named Slim.

SLIM. That's me.

GEORGE. You a jerk-line skinner?

SLIM (*in self-disparagement*). I can snap 'em around a little.

GEORGE (*terribly impressed*). That

kinda makes you Jesus Christ on this ranch, don't it?

SLIM (*obviously pleased*). Oh, nuts!

GEORGE (*chuckles*). Like the man says, "The boss tells you what to do. But if you want to know how to do it, you got to ask the mule skinner." The man says any guy that can drive twelve Arizona jack rabbits with a jerk line can fall in a toilet and come up with a mince pie under each arm.

SLIM (*laughing*). Well, I hope you get on my team. I got a pair a punks that don't know a barley bag from a blue ball. You guys ever bucked any barley?

GEORGE. Hell, yes. I ain't nothin' to scream about, but that big guy there can put up more grain alone than most pairs can.

SLIM (*looks approvingly at* GEORGE). You guys travel around together?

GEORGE. Sure. We kinda look after each other. (*Points at* LENNIE *with his thumb.*) He ain't bright. Hell of a good worker, though. Hell of a nice fella too. I've knowed him for a long time.

SLIM. Ain't many guys travel around together. I don't know why. Maybe everybody in the whole damn world is scared of each other.

GEORGE. It's a lot nicer to go 'round with a guy you know. You get used to it an' then it ain't no fun alone any more.
(*Enter* CARLSON. *Big-stomached, powerful man. His head still drips water from scrubbing and dousing.*)

CARLSON. Hello, Slim! (*He looks at* GEORGE *and* LENNIE.)

SLIM. These guys just come.

CARLSON. Glad to meet ya! My name's Carlson.

GEORGE. I'm George Milton. This here's Lennie Small.

CARLSON. Glad to meet you. He ain't very small. (*Chuckles at his own joke.*) He ain't small at all. Meant to ask you, Slim, how's your bitch? I seen she wasn't under your wagon this morning.

SLIM. She slang her pups last night. Nine of 'em. I drowned four of 'em right off. She couldn't feed that many.

CARLSON. Got five left, huh?

SLIM. Yeah. Five. I kep' the biggest.

CARLSON. What kinda dogs you think they gonna be?

SLIM. I don't know. Some kind of shepherd, I guess. That's the most kind I seen around here when she's in heat.

CARLSON (*laughs*). I had an airedale an' a guy down the road got one of them little white floozy dogs, well, she was in heat and the guy locks her up. But my airedale, named Tom he was, he et a woodshed clear down to the roots to get to her. Guy come over one day, he's sore as hell, he says, "I wouldn't mind if my bitch had pups, but Christ Almighty, this morning she slang a litter of Shetland ponies. . . ." (*Takes off his hat and scratches his head.*) Got five pups, huh! Gonna keep all of 'em?

SLIM. I don' know, gotta keep 'em awhile, so they can drink Lulu's milk.

CARLSON (*thoughtfully*). Well, looka here, Slim, I been thinkin'. That dog of Candy's so goddam old he can't hardly walks. Stinks like hell. Every time time Candy brings him in the bunkhouse, I can smell him two or three days. Why don't you get Candy to shoot his ol' dog, and give him one of them pups to raise up? I can smell that dog a mile off. Got no teeth. Can't eat. Candy feeds him milk. He can't chew nothing else. And leadin' him around

on a string so he don't bump into things . . . (*The triangle outside begins to ring wildly. Continues for a few moments, then stops suddenly.*) There she goes!
(*Outside there is a burst of voices as a group of men go by.*)

SLIM (*to* LENNIE *and* GEORGE). You guys better come on while they's still somethin' to eat. Won't be nothing left in a couple of minutes. (*Exit* SLIM *and* CARLSON. LENNIE *watches* GEORGE *excitedly.*)

LENNIE. George!

GEORGE (*rumpling his cards into a pile*). Yeah, I heard 'im, Lennie . . . I'll ask 'im!

LENNIE (*excitedly*). A brown and white one.

GEORGE. Come on, let's get dinner. I don't whether he's got a brown and white one.

LENNIE. You ask him right away, George, so he won't kill no more of 'em!

GEORGE. Sure! Come on now—let's go. (*They start for the door.*)

CURLEY (*bounces in, angrily*). You seen a girl around here?

GEORGE (*coldly*). 'Bout half an hour ago, mebbe.

CURLEY. Well, what the hell was she doin'?

GEORGE (*insultingly*). She *said* she was lookin' for you.

CURLEY (*measures both men with his eyes for a moment*). Which way did she go?

GEORGE. I don't know. I didn't watch her go. (CURLEY *scowls at him a moment and then turns and hurries out the door.*) You know, Lennie, I'm scared I'm gonna tangle with that bastard myself. I hate his guts! Jesus Christ, come on! They won't be a damn thing left to eat.

LENNIE. Will you ask him about a brown and white one?
(*They exeunt.*)

ACT TWO

SCENE I

About seven-thirty Friday evening.
Same bunkhouse interior as in last scene.
The evening light is seen coming in through the window, but it is quite dark in the interior of the bunkhouse.
From outside comes the sound of a horseshoe game. Thuds on the dirt and occasional clangs as a shoe hits the peg. Now and then voices are raised in approval or derision: "That's a good one." . . . "Goddamn right it's a good one." . . . "Here goes for a ringer. I need a ringer." . . . "Goddam near got it, too."

SLIM *and* GEORGE *come into the darkening bunkhouse together.* SLIM *reaches up and turns on the tin-shaded electric light. Sits down on a box at the table.* GEORGE *takes his place opposite.*

SLIM. It wasn't nothing. I would of had to drown most of them pups anyway. No need to thank me about that.

GEORGE. Wasn't much to you, mebbe, but it was a hell of a lot to him. Jesus Christ, I don't know how we're gonna get him to sleep in here. He'll want to stay right out in the barn. We gonna have trouble keepin' him from gettin' right in the box with them pups.

SLIM. Say, you sure was right about him. Maybe he ain't bright—but I never seen such a worker. He damn near killed his partner buckin' barley. He'd take his end of that sack—(*a gesture*)—pretty near kill his partner. God Almighty, I never seen such a strong guy.

GEORGE (*proudly*). You just tell Lennie what to do and he'll do it if it don't take no figuring.
(*Outside the sound of the horsehoe game goes on: "Son of a bitch if I can win a goddam game." . . . "Me neither. You'd think them shoes was anvils."*)

SLIM. Funny how you and him string along together.

GEORGE. What's so funny about it?

SLIM. Oh, I don't know. Hardly none of the guys ever travels around together. I hardly never seen two guys travel together. You know how the hands are. They come in and get their bunk and work a month and then they quit and go on alone. Never seem to give a damn about nobody. Jest seems kinda funny. A cuckoo like him and a smart guy like you traveling together.

GEORGE. I ain't so bright neither or I wouldn't be buckin' barley for my fifty and found. If I was bright, if I was even a little bit smart, I'd have my own place and I'd be bringin' in my own crops 'stead of doin' all the work and not gettin' what comes up out of the ground. (*He falls silent for a moment.*)

SLIM. A guy'd like to do that. Sometimes I'd like to cuss a string of mules that was my own mules.

GEORGE. It ain't so funny, him and me goin' round together. Him and me was both born in Auburn. I knowed his aunt. She took him when he was a baby and raised him up. When his aunt died Lennie jus' come along with me, out workin'. Got kinda used to each other after a little while.

SLIM. Uh huh.

GEORGE. First I used to have a hell of a lot of fun with him. Used to play jokes on him because he was too dumb to take care of himself. But, hell, he was too dumb even to know when he had a joke played on him. (*Sarcastically*) Hell, yes, I had fun! Made me seem goddam smart alongside of him.

SLIM. I seen it that way.

GEORGE. Why, he'd do any damn thing I tole him. If I tole him to walk over a cliff, over he'd go. You know that wasn't so damn much fun after a while. He never got mad about it, neither. I've beat hell out of him and he could bust every bone in my body jest with his hands. But he never lifted a finger against me.

SLIM (*braiding a bull whip*). Even if you socked him, wouldn't he?

GEORGE. No, by God! I tell you what made me stop playing jokes. One day a bunch of guys was standin' aroun' up on the Sacramento river. I was feelin' pretty smart. I turns to Lennie and I says, "Jump in."

SLIM. What happened?

GEORGE. He jumps. Couldn't swim a stroke. He damn near drowned. And he was so nice to me for pullin' him out. Clean forgot I tole him to jump in. Well, I ain't done nothin' like that no more. Makes me kinda sick tellin' about it.

SLIM. He's a nice fella. A guy don't need no sense to be a nice fella. Seems to be sometimes it's jest the other way round. Take a real smart guy, he ain't hardly ever a nice fella.

GEORGE (*stacking the scattered cards and getting his solitaire game ready again*). I ain't got no people. I seen guys that go round on the ranches alone. That ain't no good. They don't have no fun. After a while they get mean.

SLIM (*quietly*). Yeah, I seen 'em get mean. I seen 'em get so they don't want to talk to nobody. Some ways they got to. You take a bunch of guys all livin' in one room an' by God they got to mind their own business. 'Bout the only private thing a guy's got is where he come from and where he's goin'.

GEORGE. 'Course Lennie's a goddamn nuisance most of the time. But you get used to goin' round with a guy and you can't get rid of him. I mean you get used to him an' you can't get rid of bein' used to him. I'm sure drippin' at the mouth. I ain't told nobody all this before.

SLIM. Do you want to git rid of him?

GEORGE. Well, he gets in trouble all the time. Because he's so goddamn dumb. Like what happened in Weed. (*He stops, alarmed at what he has said.*) You wouldn't tell nobody?

SLIM (*calmly*). What did he do in Weed?

GEORGE. You wouldn't tell?—No, course you wouldn't.

SLIM. What did he do?

GEORGE. Well, he seen this girl in a red dress. Dumb bastard like he is he wants to touch everything he likes. Jest wants to feel of it. So he reaches out to feel this red dress. Girl lets out a squawk and that gets Lennie all mixed up. He holds on 'cause that's the only thing he can think to do.

SLIM. The hell!

GEORGE. Well, this girl squawks her head off. I'm right close and I hear all the yellin', so I comes a-running. By that time Lennie's scared to death. You know, I had to sock him over the head with a fence picket to make him let go.

SLIM. So what happens then?

GEORGE (*carefully building his solitaire hand*). Well, she runs in and tells the law she's been raped. The guys in Weed start out to lynch Lennie. So there we sit in an irrigation ditch, under water all the rest of that day. Got only our heads sticking out of water, up under the grass that grows out of the side of the ditch. That night we run outa there.

SLIM. Didn't hurt the girl none, huh?

GEORGE. Hell no, he jes' scared her.

SLIM. He's a funny guy.

GEORGE. Funny! Why, one time, you know what that big baby done! He was walking along a road—(*enter* LENNIE *through the door. He wears his coat over his shoulder like a cape and walks hunched over.*) Hi, Lennie. How do you like your pup?

LENNIE (*breathlessly*). He's brown and white jus' like I wanted. (*Goes directly to his bunk and lies down. Face to the wall and knees drawn up.*)

GEORGE (*puts down his cards deliberately*). Lennie!

LENNIE (*over his shoulder*). Huh? What you want George?

GEORGE (*sternly*). I tole ya, ya couldn't bring that pup in here.

LENNIE. What pup, George? I ain't got no pup.
(GEORGE *goes quickly over to him, grabs him by the shoulder and rolls*

him over. He picks up a tiny puppy from where LENNIE *has been concealing it against his stomach.*)

LENNIE (*quickly*). Give him to me, George.

GEORGE. You get right up and take this pup to the nest. He's got to sleep with his mother. Ya want ta kill him? Jes' born last night and ya take him out of the nest. Ya take him back or I'll tell Slim not to let you have him.

LENNIE (*pleadingly*). Give him to me, George. I'll take him back. I didn't mean no bad thing, George. Honest I didn't. I jus' want to pet him a little.

GEORGE (*giving the pup to him*). All right, you get him back there quick. And don't you take him out no more.

LENNIE (*scuttles out of the room*).

SLIM. Jesus, he's just like a kid, ain't he?

GEORGE. Sure he's like a kid. There ain't no more harm in him than a kid neither, except he's so strong. I bet he won't come in here to sleep tonight. He'll sleep right along side that box in the barn. Well, let him. He ain't doin' no harm out here.
(*The light has faded out outside and it appears quite dark outside. Enter* CANDY *leading his old dog by a string.*)

CANDY. Hello, Slim. Hello, George. Didn't neither of you play horseshoes?

SLIM. I don't like to play every night.

CANDY (*goes to his bunk and sits down, presses the old blind dog to the floor beside him*). Either you guys got a slug of whiskey? I got a gut ache.

SLIM. I ain't. I'd drink it myself if I had. And I ain't got no gut ache either.

CANDY. Goddamn cabbage give it to me. I knowed it was goin' to before I ever et it.
(*Enter* CARLSON *and* WHIT.)

CARLSON. Jesus, how that nigger can pitch shoes!

SLIM. He's plenty good.

WHIT. Damn right he is.

CARLSON. Yeah. He don't give nobody else a chance to win. (*Stops and sniffs the air. Looks around until he sees* CANDY's *dog.*) God Almighty, that dog stinks. Get him outa here, Candy. I don't know nothing that stinks as bad as ole dogs. You got to get him outa here.

CANDY (*lying down on his bunk, reaches over and pats the ancient dog, speaks softly*). I been round him so much I never notice how he stinks.

CARLSON. Well, I can't stand him in here. That stink hangs round even after he's gone. (*Walks over and stands looking down at the dog.*) Got no teeth. All stiff with rheumatism. He ain't no good to you, Candy. Why don't you shoot him?

CANDY (*uncomfortably*). Well, hell, I had him so long! Had him since he was a pup. I herded sheep with him. (*Proudly*) You wouldn't think it to look at him now. He was the best damn sheep dog I ever seen.

GEORGE. I knowed a guy in Weed that had an airedale that could herd sheep. Learned it from the other dogs.

CARLSON (*sticking to his point*). Lookit, Candy. This ole dog jus' suffers itself all the time. If you was to take him out and shoot him—right in the back of the head . . . (*leans over and points*) . . . right there, why he never'd know what hit him.

CANDY (*unhappily*). No, I couldn't do that. I had him too long.

CARLSON (*insisting*). He don't have no fun no more. He stinks like hell. Tell you what I'll do. I'll shoot him for you. Then it won't be you that done it.

CANDY (*sits up on the bunk, rubbing his whiskers nervously, speaks plaintively*). I had him from a pup.

WHIT. Let 'im alone, Carl. It ain't a guy's dog that matters. It's the way the guy feels about the dog. Hell, I had a mutt once I wouldn't a traded for a field trial pointer.

CARLSON (*being persuasive*). Well, Candy ain't being nice to him, keeping him alive. Lookit, Slim's bitch got a litter right now. I bet you Slim would give ya one of them pups to raise up, wouldn't ya, Slim?

SLIM (*studying the dog*). Yeah. You can have a pup if you want to.

CANDY (*helplessly*). Mebbe it would hurt. (*After a moment's pause, positively*) And I don't mind taking care of him.

CARLSON. Aw, he'd be better off dead. The way I'd shoot him he wouldn't feel nothin'. I'd put the gun right there. (*Points with his toe.*) Right back of the head.

WHIT. Aw, let 'im alone, Carl.

CARLSON. Why, hell, he wouldn't even quiver.

WHIT. Let 'im alone. (*He produces a magazine.*) Say, did you see this? Did you see this in the book here?

CARLSON. See what?

WHIT. Right there. Read that.

CARLSON. I don't want to read nothing. . . . It'd be all over in a minute, Candy. Come on.

WHIT. Did you see it, Slim? Go on, read it. Read it out loud.

SLIM. What is it?

WHIT. Read it.

SLIM (*reads slowly*). "Dear Editor: I read your mag for six years and I think it is the best on the market. I like stories by Peter Rand. I think he is a whing-ding. Give us more like the Dark Rider. I don't write many letters. Just thought I would tell you I think your mag is the best dime's worth I ever spen'." (*Looks up questioningly.*) What you want me to read that for?

WHIT. Go on, read the name at the bottom.

SLIM (*reading*). "Yours for Success, William Tenner." (*Looks up at* WHIT.) What ya want me to read that for?

CARLSON. Come on, Candy—what you say?

WHIT (*taking the magazine and closing it impressively. Talks to cover* CARLSON). You don't remember Bill Tenner? Worked here about three months ago?

SLIM (*thinking*). Little guy? Drove a cultivator?

WHIT. That's him. That's the guy.

CARLSON (*has refused to be drawn into this conversation*). Look, Candy. If you want me to, I'll put the old devil outa his misery right now and get it over with. There ain't nothin' left for him. Can't eat, can't see, can't hardly walk. Tomorrow you can pick one of Slim's pups.

SLIM. Sure . . . I got a lot of 'em.

CANDY (*hopefully*). You ain't got no gun.

CARLSON. The hell, I ain't. Got a Luger. It won't hurt him none at all.

CANDY. Mebbe tomorrow. Let's wait till tomorrow.

CARLSON. I don't see no reason for it. (*Goes to his bunk, pulls a bag from underneath, takes a Luger pistol out.*) Let's get it over with. We can't sleep with him stinking around in here. (*He snaps a shell into the chamber, sets the safety and puts the pistol into his hip pocket.*)

SLIM (*as* CANDY *looks toward him for help*). Better let him go, Candy.

CANDY (*looks at each person for some hope.* WHIT *makes a gesture of protest and then resigns himself. The others look away, to avoid responsibility. At last, very softly and hopelessly*). All right. Take him.
(*He doesn't look down at the dog at all. Lies back on his bunk and crosses his arms behind his head and stares at the ceiling.* CARLSON *picks up the string, helps the dog to its feet.*)

CARLSON. Come, boy. Come on, boy. (*To* CANDY, *apologetically*) He won't even feel it. (CANDY *does not move nor answer him.*) Come on, boy. That's the stuff. Come on. (*He leads the dog toward the door.*)

SLIM. Carlson?

CARLSON. Yeah.

SLIM (*curtly*). Take a shovel.

CARLSON. Oh, sure, I get you.
(*Exit* CARLSON *with the dog.* GEORGE *follows to the door, shuts it carefully and sets the latch.* CANDY *lies rigidly on his bunk. The next scene is one of silence and quick staccato speeches.*)

SLIM (*loudly*). One of my lead mules got a bad hoof. Got to get some tar on it.
(*There is a silence.*)

GEORGE (*loudly*). Anybody like to play a little euchre?

WHIT. I'll lay out a few with you.
(*They take places opposite each other at the table but* GEORGE *does not shuffle the cards. He ripples the edge of the deck. Everybody looks over at him. He stops. Silence again.*)

SLIM (*compassionately*). Candy, you can have any of them pups you want.
(*There is no answer from* CANDY. *There is a little gnawing noise on the stage.*)

GEORGE. Sounds like there was a rat under there. We ought to set a trap there.
(*Deep silence again.*)

WHIT (*exasperated*). What the hell is takin' him so long? Lay out some cards, why don't you? We ain't gonna get no euchre played this way.
(GEORGE *studies the backs of the cards. And after a long silence there is a shot in the distance. All the men start a bit, look quickly at* CANDY. *For a moment he continues to stare at the ceiling and then rolls slowly over and faces the wall.* GEORGE *shuffles the cards noisily and deals them.*)

GEORGE. Well, let's get to it.

WHIT (*still to cover the moment*). Yeah . . . I guess you guys really come here to work, huh?

GEORGE. How do you mean?

WHIT (*chuckles*). Well, you come on a Friday. You got two days to work till Sunday.

GEORGE. I don't see how you figure.

WHIT. You do if you been round these big ranches much. A guy that wants to look over a ranch comes in Saturday afternoon. He gets Saturday night supper, three meals on Sunday and he can quit Monday morning after breakfast without turning a hand. But you come to work on Friday noon. You got ta put in a day and a half no matter how ya figure it.

GEORGE (*quietly*). We're goin' stick around awhile. Me and Lennie's gonna roll up a stake.
(*Door opens and the Negro stable buck puts in his head. A lean-faced Negro with pained eyes.*

CROOKS. Mr. Slim.

SLIM (*who has been watching* CANDY *the whole time*). Huh? Oh, hello, Crooks, what's the matter?

CROOKS. You tole me to warm up tar for that mule's foot. I got it warm now.

SLIM. Oh, sure, Crooks. I'll come right out and put it on.

CROOKS. I can do it for you if you want, Mr. Slim.

SLIM (*standing up*). Naw, I'll take care of my own team.

CROOKS. Mr. Slim.

SLIM. Yeah.

CROOKS. That big new guy is messing round your pups in the barn.

SLIM. Well, he ain't doin' no harm. I give him one of them pups.

CROOKS. Just thought I'd tell ya. He's takin' 'em out of the nest and handling them. That won't do 'em no good.

SLIM. Oh, he won't hurt 'em.

GEORGE (*looks up from his cards.*) If that crazy bastard is foolin' round too much jus' kick him out.
(SLIM *follows the stable buck out.*)

WHIT (*examining his cards*). Seen the new kid yet?

GEORGE. What kid?

WHIT. Why, Curley's new wife.

GEORGE (*cautiously*). Yeah, I seen her.

WHIT. Well, ain't she a lulu?

GEORGE. I ain't seen that much of her.

WHIT. Well, you stick around and keep your eyes open. You'll see plenty of her. I never seen nobody like her. She's just workin' on everybody all the time. Seems like she's even working' on the stable buck. I don't know what the hell she wants.

GEORGE (*casually*). Been any trouble since she got here?
(*Obviously neither man is interested in the card game.* WHIT *lays down his hand and* GEORGE *gathers the cards in and lays out a solitaire hand.*)

WHIT. I see what you mean. No, they ain't been no trouble yet. She's only been here a couple of weeks. Curley's got yellow jackets in his drawers, but that's all so far. Every time the guys is around she shows up. She's lookin' for Curley. Or she thought she left somethin' layin' around and she's look-in' for that. Seems like she can't keep away from guys. And Curley's runnin' round like a cat lookin' for a dirt road. But they ain't been no trouble.

GEORGE. Ranch with a bunch of guys on it ain't no place for a girl. Specially like her.

WHIT. If she's give you any ideas you ought to come in town with us guys tomorrow night.

GEORGE. Why, what's doin'?

WHIT. Just the usual thing. We go in to Old Susy's place. Hell of a nice place. Old Susy is a laugh. Always cracking jokes. Like she says when we come up on the front porch last Saturday night: Susy opens the door and she yells over her shoulder: "Get your coats on, girls, here comes the sheriff." She never talks dirty neither. Got five girls there.

GEORGE. What does it set you back?

WHIT. Two and a half. You can get a shot of whiskey for fifteen cents. Susy got nice chairs to set in too. If a guy don't want to flop, why, he can just set in them chairs and have a couple or three shots and just pass the time of day. Susy don't give a damn. She ain't rushin' guys through, or kicking them out if they don't want to flop.

GEORGE. Might go in and look the joint over.

WHIT. Sure. Come along. It's a hell of a lot of fun—her crackin' jokes all the time. Like she says one time, she says: "I've knew people that if they got a rag rug on the floor and a kewpie doll lamp on the phonograph they think they're runnin' a parlor house." That's Gladys's house she's talkin' about. And Susy says: "I know what you boys want," she says: "My girls is clean," she says. "And there ain't no water in my whiskey," she says. "If any you guys want to look at a kewpie doll lamp and take your chance of gettin' burned, why, you know where to go." She says: "They's guys round here walkin' bowlegged because they liked to look at a kewpie doll lamp."

GEORGE. Gladys runs the other house, huh?

WHIT. Yeah.
(Enter CARLSON. CANDY looks at him.)

CARLSON. God, it's a dark night. (Goes to his bunk; starts cleaning his pistol.)

WHIT. We don't never go to Gladys's. Gladys gits three bucks, and two bits a shot and she don't crack no jokes. But Susy's place is clean and she got nice chairs. A guy can set in there like he lived there. Don't let no Manila Goo-Goos in, neither.

GEORGE. Aw, I don't know. Me and Lennie's rollin' up a stake. I might go in and set and have a shot, but I ain't puttin' out no two and a half.

WHIT. Well, a guy got to have some fun sometimes.
(Enter LENNIE. LENNIE creeps to his bunk and sits down.)

GEORGE. Didn't bring him back in, did you, Lennie?

LENNIE. No, George, honest I didn't. See?

WHIT. Say, how about this euchre game?

GEORGE. Okay. I didn't think you wanted to play.
(Enter CURLEY excitedly.)

CURLEY. Any you guys seen my wife?

WHIT. She ain't been here.

CURLEY (looks threateningly about the room). Where the hell's Slim?

GEORGE. Went out in the barn. He was goin' put some tar on a split hoof.

CURLEY. How long ago did he go?

GEORGE. Oh, five, ten minutes.
(CURLEY jumps out the door.)

WHIT (standing up). I guess maybe I'd like to see this. Curley must be spoilin' or he wouldn't start for Slim. Curley's handy, goddamn handy. But just the same he better leave Slim alone.

GEORGE. Thinks Slim's with his wife, don't he?

WHIT. Looks like it. 'Course Slim ain't. Least I don't think Slim is. But I like to see the fuss if it comes off. Come on, le's go.

GEORGE. I don't want to get mixed up

in nothing. Me and Lennie got to make a stake.

CARLSON (*finishes cleaning gun, puts it in his bag and stands up*). I'll look her over. Ain't seen a good fight in a hell of a while.
(WHIT *and* CARLSON *exeunt.*)

GEORGE. You see Slim out in the barn?

LENNIE. Sure. He tole me I better not pet that pup no more, like I said.

GEORGE. Did you see that girl out there?

LENNIE. You mean Curley's girl?

GEORGE. Yeah. Did she come in the barn?

LENNIE (*cautiously*). No—anyways I never seen her.

GEORGE. You never seen Slim talkin' to her?

LENNIE. Uh-huh. She ain't been in the barn.

GEORGE. Okay. I guess them guys ain't gonna see no fight. If they's any fightin', Lennie, ya get out of the way and stay out.

LENNIE. I don't want no fight. (GEORGE *lays out his solitaire hand.* LENNIE *picks up a face card and studies it. Turns it over and studies it again.*) Both ends the same. George, why is it both ends the same?

GEORGE. I don't know. That jus' the way they make 'em. What was Slim doin' in the barn when you seen him?

LENNIE. Slim?

GEORGE. Sure, you seen him in the barn. He tole you not to pet the pups so much.

LENNIE. Oh. Yeah. He had a can of tar

and a paint brush. I don't know what for.

GEORGE. You sure that girl didn't come in like she come in here today?

LENNIE. No, she never come.

GEORGE (*sighs*). You give me a good whorehouse every time. A guy can go in and get drunk and get it over all at once and no messes. And he knows how much it's goin' to set him back. These tarts is jus' buckshot to a guy. (LENNIE *listens with admiration, moving his lips, and* GEORGE *continues*) You remember Andy Cushman, Lennie? Went to grammar school same time as us?

LENNIE. The one that his ole lady used to make hot cakes for the kids?

GEORGE. Yeah. That's the one. You can remember if they's somepin to eat in it. (*Scores up some cards in his solitaire playing.*) Well, Andy's in San Quentin right now on account of a tart.

LENNIE. George?

GEORGE. Huh?

LENNIE. How long is it goin' be till we git that little place to live on the fat of the land?

GEORGE. I don't know. We gotta get a big stake together. I know a little place we can get cheap, but they ain't givin' it away.
(CANDY *turns slowly over and watches* GEORGE.)

LENNIE. Tell about that place, George.

GEORGE. I jus' tole you. Jus' last night.

LENNIE. Go on, tell again.

GEORGE. Well, its' ten acres. Got a little windmill. Got a little shack on it and a chicken run. Got a kitchen orchard. Cherries, apples, peaches, 'cots and nuts. Got a few berries. There's a place for alfalfa and plenty water to flood it. There's a pig pen. . . .

LENNIE (*breaking in*). And rabbits, George?

GEORGE. I could easy build a few hutches. And you could feed alfalfa to them rabbits.

LENNIE. Damn right I could. (*Excitedly*) You goddamn right I could.

GEORGE (*his voice growing warmer*). And we could have a few pigs. I'd build a smokehouse. And when we kill a pig we could smoke the hams. When the salmon run up the river we can catch a hundred of 'em. Every Sunday we'd kill a chicken or rabbit. Mebbe we'll have a cow or a goat. And the cream is so goddamn thick you got to cut it off the pan with a knife.

LENNIE (*watching him with wide eyes, softly*). We can live off the fat of the land.

GEORGE. Sure. All kinds of vegetables in the garden and if we want a little whiskey we can sell some eggs or somethin'. And we wouldn't sleep in no bunkhouse. Nobody could can us in the middle of a job.

LENNIE (*begging*). Tell about the house, George.

GEORGE. Sure. We'd have a little house. And a room to ourselves. And it ain't enough land so we'd have to work too hard. Mebbe six, seven hours a day only. We wouldn't have to buck no barley eleven hours a day. And when we put in a crop, why we'd be there to take that crop up. We'd know what come of our planting.

LENNIE (*eagerly*). And rabbits. And I'd take care of them. Tell how I'd do that, George.

GEORGE. Sure. You'd go out in the alfalfa patch and you'd have a sack. You'll fill up the sack and bring it in and put it in the rabbit cages.

LENNIE. They'd nibble and they'd nibble, the way they do. I seen 'em.

GEORGE. Every six weeks or so them does would throw a litter. So we'd have plenty rabbits to eat or sell. (*Pauses for inspiration.*) And we'd keep a few pigeons to go flying round and round the windmill, like they done when I was a kid. (*Seems entranced.*) And it'd be our own. And nobody could can us. If we don't like a guy we can say: "Get to hell out," and by God he's got to do it. And if a friend come along, why, we'd have an extra bunk. Know what we'd say? We'd say, "Why don't you spen' the night?" And by God he would. We'd have a setter dog and a couple of striped cats. (*Looks sharply at* LENNIE.) But you gotta watch out them cats don't get the little rabbits.

LENNIE (*breathing hard*). You jus' let 'em try. I'll break their goddamn necks. I'll smash them cats flat with a stick. I'd smash 'em flat with a stick. That's what I'd do.
(*They sit silently for a moment.*)

CANDY (*at the sound of his voice, both* LENNIE *and* GEORGE *jump as though caught in some secret*). You know where's a place like that?

GEORGE (*solemnly*). S'pose I do, what's that to you?

CANDY. You don't need to tell me where it's at. Might be any place.

GEORGE (*relieved*). Sure. That's right, you couldn't find it in a hundred years.

CANDY (*excitedly*). How much they want for a place like that?

GEORGE (*grudgingly*). Well, I could get it for six hundred bucks. The ole people that owns it is flat bust. And the ole lady needs medicine. Say, what's it to you? You got nothing to do with us!

CANDY (*softly*). I ain't much good with only one hand. I lost my hand right here on the ranch. That's why they didn't can me. They give me a job swampin'. And they give me two hundred and fifty dollars 'cause I lost my hand. An' I got fifty more saved up right in the bank right now. That's three hundred. And I got forty more comin' the end of the month. Tell you what . . . (*He leans forwards eagerly.*) S'pose I went in with you guys? That's three hundred and forty bucks I'd put in. I ain't much good, but I could cook and tend the chickens and hoe the garden some. How'd that be?

GEORGE (*his eyes half closed, uncertainly*). I got to think about that. We was always goin' to do it by ourselves. Me an' Lennie. I never thought of nobody else.

CANDY. I'd make a will. Leave my share to you guys in case I kicked off. I ain't got no relations nor nothing. You fellas got any money? Maybe we could go there right now.

GEORGE (*disgustedly*). We got ten bucks between us. (*He thinks.*) Say, look. If me and Lennie work a month and don't spend nothing at all, we'll have a hundred bucks. That would be four forty. I bet we could swing her for that. Then you and Lennie could go get her started and I'd get a job and make up the rest. You could sell eggs and stuff like that. (*They look at each other in amazement. Reverently*) Jesus Christ, I bet we could swing her. (*His voice is full of wonder.*) I bet we could swing 'er.

CANDY (*scratches the stump of his wrist nervously*). I got hurt four years ago. They'll can me pretty soon. Jest as soon as I can't swamp out no bunkhouses they'll put me on the county. Maybe if I give you guys my money, you'll let me hoe in the garden, even

when I ain't no good at it. And I'll wash dishes and little chicken stuff like that. But hell, I'll be on our own place. I'll be let to work on our own place. (*Miserably*) You seen what they done to my dog. They says he wasn't no good to himself nor nobody else. But when I'm that way nobody'll shoot me. I wish somebody would. They won't do nothing like that. I won't have no place to go and I can't get no more jobs.

GEORGE (*stands up*). We'll do 'er! God damn, we'll fix up that little ole place and we'll go live there. (*Wonderingly*) S'pose they was a carnival, or a circus come to town or a ball game or any damn thing. (CANDY *nods in appreciation.*) We'd just go to her. We wouldn't ask nobody if we could. Just say we'll go to her, by God, and we would. Just milk the cow and sling some grain to the chickens and go to her.

LENNIE. And put some grass to the rabbits. I wouldn't forget to feed them. When we gonna do it, George?

GEORGE (*decisively*). In one month. Right squack in one month. Know what I'm gonna do? I'm goin' write to them ole people that owns the place that we'll take 'er. And Candy'll send a hundred dollars to bind her.

CANDY (*happily*). I sure will. They got a good stove there?

GEORGE. Sure, got a nice stove. Burns coal or wood.

LENNIE. I'm gonna take my pup. I bet by Christ he likes it there.
(*The window, center backstage, swings outward.* CURLEY'S WIFE *looks in. They do not see her.*)

GEORGE (*quickly*). Now don't tell nobody about her. Jus' us three and nobody else. They'll liable to can us so we can't make no stake. We'll just go on like we was a bunch of punks. Like we was gonna buck barley the rest of our lives. And then all of a sudden, one day, bang! We get our pay and scram out of here.

CANDY. I can give you three hundred right now.

LENNIE. And not tell nobody. We won't tell nobody, George.

GEORGE. You're goddamn right we won't. (*There is a silence and then* GEORGE *speaks irritably.*) You know, seems to me I can almost smell that carnation stuff that goddamn tart dumps on herself.

CURLEY'S WIFE (*in the first part of the speech by* GEORGE *she starts to step out of sight but at the last words her face darkens with anger. At her first words everybody in the room looks around at her and remains rigid during her tirade*). Who you callin' a tart! I come from a nice home. I was brung up by nice people. Nobody never got to me before I was married. I was straight. I tell you I was good. (*A little plaintively*) I was. (*Angrily again*) You know Curley. You know he wouldn't stay with me if he wasn't sure. I tell you Curley is sure. You got no right to call me a tart.

GEORGE (*sullenly*). If you ain't a tart, what you always hangin' round guys for? You got a house an' you got a man. We don't want no trouble from you.

CURLEY'S WIFE (*pleadingly*). Sure I got a man. He ain't never home. I got nobody to talk to. I got nobody to be with. Think I can just sit home and do nothin' but cook for Curley? I want to see somebody. Just see 'em an' talk to 'em. There ain't no women. I can't walk to town. And Curley don't take me to no dances now. I tell you I jus' want to talk to somebody.

GEORGE (*boldly*). If you're just friendly what you givin' out the eye for an' floppin' your can around?

CURLEY'S WIFE (*sadly*). I just wanna be nice.
(*The sound of approaching voices: "You don't have to get mad about it, do you?" . . . "I ain't mad, but I just don't want no more questions, that's all. I just don't want no more questions."*)

GEORGE. Get goin'. We don't want no trouble.
(CURLEY'S WIFE *looks from the window and closes it silently and disappears. Enter* SLIM, *followed by* CURLEY, CARLSON *and* WHIT. SLIM's *hands are black with tar.* CURLEY *hangs close to his elbow.*)

CURLEY (*explaining*). Well, I didn't mean nothing, Slim, I jus' ast you.

SLIM. Well, you been askin' too often. I'm gettin' goddamn sick of it. If you can't look after your own wife, what you expect me to do about it? You lay off of me.

CURLEY. I'm jus' tryin' to tell you I didn't mean nothing. I just thought you might of saw her.

CARLSON. Why don't you tell her to stay to hell home where she belongs? You let her hang around the bunkhouses and pretty soon you're goin' have somethin' on your hands.

CURLEY (*whirls on* CARLSON). You keep out this 'less you want ta step outside.

CARLSON (*laughing*). Why you goddam punk. You tried to throw a scare into Slim and you couldn't make it stick. Slim throwed a scare into you. You're yellow as a frog's belly. I don't care if you're the best boxer in the country, you come for me and I'll kick your goddamn head off.

WHIT (*joining in the attack*). Glove full of vaseline!

CURLEY (*glares at him, then suddenly*

sniffs the air, like a hound). By God, she's been in *here.* I can smell— By God, she's been in here. (*To* GEORGE.) You was here. The other guys was outside. Now, God damn you—you talk.

GEORGE (*looks worried. He seems to make up his mind to face an inevitable situation. Stands up. Slowly takes off his coat, and folds it almost daintily. Speaks in an unemotional monotone.*) Somebody got to beat the hell outa you. I guess I'm elected.
(LENNIE *has been watching, fascinated. He gives his high, nervous chuckle.*)

CURLEY (*whirls on him*). What the hell you laughin' at?

LENNIE (*blankly*). Huh?

CURLEY (*exploding with rage*). Come on, you big bastard. Get up on your feet. No big son-of-a-bitch is gonna laugh at me. I'll show you who's yellow.
(LENNIE *looks helplessly at* GEORGE. *Gets up and tries to retreat upstage.* CURLEY *follows slashing at him. The others mass themselves in front of the two contestants:* "That ain't no way, Curley—he ain't done nothing to you." . . . "Lay off him, will you, Curley. He ain't no fighter." . . . "Sock him back, big guy! Don't be afraid of him!" . . . "Give him a chance, Curley. Give him a chance.")

LENNIE (*crying with terror*). George, make him leave me alone, George.

GEORGE. Get him, Lennie. Get him! (*There is a sharp cry. The gathering of men opens and* CURLEY *is flopping about, his hand lost in* LENNIE's *hand.*) Let go of him, Lennie. Let go! ("*He's got his hand!*" . . . "*Look at that, will you?*" . . . "*Jesus, what a guy!*" LENNIE *watches in terror the flopping man he holds.* LENNIE's *face is covered with blood.* GEORGE *slaps* LENNIE *in the face again and again.* CURLEY *is weak and shrunken.*) Let go his hand, Lennie.

Slim, come help me, while this guy's got any hand left.
(*Suddenly* LENNIE *lets go. He cowers away from* GEORGE.)

LENNIE. You told me to, George. I heard you tell me to.
(CURLEY *has dropped to the floor.* SLIM *and* CARLSON *bend over him and look at his hand.* SLIM *looks over at* LENNIE *with horror.*)

SLIM. We got to get him to a doctor. It looks to me like every bone in his hand is busted.

LENNIE (*crying*). I didn't wanta. I didn't wanta hurt 'im.

SLIM. Carlson, you get the candy wagon out. He'll have to go into Soledad and get his hand fixed up. (*Turns to the whimpering* LENNIE.) It ain't your fault. This punk had it comin' to him. But Jesus—he ain't hardly got no hand left.

GEORGE (*moving near*). Slim, will we git canned now? Will Curley's ole man can us now?

SLIM. I don't know. (*Kneels down beside Curley*). You got your sense enough to listen? (CURLEY *nods.*) Well, then you listen. I think you got your hand caught in a machine. If you don't tell nobody what happened, we won't. But you jest tell and try to get this guy canned and we'll tell everybody. And then will you get the laugh! (*Helps* CURLEY *to his feet.*) Come on now. Carlson's goin' to take you in to a doctor. (*Starts for the door, turns back to* LENNIE.) Le's see your hands. (LENNIE *sticks out both hands.*) Christ Almighty!

GEORGE. Lennie was just scairt. He didn't know what to do. I tole you nobody ought never to fight him. No, I guess it was Candy I tole.

CANDY (*solemnly*). That's just what you done. Right this morning when

Curley first lit into him. You says he better not fool with Lennie if he knows what's good for him.

(*They all leave the stage except* GEORGE *and* LENNIE *and* CANDY.)

GEORGE (*to* LENNIE, *very gently*). It ain't your fault. You don't need to be scairt no more. You done jus' what I tole you to. Maybe you better go in the washroom and clean up your face. You look like hell.

LENNIE. I didn't want no trouble.

GEORGE. Come on—I'll go with you.

LENNIE. George?

GEORGE. What you want?

LENNIE. Can I still tend the rabbits, George?
(*They exeunt together, side by side, through the door of the bunkhouse.*)

SCENE II

Ten o'clock Saturday evening.

The room of the stable buck, a lean-to off the barn. There is a plank door up stage center; a small square window center right. On one side of the door a leather working bench with tools racked behind it, and on the other racks with broken and partly mended harnesses, collars, hames, traces, etc. At the left upstage CROOKS' *bunk. Over it two shelves. On one a great number of medicines in cans and bottles. And on the other a number of tattered books and a big alarm clock. In the corner right upstage a single-barreled shotgun and on the floor beside it a pair of rubber boots. A large pair of gold spectacles hangs on a nail over* CROOKS' *bunk.*
The entrance leads into the barn proper. From that direction and during the whole scene come the sounds of horses eating, stamping, jingling their halter chains and now and then whinnying.
Two empty nail kegs are in the room to be used as seats. Single unshaded small-candle-power carbon light hanging from its own cord.
As the curtain rises, we see CROOKS *sitting on his bunk rubbing his back with liniment. He reaches up under his shirt to do this. His face is lined with pain. As he rubs he flexes his muscles and shivers a little.*
LENNIE *appears in the open doorway, nearly filling the opening. Then* CROOKS, *sensing his presence, raises his eyes, stiffens and scowls.*
LENNIE *smiles in an attempt to make friends.*

CROOKS (*sharply*). You got no right to come in my room. This here's my room. Nobody got any right in here but me.

LENNIE (*fawning*). I ain't doin' nothing. Just come in the barn to look at my pup, and I seen your light.

CROOKS. Well, I got a right to have a light. You go on and get out of my room. I ain't wanted in the bunkhouse and you ain't wanted in my room.

LENNIE (*ingenuously*). Why ain't you wanted?

CROOKS (*furiously*). 'Cause I'm black. They play cards in there. But I can't play because I'm black. They say I stink. Well, I tell you all of you stink to me.

LENNIE (*helplessly*). Everybody went into town. Slim and George and everybody. George says I got to stay here and not get into no trouble. I seen your light.

CROOKS. Well, what do you want?

LENNIE. Nothing . . . I seen your light. I thought I could jus' come in and set.

CROOKS (*stares at* LENNIE *for a moment, takes down his spectacles and adjusts them over his ears; says in a complaining tone*). I don't know what you're doin' in the barn anyway. You ain't no skinner. There's no call for a bucker to come into the barn at all. You've got nothing to do with the horses and mules.

LENNIE (*patiently*). The pup. I come to see my pup.

CROOKS. Well, God damn it, go and see your pup then. Don't go no place where you ain't wanted.

LENNIE (*advances a step into the room, remembers and backs to the door again*). I looked at him a little. Slim says I ain't to pet him very much.

CROOKS (*the anger gradually going out of his voice*). Well, you been taking him out of the nest all the time. I wonder the ole lady don't move him some place else.

LENNIE (*moving into the room*). Oh, she don't care. She lets me.

CROOKS (*scowls and then gives up*). Come on in and set awhile. Long as you won't get out and leave me alone, you might as well set down. (*A little more friendly*) All the boys gone into town, huh?

LENNIE. All but old Candy. He jus' sets in the bunkhouse sharpening his pencils. And sharpening and figurin'.

CROOKS (*adjusting his glasses*). Figurin'? What's Candy figurin' about?

LENNIE. 'Bout the land. 'Bout the little place.

CROOKS. You're nuts. You're crazy as a wedge. What land you talkin' about?

LENNIE. The land we're goin' ta get. And a little house and pigeons.

CROOKS. Just nuts. I don't blame the guy you're traveling with for keeping you out of sight.

LENNIE (*quietly*). It ain't no lie. We're gonna do it. Gonna get a little place and live on the fat of the land.

CROOKS (*settling himself comfortably on his bunk*). Set down. Set down on that nail keg.

LENNIE (*hunches over on the little barrel*). You think it's a lie. But it ain't no lie. Ever' word's the truth. You can ask George.

CROOKS (*puts his dark chin on his palm*). You travel round with George, don't you?

LENNIE (*proudly*). Sure, me and him goes ever' place together.

CROOKS (*after a pause, quietly*). Sometimes he talks and you don't know what the hell he's talkin' about. Ain't that so? (*Leans forward.*) Ain't that so?

LENNIE. Yeah. Sometimes.

CROOKS. Just talks on. And you don't know what the hell it's all about.

LENNIE. How long you think it'll be before them pups will be old enough to pet?

CROOKS (*laughs again*). A guy can talk to you and be sure you won't go blabbin'. A couple of weeks and them pups will be all right. (*Musing*) George knows what he's about. Just talks and you don't understand nothing. (*Mood gradually changes to excitement.*) Well, this is just a nigger talkin' and a busted-back nigger. It don't mean nothing, see. You couldn't remember it anyway. I seen it over and over—a guy talking to another guy and it don't make no difference if he don't hear or understand. The thing is they're talkin'. (*He pounds his knee with his hand.*) George can tell you screwy things and it don't matter. It's just the talkin'. It's just bein' with another guy, that's all. (*His voice becomes soft and malicious.*) S'pose George don't come back no more? S'pose he took a powder and just ain't comin' back. What you do then?

LENNIE (*trying to follow* CROOKS). What? What?

CROOKS. I said s'pose George went into town tonight and you never heard of him more. (*Presses forward.*) Just s'pose that.

LENNIE (*sharply*). He won't do it. George wouldn't do nothing like that. I been with George a long time. He'll come back tonight. . . . (*Doubt creeps into his voice.*) Don't you think he will?

CROOKS (*delighted with his torture*). Nobody can tell what a guy will do. Let's say he wants to come back and can't. S'pose he gets killed or hurt so he can't come back.

LENNIE (*in terrible apprehension*). I don't know. Say, what you doin' anyway? It ain't true. George ain't got hurt.

CROOKS (*cruelly*). Want me to tell you what'll happen? They'll take you to the bobby hatch. They'll tie you up with a collar like a dog. Then you'll be jus' like me. Livin' in a kennel.

LENNIE (*furious, walks over towards* CROOKS). Who hurt George?

CROOKS (*recoiling from him with fright*). I was jus' supposin'. George ain't hurt. He's all right. He'll be back all right.

LENNIE (*standing over him*). What you supposin' for? Ain't nobody goin' to s'pose any hurt to George.

CROOKS (*trying to calm him*). Now set down. George ain't hurt. Go on now, set down.

LENNIE (*growling*). Ain't nobody gonna talk no hurt to George.

CROOKS (*very gently*). Maybe you can see now. You got George. You know he's comin' back. S'pose you didn't have nobody. S'pose you couldn't go in the bunkhouse and play rummy, 'cause you was black. How would you like that? S'pose you had to set out here and read books. Sure, you could play horseshoes until it got dark, but then you got to read books. Books ain't no good. A guy needs somebody . . . to be near him. (*His tone whines.*) A guy goes nuts if he ain't got nobody. Don't make no difference who it is as long as he's with you. I tell you a guy gets too lonely, he gets sick.

LENNIE (*reassuring himself*). George gonna come back. Maybe George come back already. Maybe I better go see.

CROOKS (*more gently*). I didn't mean to scare you. He'll come back. I was talkin' about myself.

LENNIE (*miserably*). George won't go away and leave me. I know George won't do that.

CROOKS (*continuing dreamily*). I remember when I was a little kid on my ole man's chicken ranch. Had two brothers. They was always near me, always there. Used to sleep right in the same room. Right in the same bed, all three. Had a strawberry patch. Had an alfalfa patch. Used to turn the chickens out in the alfalfa on a sunny morning. Me and my brothers would set on the fence and watch 'em—white chickens they was.

LENNIE (*interested*). George says we're gonna have alfalfa.

CROOKS. You're nuts.

LENNIE. We are too gonna get it. You ask George.

CROOKS (*scornfully*). You're nuts. I seen hundreds of men come by on the road and on the ranches, bindles on their back and that same damn thing in their head. Hundreds of 'em. They come and they quit and they go on. And every damn one of 'em is got a little piece of land in his head. And never a goddamn one of 'em gets it. Jus' like heaven. Everybody wants a little piece of land. Nobody never gets to heaven. And nobody gets no land.

LENNIE. We are too.

CROOKS. It's jest in your head. Guys all the time talkin' about it, but it's jest in your head. (*The horses move restlessly. One of them whinnies.*) I guess somebody's out there. Maybe Slim. (*Pulls himself painfully upright and moves toward the door. Calls*) That you, Slim?

CANDY (*from outside*). Slim went in town. Say, you seen Lennie?

CROOKS. You mean the big guy?

CANDY. Yes. Seen him around any place?

CROOKS (*goes back to his bunk and sits down, says shortly*). He's in here.

CANDY (*stands in the doorway, scratching his wrist. Makes no attempt to enter*). Look, Lennie, I been figuring something out. About the place.

CROOKS (*irritably*). You can come in if you want.

CANDY (*embarrassed*). I don't know. Course if you want me to.

CROOKS. Oh, come on in. Everybody's comin' in. You might just as well. Gettin' to be a goddamn race track. (*He tries to conceal his pleasure.*)

CANDY (*still embarrassed*). You've got a nice cozy little place in here. Must be nice to have a room to yourself this way.

CROOKS. Sure. And a manure pile under the window. All to myself. It's swell.

LENNIE (*breaking in*). You said about the place.

CANDY. You know, I been here a long time. An' Crooks been here a long time. This is the first time I ever been in his room.

CROOKS (*darkly*). Guys don't come in a colored man's room. Nobody been here but Slim.

LENNIE (*insistently*). The place. You said about the place.

CANDY. Yeah. I got it all figured out. We can make some real money on them rabbits if we go about it right.

LENNIE. But I get to tend 'em. George says I get to tend 'em. He promised.

CROOKS (*brutally*). You guys is just kiddin' yourselves. You'll talk about it a hell of a lot, but you won't get no land. You'll be a swamper here until they take you out in a box. Hell, I seen too many guys.

CANDY (*angrily*). We're gonna do it. George says we are. We got the money right now.

CROOKS. Yeah. And where is George now? In town in a whorehouse. That's where your money's goin'. I tell you I seen it happen too many times.

CANDY. George ain't got the money in town. The money's in the bank. Me and Lennie and George. We gonna have a room to ourselves. We gonna have a dog and chickens. We gonna have green corn and maybe a cow.

CROOKS (*impressed*). You say you got the money?

CANDY. We got most of it. Just a little bit more to get. Have it all in one month. George's got the land all picked out too.

CROOKS (*exploring his spine with his hands*). I've never seen a guy really do it. I seen guys nearly crazy with loneliness for land, but every time a whorehouse or a blackjack game took it away from him. (*Hesitates and then speaks timidly.*) If you guys would want a hand to work for nothin'—just his keep, why I'd come and lend a hand. I ain't so crippled I can't work like a son-of-a-bitch if I wanted to.

GEORGE (*strolls through the door, hands in pockets, leans against the wall, speaks in a half-satiric, rather gentle voice*). You couldn't go to bed like I told you, could you, Lennie? Hell, no—you got to get out in society an' flap your mouth. Holdin' a convention out here.

LENNIE (*defending himself*). You was gone. There wasn't nobody in the bunkhouse. I ain't done no bad things, George.

GEORGE (*still casually*). Only time I get any peace is when you're asleep. If you ever get walkin' in your sleep I'll chop off your head like a chicken. (*Chops with his hand.*)

CROOKS (*coming to* LENNIE's *defense*). We was jus' settin' here talkin'. Ain't no harm in that.

GEORGE. Yeah. I heard you. (*A weariness has settled on him.*) Got to be here ever' minute, I guess. Got to

watch ya. (*To* CROOKS) It ain't nothing against you, Crooks. We just wasn't gonna tell nobody.

CANDY (*tries to change subject*). Didn't you have no fun in town?

GEORGE. Oh! I set in a chair and Susy was crackin' jokes an' the guys was startin' to raise a little puny hell. Christ Almighty—I never been this way before. I'm jus' gonna set out a dime and a nickel for a shot an' I think what a hell of a lot of bulk carrot seed you can get for fifteen cents.

CANDY. Not in them damn little envelopes—but bulk seed—you sure can.

GEORGE. So purty soon I come back. I can't think of nothing else. Them guys slingin' money around got me jumpy.

CANDY. Guy got to have *some* fun. I was to a parlor house in Bakersfield once. God Almighty, what a place. Went upstairs on a red carpet. They was big pitchers on the wall. We set in big sof' chairs. They was cigarettes on the table—an' they was *free*. Purty soon a Jap come in with drinks on a tray an' them *drinks* was free. Take all you want. (*In a reverie*) Purty soon the girls come in an' they was jus' as polite an' nice an' quiet an' purty. Didn't seem like hookers. Made ya kinda scared to ask 'em. . . . That was a long time ago.

GEORGE. Yeah? An' what'd them sof' chairs set you back?

CANDY. Fifteen bucks.

GEORGE (*scornfully*). So ya got a cigarette an' a whiskey an' a look at a purty dress an' it cost ya twelve and a half bucks extra. You shot a week's pay to walk on that red carpet.

CANDY (*still entranced with his memory*). A week's pay? Sure. But I worked weeks all my life. I can't remember none of them weeks. But . . . that was nearly twenty years ago. And I can remember that. Girl I went with was named Arline. Had on a pink silk dress.

GEORGE (*turns suddenly and looks out the door into the dark barn, speaks savagely*). I s'pose ya lookin' for Curley? (CURLEY'S WIFE *appears in the door.*) Well, Curley ain't here.

CURLEY'S WIFE (*determined now*). I know Curley ain't here. I wanted to ast Crooks somepin'. I didn't know you guys was here.

CANDY. Didn't George tell you before—we don't want nothing to do with you. You know damn well Curley ain't here.

CURLEY'S WIFE. I know where Curley went. Got his arm in a sling an' he went anyhow. I tell ya I come out to ast Crooks somepin'.

CROOKS (*apprehensively*). Maybe you better go along to your own house. You hadn't ought to come near a colored man's room. I don't want no trouble. You don't want to ask me nothing.

CANDY (*rubbing his wrist stump*). You got a husband. You got no call to come foolin' around with other guys, causin' trouble.

CURLEY'S WIFE (*suddenly angry*). I try to be nice an' polite to you lousy bindle bums—but you're too good. I tell ya I could of went with shows. An'—an' a guy wanted to put me in pitchers right in Hollywood. (*Looks about to see how she is impressing them. Their eyes are hard.*) I come out here to ast somebody somepin' an'——

CANDY (*stands up suddenly and knocks his nail keg over backward, speaks angrily*). I had enough. You ain't wanted here. We tole you, you ain't. Callin' us bindle stiffs. You got floozy idears what

us guys amounts to. You ain't got sense enough to see us guys ain't bindle stiffs. S'pose you could get us *canned* —s'pose you *could*. You think we'd hit the highway an' look for another two-bit job. You don't know we got our own ranch to go to an' our own house an' fruit trees. An' we got friends. That's what we got. Maybe they was a time when we didn't have nothing, but that ain't so no more.

CURLEY'S WIFE. You damn ol' goat. If you had two bits, you'd be in Soledad gettin' a drink an' suckin' the bottom of the glass.

GEORGE. Maybe she could ask Crooks what she come to ask an' then get the hell home. I don't think she come to ask nothing.

CURLEY'S WIFE. What happened to Curley's hand? (CROOKS *laughs.* GEORGE *tries to shut him up.*) So it wasn't no machine. Curley didn't act like he was tellin' the truth. Come on, Crooks—what happened?

CROOKS. I wasn't there. I didn't see it.

CURLEY'S WIFE (*eagerly*). What happened? I won't let on to Curley. He says he caught his han' in a gear. (CROOKS *is silent.*) Who done it?

GEORGE. Didn't nobody do it.

CURLEY'S WIFE (*turns slowly to* GEORGE). So *you* done it. Well, he had it comin'.

GEORGE. I didn't have no fuss with Curley.

CURLEY'S WIFE (*steps near him, smiling*). Maybe now you ain't scared of him no more. Maybe you'll talk to me sometimes now. Ever'body was scared of him.

GEORGE (*speaks rather kindly*). Look! I didn't sock Curley. If he had trouble, it ain't none of our affair. Ask Curley about it. Now listen. I'm gonna try to tell ya. We tole you to get the hell out and it don't do no good. So I'm gonna tell you another way. Us guys got somepin' we're gonna do. If you stick around you'll gum up the works. It ain't your fault. If a guy steps on a round pebble an' falls down an' breaks his neck, it ain't the pebble's fault, but the guy wouldn't of did it if the pebble wasn't there.

CURLEY'S WIFE (*puzzled*). What you talkin' about pebbles? If you didn't sock Curley, who did? (*She looks at the others, then steps quickly over to* LENNIE.) Where'd you get them bruises on your face?

GEORGE. I tell you he got his hand caught in a machine.

LENNIE (*looks anxiously at* GEORGE, *speaks miserably*). He caught his han' in a machine.

GEORGE. So now get out of here.

CURLEY'S WIFE (*goes close to* LENNIE, *speaks softly and there is a note of affection in her voice*). So . . . it was

you. Well . . . maybe you're dumb like they say . . . an' maybe . . . you're the only guy on the ranch with guts. (*She puts her hand on* LENNIE's *shoulder. He looks up in her face and a smile grows on his face. She strokes his shoulder.*) You're a nice fella.

GEORGE (*suddenly leaps at her ferociously, grabs her shoulder and whirls her around*). Listen . . . you! I tried to give you a break. Don't you walk into nothing! We ain't gonna let you mess up what we're gonna do. You let this guy alone an' get the hell out of here.

CURLEY'S WIFE (*defiant but slightly frightened*). You ain't tellin' me what to do. (THE BOSS *appears in the door, stands legs spread, thumbs hooked over his belt.*) I got a right to talk to anybody I want to.

GEORGE. Why, you—(GEORGE, *furious, steps close—his hand is raised to strike her. She cowers a little.* GEORGE *stiffens, seeing* BOSS, *frozen in position. The others see* BOSS *too. Girl retreats slowly.* GEORGE's *hand drops slowly to his side—he takes two slow backward steps. Hold the scene for a moment.*)

ACT THREE

SCENE I

Mid-afternoon Sunday.
One end of a great barn. Backstage the hay slopes up sharply against the wall. High in the upstage wall is a large hay window. On each side are seen the hay racks, behind which are the stalls with the horses in them. Throughout this scene the horses can be heard in their stalls, rattling their halter chains and chewing at the hay.
The entrance is downstage right.
The boards of the barn are not close together. Streaks of afternoon sun come between the boards, made visible by dust in the air. From outside comes the clang of horseshoes on the playing peg, shouts of men encouraging or jeering. In the barn there is a feeling of quiet and humming and lazy warmth. Curtain rises on LENNIE *sitting in the hay, looking down at a little dead puppy in front of him. He puts out his big hand and strokes it clear from one end to the other.*

LENNIE (*softly*). Why do you got to get killed? You ain't so little as mice. I didn't bounce you hard. (*Bends the pup's head up and looks in its face.*) Now maybe George ain't gonna let me tend no rabbits if he finds out you got killed. (*He scoops a little hollow and lays the puppy in it out of sight and covers it over with hay. He stares at the mound he has made.*) This ain't no bad thing like I got to hide in the brush. I'll tell George I found it dead. (*He unburies the pup and inspects it. Twists its ears and works his fingers in its fur. (Sorrowfully*) But he'll know. George always knows. He'll say: "You done it. Don't try to put nothin' over on me." And he'll say: "Now just for that you don't get to tend no—you-know-whats." (*His anger rises. Addresses the pup.*) God damn you. Why do you got to get killed? You ain't so little as mice. (*Picks up the pup and hurls it from him and turns his back on it. He sits bent over his knees moaning to himself.*) Now he won't let me. . . . Now he won't let me. (*Outside there is a clang of horseshoes on the iron stake and a little chorus of cries.* LENNIE *gets up and brings the pup back and lays it in the hay and sits down. He mourns.*) You wasn't big enough. They tole me and tole me you wasn't. I didn't know you'd get killed so easy. Maybe George won't care. This here goddamn little son-of-a-bitch wasn't nothin' to George.

CANDY (*voice from behind the stalls*). Lennie, where you at? (LENNIE *frantically buries the pup under the hay.* CANDY *enters excitedly.*) Thought I'd find ya here. Say . . . I been talkin' to Slim. It's okay. We ain't gonna get the can. Slim been talkin' to the boss. Slim tol' the boss you guys is good buckers. The boss got to move that grain. 'Member what hell the boss give us las' night? He tol' Slim he got his eye on you an' George. But you ain't gonna get the can. Oh! an' say. The boss give Curley's wife hell, too. Tole her never to go near the men no more. Give her worse hell than you an' George. (*For the first time notices* LENNIE's *dejection.*) Ain't you glad?

LENNIE. Sure.

CANDY. You ain't sick?

LENNIE. Uh-uh!

CANDY. I got to go tell George. See you later. (*Exits.*)

(LENNIE, *alone, uncovers the pup. Lies down in the hay and sinks deep in it. Puts the pup on his arm and strokes it.* CURLEY'S WIFE *enters secretly. A little mound of hay conceals* LENNIE *from her. In her hand she carries a small suitcase, very cheap. She crosses the barn and buries the case in the hay. Stands up and looks to see whether it can be seen.* LENNIE *watching her quietly tries to cover the pup with hay. She sees the movement.*)

CURLEY'S WIFE. What—what you doin' here?

LENNIE (*sullenly*). Jus' settin' here.

CURLEY'S WIFE. You seen what I done.

LENNIE. Yeah! you brang a valise.

CURLE'S WIFE (*comes near to him*). You won't tell—will you?

LENNIE (*still sullen*). I ain't gonna have nothing to do with you. George tole me. I ain't to talk to you or nothing. (*Covers the pup a little more.*)

CURLEY'S WIFE. George give you all your orders?

LENNIE. Not talk nor nothing.

CURLEY'S WIFE. You won't tell about that suitcase? I ain't gonna stay here no more. Tonight I'm gonna get out. Come here an' get my stuff an' get out. I ain't gonna be run over no more. I'm gonna go in pitchers. (*Sees* LENNIE'S *hand stroking the pup under the hay.*) What you got there?

LENNIE. Nuthing. I ain't gonna talk to you. George says I ain't.

CURLEY'S WIFE. Listen: The guys got a horseshoe tenement out there. It's only four o'clock. Them guys ain't gonna leave that tenement. They got

money bet. You don't need to be scared to talk to me.

LENNIE (*weakening a little*). I ain't supposed to.

CURLEY'S WIFE (*watching his buried hand*). What you got under there?

LENNIE (*his woe comes back to him*). Jus' my pup. Jus' my little ol' pup. (*Sweeps the hay aside.*)

CURLEY'S WIFE. Why! He's dead.

LENNIE (*explaining sadly*). He was so little. I was jus' playin' with him—an' he made like he's gonna bite me—an' I made like I'm gonna smack him—an'—I done it. An' then he was dead.

CURLEY'S WIFE (*consolingly*). Don't you worry none. He was just a mutt. The whole country is full of mutts.

LENNIE. It ain't that so much. George gonna be mad. Maybe he won't let me —what he said I could tend.

CURLEY'S WIFE (*sits down in the hay beside him, speaks soothingly*). Don't you worry. Them guys got money bet on that horseshoe tenement. They ain't gonna leave it. And tomorra I'll be gone. I ain't gonna let them run over me.

(*In the following scene it is apparent that neither is listening to the other and yet as it goes on, as a happy tone increases, it can be seen that they are growing closer together.*)

LENNIE. We gonna have a little place an' raspberry bushes.

CURLEY'S WIFE. I ain't meant to live like this. I come from Salinas. Well, a show come through an' I talked to a guy that was in it. He says I could go with the show. My ol' lady wouldn't let me, 'cause I was on'y fifteen. I wouldn't be no place like this if I had went with that show, you bet.

LENNIE. Gonna take a sack an' fill it up with alfalfa an'—

CURLEY'S WIFE (*hurrying on*). 'Nother time I met a guy an' he was in pitchers. Went out to the Riverside Dance Palace with him. He said he was gonna put me in pitchers. Says I was a natural. Soon's he got back to Hollywood he was gonna write me about it. (*Looks impressively at* LENNIE.) I never got that letter. I think my ol' lady stole it. Well, I wasn't gonna stay no place where they stole your letters. So I married Curley. Met *him* out to the Riverside Dance Palace too.

LENNIE. I hope George ain't gonna be mad about this pup.

CURLEY'S WIFE. I ain't tol' this to nobody before. Maybe I oughtn' to. I don't like Curley. He ain't a nice fella. I might a stayed with him but last night him an' his ol' man both lit into me. I don't have to stay here. (*Moves closer and speaks confidentially.*) Don't tell nobody till I get clear away. I'll go in the night an' thumb a ride to Hollywood.

LENNIE. We gonna get out a here purty soon. This ain't no nice place.

CURLEY'S WIFE (*ecstatically*). Gonna get in the movies an' have nice clothes —all them nice clothes like they wear. An' I'll set in them big hotels and they'll take pitchers of me. When they have them openings I'll go an' talk in the radio . . . an' it won't cost me nothing 'cause I'm in the pitcher. (*Puts her hand on* LENNIE's *arm for a moment.*) All them nice clothes like they wear . . . because this guy says I'm a natural.

LENNIE. We gonna go way . . . far away from here.

CURLEY'S WIFE. 'Course, when I run away from Curley, my ol' lady won't never speak to me no more. She'll think I ain't decent. That's what she'll say.

(*Defiantly*) Well, we really ain't decent, no matter how much my ol' lady tries to hide it. My ol' man was a drunk. They put him away. There! Now I told.

LENNIE. George an' me was to the Sacramento Fair. One time I fell in the river an' George pulled me out an' saved me, an' then we went to the Fair. They got all kinds of stuff there. We seen long-hair rabbits.

CURLEY'S WIFE. My ol' man was a sign-painter when he worked. He used to get drunk an' paint crazy pictures an' waste paint. One night when I was a little kid, him an' my ol' lady had an awful fight. They was always fightin'. In the middle of the night he come into my room, and he says, "I can't stand this no more. Let's you an' me go away." I guess he was drunk. (*Her voice takes on a curious wondering tenderness.*) I remember in the night —walkin' down the road, and the trees was black. I was pretty sleepy. He picked me up, an' he carried me on his back. He says, "We gonna live together because you're my own little girl, an' not no stranger. No arguin' and fightin'," he says, "because you're my little daughter." (*Her voice becomes soft.*) He says, "Why you'll bake little cakes for me, an' I'll paint pretty pitchers all over the wall." (*Sadly*) In the morning they caught us . . . an' they put him away. (*Pause.*) I wish we'd a' went.

LENNIE. Maybe if I took this here pup an' throwed him away George wouldn't never know.

CURLEY'S WIFE. They locked him up for a drunk, and in a little while he died.

LENNIE. Then maybe I could tend the rabbits without no trouble.

CURLEY'S WIFE. Don't you think of nothing but rabbits? (*Sound of horse-*

shoe on metal.) Somebody made a ringer.

LENNIE (*patiently*). We gonna have a house and a garden, an' a place for alfalfa. And I take a sack and get it all full of alfalfa, and then I take it to the rabbits.

CURLEY'S WIFE. What makes you so nuts about rabbits?

LENNIE (*moves close to her*). I like to pet nice things. Once at a fair I seen some of them long-hair rabbits. And they was nice, you bet. (*Despairingly*) I'd even pet mice, but not when I could get nothin' better.

CURLEY'S WIFE (*giggles*). I think you're nuts.

LENNIE (*earnestly*). No, I ain't. George says I ain't. I like to pet nice things with my fingers. Soft things.

CURLEY'S WIFE. Well, who don't? Everybody likes that. I like to feel silk and velvet. You like to feel velvet?

LENNIE (*chuckling with pleasure*). You bet, by God. And I had some too. A lady give me some. And that lady was —my Aunt Clara. She give it right to me. . . . (*Measuring with his hands*) 'Bout this big a piece. I wisht I had that velvet right now. (*He frowns.*) I lost it. I ain't seen it for a long time.

CURLEY'S WIFE (*laughing*). You're nuts. But you're a kinda nice fella. Jus' like a big baby. A person can see kinda what you mean. When I'm doin' my hair sometimes I jus' set there and stroke it, because it's so soft. (*Runs her fingers over the top of her head.*) Some people got kinda coarse hair. You take Curley, his hair's just like wire. But mine is soft and fine. Here, feel. Right here. (*Takes* LENNIE'S *hand and puts it on her head.*) Feel there and see how soft it is. (LENNIE'S *fingers fall to stroking her hair.*) Don't you muss it up.

LENNIE. Oh, that's nice. (*Strokes harder.*) Oh, that's nice.

CURLEY'S WIFE. Look out now, you'll muss it. (*Angrily*) You stop it now, you'll mess it all up. (*She jerks her head sideways and* LENNIE'S *fingers close on her hair and hang on. In a panic*) Let go. (*She screams.*) You let go. (*She screams again. His other hand closes over her mouth and nose.*)

LENNIE (*begging*). Oh, please don't do that. George'll be mad. (*She struggles violently to be free. A soft screaming comes from under* LENNIE'S *hand. Crying with fright*) Oh, please don't do none of that. George gonna say I done a bad thing. (*He raises his hand from her mouth and a hoarse cry escapes. Angrily*) Now don't. I don't want you to yell. You gonna get me in trouble just like George says you will. Now don't you do that. (*She struggles more.*) Don't you go yellin'. (*He shakes her violently. Her neck snaps sideways and she lies still. Looks down at her and cautiously removes his hand from over her mouth.*) I don't wanta hurt you. But George will be mad if you yell. (*When she doesn't answer he bends closely over her. He lifts her arm and lets it drop. For a moment he seems bewildered.*) I done a bad thing. I done another bad thing. (*He paws up the hay until it partly covers her. The sound of the horseshoe game comes from the outside. And for the first time* LENNIE *seems conscious of it. He crouches down and listens.*) Oh, I done a real bad thing. I shouldn't a did that. George will be mad. And . . . he said . . . and hide in the brush till he comes. . . . He's gonna be mad . . . in the brush till he comes. That's what he said (*He picks up the puppy from beside the girl.*) I'll throw him away. It's bad enough like it is.
(*He puts the pup under his coat, creeps to the barn wall and peers out between the cracks and then he creeps around to the end of the manger and disappears. The stage is vacant except for* CURLEY'S WIFE. *She lies in the hay*

half covered up and she looks very young and peaceful. Her rouged cheeks and red lips make her seem alive and sleeping lightly. For a moment the stage is absolutely silent. Then the horses stamp on the other side of the feeding rack. The halter chains clink and from outside men's voices come loud and clear.)

CANDY (offstage). Lennie! Oh, Lennie, you in there? (He enters.) I been fig- urin' some more, Lennie. Tell you what we can do. (Sees CURLEY'S WIFE and stops. Rubs his white whiskers.) I didn't know you was here. You was tol' not to be here. (He steps near her.) You oughtn't to sleep out here. (He is right beside her and looks down.) Oh, Jesus Christ! (Goes to the door and calls softly) George, George! Come here . . . George!

GEORGE (enters). What do you want?

CANDY (points at CURLEY'S WIFE). Look.

GEORGE. What's the matter with her? (Steps up beside her.) Oh, Jesus Christ! (Kneels beside her and feels her heart and her wrist. Finally stands up slowly and stiffly. From this time on through the rest of the scene GEORGE is wooden.)

CANDY. What done it?

GEORGE (coldly). Ain't you got any idea? (CANDY looks away.) I should of knew. I guess way back in my head I did.

CANDY. What we gonna do now, George? What we gonna do now?

GEORGE (answering slowly and dully). Guess . . . we gotta . . . tell . . . the guys. Guess we got to catch him and lock him up. We can't let him get away. Why, the poor bastard would starve. (He tries to reassure himself.) Maybe they'll lock him up and be nice to him.

CANDY (excitedly). You know better'n that, George. You know Curley's gonna want to get him lynched. You know how Curley is.

GEORGE. Yeah. . . . Yeah . . . that's right. I know Curley. And the other guys too (He looks back at CURLEY'S WIFE.)

CANDY (pleadingly). You and me can get that little place can't we, George? You and me can go there and live nice, can't we? Can't we? (CANDY drops his head and looks down at the hay to in- dicate that he knows.)

GEORGE (shakes his head slowly). It was somethin' me and him had. (Softly) I think I knowed it from the very first. I think I knowed we'd never do her. He used to like to hear about it so much. I got fooled to thinkin' maybe we would. (CANDY starts to speak but doesn't.)

GEORGE (as though repeating a lesson). I'll work my month and then I'll take my fifty bucks. I'll stay all night in some lousy cat-house or I'll set in a pool room until everybody goes home. An' then—I'll come back an' work an- other month. And then I'll have fifty bucks more.

CANDY. He's such a nice fellow. I didn't think he'd a done nothing like this.

GEORGE (gets a grip on himself and straightens his shoulders). Now listen. We gotta tell the guys. I guess they've gotta bring him in. They ain't no way out. Maybe they won't hurt him. I ain't gonna let 'em hurt Lennie. (Sharply) Now you listen. The guys might think I was in on it. I'm gonna go in the bunkhouse. Then in a minute you come out and yell like you just seen her. Will you do that? So the guy's won't think I was in on it?

CANDY. Sure, George. Sure, I'll do that.

GEORGE. Okay. Give me a couple of minutes then. And then you yell your head off. I'm goin' now. (GEORGE *exits.*)

CANDY (*watches him go, looks helplessly back at* CURLEY'S WIFE; *his next words are in sorrow and in anger*). You goddam tramp. You done it, didn't you? Everybody knowed you'd mess things up. You just wasn't no good. (*His voice shakes.*) I could of hoed in the garden and washed dishes for them guys. . . . (*Pauses for a moment and then goes into a sing-song repeating the old words.*) If there was a circus or a baseball game . . . we would o' went to her . . . just said to hell with work and went to her. And they'd been a pig and chickens . . . and in the winter a little fat stove. An' us jus' settin' there . . . settin' there. . . . (*His eyes blind with tears and he goes weakly to the entrance of the barn. Tries for a moment to break a shout out of his throat before he succeeds.*) Hey, you guys! Come here! Come here!
(*Outside the noise of the horseshoe game stops. The sound of discussion and then the voices come closer:* "What's the matter?" . . . "Who's that?" . . . It's Candy." . . . "Something must have happened."
Enter SLIM and CARLSON, young WHIT and CURLEY, CROOKS in the back, keeping out of attention range. And last of all GEORGE. GEORGE has put on his blue denim coat and buttoned it. His black hat is pulled down low over his eyes. "What's the matter?" . . . What's happened?"
A gesture from CANDY.
The men stare at CURLEY'S WIFE. SLIM goes over to her, feels her wrist and touches her cheek with his fingers. His hand goes under her slightly twisted neck.
CURLEY comes near. For a moment he seems shocked. Looks around helplessly and suddenly he comes to life.*)

CURLEY. I know who done it. That big son-of-a-bitch done it. I know he done it. Why, everybody else was out there playing horseshoes. (*Working himself into a fury.*) I'm gonna get him. I'm gonna get my shotgun. Why, I'll kill the big son-of-a-bitch myself. I'll shoot him in the guts. Come on, you guys. (*He runs out of the barn.*)

CARLSON. I'll go get my Luger. (*He runs out too.*)

SLIM (*quietly to* GEORGE). I guess Lennie done it all right. Her neck's busted. Lennie could o' did that. (GEORGE *nods slowly. Half-questioning*) Maybe like that time in Weed you was tellin' me about. (GEORGE *nods. Gently*) Well. I guess we got to get him. Where you think he might o' went?

GEORGE (*struggling to get words out*). I don't know.

SLIM. I guess we gotta get him.

GEORGE (*stepping close and speaking passionately*). Couldn't we maybe bring him in and lock him up? He's nuts, Slim, he never done this to be mean.

SLIM. If we could only keep Curley in. But Curley wants to shoot him. (*He thinks.*) And s'pose they lock him up, George, and strap him down and put him in a cage, that ain't no good.

GEORGE. I know. I know.

SLIM. I think there's only one way to get him out of it.

GEORGE. I know.

CARLSON (*enters running*). The bastard stole my Luger. It ain't in my bag.

CURLEY (*enters carrying a shotgun in his good hand. Officiously*). All right, you boys. The nigger's got a shotgun. You take it, Carlson.

WHIT. Only cover around here is down by the river. He might have went there.

CURLEY. Don't give him no chance. Shoot for his guts, that'll double him over.

WHIT. I ain't got a gun.

CURLEY. Go in and tell my old man. Get a gun from him. Let's go now. (*Turns suspiciously on* GEORGE.) You're comin' with us, fella!

GEORGE. Yeah. I'll come. But listen, Curley, the poor bastard's nuts. Don't shoot him, he didn't know what he was doin'.

CURLEY. Don't shoot him! He's got Carlson's Luger, ain't he?

GEORGE (*weakly*). Maybe Carlson lost his gun.

CARLSON. I seen it this morning. It's been took.

SLIM (*looking down at* CURLEY'S WIFE). Curley, maybe you better stay here with your wife.
(*The light is fading into evening.* CURLEY *hesitates. Seems almost to weaken, then he hardens again.*)

CURLEY. Naw, I'm gonna shoot the guts out of that big bastard, I'm gonna get him myself. Come on, you guys.

SLIM (*to* CANDY). You stay here then, Candy. The rest of us better get goin'. (*They walk out,* SLIM *and* GEORGE *last. Exeunt all but* CANDY. *He squats in the hay, watching the face of* CURLEY'S WIFE.)

CANDY. Poor bastard.

SCENE II

Evening.
The river bank again.
Light from the setting sun shines on the low brown hills. Among the trees by the river, the shade is deep with evening feeling.
Sounds: distant barking of dogs and the quiet call of quail.

The curtain rises on an empty stage.
There is a sudden whistle of evening wind that stirs the trees and scuds the leaves on the ground.
The stage is still again. LENNIE *enters as silently as a bear. He is bent over and wary. On stage he looks behind him. Then he takes from under his coat the dead pup, lays it on the ground and, going to the river, lies on his stomach and drinks.*
He returns to the dead pup, sits down beside it.

LENNIE. George gonna give me hell . . . I bet. I . . . won't tell him. I'll bury him. (*Begins to scoop a hole in the sand in front of him. Softly*) But I didn't forget, you bet. I come right here. Hide in the brush an' wait for George. (*Works carefully at his little grave, shaping the hole. At last he picks up the pup and lays it in the hole. Mourning*) He gonna give me hell. He gonna wish he was alone. (*Ad-* justs the puppy in the hole, turning it around to make it fit better. Defiantly*) Well . . . I can go right up in the hills an' find a cave. 'Course I wouldn't never have no ketchup. (*Begins packing sand down carefully about the pup, patting it as he does in beat with his words.*) I'll — go — away — go — away. (*Every word a pat. Fills the grave carefully, smooths the sand over it.*) There now. (*Gathers leaves and scat-*

ters them over the place. Gets up on his knees and cocks his head to inspect the job.) Now. I won't never tell George. (Sinks back to a sitting position.) He'll know. He always knows. (Far off sound of voices approaching. They come closer during the scene. Suddenly there is the clicking warning of a cock-quail and then the drum of the flock's wings. GEORGE enters silently, but hurriedly.)

GEORGE (in a hoarse whisper). Get in the tules—quick.

LENNIE. I ain't done nothing, George. (The voices are very close.)

GEORGE (frantically). Get in the tules —damn you. (Voices are nearly there. GEORGE half pushes LENNIE down among the tules. The tops rustle showing his crawling progress.)

WHIT (offstage). There's George. (Enters.) Better not get so far ahead. You ain't got a gun. (Enter SLIM, CARLSON, BOSS, CURLEY, and three other ranch hands. They are armed with shotguns and rifles.)

CARLSON. He musta come this way. Them prints in the sand was aimed this way.

SLIM (has been regarding GEORGE). Now look. We ain't gonna find him stickin' in a bunch this way. We got to spread out.

CURLEY. Brush is pretty thick here. He might be lying in the brush. (Steps toward the tules. GEORGE moves quickly after him.)

SLIM (seeing the move speaks quickly). Look—(pointing)—up there's the county road an' open fields an' over there's the highway. Le's spread out an' cover the brush.

BOSS. Slim's right. We got to spread.

SLIM. We better drag up to the roads an' then drag back.

CURLEY. 'Member what I said—shoot for his guts.

SLIM. Okay, move out. Me an' George'll go up to the county road. You guys get the highway an' drag back.

BOSS. If we get separated, we'll meet here. Remember this place.

CURLEY. All I care is getting the bastard. (The men move off-stage right, talking. SLIM and GEORGE move slowly up-stage listening to the voices that grow fainter and fainter.)

SLIM (softly to GEORGE). Where is he? (GEORGE looks at him in the eyes for a long moment. Finally trusts him and points with his thumb toward the tules.)

SLIM. You want—I should—go away? (GEORGE nods slowly, looking at the ground. SLIM starts away, comes back, tries to say something, instead puts his hand on GEORGE's shoulder for a second, and then hurries off upstage.)

GEORGE (moves woodenly toward the bank and the tule clump and sits down). Lennie! (The tules shiver again and LENNIE emerges dripping.)

LENNIE. Where's them guys goin'? (Long pause.)

GEORGE. Huntin'.

LENNIE. Whyn't we go with 'em? I like huntin'. (Waits for an answer. GEORGE stares across the river.) Is it 'cause I done a bad thing?

GEORGE. It don't make no difference.

LENNIE. Is that why we can't go huntin' with them guys?

GEORGE (*woodenly*). It don't make no difference. . . . Sit down, Lennie. Right there. (*The light is going now. In the distance there are shouts of men.* GEORGE *turns his head and listens to the shouts.*)

LENNIE. George!

GEORGE. Yeah?

LENNIE. Ain't you gonna give me hell?

GEORGE. Give ya hell?

LENNIE. Sure. . . . Like you always done before. Like—"If I didn' have you I'd take my fifty bucks . . ."

GEORGE (*softly as if in wonder*). Jesus Christ, Lennie, you can't remember nothing that happens. But you remember every word I say!

LENNIE. Well, ain't you gonna say it?

GEORGE (*reciting*). "If I was alone I —could live—so easy. (*His voice is monotonous.*) I could get a job and not have no mess. . . ."

LENNIE. Go on, go on! "And when the end of the month come . . ."

GEORGE. "And when the end of the month come, I could take my fifty bucks and go to—a cat-house. . . ."

LENNIE (*eagerly*). Go on, George, ain't you gonna give me no more hell?

GEORGE. No!

LENNIE. I can go away. I'll go right off in the hills and find a cave if you don't want me.

GEORGE (*speaks as though his lips were stiff*). No, I want you to stay here with me.

LENNIE (*craftily*). Then tell me like you done before.

GEORGE. Tell you what?

LENNIE. 'Bout the other guys and about us!

GEORGE (*recites again*). "Guys like us got no families. They got a little stake and then they blow it in. They ain't got nobody in the world that gives a hoot in hell about 'em!"

LENNIE (*happily*). "But not *us*." Tell about us now.

GEORGE. "But not us."

LENNIE. "Because . . ."

GEORGE. "Because I got you and . . ."

LENNIE (*triumphantly*). "And I got you. We got each other," that's what, that gives a hoot in hell about us. (*A breeze blows up the leaves and then they settle back again. There are the shouts of men again. This time closer.*)

GEORGE (*takes off his hat; shakily*). Take off your hat, Lennie. The air feels fine!

LENNIE (*removes his hat and lays it on the ground in front of him*). Tell how it's gonna be. (*Again the sound of men.* GEORGE *listens to them.*)

GEORGE. Look acrost the river, Lennie, and I'll tell you like you can almost see it. (LENNIE *turns his head and looks across the river.*) "We gonna get a little place . . . (*Reaches in his side pocket and brings out* CARLSON's *Luger. Hand and gun lie on the ground behind* LENNIE's *back. He stares at the back of* LENNIE's *head at the place where spine and skull are joined. Sounds of men's voices talking offstage.*)

LENNIE. Go on! (GEORGE *raises the gun, but his hand shakes and he drops his hand on to the ground.*) Go on! How's it gonna be? "We gonna get a little place. . . ."

GEORGE (*thickly*). "We'll have a cow. And we'll have maybe a pig and chickens—and down the flat we'll have a . . . little piece of alfalfa. . . ."

LENNIE (*shouting*). "For the rabbits!"

GEORGE. "For the rabbits!"

LENNIE. "And I get to tend the rabbits?"

GEORGE. "And you get to tend the rabbits!"

LENNIE (*giggling with happiness*). "And live on the fat o' the land!"

GEORGE. Yes. (LENNIE *turns his head. Quickly*) Look over there, Lennie. Like you can really see it.

LENNIE. Where?

GEORGE. Right acrost that river there. Can't you almost see it?

LENNIE (*moving*). Where, George?

GEORGE. It's over there. You keep lookin', Lennie. Just keep lookin'.

LENNIE. I'm lookin', George. I'm lookin'.

GEORGE. That's right. It's gonna be nice there. Ain't gonna be no trouble, no fights. Nobody ever gonna hurt nobody, or steal from 'em. It's gonna be—nice.

LENNIE. I can see it, George. I can see it! Right over there! I can see it! (GEORGE *fires.* LENNIE *crumples; falls behind the brush. The voices of the men in the distance.*)

The Time of Your Life

BY WILLIAM SAROYAN

CHARACTERS

THE TIME OF YOUR LIFE was produced by Eddie Dowling in conjunction with The Guild Theatre, and directed by Mr. Dowling and the author. It was first performed in New Haven at the Shubert Theatre, Saturday evening, October 7, 1939. From New Haven it moved to the Plymouth Theatre in Boston for a run of two weeks. It opened in New York at the Booth Theatre on Wednesday, October 25.

This is the cast which opened the play:

THE NEWSBOY	*Ross Bagdasarian*
THE DRUNKARD	*John Farrell*
WILLIE	*Will Lee*
JOE	*Eddie Dowling*
NICK	*Charles de Sheim*
TOM	*Edward Andrews*
KITTY DUVAL	*Julie Haydon*
DUDLEY	*Curt Conway*
HARRY	*Gene Kelly*
WESLEY	*Reginald Beane*
LORENE	*Nene Vibber*
BLICK	*Grover Burgess*
ARAB	*Houseley Stevens, Sr.*
MARY L.	*Celeste Holme*
KRUPP	*William Bendix*
McCARTHY	*Tom Tully*
KIT CARSON	*Len Doyle*
NICK'S MA	*Michelette Burani*
SAILOR	*Randolph Wade*
ELSIE	*Cathie Bailey*
A KILLER	*Evelyn Geller*
HER SIDE KICK	*Mary Cheffey*
A SOCIETY LADY	*Eva Leonard Boyne*
A SOCIETY GENTLEMAN	*Ainsworth Arnold*
FIRST COP	*Randolph Wade*
SECOND COP	*John Farrell*

THE PLACE

Nick's Pacific Street Saloon, Restaurant, and Entertainment Palace at the foot of Embarcadero, in San Franciso. A suggestion of room 21 at The New York Hotel, upstairs, around the corner.

THE TIME

Afternoon and night of a day in October, 1939.

The Time of Your Life

ACT ONE

Nick's is an American place: a San Francisco waterfront honky-tonk.
At a table, JOE: *always calm, always quiet, always thinking, always eager, always bored, always superior. His expensive clothes are casually and youthfully worn and give him an almost boyish appearance. He is thinking.*
Behind the bar, NICK: *a big red-headed young Italian-American with an enormous naked woman tattooed in red on the inside of his right arm. He is studying* The Racing Form.
The ARAB, *at his place at the end of the bar. He is a lean old man with a rather ferocious old-country mustache, with the ends twisted up. Between the thumb and forefinger of his left hand is the Mohammedan tattoo indicating that he has been to Mecca. He is sipping a glass of beer.*
It is about eleven-thirty in the morning. SAM *is sweeping out. We see only his back. He disappears into the kitchen. The* SAILOR *at the bar finishes his drink and leaves, moving thoughtfully, as though he were trying very hard to discover how to live.*

The NEWSBOY *comes in.*

NEWSBOY (*cheerfully*). Good-morning, everybody. (*No answer. To* NICK.) Paper, Mister? (NICK *shakes his head, no. The* NEWSBOY *goes to* JOE.) Paper, Mister? (JOE *shakes his head, no. The* NEWSBOY *walks away, counting papers.*)

JOE (*noticing him*). How many you got?

NEWSBOY. Five.
(JOE *gives him a quarter, takes all the papers, glances at the headlines with irritation, throws them away. The* NEWSBOY *watches carefully, then goes.*)

ARAB (*picks up paper, looks at headlines, shakes head as if rejecting everything else a man might say about the world*). No foundation. All the way down the line.
(*The* DRUNK *comes in. Walks to the telephone, looks for a nickel in the chute, sits down at* JOE's *table.* NICK

takes the DRUNK out. The DRUNK returns.)

DRUNK (*champion of the Bill of Rights*). This is a free country, ain't it?
(WILLIE, *the marble-game maniac, explodes through the swinging doors and lifts the forefinger of his right hand comically, indicating one beer. He is a very young man, not more than twenty. He is wearing heavy shoes, a pair of old and dirty corduroys, a light green turtle-neck jersey with a large letter "F" on the chest, an oversize two-button tweed coat, and a green hat, with the brim up.* NICK *sets out a glass of beer for him, he drinks it, straightens up vigorously, saying Aaah, makes a solemn face, gives* NICK *a one-finger salute of adieu, and begins to leave, refreshed and restored in spirit. He walks by the marble game, halts suddenly, turns, studies the contraption, gestures as if to say, Oh, no. Turns to go, stops,*

219

returns to the machine, studies it, takes a handful of small coins out of his pants pocket, lifts a nickel, indicates with a gesture, One game, no more. Puts the nickel in the slot, pushes in the slide, making an interesting noise.)

NICK. You can't beat that machine.

WILLIE. Oh, yeah?

(*The marbles fall, roll and take their place. He pushes down the lever, placing one marble in position. Takes a very deep breath, walks in a small circle, excited at the beginning of great drama. Stands straight and pious before the contest. Himself vs. the machine. Willie vs. Destiny. His skill and daring vs. the cunning and trickery of the novelty industry of America, and the whole challenging world. He is the last of the American pioneers, with nothing more to fight but the machine, with no other reward than lights going on and off, and six nickels for one. Before him is the last champion, the machine. He is the last challenger, the young man with nothing to do in the world.* WILLIE *grips the knob delicately, studies the situation carefully, draws the knob back, holds it a moment, and then releases it. The first marble rolls out among the hazards, and the contest is on. At the very beginning of the play "The Missouri Waltz" is coming from the phonograph. The music ends here.*
This is the signal for the beginning of the play.
JOE *suddenly comes out of his reverie. He whistles the way people do who are calling a cab that's about a block away, only he does it quietly.* WILLIE *turns around, but* JOE *gestures for him to return to his work.* NICK *looks up from The Racing Form.*)

JOE (*calling*). Tom. (*To himself*) Where the hell is he, every time I need him? (*He looks around calmly: the nickel-in-the-slot phonograph in the corner; the open public telephone; the stage; the marble-game; the bar; and*

so on. He calls again, this time very loud.) Hey, Tom.

NICK (*with morning irritation*). What do you want?

JOE (*without thinking*). I want the boy to get me a watermelon, that's what I want. What do *you* want? Money, or love, or fame, or what? You won't get them studying The Racing Form.

NICK. I like to keep abreast of the times. (TOM *comes hurrying in. He is a great big man of about thirty or so who appears to be much younger because of the childlike expression of his face: handsome, dumb, innocent, troubled, and a little bewildered by everything. He is obviously adult in years, but it seems as if by all rights he should still be a boy. He is defensive as clumsy, self-conscious, overgrown boys are. He is wearing a flashy cheap suit.* JOE *leans back and studies him with casual disapproval.* TOM *slackens his pace and becomes clumsy and embarrassed, waiting for the bawling-out he's pretty sure he's going to get.*)

JOE (*objectively, severely, but a little amused*). Who saved your life?

TOM (*sincerely*). You did, Joe. Thanks.

JOE (*interested*). How'd I do it?

TOM (*confused*). What?

JOE (*even more interested*). *How'd I do it?*

TOM. Joe, you know how you did it.

JOE (*softly*). I want you to answer me. How'd I save your life? I've forgotten.

TOM (*remembering, with a big sorrowful smile*). You made me eat all that chicken soup three years ago when I was sick and hungry.

JOE (*fascinated*). *Chicken soup?*

TOM (*eagerly*). Yeah.

JOE. Three years? Is it that long?

TOM (*delighted to have the information*). Yeah, sure, 1937. 1938. 1939. This is 1939, Joe.

JOE (*amused*). Never mind what year it is. Tell me the whole story.

TOM. You took me to the doctor. You gave me money for food and clothes, and paid my room rent. Aw, Joe, you know all the different things you did. (JOE *nods, turning away from* TOM *after each question.*)

JOE. You in good health now?

TOM. Yeah, Joe.

JOE. You got clothes?

TOM. Yeah, Joe.

JOE. You eat three times a day. Sometimes four?

TOM. Yeah, Joe. Sometimes five.

JOE. You got a place to sleep?

TOM. Yeah, Joe.
(JOE *nods. Pauses. Studies* TOM *carefully.*)

JOE. Then, where the hell have you been?

TOM (*humbly*). Joe, I was out in the street listening to the boys. They're talking about the trouble down here on the waterfront.

JOE (*sharply*). I want you to be around when I need you.

TOM (*pleased that the bawling-out is over*). I won't do it again. Joe, one guy out there says there's got to be a revolution before anything will ever be all right.

JOE (*impatiently*). I know all about it. Now, here. Take this money. Go up to the Emporium. You know where the Emporium is?

TOM. Yeah, sure, Joe.

JOE. All right. Take the elevator and go up to the fourth floor. Walk around to the back, to the toy department. Buy me a couple of dollars' worth of toys and bring them here.

TOM (*amazed*). Toys? What *kind* of toys, Joe?

JOE. Any kind of toys. Little ones that I can put on this table.

TOM. What do you want toys for, Joe?

JOE (*mildly angry*). What?

TOM. All right, all right. You don't have to get sore at *everything*. What'll people think, a big guy like me buying toys?

JOE. *What people?*

TOM. Aw, Joe, you're always making me do crazy things for you, and *I'm* the guy that gets embarrassed. You just sit in this place and make me do all the dirty work.

JOE (*looking away*). Do what I tell you.

TOM. O.K., but I wish I knew *why*. (*He makes to go.*)

JOE. Wait a minute. Here's a nickel. Put it in the phonograph. Number seven. I want to hear that waltz again.

TOM. Boy, I'm glad *I* don't have to stay and listen to it. Joe, what do you hear in that song anyway? We listen to that song ten times a day. Why can't we hear number six, or two, or nine? There are a lot of other numbers.

JOE (*emphatically*). Put the nickel in

the phonograph. (*Pause.*) Sit down and wait till the music's over. Then go get me some toys.

TOM. O.K. O.K.

JOE (*loudly*). Never mind being a martyr about it either. The cause isn't worth it.

(TOM *puts the nickel into the machine, with a ritual of impatient and efficient movement which plainly shows his lack of sympathy or enthusiasm. His manner also reveals, however, that his lack of sympathy is spurious and exaggerated. Actually, he is fascinated by the music, but is so confused by it that he pretends he dislikes it.*

The music begins. It is another variation of "The Missouri Waltz," played dreamily and softly, with perfect orchestral form, and with a theme of weeping in the horns repeated a number of times.

At first TOM *listens with something close to irritation, since he can't understand what is so attractive in the music to* JOE, *and what is so painful and confusing in it to himself. Very soon, however, he is carried away by the melancholy story of grief and nostalgia of the song.*

He stands, troubled by the poetry and confusion in himself.

JOE, *on the other hand, listens as if he were not listening, indifferent and unmoved. What he's interested in is* TOM. *He turns and glances at* TOM.

KITTY DUVAL, *who lives in a room in The New York Hotel, around the corner, comes beyond the swinging doors quietly, and walks slowly to the bar, her reality and rhythm a perfect accompaniment to the sorrowful American music, which is her music, as it is Tom's. Which the world drove out of her, putting in its place brokenness and all manner of spiritually crippled forms. She seems to understand this, and is angry. Angry with herself, full of hate for the poor world, and full of pity and contempt for its tragic, unbelievable, confounded people. She is a small powerful girl, that kind of delicate and* rugged beauty which no circumstance of evil or ugly reality can destroy. This beauty is that element of the immortal which is in the seed of good and common people, and which is kept alive in some of the female of our kind, no matter how accidentally or pointlessly they may have entered the world. KITTY DUVAL *is somebody. There is an angry purity, and a fierce pride, in her. In her stance, and way of walking, there is grace and arrogance.* JOE *recognizes her as a great person immediately. She goes to the bar.*)

KITTY. Beer. (NICK *places a glass of beer before her mechanically. She swallows half the drink, and listens to the music again.*)

(TOM *turns and sees her. He becomes dead to everything in the world but her. He stands like a lump, fascinated and undone by his almost religious adoration for her.* JOE *notices* TOM.)

JOE (*gently*). Tom. (TOM *begins to move toward the bar, where* KITTY *is standing. Loudly*) Tom. (TOM *halts, then turns, and* JOE *motions to him to come over to the table.* TOM *goes over. Quietly*) Have you got everything straight?

TOM (*out of the world*). What?

JOE. What do you mean, what? I just gave you some instructions.

TOM (*pathetically*). What do you want, Joe?

JOE. I want you to come to your senses. (*He stands up quietly and knocks* TOM's *hat off.* TOM *picks up his hat quickly.*)

TOM. I got it, Joe. I got it. The Emporium. Fourth floor. In the back. The toy department. Two dollars' worth of toys. That you can put on a table.

KITTY (*to herself*). Who the hell is he to push a big man like that around?

JOE. I'll expect you back in a half hour. Don't get side-tracked anywhere. Just do what I tell you.

TOM (*pleadingly*). Joe? Can't I bet four bits on a horse race? There's a long shot—Precious Time—that's going to win by ten lengths. I got to have money.
(JOE *points to the street.* TOM *goes out.* NICK *is combing his hair, looking in the mirror.*)

NICK. I thought you wanted him to get you a watermelon.

JOE. I forgot. (*He watches* KITTY *a moment. To* KITTY, *clearly, slowly, with great compassion.*) What's the dream?

KITTY (*moving to* JOE, *coming to*). What?

JOE (*holding the dream for her*). What's the dream, now?

KITTY (*coming still closer*). What dream?

JOE. What dream! The dream you're dreaming.

NICK. Suppose he did bring you a watermelon? What the hell would you do with it?

JOE (*irritated*). I'd put it on this table. I'd look at it. Then I'd eat it. What do you *think* I'd do with it, sell it for a profit?

NICK. How should I know what *you'd* do with *anything*? What I'd like to know is, where do you get your money from? What work do you do?

JOE (*looking at* KITTY). Bring us a bottle of champagne.

KITTY. Champagne?

JOE (*simply*). Would you rather have something else?

KITTY. What's the big idea?

JOE. I thought you might like some champagne. I myself am very fond of it.

KITTY. Yeah, but what's the big idea? You can't push *me* around.

JOE (*gently but severely*). It's not in my nature to be unkind to another human being. I have only contempt for wit. Otherwise I might say something obvious, therefore cruel, and perhaps untrue.

KITTY. You be careful what you think about me.

JOE (*slowly, not looking at her*). I have only the noblest thoughts for both your person, and your spirit.

NICK (*having listened carefully and not being able to make it out*). What are you talking about?

KITTY. You shut up. You—

JOE. He owns this place. He's an important man. All kinds of people come to him looking for work. Comedians. Singers. Dancers.

KITTY. I don't care. He can't call me names.

NICK. All right, sister. I know how it is with a two-dollar whore in the morning.

KITTY (*furiously*). Don't you dare call me names. I used to be in burlesque.

NICK. If you were ever in burlesque, I used to be Charlie Chaplin.

KITTY (*angry and a little pathetic*). I *was* in burlesque. I played the burlesque circuit from coast to coast. I've had flowers sent to me by European royalty. I've had dinner with young men of wealth and social position.

NICK. You're dreaming.

KITTY (*to* JOE). *I was in burlesque.* Kitty Duval. That was my name. Life-size photographs of me in costume in front of burlesque theaters all over the country.

JOE (*gently, coaxingly*). I believe you. Have some champagne.

NICK (*going to table, with champagne bottle and glasses*). There he goes again.

JOE. Miss Duval?

KITTY (*sincerely, going over*). That's not my *real* name. That's my *stage* name.

JOE. I'll call you by your stage name.

NICK (*pouring*). All right, sister, make up your mind. Are you going to have champagne with him, or not?

JOE. Pour the lady some wine.

NICK. O.K., Professor. Why you come to this joint instead of one of the high-class dumps uptown is more than I can understand. Why don't you have champagne at the St. Francis? Why don't you drink with a lady?

KITTY (*furiously*). Don't you call me names—you dentist.

JOE. Dentist?

NICK (*amazed, loudly*). What kind of cussing is that? (*Pause. Looking at* KITTY, *then at* JOE, *bewildered*) This guy doesn't belong here. The only reason I've got champagne is because *he* keeps ordering it all the time. (*To* KITTY) Don't think you're the only one he drinks champagne with. He drinks with *all* of them. (*Pause.*) He's crazy. Or something.

JOE (*confidentially*). Nick, I think

you're going to be all right in a couple of centuries.

NICK. I'm sorry, I don't understand your English.
(JOE lifts his glass.
KITTY *slowly lifts her, not quite sure of what's going on.*)

JOE (*sincerely*). To the spirit, Kitty Duval.

KITTY (*beginning to understand, and very grateful, looking at him*). Thank you. (*They drink.*)

JOE (*calling*). Nick.

NICK. Yeah?

JOE. Would you mind putting a nickel in the machine again? Number—

NICK. Seven. I know. I know. I don't mind at all, Your Highness, although, personally, I'm not a lover of music. (*Going to the machine*) As a matter of fact I think Tchaikowsky was a dope.

JOE. Tchaikowsky? Where'd you ever hear of Tchaikowsky?

NICK. He was a dope.

JOE. Yeah. Why?

NICK. They talked about him on the radio one Sunday morning. He was a sucker. He let a woman drive him crazy.

JOE. I see.

NICK. I stood behind that bar listening to the God damn stuff and cried like a baby. *None but the lonely heart!* He was a dope.

JOE. What made you cry?

NICK. What?

JOE (*sternly*). What made you cry, Nick?

NICK (*angry with himself*). I don't know.

JOE. I've been underestimating you, Nick. Play number seven.

NICK. They get everybody worked up. They give everybody stuff they shouldn't have. (NICK *puts the nickel into the machine and the Waltz begins again. He listens to the music. Then studies The Racing Form.*)

KITTY (*to herself, dreaming*). I like champagne, and everything that goes with it. Big houses with big porches, and big rooms with big windows, and big lawns, and big trees, and flowers growing everywhere, and big shepherd dogs sleeping in the shade.

NICK. I'm going next door to Frankie's to make a bet. I'll be right back.

JOE. Make one for me.

NICK (*going to* JOE). Who do you like?

JOE (*giving him money*). Precious Time.

NICK. *Ten dollars?* Across the board?

JOE. No. On the nose.

NICK. O.K. (*He goes.*)

DUDLEY R. BOSTWICK, *as he calls himself, breaks through the swinging doors, and practically flings himself upon the open telephone beside the phonograph.* DUDLEY *is a young man of about twenty-four or twenty-five, ordinary and yet extraordinary. He is smallish, as the saying is, neatly dressed in bargain clothes, over-worked and irritated by the routine and dullness and monotony of his life, apparently nobody and nothing, but in reality a great personality. The swindled young man. Educated, but without the least real understanding. A brave, dumb, salmon-spirit struggling for life in weary, stupefied flesh, dueling ferociously with a banal mind which has been only irritated by what it has been taught. He is a great personality because, against all these handicaps, what he wants is simple and basic: a woman. This urgent and violent need, common yet miraculous enough in itself, considering the unhappy environment of the animal, is the force which elevates him from nothingness to greatness. A ridiculous greatness, but in the nature of things beautiful to behold. All that he has been taught, and everything he believes, is phony, and yet he himself is real, almost super-real, because of this indestructible force in himself. His face is ridiculous. His personal rhythm is tense and jittery. His speech is shrill and violent. His gestures are wild. His ego is disjointed and epileptic. And yet deeply he possesses the same wholeness of spirit, and directness of energy, that is in all species of animals. There is little innate or cultivated spirit in him, but there is no absence of innocent animal force. He is a young man who has been taught that he has a chance, as a person, and believes it. As a matter of fact, he hasn't a chance in the world, and should have been told by somebody, or should not have had his natural and valuable ignorance spoiled by education, ruining an otherwise perfectly good and charming member of the human race.*

At the telephone he immediately begins to dial furiously, hesitates, changes his mind, stops dialing, hangs up furiously, and suddenly begins again.

Not more than half a minute after the firecracker arrival of DUDLEY R. BOSTWICK, *occurs the polka-and-waltz arrival of* HARRY.

HARRY *is another story.*

He comes in timidly, turning about uncertainly, awkward, out of place everywhere, embarrassed and encumbered by the contemporary costume, sick at heart, but determined to fit in somewhere. His arrival constitutes a dance. His clothes don't fit. The pants are a little too large. The coat, which doesn't match, is also a little too large, and loose.

He is a dumb young fellow, but he has ideas. A philosophy, in fact. His philosophy is simple and beautiful. The world is sorrowful. The world needs laughter. HARRY *is funny. The world needs* HARRY. HARRY *will make the world laugh.*

He has probably had a year or two of high school. He has also listened to the boys at the pool room.

He's looking for NICK. *He goes to the* ARAB, *and says, Are you Nick? The* ARAB *shakes his head. He stands at the bar, waiting. He waits very busily.*)

HARRY (*as* NICK *returns*). You Nick?

NICK (*very loudly*). I am Nick.

HARRY (*acting*). Can you use a great comedian?

NICK (*behind the bar*). Who, for instance?

HARRY (*almost angry*). Me.

NICK. You? What's funny about you? (DUDLEY *at the telephone, is dialing. Because of some defect in the apparatus the dialing is very loud.*)

DUDLEY. Hello. Sunset 7349? May I speak to Miss Elsie Mandelspiegel? (*Pause.*)

HARRY (*with spirit and noise, dancing*). I dance and do gags and stuff.

NICK. In costume? Or are you wearing your costume?

DUDLEY. All I need is a cigar.

KITTY (*continuing the dream of grace*). I'd walk out of the house, and stand on the porch, and look at the trees, and smell the flowers, and run across the lawn, and lie down under a tree, and read a book. (*Pause.*) A book of poems, maybe.

DUDLEY (*very, very clearly*). Elsie Mandelspiegel. (*Impatiently*) She has a room on the fourth floor. She's a nurse at the Southern Pacific Hospital. Elsie Mandelspiegel. She works at night. Elsie. Yes. (*He begins waiting again.*)

(WESLEY, *a colored boy, comes to the bar and stands near* HARRY, *waiting.*)

NICK. Beer?

WESLEY. No, sir. I'd like to talk to you.

NICK (*to* HARRY). All right. Get funny.

HARRY (*getting funny, an altogether different person, an actor with great energy, both in power of voice, and in force and speed of physical gesture*). Now, I'm standing on the corner of Third and Market. I'm looking around. I'm figuring it out. There it is. Right in front of me. The whole city. The whole world. People going by. They're going somewhere. I don't know where, but they're going. I ain't going *anywhere*. Where the hell can you go? I'm figuring it out. All right, I'm a citizen. A fat guy bumps his stomach into the face of an old lady. They were in a hurry. Fat and old. *They bumped.* Boom. I don't know. It may mean war. *War.* Germany. England. Russia. I don't know for sure. (*Loudly, dramatically, he salutes, about faces, presents arms, aims, and fires.*) WAAAAAR. (*He blows a call to arms.* NICK *gets sick of this, indicates with a gesture that* HARRY *should hold it, and goes to* WESLEY.)

NICK. What's on your mind?

WESLEY (*confused*). Well—

NICK. Come on. Speak up. Are you hungry, or what?

WESLEY. Honest to God, I ain't hungry. All I want is a job. I don't want no charity.

NICK. Well, what can you do, and how good are you?

WESLEY. I can run errands, clean up, wash dishes, anything.

DUDLEY (*on the telephone, very eagerly*). Elsie? Elsie, this is Dudley. Elsie, I'll jump in the bay if you don't marry me. Life isn't worth living without you. I can't sleep. I can't think of anything but you. All the time. Day and night and night and day. Elsie, I love you. I love you. What? (*Burning up*) Is this Sunset 7-3-4-9? (*Pause*) 7943? (*Calmly, while* WILLIE *begins making a small racket*) Well, what's *your* name? Lorene? Lorene Smith? I thought you were Elsie Mandelspiegel. What? Dudley. Yeah. Dudley R. Bostwick. Yeah. R. It stands for Raoul, but I never spell it out. I'm pleased to meet *you*, too. What? There's a lot of noise around here. (WILLIE *stops hitting the marble-game.*) Where am I? At Nick's, on Pacific Street. I work at the S. P. I told them I was sick and they gave me the afternoon off. Wait a minute. I'll ask them. I'd like to meet *you*, too. Sure. I'll ask them. (*Turns around to* NICK.) What's this address?

NICK. Number 3 Pacific Street, you cad.

DUDLEY. Cad? You don't know how I've been suffering on account of Elsie. I take things too ceremoniously. I've got to be more lackadaisical. (*Into telephone*) Hello, Elenore? I mean, Lorene. It's number 3 Pacific Street. Yeah. Sure. I'll wait for you. How'll you know me? You'll *know* me. I'll recognize *you*. Good-by, now. (*He hangs up.*)

HARRY (*continuing his monologue, with gestures, movements, and so on*). I'm standing there. I didn't do anything to anybody. Why should *I* be a soldier? (*Sincerely, insanely*) BOOOOOOOOM. WAR! O.K. War. *I* retreat. *I* hate war. I move to Sacramento.

NICK (*shouting*). All right, Comedian. Lay off a minute.

HARRY (*broken-hearted, going to* WILLIE). Nobody's got a sense of humor any more. The world's dying for comedy like never before, but nobody knows how to *laugh*.

NICK (*to* WESLEY). Do you belong to the union?

WESLEY. What union?

NICK. For the love of Mike, where've you been? Don't you know you can't come into a place and ask for a job and get one and go to work, just like that. You've got to belong to one of the unions.

WESLEY. I didn't know. I got to have a job. Real soon.

NICK. Well, you've got to belong to a union.

WESLEY. I don't want any favors. All I want is a chance to earn a living.

NICK. Go on into the kitchen and tell Sam to give you some lunch.

WESLEY. Honest, I ain't hungry.

DUDLEY (*shouting*). What I've gone through for Elsie.

HARRY. I've got all kinds of funny ideas in my head to help make the world happy again.

NICK (*holding* WESLEY). *No, he isn't* hungry.
(WESLEY *almost faints from hunger.* NICK *catches him just in time. The* ARAB *and* NICK *go off with* WESLEY *into the kitchen.*)

HARRY (*to* WILLIE). See if you think this is funny. It's my own idea. I created this dance myself. It comes after the monologue. (HARRY *begins to dance.* WILLIE *watches a moment, and then goes back to the game. It's a goofy dance, which* HARRY *does with great sorrow, but much energy.*)

DUDLEY. Elsie. Aw, gee, Elsie. What the hell do I want to see Lorene Smith for? Some girl I don't know.
(JOE *and* KITTY *have been drinking in silence. There is no sound now except the soft shoe shuffling of* HARRY, *the Comedian.*)

JOE. What's the dream now, Kitty Duval?

KITTY (*dreaming the words and pictures*). I dream of home. Christ, I always dream of home. I've no *home.* I've no place. But I always dream of all of us together again. We had a farm in Ohio. There was nothing good about it. It was always sad. There was always trouble. But I always dream about it as if I could go back and Papa would be there and Mamma and Louie and my little brother Stephen and my sister Mary. I'm Polish. Duval! My name isn't Duval, it's Koranovsky. Katerina Koranovsky. We lost everything. The house, the farm, the trees, the horses, the cows, the chickens. Papa died. He was old. He was thirteen years older than Mamma. We moved to Chicago. We tried to work. We tried to stay together. Louie got in trouble. The fellows he was with killed him for something. I don't know what. Stephen ran away from home. Seventeen years old. I don't know where he is. Then Mamma died. (*Pause.*) What's the dream? I dream of home.
(NICK *comes out of the kitchen with* WESLEY.)

NICK. Here. Sit down here and rest. That'll hold you for a *while.* Why didn't you tell me you were hungry? You all right now?

WESLEY (*sitting down in the chair at the piano*). Yes, I am. Thank you. I didn't know I was *that* hungry.

NICK. Fine. (*To* HARRY *who is danc-*

ing) Hey. What the hell do you think you're doing?

HARRY (*stopping*). That's my own idea. I'm a natural-born dancer and comedian.
(WESLEY *begins slowly, one note, one chord at a time, to play the piano.*)

NICK. You're no good. Why don't you try some other kind of work? Why don't you get a job in a store, selling something? What do you want to be a comedian for?

HARRY. I've got something for the world and they haven't got sense enough to let me give it to them. Nobody knows me.

DUDLEY. Elsie. Now I'm waiting for some dame I've never seen before. Lorene Smith. Never saw her in my life. Just happened to get the wrong number. She turns on the personality, and I'm a cooked Indian. Give me a beer, please.

HARRY. Nick, you've got to see my act. It's the greatest thing of its kind in America. All I want is a chance. No salary to begin. Let me try it out tonight. If I don't wow 'em, O.K., I'll go home. If vaudeville wasn't dead, a guy like me would have a chance.

NICK. You're not funny. You're a sad young punk. What the hell do you want to try to be funny for? You'll break everybody's heart. What's there for you to be funny about? You've been poor all your life, haven't you?

HARRY. I've been poor all right, but don't forget that some things count more than some other things.

NICK. What counts more, for instance, than what else, for instance?

HARRY. Talent, for instance, counts more than money, for instance, that's what, and I've got talent. I get new ideas night and day. Everything comes natural to me. I've got style, but it'll take me a little time to round it out. That's all.

(*By now* WESLEY *is playing something of his own which is very good and out of the world. He plays about half a minute, after which* HARRY *begins to dance.*)

NICK (*watching*). I run the lousiest dive in Frisco, and a guy arrives and makes me stock up with champagne. The whores come in and holler at me that they're ladies. Talent comes in and begs me for a chance to show itself. Even society people come here once in a while. I don't know what for. Maybe it's liquor. Maybe it's the location. Maybe it's my personality. Maybe it's the crazy personality of the joint. The old honky-tonk. (*Pause.*) Maybe they can't feel at home anywhere else.

(*By now* WESLEY *is really playing, and* HARRY *is going through a new routine.* DUDLEY *grows sadder and sadder.*)

KITTY. Please dance with me.

JOE (*loudly*). I never learned to dance.

KITTY. Anybody can dance. Just hold me in your arms.

JOE. I'm very fond of you. I'm *sorry.* I *can't* dance. I wish to God I could.

KITTY. Oh, please.

JOE. Forgive me. I'd like to very much. (KITTY *dances alone.* TOM *comes in with a package. He sees* KITTY *and goes ga-ga again. He comes out of the trance and puts the bundle on the table in front of* JOE.)

JOE (*taking the package*). What'd you get?

TOM. Two dollars' worth of toys. That's what you sent me for. The girl asked me what I wanted with toys. I didn't know what to tell her. (*He stares at* KITTY, *then back at* JOE.) Joe? I've got to have some money. After all you've

done for me, I'll do anything in the world for you, but, Joe, you got to give me some money once in a while.

JOE. What do you want it for?
(TOM *turns and stares at* KITTY *dancing.*)

JOE (*noticing*). Sure. Here. Here's five. (*Shouting*) Can you dance?

TOM (*proudly*). I got second prize at the Palomar in Sacramento five years ago.

JOE (*loudly, opening package*). O.K., dance with her.

TOM. You mean *her?*

JOE (*loudly*). I mean Kitty Duval, the burlesque queen. I mean the queen of the world burlesque. Dance with her. She wants to dance.

TOM (*worshiping the name Kitty Duval, helplessly*). Joe, can I tell you something?

JOE (*he brings out a toy and winds it*). You don't have to. I know. You love her. You *really* love her. I'm not blind. I know. But take care of yourself. Don't get sick that way again.

NICK (*looking at and listening to* WESLEY *with amazement*). Comes in here and wants to be a dish-washer. Faints from hunger. And then sits down and plays better than Heifetz.

JOE. Heifetz plays the violin.

NICK. All right, don't get careful. He's good, ain't he?

TOM (*to* KITTY). Kitty.

JOE (*he lets the toy go, loudly*). Don't talk. Just *dance.*
(TOM *and* KITTY *dance.* NICK *is at the bar, watching everything.* HARRY *is dancing.* DUDLEY *is grieving into his beer.* LORENE SMITH, *about thirty-*

seven, very overbearing and funny-looking, comes to the bar.)

NICK. What'll it be, lady?

LORENE (looking about and scaring all the young men). I'm looking for the young man I talked to on the telephone. Dudley R. Bostwick.

DUDLEY (jumping, running to her, stopping, shocked). Dudey R. (Slowly) Bostwick? Oh, yeah. He left here ten minutes ago. You mean Dudley Bostwick, that poor man on crutches?

LORENE. Crutches?

DUDLEY. Yeah. Dudley Bostwick. That's what he said his name was. He said to tell you not to wait.

LORENE. Well. (She begins to go, turns around.) Are you sure you're not Dudley Bostwick?

DUDLEY. Who—me? (Grandly) My name is Roger Tenefrancia. I'm a French-Canadian. I never saw the poor fellow before.

LORENE. It seems to me your voice is like the voice I heard over the telephone.

DUDLEY. A coincidence. An accident. A quirk of fate. One of those things. Dismiss the thought. That poor cripple hobbled out of here ten minutes ago.

LORENE. He said he was going to commit suicide. I only wanted to be of help. (She goes.)

DUDLEY. Be of help? What kind of help could she be, of? (DUDLEY runs to the telephone in the corner.) Gee whiz. Elsie. Gee whiz. I'll never leave you again. (He turns the pages of a little address book.) Why do I always forget the number? I've tried to get her on the phone a hundred times this week and I still forget the number. She won't come to the phone, but I keep

trying anyway. She's out. She's not in. She's working. I get the wrong number. Everything goes haywire. I can't sleep. (Defiantly) She'll come to the phone one of these days. If there's anything to true love at all, she'll come to the phone. Sunset 7349. (He dials the number, as JOE goes on studying the toys. They are one big mechanical toy, whistles, and a music box. JOE blows into the whistles, quickly, by way of getting casually acquainted with them.) TOM and KITTY stop dancing. TOM stares at her.)

DUDLEY. Hello. Is this Sunset 7349? May I speak to Elsie? Yes. (Emphatically, and bitterly) No, this is not Dudley Bostwick. This is Roger Tenefrancia of Montreal, Canada. I'm a childhood friend of Miss Mandelspiegel. We went to kindergarten together. (Hand over phone) God damn it. (Into phone) Yes. I'll wait, thank you.

TOM. I love you.

KITTY. You want to go to my room? (TOM can't answer.) Have you got two dollars?

TOM (shaking his head with confusion). I've got five dollars, but I love you.

KITTY (looking at him). You want to spend all that money? (TOM embraces her. They go. JOE watches. Goes back to the toy.)

JOE. Where's that longshoreman, McCarthy?

NICK. He'll be around.

JOE. What do you think he'll have to say today?

NICK. Plenty, as usual. I'm going next door to see who won that third race at Laurel.

JOE. Precious Time won it.

NICK. That's what you think. (*He goes.*)

JOE (*to himself*). A horse named McCarthy is running in the sixth race today.

DUDLEY (*on the phone*). Hello. Hello, Elsie? Elsie? (*His voice weakens; also his limbs.*) My God. She's come to the phone. Elsie, I'm at Nick's on Pacific Street. You've got to come here and talk to me. Hello. Hello, Elsie? (*Amazed*) Did she hang up? Or was I disconnected? (*He hangs up and goes to bar.*)
(WESLEY *is still playing the piano.* HARRY *is still dancing.* JOE *has wound up the big mechanical toy and is watching it work.* NICK *returns.*)

NICK (*watching the toy*). Say. That's some gadget.

JOE. How much did I win?

NICK. How do you know you *won*?

JOE. Don't be silly. He said Precious Time was going to win by ten lengths, didn't he? He's in love, isn't he?

NICK. O.K. I don't know why, but Precious Time won. You got eighty for ten. How do you do it?

JOE (*roaring*). Faith. Faith. How'd he win?

NICK. By a nose. Look him up in The Racing Form. The slowest, the cheapest, the worst horse in the race, and the worse jockey. What's the matter with my luck?

JOE. How much did you lose?

NICK. Fifty cents.

JOE. You should never gamble.

NICK. Why not?

JOE. You always bet fifty cents. You've got no more faith than a flea, that's why.

HARRY (*shouting*). How do you like this, Nick? (*He is really busy now, all legs and arms.*)

NICK (*turning and watching*). Not bad. Hang around. You can wait table. (*To* WESLEY) Hey. Wesley. Can you play that again tonight?

WESLEY (*turning, but still playing the piano*). I don't know for sure, Mr. Nick. I can play *something*.

NICK. Good. You hang around, too. (*He goes behind the bar.*)
(*The atmosphere is now one of warm, natural, American ease; every man innocent and good; each doing what he believes he should do, or what he must do. There is deep American naïveté and faith in the behavior of each person. No one is competing with anyone else. No one hates anyone else. Every man is living, and letting live. Each man is following his destiny as he feels it should be followed; or is abandoning it as he feels it must, by now, be abandoned; or is forgetting it for the moment as he feels he should forget it. Although everyone is dead serious, there is unmistakable smiling and humor in the scene; a sense of the human body and spirit emerging from the world-imposed state of stress and fretfulness, fear and awkwardness, to the more natural state of casualness and grace. Each person belongs to the environment, in his own person, as himself:* WESLEY *is playing better than ever.* HARRY *is hoofing better than ever.* NICK *is behind the bar shining glasses.* JOE *is smiling at the toy and studying it.* DUDLEY, *although still troubled, is at least calm now and full of melancholy poise.* WILLIE, *at the marble game, is happy. The* ARAB *is deep in his memories, where he wants to be.*
Into this scene and atmosphere comes BLICK.
BLICK *is the sort of human being you*

dislike at sight. He is no different from anybody else physically. His face is an ordinary face. There is nothing obviously wrong with him, and yet you know that it is impossible, even by the most generous expansion of understanding, to accept him as a human being. He is the strong man without strength—strong only among the weak—the weakling who uses force on the weaker.

BLICK *enters casually, as if he were a customer, and immediately* HARRY *begins slowing down.*)

BLICK (*oily, and with mock-friendliness*). Hello, Nick.

NICK (*stopping his work and leaning across the bar*). What do you want to come here for? You're too big a man for a little honky-tonk.

BLICK (*flattered*). Now, Nick.

NICK. Important people never come here. *Here.* Have a drink. (*Whiskey bottle.*)

BLICK. Thanks, I don't drink.

NICK (*drinking the drink himself*). Well, why don't you?

BLICK. I have responsibilities.

NICK. You're head of the lousy Vice Squad. There's no vice here.

BLICK (*sharply*). Streetwalkers are working out of this place.

NICK (*angry*). What do you want?

BLICK (*loudly*). I just want you to know that it's got to stop.
(*The music stops. The mechanical toy runs down. There is absolute silence, and a strange fearfulness and disharmony in the atmosphere now.* HARRY *doesn't know what to do with his hands or feet.* WESLEY'S *arms hang at his sides.* JOE *quietly pushes the toy to one side of the table eager to study*

what is happening. WILLIE *stops playing the marble game, turns around and begins to wait.* DUDLEY *straightens up very, very vigorously, as if to say: "Nothing can scare me. I know love is the only thing." The* ARAB *is the same as ever, but watchful.* NICK *is arrogantly aloof. There is a moment of this silence and tension, as though* BLICK *were waiting for everybody to acknowledge his presence. He is obviously flattered by the acknowledgment of* HARRY, DUDLEY, WESLEY, *and* WILLIE, *but a little irritated by* NICK'S *aloofness and unfriendliness.*)

NICK. Don't look at me. I can't tell a streetwalker from a lady. You married?

BLICK. You're not asking *me* questions. *I'm* telling *you.*

NICK (*interrupting*). You're a man of about forty-five or so. You *ought* to know better.

BLICK (*angry*). Streetwalkers are working out of this place.

NICK (*beginning to shout*). Now, don't start any trouble with me. People come here to drink and loaf around. I don't care who they are.

BLICK. Well, I do.

NICK. The only way to find out if a lady is a streetwalker is to walk the streets with her, go to bed, and make sure. You wouldn't want to do that. You'd *like* to, of course.

BLICK. Any more of it, and I'll have your joint closed.

NICK (*very casually, without ill-will*). Listen. I've got no use for you, or anybody like you. You're out to change the world from something bad to something worse. Something like yourself.

BLICK (*furious pause, and contempt*).

THE TIME OF YOUR LIFE

I'll be back tonight. (*He begins to go.*)

NICK (*very angry but very calm*). Do yourself a big favor and don't come back tonight. Send somebody else. I don't like your personality.

BLICK (*casually, but with contempt*). Don't break any laws. I don't like yours, either. (*He looks the place over, and goes.*)
(*There is a moment of silence. Then* WILLIE *turns and puts a new nickel in the slot and starts a new game.* WESLEY *turns to the piano and rather falteringly begins to play. His heart really isn't in it.* HARRY *walks about, unable to dance.* DUDLEY *lapses into his customary melancholy, at a table.* NICK *whistles a little: suddenly stops.* JOE *winds the toy.*)

JOE (*comically*). Nick. You going to kill that man?

NICK. I'm disgusted.

JOE. Yeah? Why?

NICK. Why should I get worked up over a guy like that? Why should I hate *him?* He's nothing. He's nobody. He's a mouse. But every time he comes into this place I get burned up. He doesn't want to drink. He doesn't want to sit down. He doesn't want to take things easy. Tell me one thing?

JOE. Do my best.

NICK. What's a punk like *that* want to go out and try to change the world for?

JOE (*amazed*). Does *he* want to change the world, too?

NICK (*irritated*). You know what I mean. What's he want to bother people for? He's *sick.*

JOE (*almost to himself, reflecting on the fact that Blick too wants to change the*

world). I guess he wants to change the world at that.

NICK. So I go to work and hate him.

JOE. It's not him, Nick. It's everything.

NICK. Yeah, *I know.* But I've still got no use for him. He's no good. You know what I mean? He hurts little people. (*Confused*) One of the girls tried to commit suicide on account of him. (*Furiously*) I'll break his head if he hurts anybody around here. This is *my* joint. (*Afterthought*) Or anybody's *feelings,* either.

JOE. He may not be so bad, deep down underneath.

NICK. I know all about him. He's no good.
(*During this talk* WESLEY *has really begun to play the piano, the toy is rattling again, and little by little* HARRY *has begun to dance.* NICK *has come around the bar, and now, very much like a child—forgetting all his anger— is watching the toy work. He begins to smile at everything: turns and listens to* WESLEY: *watches* HARRY: *nods at the* ARAB: *shakes his head at* DUDLEY: *and gestures amiably about* WILLIE. *It's his joint all right.
It's a good, low-down, honky-tonk American place that lets people alone.*)

NICK. I've got a good joint. There's nothing wrong here. Hey. Comedian. Stick to the dancing tonight. I think you're O.K. Wesley? Do some more of that tonight. That's fine!

HARRY. Thanks, Nick. Gosh, I'm on my way at last. (*On telephone*) Hello, Ma? Is that you, Ma? Harry. I got the job. (*He hangs up and walks around, smiling.*)

NICK (*watching the toy all this time*). Say, that really is something. What is that, anyway?
(MARY L. *comes in.*)

JOE (*holding it toward* NICK, *and* MARY L.). Nick, this is a toy. A contraption devised by the cunning of man to drive boredom, or grief, or anger out of children. A noble gadget. A gadget, I might say, infinitely nobler than any other I can think of at the moment. (*Everybody gathers around* JOE'*s table to look at the toy. The toy stops working.* JOE *winds the music box. Lifts a whistle: blows it, making a very* strange, funny and sorrowful sound.) Delightful. Tragic, but delightful. (WESLEY *plays the music-box theme on the piano.* MARY L. *takes a table.*) NICK. Joe. That girl, Kitty. What's she mean, calling me a dentist? I wouldn't hurt anybody, let alone a tooth. (NICK *goes to* MARY L.'*s table.* HARRY *imitates the toy. Dances. The piano music comes up, the light dims slowly, while the piano solo continues.*)

ACT TWO

An hour later. All the people who were at Nick's when the curtain came down are still there. JOE *at his table, quietly shuffling and turning a deck of cards, and at the same time watching the face of the woman, and looking at the initials on her handbag, as though they were the symbols of the lost glory of the world. The* WOMAN, *in turn, very casually regards* JOE *occasionally. Or rather senses him; has sensed him in fact the whole hour. She is mildly tight on beer, and* JOE *himself is tight, but as always completely under control; simply sharper. The others are about, at tables, and so on.*

JOE. Is it Madge—Laubowitz?

MARY. Is what *what?*

JOE. Is the name Mabel Lepescu?

MARY. What name?

JOE. The name the initials M. L. stand for. The initials on your bag.

MARY. No.

JOE (*after a long pause, thinking deeply what the name might be, turning a card, looking into the beautiful face of the woman*). Margie Longworthy?

MARY (*all this is very natural and sincere, no comedy on the part of the people involved: they are both solemn, being drunk*). No.

JOE (*his voice higher-pitched, as though he were growing a little alarmed*). Midge Laurie? (MARY *shakes her head.*) My initials are J. T.

MARY (*pause*). John?

JOE. No. (*Pause.*) Martha Lancaster?

MARY. No. (*Slight pause.*) Joseph?

JOE. Well, not exactly. That's my first name, but everybody calls me Joe. The last name is the tough one. I'll help you a little. I'm Irish. (*Pause.*) Is it just plain Mary?

MARY. Yes, it is. I'm Irish, too. At least on my father's side. English on my mother's side.

JOE. I'm Irish on both sides. Mary's one of my favorite names. I guess that's why I didn't think of it. I met a girl in Mexico City named Mary once. She was an American from Philadelphia. She got married there. In Mexico City, I mean. While I was *there*. We were in love, too. At least *I* was. You never know about anyone else. They were engaged, you see, and her mother was with her, so they went through with it.

Must have been six or seven years ago. She's probably got three or four children by this time.

MARY. Are you still in love with her?

JOE. Well—no. To tell you the truth, I'm not sure. I guess I am. I didn't even know she was engaged until a couple of days before they got married. I thought *I* was going to marry her. I kept thinking all the time about the kind of kids we would be likely to have. My favorite was the third one. The first two were fine. Handsome and fine and intelligent, but that third one was different. Dumb and goofy-looking. I liked *him* a lot. When she told me she was going to be married, I didn't feel so bad about the first two, it was that dumb one.

MARY (*after a pause of some few seconds*). What do you do?

JOE. Do? To tell you the truth, nothing.

MARY. Do you always drink a great deal?

JOE (*scientifically*). Not *always*. Only when I'm awake. I sleep seven or eight hours every night, you know.

MARY. How nice. I mean to drink when you're awake.

JOE (*thoughtfully*). It's a privilege.

MARY. Do you really *like* to drink?

JOE (*positively*). As much as I like to *breathe*.

MARY (*beautifully*). Why?

JOE (*dramatically*). Why do I like to drink? (*Pause.*) Because I don't like to be gypped. Because I don't like to be dead most of the time and just a little alive every once in a long while. (*Pause.*) If I don't drink, I become fascinated by unimportant things—like everybody else. I get busy. Do things. All

kinds of little stupid things, for all kinds of little stupid reasons. Proud, selfish, *ordinary* things. I've done them. Now I don't do anything. *I live all the time.* Then I go to sleep. (*Pause.*)

MARY. Do you sleep well?

JOE (*taking it for granted*). Of course.

MARY (*quietly, almost with tenderness*). What are your plans?

JOE (*loudly, but also tenderly*). Plans? I haven't *got* any. *I just get up.*

MARY (*beginning to understand everything*). Oh, yes. Yes, of course. (DUDLEY *puts a nickel in the phonograph.*)

JOE (*thoughtfully*). Why do I drink? (*Pause, while he thinks about it. The thinking appears to be profound and complex, and has the effect of giving his face a very comical and naive expression.*) That question calls for a pretty complicated answer. (*He smiles abstractly.*)

MARY. Oh, I didn't mean—

JOE (*swiftly, gallantly*). No. No. I *insist*. I *know* why. It's just a matter of finding words. Little ones.

MARY. It really doesn't matter.

JOE (*seriously*). Oh, yes, it does. (*Clinically*) Now, why do I drink? (*Scientifically*) No. Why does *anybody* drink? (*Working it out*) Every day has twenty-four hours.

MARY (*sadly, but brightly*). Yes, that's true.

JOE. Twenty-four hours. Out of the twenty-four hours at least twenty-three and a half are—my God, I don't know why—dull, dead, boring, empty, and murderous. Minutes on the clock, *not time of living.* It doesn't make any difference who you are or what you do, twenty-three and a half hours of the twenty-four are spent *waiting.*

MARY. Waiting?

JOE (*gesturing, loudly*). And the more you wait, the less there is to wait *for.*

MARY (*attentively, beautifully his student*). Oh?

JOE (*continuing*). That goes on for days and days, and weeks and months and years, and years, and the first thing you know *all* the years are dead. All the minutes are dead. You yourself are dead. There's nothing to wait for any more. Nothing except *minutes* on the *clock.* No time of life. Nothing but minutes, and idiocy. Beautiful, bright, intelligent idiocy. (*Pause.*) Does that answer your question?

MARY (*earnestly*). I'm afraid it does. Thank you. You shouldn't have gone to all the trouble.

JOE. No trouble at all. (*Pause.*) You have children?

MARY. Yes. Two. A son and a daughter.

JOE (*delighted*). How swell. Do they look like you?

MARY. Yes.

JOE. Then why are you sad?

MARY. I was always sad. It's just that after I was married I was allowed to drink.

JOE (*eagerly*). Who are you waiting for?

MARY. No one.

JOE (*smiling*). I'm not waiting for anybody, either.

MARY. My husband, of course.

JOE. Oh, sure.

MARY. He's a lawyer.

JOE (*standing, leaning on the table*). He's a great guy. I like him. I'm very fond of him.

MARY (*listening*). You have responsibilities?

JOE (*loudly*). One, and *thousands.* As a matter of fact, I feel responsible to everybody. At least to everybody I meet. I've been trying for three years to find out if it's possible to live what I think is a civilized life. I mean a life that can't hurt any other life.

MARY. You're famous?

JOE. Very. Utterly unknown, but very famous. Would you like to dance?

MARY. All right.

JOE (*loudly*). I'm *sorry.* I don't dance. I didn't think you'd like to.

MARY. To tell you the truth, I don't like to dance at all.

JOE (*proudly. Commentator*). I can hardly walk.

MARY. You mean you're tight?

JOE (*smiling*). No. I mean *all* the time.

MARY (*looking at him closely*). Were you ever in Paris?

JOE. In 1929, and again in 1934.

MARY. What month of 1934?

JOE. Most of April, all of May, and a little of June.

MARY. I was there in November and December that year.

JOE. We were there almost at the same time. You were married?

MARY. Engaged. (*They are silent a moment, looking at one another. Quietly and with great charm*) Are you *really* in love with me?

JOE. Yes.

MARY. Is it the champagne?

JOE. Yes. Partly, at least. (*He sits down.*)

MARY. If you don't see me again, will you be very unhappy?

JOE. Very.

MARY (*getting up*). I'm so pleased. (*JOE is deeply grieved that she is going. In fact, he is almost panic-stricken about it, getting up in a way that is full of furious sorrow and regret.*) I must go now. Please don't get up. (*JOE is up, staring at her with amazement.*) Good-by.

JOE (*simply*). Good-by.
(*The WOMAN stands looking at him a moment, then turns and goes. JOE stands staring after her for a long time. Just as he is slowly sitting down again, the NEWSBOY enters, and goes to Joe's table.*)

NEWSBOY. Paper, Mister?

JOE. How many you got this time?

NEWSBOY. Eleven.
(*JOE buys them all, looks at the lousy headlines, throws them away.
The NEWSBOY looks at JOE, amazed. He walks over to NICK at the bar.*)

NEWSBOY (*troubled*). Hey, Mister, do you own this place?

NICK (*casually but emphatically*). I own this place.

NEWSBOY. Can you use a great lyric tenor?

NICK (*almost to himself*). Great lyric tenor? (*Loudly*) Who?

NEWSBOY (*loud and the least bit angry*). Me. I'm getting too big to sell papers. I don't want to holler headlines all the time. I want to *sing*. You can use a great lyric tenor, can't you?

NICK. What's lyric about you?

NEWSBOY (*voice high-pitched, confused*). My voice.

NICK. Oh. (*Slight pause, giving in*) All right, then—sing!
(*The NEWSBOY breaks into swift and beautiful song: "When Irish Eyes Are Smiling." NICK and JOE listen carefully: NICK with wonder, JOE with amazement and delight.*)

NEWSBOY (*singing*)
When Irish eyes are smiling,
Sure 'tis like a morn in Spring.
In the lilt of Irish laughter,
You can hear the angels sing.
When Irish hearts are happy,
All the world seems bright and gay.
But when Irish eyes are smiling—

NICK (*loudly, swiftly*). Are you Irish?

NEWSBOY (*speaking swiftly, loudly, a little impatient with the irrelevant question*). No, I'm Greek. (*He finishes the song, singing louder than ever.*) Sure they steal your heart away. (*He turns to NICK dramatically, like a vaudeville singer begging his audience for applause. NICK studies the boy eagerly. JOE gets to his feet and leans toward the BOY and NICK.*)

NICK. Not bad. Let me hear you again about a year from now.

NEWSBOY (*thrilled*). Honest?

NICK. Yeah. Along about November 7th, 1940.

NEWSBOY (*happier than ever before in*

his life, running over to JOE). Did you hear it too, Mister?

JOE. Yes, and it's great. What part of Greece?

NEWSBOY. Salonica. Gosh, Mister. Thanks.

JOE. Don't wait a year. Come back with some papers a little later. You're a great singer.

NEWSBOY (*thrilled and excited*). Aw, thanks, Mister. So long. (*Running, to* NICK) Thanks, Mister. (*He runs out.* JOE *and* NICK *look at the swinging doors.* JOE *sits down.* NICK *laughs.*)

NICK. Joe, people are so wonderful. Look at that kid.

JOE. Of course they're wonderful. Every one of them is wonderful.
(MC CARTHY *and* KRUPP *come in, talking.*
MC CARTHY *is a big man in work clothes, which make him seem very young. He is wearing black jeans, and a blue workman's shirt. No tie. No hat. He has broad shoulders, a lean intelligent face, thick black hair. In his right back pocket is the longshoreman's hook. His arms are long and hairy. His sleeves are rolled up to just below his elbows. He is a casual man, easy-going in movement, sharp in perception, swift in appreciation of charm or innocence or comedy, and gentle in spirit. His speech is clear and full of warmth. His voice is powerful, but modulated. He enjoys the world, in spite of the mess it is, and he is fond of people, in spite of the mess they are.*
KRUPP *is not quite as tall or broad-shouldered as* MC CARTHY. *He is physically encumbered by his uniform, club, pistol, belt, and cap. And he is plainly not at home in the role of policeman. His movement is stiff and unintentionally pompous. He is a naive man, essentially good. His understanding is less than McCarthy's, but he is honest and he doesn't try to bluff.*)

KRUPP. You don't understand what I mean. Hi-ya, Joe.

JOE. Hello, Krupp.

MC CARTHY. Hi-ya, Joe.

JOE. Hello, McCarthy.

KRUPP. Two beers, Nick. (*To* MC CARTHY) All I do is carry out orders, carry out orders. I don't know what the idea is behind the order. Who it's for, or who it's against, or why. All I do is carry it out.
(NICK *gives them beer.*)

MC CARTHY. You don't read enough.

KRUPP. I do read. I read *The Examiner* every morning. *The Call-Bulletin* every night.

MC CARTHY. And carry out orders. What are the orders now?

KRUPP. To keep the peace down here on the waterfront.

MC CARTHY. Keep it for who? (*To* JOE) Right?

JOE (*sorrowfully*). Right.

KRUPP. How do I know for who? The peace. Just keep it.

MC CARTHY. It's got to be kept for somebody. Who would you suspect it's kept for?

KRUPP. For citizens!

MC CARTHY. I'm a citizen!

KRUPP. All right, I'm keeping it for you.

MC CARTHY. By hitting me over the head with a club? (*To* JOE) Right?

JOE (*melancholy, with remembrance*). I don't know.

KRUPP. Mac, you know I never hit you over the head with a club.

MC CARTHY. But you will if you're on duty at the time and happen to stand on the opposite side of myself, on duty.

KRUPP. We went to Mission High together. We were always good friends. The only time we ever fought was that time over Alma Haggerty. Did *you* marry Alma Haggerty? (*To* JOE) Right?

JOE. Everything's right.

MC CARTHY. No. Did you? (*To* JOE) Joe, are you with me or against me?

JOE. I'm with everybody. One at a time.

KRUPP. No. And that's just what I mean.

MC CARTHY. You mean neither one of us is going to marry the thing we're fighting for?

KRUPP. *I don't even know what it is.*

MC CARTHY. You don't read enough, I tell you.

KRUPP. Mac, you don't know what you're fighting for, either.

MC CARTHY. It's so simple, it's fantastic.

KRUPP. All right, what are you fighting for?

MC CARTHY. For the rights of the inferior. Right?

JOE. Something like that.

KRUPP. The who?

MC CARTHY. The inferior. The world full of Mahoneys who haven't got what it takes to make monkeys out of everybody else, near by. The men who were created equal. Remember?

KRUPP. Mac, you're not inferior.

MC CARTHY. I'm a longshoreman. And an idealist. I'm a man with too much brawn to be an intellectual, exclusively. I married a small, sensitive, cultured woman so that my kids would be sissies instead of suckers. A strong man with any sensibility has no choice in this world but to be a heel, or a *worker*. I haven't the heart to be a heel, so I'm a worker. I've got a son in high school who's already thinking of being a writer.

KRUPP. I wanted to be a writer once.

JOE. Wonderful. (*He puts down the paper, looks at* KRUPP *and* MC CARTHY.)

MC CARTHY. They *all* wanted to be writers. Every maniac in the world that ever brought about the murder of people through war started out in an attic or a basement writing poetry. It stank. So they got even by becoming important heels. And it's still going on.

KRUPP. Is it really, Joe?

JOE. Look at today's paper.

MC CARTHY. Right now on Telegraph Hill is some punk who is trying to be Shakespeare. Ten years from now he'll be a senator. Or a communist.

KRUPP. Somebody ought to do something about it.

MC CARTHY (*mischievously, with laughter in his voice*). The thing to do is to have more magazines. Hundreds of them. *Thousands.* Print everything they write, so they'll believe they're immortal. That way keep them from going haywire.

KRUPP. Mac, you ought to be a writer yourself.

MC CARTHY. I hate the tribe. They're mischief-makers. Right?

JOE (*swiftly*). Everything's right. Right and wrong.

KRUPP. Then why do you read?

MC CARTHY (*laughing*). It's relaxing. It's soothing. (*Pause.*) The lousiest people born into the world are writers. Language is all right. It's the people who use language that are lousy. (*The* ARAB *has moved a little closer, and is listening carefully. To the* ARAB) What do you think, Brother?

ARAB (*after making many faces, thinking very deeply*). No foundation. All the way down the line. What. Whatnot. Nothing. I go walk and look at sky. (*He goes.*)

KRUPP. What? What-not? (*To* JOE) What's that mean?

JOE (*slowly, thinking, remembering*). What? What-not? That means this side, Inhale, exhale. What: birth. What-not: death. The inevitable, the astounding, the magnificent seed of growth and decay in all things. Beginning, and end. That man, in his own way, is a prophet. He is one who, with the help of *beer*, is able to reach that state of deep understanding in which what and whatnot, the reasonable and the unreasonable, are *one*.

MC CARTHY. Right.

KRUPP. If you can understand that kind of talk, how can you be a longshoreman?

MC CARTHY. I come from a long line of McCarthys who never married or slept with anything but the most powerful and quarrelsome flesh. (*He drinks beer.*)

KRUPP. I could listen to you two guys for hours, but I'll be damned if I know what the hell you're talking about.

MC CARTHY. The consequence is that all the McCarthys are too great and too strong to be heroes. Only the weak and unsure perform the heroic. They've *got* to. The more heroes you have, the worse the history of the world becomes. Right?

JOE. Go outside and look at it.

KRUPP. You sure can philos—philosoph — Boy, you can talk.

MC CARTHY. I wouldn't talk this way to anyone but a man in uniform, and a man who couldn't understand a word of what I was saying. The party I'm speaking of, my friend, is YOU.
(*The phone rings.*
HARRY *gets up from his table suddenly and begins a new dance.*)

KRUPP (*noticing him, with great authority*). Here. Here. What do you think you're doing?

HARRY (*stopping*). I just got an idea for a new dance. I'm trying it out. Nick. Nick, the phone's ringing.

KRUPP (*to* MC CARTHY). Has he got a right to do that?

MC CARTHY. The living have danced from the beginning of time. I might even say, the dance and the life have moved along together, until now we have—(*To* HARRY) Go into your dance, son, and show us what we have.

HARRY. I haven't got it worked out *completely* yet, but it starts out like this. (*He dances.*)

NICK (*on phone*). Nick's Pacific Street Restaurant, Saloon, and Entertainment Palace. Good afternoon. Nick speaking. (*Listens*) Who? (*Turns around.*) Is there a Dudley Bostwick in the joint? (DUDLEY *jumps to his feet and goes to phone.*)

DUDLEY (*on phone*). Hello. Elsie? (*Listens*) You're coming down? (*Elated. To the saloon*) She's coming down. (*Pause.*) No. I won't drink. Aw, gosh, Elsie. (*He hangs up, looks about him strangely, as if he were just born, walks around touching things, putting chairs in place, and so on.*)

MC CARTHY (*to* HARRY). Splendid. Splendid.

HARRY. Then I go into this little routine. (*He demonstrates.*)

KRUPP. Is that good, Mac?

MC CARTHY. It's awful, but it's honest and ambitious, like everything else in this great country.

HARRY. Then I work along into this. (*He demonstrates.*) And *this* is where I *really* get going. (*He finishes the dance.*)

MC CARTHY. Excellent. A most satisfying demonstration of the present state of the American body and soul. Son, you're a genius.

HARRY (*delighted, shaking hands with* MC CARTHY). I go on in front of an audience for the first time in my life tonight.

MC CARTHY. They'll be delighted. Where'd you learn to dance?

HARRY. Never took a lesson in my life. I'm a natural-born dancer. And *comedian,* too.

MC CARTHY (*astounded*). You can make people *laugh?*

HARRY (*dumbly*). I can be funny, but they won't laugh.

MC CARTHY. That's odd. Why not?

HARRY. I don't know. They just won't laugh.

MC CARTHY. Would you care to be funny now?

HARRY. I'd like to try out a new monologue I've been thinking about.

MC CARTHY. Please do. I promise you if it's funny I shall *roar* with laughter.

HARRY. This is it. (*Goes into the act, with much energy.*) I'm up at Sharkey's on Turk Street. It's a quarter to nine, daylight saving. Wednesday, the eleventh. What I've got is a headache and a 1918 nickel. What I *want* is a cup of coffee. If I buy a cup of coffee with the nickel, I've got to walk home. I've got an eight-ball problem. George the Greek is shooting a game of snooker with Pedro the Filipino. *I'm in rags.* They're wearing thirty-five dollar suits, made to order. I haven't got a cigarette. They're smoking Bobby Burns panatelas. I'm thinking it over, like I always do. George the Greek is in a tough spot. If I buy a cup of coffee, I'll want another cup. What happens? My *ear* aches! My ear. George the Greek takes the cue. Chalks it. Studies the table. Touches the cue-ball delicately. Tick. What happens? He makes the three-ball! What do I do? I get confused. *I go out and buy a morning paper.* What the hell do I want with a morning paper? What I want is a cup of coffee, and a good used car. I go out and buy a morning paper. Thursday, the twelfth. Maybe the headline's about *me.* I take a quick look. *No. The headline is not about me.* It's about Hitler. Seven thousand miles away. I'm here. Who the hell is Hitler? Who's behind the eight-ball? I turn around. *Everybody's behind the eight-ball!*
(*Pause.* KRUPP *moves toward* HARRY *as if to make an important arrest.* HARRY *moves to the swinging doors.* MC-CARTHY *stops* KRUPP.)

MC CARTHY (*to* HARRY). It's the funniest thing I've ever heard. Or *seen,* for that matter.

HARRY (*coming back to* MC CARTHY). Then, why don't you laugh?

MC CARTHY. I don't know, *yet.*

HARRY. I'm always getting funny ideas that nobody will laugh at.

MC CARTHY (*thoughtfully*). It may be that you've stumbled headlong into a new kind of comedy.

HARRY. Well, what good is it if it doesn't make anybody laugh?

MC CARTHY. There are *kinds* of laughter, son. I must say, in all truth, that I *am* laughing, although not *out loud.*

HARRY. I want to *hear* people laugh. *Out loud.* That's why I keep thinking of funny things to say.

MC CARTHY. Well. They may catch on in time. Let's go, Krupp. So long, Joe. (MC CARTHY *and* KRUPP *go.*)

JOE. So long. (*After a moment's pause*) Hey, Nick.

NICK. Yeah.

JOE. Bet McCarthy in the last race.

NICK. You're crazy. That horse is a double-crossing, no good—

JOE. Bet everything you've got on McCarthy.

NICK. I'm not betting a nickel on him. *You* bet everything you've got on McCarthy.

JOE. I don't need money.

NICK. What makes you think McCarthy's going to win?

JOE. McCarthy's name's McCarthy, isn't it?

NICK. Yeah. So what?

JOE. The *horse* named McCarthy is going to win, *that's all.* Today.

NICK. Why?

JOE. You do what I tell you, and everything will be all right.

NICK. McCarthy likes to talk, that's all. (*Pause.*) Where's Tom?

JOE. He'll be around. He'll be miserable, but he'll be around. Five or ten minutes more.

NICK. You don't believe that Kitty, do you? About being in burlesque?

JOE (*very clearly*). I believe dreams sooner than statistics.

NICK (*remembering*). She sure is somebody. Called me a dentist. (TOM, *turning about, confused, troubled, comes in, and hurries to* JOE's *table.*)

JOE. What's the matter?

TOM. Here's your five, Joe. I'm in trouble again.

JOE. If it's not organic, it'll cure itself. If it is organic, science will cure it. What is it, organic or non-organic?

TOM. Joe. I don't know— (*He seems to be completely broken-down.*)

JOE. What's eating you? I want you to go on an errand for me.

TOM. It's Kitty.

JOE. What about her?

TOM. She's up in her room, crying.

JOE. Crying?

TOM. Yeah, she's been crying for over an hour. I been talking to her all this time, but she won't stop.

JOE. What's she crying about?

TOM. I don't know. I couldn't understand anything. She kept crying and telling me about a big house and collie dogs all around and flowers and one of her brother's dead and the other one lost somewhere. Joe, I can't stand Kitty crying.

JOE. You want to marry the girl?

TOM (nodding). Yeah.

JOE (curious and sincere). Why?

TOM. I don't know why, exactly, Joe. (Pause.) Joe, I don't like to think of Kitty out in the streets. I guess I love her, that's all.

JOE. She's a nice girl.

TOM. She's like an angel. She's not like those other streetwalkers.

JOE (swiftly). Here. Take all this money and run next door to Frankie's and bet it on the nose of McCarthy.

TOM (swiftly). All this money, Joe? McCarthy?

JOE. Yeah. Hurry.

TOM (going). Ah, Joe. If McCarthy wins we'll be rich.

JOE. Get going, will you?
(TOM runs out and nearly knocks over the ARAB coming back in. NICK fills him a beer without a word.)

ARAB. No foundation, anywhere. Whole world. No foundation. All the way down the line.

NICK (angry). McCarthy! Just because you got a little lucky this morning, you have to go to work and throw away eighty bucks.

JOE. He wants to marry her.

NICK. Suppose she doesn't want to marry him?

JOE (amazed). Oh, yeah. (Thinking) Now, why wouldn't she want to marry a nice guy like Tom?

NICK. She's been in burlesque. She's had flowers sent to her by European royalty. She's dined with young men of quality and social position. She's above Tom.
(TOM comes running in.)

TOM (disgusted). They were running when I got there. Frankie wouldn't take the bet. McCarthy didn't get a call till the stretch. I thought we were going to save all this money. Then Mc-Carthy won by two lengths.

JOE. What'd he pay, fifteen to one?

TOM. Better, but Frankie wouldn't take the bet.

NICK (throwing a dish towel across the room). Well, for the love of Mike.

JOE. Give me the money.

TOM (giving back the money). We would have had about a thousand five hundred dollars.

JOE (bored, casually, inventing). Go up to Schwabacher-Frey and get me the biggest Rand-McNally map of the nations of Europe they've got. On your way back stop at one of the pawn shops on Third Street, and buy me a good revolver and some cartridges.

TOM. She's up in her room crying, Joe.

JOE. Go get me those things.

NICK. What are you going to do, study the map, and then go out and shoot somebody?

JOE. I want to read the names of some European towns and rivers and valleys and mountains.

NICK. What do you want with the revolver?

JOE. I want to study it. I'm interested in things. Here's twenty dollars, Tom. Now go get them things.

TOM. A big map of Europe. And a revolver.

JOE. Get a good one. Tell the man you don't know anything about firearms and you're trusting him not to fool you. Don't pay more than ten dollars.

TOM. Joe, you got something on your mind. Don't go fool with a revolver.

JOE. Be sure it's a good one.

TOM. Joe.

JOE (*irritated*). What, Tom?

TOM. Joe, what do you send me out for crazy things for all the time?

JOE (*angry*). They're not crazy, Tom. Now, get going.

TOM. What about Kitty, Joe?

JOE. Let her cry. It'll do her good.

TOM. If she comes in here while I'm gone, talk to her, will you, Joe? Tell her about me.

JOE O.K. Get going. Don't load that gun. Just buy it and bring it here.

TOM (*going*). You won't catch me loading any gun.

JOE. Wait a minute. Take these toys away.

TOM. Where'll I take them?

JOE. Give them to some kid. (*Pause.*) No. Take them up to Kitty. Toys stopped me from crying once. That's the reason I had you buy them. I wanted to see if I could find out *why* they stopped me from crying. I remember they seemed awfully stupid at the time.

TOM. Shall I, Joe? Take them up to Kitty? Do you think they'd stop *her* from crying?

JOE. They might. You get curious about the way they work and you forget whatever it is you're remembering that's making you cry. That's what they're for.

TOM. Yeah. Sure. The girl at the store asked me what I wanted with toys. I'll take them up to Kitty. (*Tragically*) She's like a little girl. (*He goes.*)

WESLEY. Mr. Nick, can I play the piano again?

NICK. Sure. Practice all you like—until I tell you to stop.

WESLEY. You going to pay me for playing the piano?

NICK. Sure. I'll give you enough to get by on.

WESLEY (*amazed and delighted*). Get money for playing the piano? (*He goes to the piano and begins to play quietly.* HARRY *goes up on the little stage and listens to the music. After a while he begins a soft shoe dance.*)

NICK. What were you crying about?

JOE. My mother.

NICK. What about her?

JOE. She was dead. I stopped crying when they gave me the toys.
(NICK'S MOTHER, *a little old woman of sixty or so, dressed plainly in black, her face shining, comes in briskly, chattering loudly in Italian, gesturing.* NICK *is delighted to see her.*)

NICK'S MOTHER. (*in Italian*). Everything all right, Nickie?

NICK (*in Italian*). Sure, Mamma.
(NICK'S MOTHER *leaves as gaily and as*

noisily as she came, after half a minute of loud Italian family talk.)

JOE. Who was that?

NICK (*to* JOE, *proudly and a little sadly*). My mother. (*Still looking at the swinging doors.*)

JOE. What'd she say?

NICK. Nothing. Just wanted to see me. (*Pause.*) What do you want with that gun?

JOE. I study things, Nick.
(*An old man who looks as if he might have been* KIT CARSON *at one time walks in importantly, moves about, and finally stands at* JOE's *table.*)

KIT CARSON. Murphy's the name. Just an old trapper. Mind if I sit down?

JOE. Be delighted. What'll you drink?

KIT CARSON (*sitting down*). Beer. Same as I've been drinking. And thanks.

JOE (*to* NICK). Glass of beer, Nick.
(NICK *brings the beer to the table,* KIT CARSON *swallows it in one swig, wipes his big white mustache with the back of his right hand.*)

KIT CARSON (*moving in*). I don't suppose you ever fell in love with a midget weighing thirty-nine pounds?

JOE (*studying the man*). Can't say I have, but have another beer.

KIT CARSON (*intimately*). Thanks, thanks. Down in Gallup, twenty years ago. Fellow by the name of Rufus Jenkins came to town with six white horses and two black ones. Said he wanted a man to break the horses for him because his left leg was wood and he couldn't do it. Had a meeting at Parker's Mercantile Store and finally came to blows, me and Henry Walpal. Bashed his head with a brass cuspidor

and ran away to Mexico, but he didn't die.

Couldn't speak a word. Took up with a cattle-breeder named Diego, educated in California. Spoke the language better than you and me. Said, Your job, Murph, is to feed them prize bulls. I said, Fine, what'll I feed them? He said, Hay, lettuce, salt, beer, and aspirin.

Came to blows two days later over an accordion he claimed I stole. I had borrowed it. During the fight I busted it over his head; ruined one of the finest accordions I ever saw. Grabbed a horse and rode back across the border. Texas. Got to talking with a fellow who looked honest. Turned out to be a Ranger who was looking for me.

JOE. Yeah. You were saying, a thirty-nine pound midget.

KIT CARSON. Will I ever forget that lady? Will I ever get over that amazon of small proportions?

JOE. Will you?

KIT CARSON. If I live to be sixty.

JOE. Sixty? You look more than sixty now.

KIT CARSON. That's trouble showing in my face. Trouble and complications. I was fifty-eight three months ago.

JOE. That accounts for it, then. Go ahead, tell me more.

KIT CARSON. Told the Texas Ranger my name was Rothstein, mining engineer from Pennsylvania, looking for something worth while. Mentioned two places in Houston. Nearly lost an eye early one morning, going down the stairs. Ran into a six-footer with an iron claw where his right hand was supposed to be. Said, You broke up my home. Told him I was a stranger in Houston. The girls gathered at the top of the stairs to see a fight. Seven of them. Six feet and an iron claw. That's bad on the nerves. Kicked him in the mouth when he swung for my head with the claw. Would have lost an eye except for quick thinking. He rolled into the gutter and pulled a gun. Fired seven times. I was back upstairs. Left the place an hour later, dressed in silk and feathers, with a hat swung around over my face. Saw him standing on the corner, waiting. Said, Care for a wiggle? Said he didn't. I went on down the street and left town. I don't suppose you ever had to put a dress on to save your skin, did you?

JOE. No, and I never fell in love with a midget weighing thirty-nine pounds. Have another beer?

KIT CARSON. Thanks. (*Swallows glass of beer.*) Ever try to herd cattle on a bicycle?

JOE. No. I never got around to that.

KIT CARSON. Left Houston with sixty cents in my pocket, gift of a girl named Lucinda. Walked fourteen miles in fourteen hours. Big house with barbwire all around, and big dogs. One thing I never could get around. Walked past the gate, anyway, from hunger, and thirst. Dogs jumped up and came for me. Walked right into them, growing older every second. Went up to the door and knocked. Big negress opened the door, closed it quick. Said, On your way, white trash.

Knocked again. Said, On your way. Again. On your way. Again. This time the old man himself opened the door, ninety, if he was a day. Sawed-off shotgun, too.

Said, I ain't looking for trouble, Father. I'm hungry and thirsty, name's Cavanaugh.

Took me in and made mint juleps for the two of us.

Said, Living here alone, Father?

Said, Drink and ask no questions. Maybe I am and maybe I ain't. You saw the lady. Draw your own conclusions.

I'd heard of that, but didn't wink out of tact. If I told you that old Southern gentleman was my grandfather you wouldn't believe me, would you?

JOE. I might.

KIT CARSON. Well, it so happens he wasn't. Would have been romantic if he had been, though.

JOE. Where did you herd cattle on a bicycle?

KIT CARSON. Toledo, Ohio, 1918.

JOE. Toledo, Ohio? They don't herd cattle in Toledo.

KIT CARSON. They don't any more. They did in 1918. One fellow did, leastaways. Bookkeeper named Sam Gold. Straight from the East Side, New York. Sombrero, lariats, Bull Durham, two head of cattle and two bicycles. Called his place The Gold Bar Ranch, two acres, just outside the city limits.

That was the year of the War, you'll remember.

JOE. Yeah, I remember, but how about herding them two cows on a bicycle? How'd you do it?

KIT CARSON. Easiest thing in the world. Rode no hands. Had to, otherwise couldn't lasso the cows. Worked for Sam Gold till the cows ran away. Bicycles scared them. They went into Toledo. Never saw hide nor hair of them again. Advertised in every paper, but never got them back. Broke his heart. Sold both bikes and returned to New York.

Took four aces from a deck of red

cards and walked to town. Poker. Fellow in the game named Chuck Collins, liked to gamble. Told him with a smile I didn't suppose he'd care to bet a hundred dollars I wouldn't hold four aces the next hand. Called it. My cards were red on the blank side. The other cards were blue. Plumb forgot all about it. Showed him four aces. Ace of spades, ace of clubs, ace of diamonds, ace of hearts. I'll remember them four cards if I live to be sixty. Would have been killed on the spot except for the hurricane that year.

JOE. Hurricane?

KIT CARSON. You haven't forgotten the Toledo hurricane of 1918, have you?

JOE. No. There was no hurricane in Toledo in 1918, or any other year.

KIT CARSON. For the love of God, then what do you suppose that commotion was? And how come I came to in Chicago, dream-walking down State Street?

JOE. I guess they scared you.

KIT CARSON. No, that wasn't it. You go back to the papers of November 1918, and I think you'll find there was a hurricane in Toledo. I remember sitting on the roof of a two-story house, floating northwest.

JOE (seriously). Northwest?

KIT CARSON. Now, son, don't tell me you don't believe me, either?

JOE (Pause. Very seriously, energetically and sharply). Of course I believe you. Living is an art. It's not bookkeeping. It takes a lot of rehearsing for a man to get to be himself.

KIT CARSON (thoughtfully, smiling and amazed). You're the first man I've ever met who believes me.

JOE (seriously). Have another beer. (TOM comes in with the Rand-McNally book, the revolver, and the box of cartridges. KIT goes to bar.)

JOE (to TOM). Did you give her the toys?

TOM. Yeah, I gave them to her.

JOE. Did she stop crying?

TOM. No. She started crying harder than ever.

JOE. That's funny. I wonder why.

TOM. Joe, if I was a minute earlier, Frank would have taken the bet and now we'd have about a thousand five hundred dollars. How much of it would you have given me, Joe?

JOE. If she'd marry you—all of it.

TOM. Would you, Joe?

JOE (opening packages, examining book first, and revolver next). Sure. In this realm there's only one subject, and you're it. It's my duty to see that my subject is happy.

TOM. Joe, do you think we'll ever have eighty dollars for a race sometime again when there's a fifteen-to-one shot that we like, weather good, track fast, they get off to a good start, our horse doesn't get a call till the stretch, we think we're going to lose all that money, and then it wins, by a nose?

JOE. I didn't quite get that.

TOM. You know what I mean.

JOE. You mean the impossible. No, Tom, we won't. We were just a little late, that's all.

TOM. We might, Joe.

JOE. It's not likely.

TOM. Then how am I ever going to make enough money to marry her?

JOE. I don't know, Tom. Maybe you aren't.

TOM. Joe, I got to marry Kitty. (*Shaking his head*) You ought to see the crazy room she lives in.

JOE. What kind of a room is it?

TOM. It's little. It crowds you in. It's bad, Joe. Kitty don't belong in a place like that.

JOE. You want to take her away from there?

TOM. Yeah. I want her to live in a house where there's room enough to live. Kitty ought to have a garden, or something.

JOE. You want to take care of her?

TOM. Yeah, sure, Joe. I ought to take care of somebody good that makes me feel like *I'm* somebody.

JOE. That means you'll have to get a job. What can you do?

TOM. I finished high school, but I don't know what I can do.

JOE. Sometimes when you think about it, what do you think you'd like to do?

TOM. Just sit around like you, Joe, and have somebody run errands for me and drink champagne and take things easy and never be broke and never worry about money.

JOE. That's a noble ambition.

NICK (*to* JOE). How do you do it?

JOE. I really don't know, but I think you've got to have the full co-operation of the Good Lord.

NICK. I can't understand the way you talk.

TOM. Joe, shall I go back and see if I can get her to stop crying?

JOE. Give me a hand and I'll go with you.

TOM (*amazed*). What! You're going to get up already?

JOE. She's crying, isn't she?

TOM. She's crying. Worse than ever now.

JOE. I thought the toys would stop her.

TOM. I've seen you sit in one place from four in the morning till two the next morning.

JOE. At my best, Tom, I don't travel by foot. That's all. Come on. Give me a hand. I'll find some way to stop her from crying.

TOM (*helping* JOE). Joe, I never did tell you. You're a different kind of a guy.

JOE (*swiftly, a little angry*). Don't be silly. I don't understand things. I'm trying to understand them.
(JOE *is a little drunk. They go out together. The lights go down slowly, while* WESLEY *plays the piano, and come up slowly on:*)

ACT THREE

A cheap bed in Nick's to indicate room 21 of The New York Hotel, upstairs, around the corner from Nick's. The bed can be at the center of Nick's, or up on the little stage. Everything in Nick's is the same, except that all the people are silent, immobile and in darkness, except WESLEY who is playing the piano softly and sadly. KITTY DUVAL, *in a dress she has carried around with her from the early days in Ohio, is seated on the bed, tying a ribbon in her hair. She looks at herself in a hand mirror. She is deeply grieved at the change she sees in herself. She takes off the ribbon, angry and hurt. She lifts a book from the bed and tries to read. She begins to sob again. She picks up an old picture of herself and looks at it. Sobs harder than ever, falling on the bed and burying her face. There is a knock, as if at the door.*

KITTY (*sobbing*). Who is it?

TOM'S VOICE. Kitty, it's me. Tom. Me and Joe.
(JOE, *followed by* TOM, *comes to the bed quietly.* JOE *is holding a rather large toy carousel.* JOE *studies* KITTY *a moment.*
He sets the toy carousel on the floor, at the foot of Kitty's bed.)

TOM (*standing over* KITTY *and bending down close to her*). Don't cry any more, Kitty.

KITTY (*not looking, sobbing*). I don't like this life.
(JOE *starts the carousel which makes a strange, sorrowful, tinkling music. The music begins slowly, becomes swift, gradually slows down, and ends.* JOE *himself is interested in the toy, watches and listens to it carefully.*)

TOM (*eagerly*). Kitty. Joe got up from his chair at Nick's just to get you a toy and come here. This one makes music. We rode all over town in a cab to get it. Listen.
(KITTY *sits up slowly, listening, while* TOM *watches her. Everything happens slowly and somberly.* KITTY *notices the photograph of herself when she was a little girl. Lifts it, and looks at it again.*)

TOM (*looking*). Who's that little girl, Kitty?

KITTY. That's me. When I was seven.
(KITTY *hands the photo to* TOM.)

TOM (*looking, smiling*). Gee, you're pretty, Kitty.
(JOE *reaches up for the photograph, which* TOM *hands to him.* TOM *returns to* KITTY *whom he finds as pretty now as she was at seven.* JOE *studies the photograph.* KITTY *looks up at* TOM. *There is no doubt that they really love one another.* JOE *looks up at them.*)

KITTY. Tom?

TOM (*eagerly*). Yeah, Kitty.

KITTY. Tom, when you were a little boy what did you want to be?

TOM (*a little bewildered, but eager to please her*). What, Kitty?

KITTY. Do you remember when you were a little boy?

TOM (*thoughtfully*). Yeah, I remember sometimes, Kitty.

KITTY. What did you want to be?

TOM (*Looks at* JOE. JOE *holds Tom's*

eyes a moment. Then TOM *is able to speak*). Sometimes I wanted to be a locomotive engineer. Sometimes I wanted to be a policeman.

KITTY. I wanted to be a great actress. (*She looks up into Tom's face.*) Tom, didn't you ever want to be a doctor?

TOM (*Looks at* JOE. JOE *holds Tom's eyes again, encouraging Tom by his serious expression to go on talking*). Yeah, now I remember. Sure, Kitty. I wanted to be a doctor—*once.*

KITTY (*smiling sadly*). I'm so glad. Because I wanted to be an actress and have a young doctor come to the theater and see me and fall in love with me and send me flowers. (JOE *pantomimes to* TOM, *demanding that he go on talking.*)

TOM. I would do that, Kitty.

KITTY. I wouldn't know who it was, and then one day I'd see him in the street and fall in love with him. I wouldn't know *he* was the one who was in love with me. I'd think about him all the time. I'd dream about him. I'd dream of being near him the rest of my life. I'd dream of having children that looked like him. I wouldn't be an actress all the time. Only until I found him and fell in love with him. After that we'd take a train and go to beautiful cities and see the wonderful people everywhere and give money to the poor and whenever people were sick he'd go to them and make them well again. (TOM *looks at* JOE, *bewildered, confused, and full of sorrow.* KITTY *is deep in memory, almost in a trance.*)

JOE (*gently*). Talk to her, Tom. Be the wonderful young doctor she dreamed about and never found. Go ahead. Correct the errors of the world.

TOM. Joe. (*pathetically*) I don't know what to say. (*There is rowdy singing in the hall. A* loud *young* VOICE *sings*: "Sailing, sailing, over the bounding main.")

VOICE. Kitty. Oh, Kitty! (KITTY *stirs, shocked, coming out of the trance.*) Where the hell are you? Oh, Kitty. (TOM *jumps up, furiously.*)

WOMAN'S VOICE (*in the hall*). Who you looking for, Sailor Boy?

VOICE. The most beautiful lay in the world.

WOMAN'S VOICE. Don't go any further.

VOICE (*with impersonal contempt*). You? No. Not you. Kitty. You stink.

WOMAN'S VOICE (*rasping, angry*). Don't you dare talk to me that way. You pickpocket.

VOICE (*still impersonal, but louder*). Oh, I see. Want to get tough, hey? Close the door. Go hide.

WOMAN'S VOICE. You pickpocket. All of you. (*The door slams.*)

VOICE (*roaring with laughter which is very sad*). Oh—Kitty. Room 21. Where the hell is that room?

TOM (*to* JOE). Joe, I'll kill him.

KITTY (*fully herself again, terribly frightened*). Who is it? (*She looks long and steadily at* TOM *and* JOE. TOM *is standing, excited and angry.* JOE *is completely at ease, his expression full of pity.* KITTY *buries her face in the bed.*)

JOE (*gently*). Tom. Just take him away.

VOICE. Here it is. Number 21. Three naturals. Heaven. My blue heaven. The west, a nest, and you. Just Molly and me. (*Tragically*) Ah, to hell with everything.

(*A young* SAILOR, *a good-looking boy of no more than twenty or so, who is only drunk and lonely, comes to the bed, singing sadly.*)

SAILOR. Hi-ya, Kitty. (*Pause.*) Oh. Visitors. Sorry. A thousand apologies. (*To* KITTY) I'll come back later.

TOM (*taking him by the shoulders, furiously*). If you do, I'll kill you. (JOE *holds* TOM. TOM *pushes the frightened boy away.*)

JOE (*somberly*). Tom. You stay here with Kitty. I'm going down to Union Square to hire an automobile. I'll be back in a few minutes. We'll ride out to the ocean and watch the sun go down. Then we'll ride down the Great Highway to Half Moon Bay. We'll have supper down there, and you and Kitty can dance.

TOM (*stupefied, unable to express his amazement and gratitude*). Joe, you mean you're going to go on an errand for *me?* You mean you're not going to send me?

JOE. That's right.
(*He gestures toward* KITTY, *indicating that* TOM *shall talk to her, protect the innocence in her which is in so much danger when* TOM *isn't near, which* TOM *loves so deeply.* JOE *leaves.* TOM *studies* KITTY, *his face becoming childlike and somber. He sets the carousel into motion, listens, watching* KITTY, *who lifts herself slowly, looking only at* TOM. TOM *lifts the turning carousel and moves it slowly toward* KITTY, *as though the toy were his heart. The piano music comes up loudly and the lights go down, while* HARRY *is heard dancing swiftly.*)

ACT FOUR

A little later.
WESLEY, *the colored boy, is at the piano.*
HARRY *is on the little stage, dancing.*
NICK *is behind the bar.*
The ARAB *is in his place.*
KIT CARSON *is asleep on his folded arms.*

The DRUNKARD *comes in. Goes to the telephone for the nickel that might be in the return-chute.* NICK *comes to take him out. He gestures for* NICK *to hold on a minute. Then produces a half dollar.* NICK *goes behind the bar to serve the* DRUNKARD *whiskey.*

THE DRUNKARD. To the old, God bless them. (*Another*) To the new, God love them. (*Another*) To—children and small animals, like little dogs that don't bite. (*Another. Loudly*) To reforestation. (*Searches for money. Finds some.*) To—President Taft. (*He goes out.*)
(*The telephone rings.*)

KIT CARSON (*jumping up, fighting*). Come on, *all* of you, if you're looking for trouble. I never asked for quarter and I always gave it.

NICK (*reproachfully*). Hey, Kit Carson.

DUDLEY (*on the phone*). Hello. Who? Nick? Yes. He's here. (*To* NICK) It's for you. I think it's important.

NICK (*going to the phone*). Important! *What's* important?

DUDLEY. He sounded like big-shot.

NICK. Big *what?* (*To* WESLEY *and* HARRY) Hey, you. Quiet. I want to hear this important stuff.

(WESLEY *stops playing the piano.* HARRY *stops dancing.* KIT CARSON *comes close to* NICK.)

KIT CARSON. If there's anything I can do, name it. I'll do it for you. I'm fifty-eight years old; been through three wars; married four times; the father of countless children whose *names* I don't even know. I've got no money. I live from hand to mouth. But if there's anything I can do, name it. I'll do it.

NICK (*patiently*). Listen, Pop. For a moment, please sit down and go back to sleep—*for me.*

KIT CARSON. I can do that, too. (*He sits down, folds his arms, and puts his head into them. But not for long. As* NICK *begins to talk, he listens carefully, gets to his feet, and then begins to express in pantomime the moods of each of* NICK's *remarks.*)

NICK (*on phone*). Yeah? (*Pause*) Who? Oh, I see. (*Listens*) Why don't you leave them alone? (*Listens*) The church-people? Well, to hell with the church-people. I'm a Catholic myself. (*Listens*) All right. I'll send them away. I'll tell them to lay low for a couple of days. Yeah, I know how it is. (*Nick's daughter* ANNA *comes in shyly, looking at her father, and stands unnoticed by the piano.*) What? (*Very angry*) Listen. I don't like that Blick. He was here this morning, and I told him not to come back. I'll keep the girls out of here. You keep Blick out of here. (*Listens*) I know his brother-in-law is important, but I don't want him to come down here. He looks for trouble everywhere, and he always finds it. I don't break any laws. I've got a dive in the lousiest part of town. Five years nobody's been robbed, murdered, or gypped. I leave people alone. Your swanky joints uptown make trouble for

you every night. (NICK *gestures to* WESLEY—*keeps listening on the phone—puts his hand over the mouthpiece. To* WESLEY *and* HARRY) Start playing again. My ears have got a headache. Go into your dance, son. (WESLEY *begins to play again.* HARRY *begins to dance.* NICK, *into mouthpiece*) Yeah. I'll keep them out. Just see that Blick doesn't come around and start something. (*Pause*) O.K. (*He hangs up.*)

KIT CARSON. Trouble coming?

NICK. That lousy Vice Squad again. It's that gorilla Blick.

KIT CARSON. Anybody at all. You can count on me. What kind of a gorilla is this gorilla Blick?

NICK. Very dignified. Toenails on his fingers.

ANNA (*to* KIT CARSON, *with great, warm, beautiful pride, pointing at* NICK). That's my father.

KIT CARSON (*leaping with amazement at the beautiful voice, the wondrous face, the magnificent event*). Well, bless your heart, child. Bless your lovely heart. I had a little daughter point me out in a crowd once.

NICK (*surprised*). Anna. What the hell are you doing here? Get back home where you belong and help Grandma cook me some supper. (ANNA *smiles at her father, understanding him, knowing that his words are words of love. She turns and goes, looking at him all the way out, as much as to say that she would cook for him the rest of her life.* NICK *stares at the swinging doors.* KIT CARSON *moves toward them, two or three steps.* ANNA *pushes open one of the doors and peeks in, to look at her father again. She waves to him. Turns and runs.* NICK *is very sad. He doesn't know what to do. He gets a glass and a bottle. Pours himself a drink. Swallows some. It isn't enough, so he pours more and swallows the whole drink.*)

(*To himself*) My beautiful, beautiful baby. Anna, she is you again. (*He brings out a handkerchief, touches his eyes, and blows his nose.* KIT CARSON *moves close to* NICK, *watching* NICK's *face.* NICK *looks at him. Loudly, almost making* KIT *jump*) You're broke, aren't you?

KIT CARSON. Always. Always.

NICK. All right. Go into the kitchen and give Sam a hand. Eat some food and when you come back you can have a couple of beers.

KIT CARSON (*studying* NICK). Anything at all. I know a good man when I see one. (*He goes.*)
(ELSIE MANDELSPIEGEL *comes into* Nick's. *She is a beautiful, dark girl, with a sorrowful, wise, dreaming face, almost on the verge of tears, and full of pity. There is an aura of dream about her. She moves softly and gently, as if everything around her were unreal and pathetic.* DUDLEY *doesn't notice her for a moment or two. When he does finally see her, he is so amazed, he can barely move or speak. Her presence has the effect of changing him completely. He gets up from his chair, as if in a trance, and walks toward her, smiling sadly.*)

ELSIE (*looking at him*). Hello, Dudley.

DUDLEY (*broken-hearted*). Elsie.

ELSIE. I'm sorry. (*Explaining*) So many people are sick. Last night a little boy died. I love you, but— (*She gestures, trying to indicate how hopeless love is. They sit down.*)

DUDLEY (*staring at her, stunned and quieted*). Elsie. You'll never know how glad I am to see you. Just to see you. (*Pathetically*) I was afraid I'd never see you again. It was driving me crazy. I didn't want to live. Honest. (*He shakes his head mournfully, with dumb and beautiful affection.* TWO STREET-WALKERS *come in, and pause near* DUD-LEY, *at the bar.*) I know. You told me before, but I can't help it, Elsie. I love you.

ELSIE (*quietly, somberly, gently, with great compassion*). I know you love me, and I love you, but don't you see love is impossible in this world?

DUDLEY. Maybe it isn't, Elsie.

ELSIE. Love is for birds. They have wings to fly away on when it's time for flying. For tigers in the jungle because they don't know their end. We know *our* end. Every night I watch over poor, dying men. I hear them breathing, crying, talking in their sleep. Crying for air and water and love, for mother and field and sunlight. *We* can never know love or greatness. We *should* know both.

DUDLEY (*deeply moved by her words*). Elsie, I love you.

ELSIE. You want to live. *I* want to live, too, but where? Where can we escape our poor world?

DUDLEY. Elsie, we'll find a place.

ELSIE (*smiling at him*). All right. We'll try again. We'll go together to a room in a cheap hotel, and dream that the world is beautiful, and that living is full of love and greatness. But in the morning, can we forget debts, and duties, and the cost of ridiculous things?

DUDLEY (*with blind faith*). Sure, we can, Elsie.

ELSIE. All right, Dudley. Of course. Come on. The time for the new pathetic war has come. Let's hurry, before they dress you, stand you in line, hand you a gun, and have you kill and be killed. (ELSIE *looks at him gently, and takes his hand.* DUDLEY *embraces her shyly, as if he might hurt her. They go, as if they were a couple of young animals. There is a moment of silence. One of the* STREETWALKERS *bursts out laughing.*)

KILLER. Nick, what the hell kind of a joint are you running?

NICK. Well, it's not out of the world. It's on a street in a city, and people come and go. They bring whatever they've got with them and they say what they must say.

THE OTHER STREETWALKER. It's floozies like her that raise hell with our racket.

NICK (*remembering*). Oh, yeah. Finnegan telephoned.

KILLER. That mouse in elephant's body?

THE OTHER STREETWALKER. What the hell does *he* want?

NICK. Spend your time at the movies for the next couple of days.

KILLER. They're all lousy. (*Mocking*) All about love.

NICK. Lousy or not lousy, for a couple of days the flat-foots are going to be romancing you, so stay out of here, and lay low.

KILLER. I always was a pushover for a man in uniform, with a badge, a club and a gun.
(KRUPP *comes into the place. The* GIRLS *put down their drinks.*)

NICK. O.K., get going.
(*The* GIRLS *begin to leave and meet* KRUPP.)

THE OTHER STREETWALKER. We was just going.

KILLER. We was formerly models at Magnin's.
(*They go.*)

KRUPP (*at the bar*). The strike isn't enough, so they've got to put us on the tails of the girls, too. I don't know. I wish to God I was back in the Sunset holding the hands of kids going home from school, where I belong. I don't like trouble. Give me a beer. (NICK *gives him a beer. He drinks some.*) Right now, McCarthy, my best friend, is with sixty strikers who want to stop the finks who are going to try to unload the *Mary Luckenbach* tonight. Why the hell McCarthy ever became a longshoreman instead of a professor of some kind is something I'll never know.

NICK. Cowboys and Indians, cops and robbers, longshoremen and finks.

KRUPP. They're all guys who are trying to be happy; trying to make a living; support a family; bring up children; enjoy sleep. Go to a movie; take a drive on Sunday. They're all good guys, so out of nowhere, comes trouble. All they want is a chance to get out of debt and relax in front of a radio while Amos and Andy go through their act. What the hell do they always want to make trouble for? I been thinking everything over, Nick, and you know what I think?

NICK. No. What?

KRUPP. I think we're all crazy. It came to me while I was on my way to Pier 27. All of a sudden it hit me like a ton of bricks. A thing like that never happened to me before. Here we are in this wonderful world, full of all the wonderful things—here we are—all of us, and look at us. Just look at us. We're crazy. We're nuts. We've got everything, but we always feel lousy and dissatisfied just the same.

NICK. Of course we're crazy. Even so, we've got to go on living together. (*He waves at the people in his joint.*)

KRUPP. There's no hope. I don't suppose it's right for an officer of the law to feel the way I feel, but, by God, right or not right, that's how I feel. Why are we all so lousy? This is a good world. It's wonderful to get up in the morning and go out for a little walk and smell the trees and see the streets and the kids going to school and the clouds in the sky. It's wonderful just to be able to move around and whistle a song if you feel like it, or maybe try to sing one. This is a nice world. So why do they make all the trouble?

NICK. I don't know. Why?

KRUPP. We're crazy, that's why. We're no good any more. All the corruption everywhere. The poor kids selling themselves. A couple of years ago they were in grammar school. Everybody trying to get a lot of money in a hurry. Everybody betting the horses. Nobody going quietly for a little walk to the ocean. Nobody taking things easy and not wanting to make some kind of a killing. Nick, I'm going to quit being a cop. Let somebody else keep law and order. The stuff I hear about at headquarters. I'm thirty-seven years old, and I still can't get used to it. The only trouble is, the wife'll raise hell.

NICK. Ah, the wife.

KRUPP. She's a wonderful woman, Nick. We've got two of the swellest boys in the world. Twelve and seven years old. (*The* ARAB *gets up and moves closer to listen.*)

NICK. I didn't know that.

KRUPP. Sure. But what'll I do? I've wanted to quit for seven years. I wanted to quit the day they began putting me through the school. I didn't quit. What'll I do if I quit? Where's money going to be coming in from?

NICK. That's one of the reasons we're all crazy. We don't know where it's going to be coming in from, except from wherever it happens to be coming in from at the time, which we don't usually like.

KRUPP. Every once in a while I catch myself being mean, hating people just because they're down and out, broke and hungry, sick or drunk. And then when I'm with the stuffed shirts at headquarters, all of a sudden I'm nice to them, trying to make an impression. On who? People I don't like. And I feel disgusted. (*With finality*) I'm going to quit. That's all. Quit. Out. I'm going to give them back the uniform and the gadgets that go with it. I don't want any part of it. This is a good world. What do they want to make all the trouble for all the time?

ARAB (*quietly, gently, with great understanding*). No foundation. All the way down the line.

KRUPP. What?

ARAB. No foundation. No foundation.

KRUPP. I'll say there's no foundation.

ARAB. All the way down the line.

KRUPP (*to* NICK). Is that all he ever says?

NICK. That's all he's been saying *this* week.

KRUPP. What is he, anyway?

NICK. He's an Arab, or something like that.

KRUPP. No, I mean what's he do for a living?

NICK (*to* ARAB). What do you do for a living, brother?

ARAB. Work. Work all my life. All my life, work. From small boy to old man, work. In old country, work. In new country, work. In New York. Pittsburgh. Detroit. Chicago. Imperial Valley. San Francisco. Work. No beg. Work. For what? Nothing. Three boys in old country. Twenty years, not see. Lost. Dead. Who knows? What. What-not. No foundation. All the way down the line.

KRUPP. What'd he say last week?

NICK. Didn't say anything. Played the harmonica.

ARAB. Old country song, I play. (*He brings a harmonica from his back pocket.*)

KRUPP. Seems like a nice guy.

NICK. Nicest guy in the world.

KRUPP (*bitterly*). But crazy. Just like all the rest of us. Stark raving mad. (WESLEY *and* HARRY *long ago stopped playing and dancing. They sat at a table together and talked for a while; then began playing casino or rummy. When the* ARAB *begins his solo on the harmonica, they stop their game to listen.*)

WESLEY. You hear that?

HARRY. That's *something*.

WESLEY. That's crying. That's crying.

HARRY. I want to make people laugh.

WESLEY. That's deep, deep crying. That's crying a long time ago. That's crying a thousand years ago. Some place five thousand miles away.

HARRY. Do you think you can play to that?

WESLEY. I want to *sing* to that, but I can't *sing*.

HARRY. You try and play to that. I'll try to dance. (WESLEY *goes to the piano, and after closer listening, he begins to accompany the harmonica solo.* HARRY *goes to the little stage and after a few efforts begins to dance to the song. This keeps up quietly for some time.* KRUPP *and* NICK *have been silent, and deeply moved.*)

KRUPP (*softly*). Well, anyhow, Nick.

NICK. Hmmmmmmm?

KRUPP. What I said. Forget it.

NICK. Sure.

KRUPP. It gets me down once in a while.

NICK. No harm in talking.

KRUPP (*the* POLICEMAN *again, loudly*). Keep the girls out of here.

NICK (*loud and friendly*). Take it easy. (*The music and dancing are now at their height.*)

ACT FIVE

That evening. Fog-horns are heard throughout the scene. A man in evening clothes and a top hat, and his woman, also in evening clothes, are entering.

WILLIE *is still at the marble game.* NICK *is behind the bar.* JOE *is at his table, looking at the book of maps of the countries of Europe. The box containing the revolver and the box containing the cartridges are on the table, beside his glass. He is at peace, his hat tilted back on his head, a calm expression on his face.* TOM *is leaning against the bar, dreaming of love and Kitty. The* ARAB *is gone.* WESLEY *and* HARRY *are gone.* KIT CARSON *is watching the boy at the marble game.*

LADY. Oh, come on, please. (*The gentleman follows miserably.*
The SOCIETY MAN *and* WIFE *take a table.* NICK *gives them a menu.*
Outside, in the street, the Salvation Army people are playing a song. Big drum, tambourines, cornet and singing. They are singing, "The Blood of the Lamb." The music and words come into the place faintly and comically. This is followed by an old sinner testifying. It is the DRUNKARD. *His words are not intelligible, but his message is unmistakable. He is saved. He wants to sin no more. And so on.*)

DRUNKARD (*testifying, unmistakably drunk*). Brothers and sisters. I was a sinner. I chewed tobacco and chased women. Oh, I sinned, brothers and sisters. And then I was saved. Saved by the Salvation Army. God forgive me.

JOE. Let's see now. Here's a city. Pribor. Czecho-slovakia. Little, lovely, lonely Czecho-slovakia. I wonder what kind of a place Pribor was? (*Calling*) Pribor! *Pribor!*
(TOM *leaps.*)

LADY. What's the matter with him?

MAN (*crossing his legs, as if he ought to go to the men's room*). Drunk.

TOM. Who you calling, Joe?

JOE. Pribor.

TOM. Who's Pribor?

JOE. He's a Czech. And a Slav. A Czecho-slovakian.

LADY. How interesting.

MAN (*uncrosses legs*). He's drunk.

JOE. Tom, Pribor's a city in Czecho-slovakia.

TOM. Oh. (*Pause.*) You sure were nice to her, Joe.

JOE. Kitty Duval? She's one of the finest people in the world.

TOM. It sure was nice of you to hire an automobile and take us for a drive along the ocean-front and down to Half Moon Bay.

JOE. Those three hours were the most delightful, the most somber, and the most beautiful I have ever known.

TOM. Why, Joe?

JOE. Why? I'm a student. (*Lifting his voice*) Tom (*Quietly*) I'm a student. I study all things. All. All. And when my study reveals something of beauty in a place or in a person where by all rights only ugliness or death should be revealed, then I know how full of goodness this life is. And that's a good thing to know. That's a truth I shall always seek to verify.

LADY. Are you *sure* he's drunk?

MAN (*crossing his legs*). He's either drunk, or just naturally crazy.

TOM. Joe?

JOE. Yeah.

TOM. You won't get sore or anything?

JOE (*impatiently*). What is it, Tom?

TOM. Joe, where do you get all that money? You paid for the automobile. You paid for supper and the two bottles of champagne at the Half Moon Bay Restaurant. You moved Kitty out of the New York Hotel around the corner to the St. Francis Hotel on Powell Street. I saw you pay her rent. I saw you give her money for new clothes. Where do you get all that money, Joe? Three years now and I've never asked.

JOE (*looking at* TOM *sorrowfully, a little irritated, not so much with* TOM *as with the world and himself, his own superiority. He speaks clearly, slowly and solemnly*). Now don't be a fool, Tom. Listen carefully. If anybody's got any money—to hoard or to throw away—you can be sure he stole it from other people. Not from rich people who can spare it, but from poor people who can't. From their lives and from their dreams. I'm no exception. I *earned* the money I throw away. I stole it like everybody else does. I hurt people to get it. Loafing around this way, I *still* earn money. The money itself earns *more*. I *still* hurt people. I don't know who they are, or where they are. If I did, I'd feel worse than I do. I've got a Christian conscience in a world that's got no conscience at all. The world's trying to get some sort of a *social* conscience, but it's having a devil of a time trying to do *that*. I've got money. I'll always have money, as long as this world stays the way it is. I

don't work. I don't make anything. (*He sips.*) I drink. I worked when I was a kid. I worked *hard*. I mean hard, Tom. People are supposed to enjoy living. I got tired. (*He lifts the gun and looks at it while he talks.*) I decided to get even on the world. Well, you can't enjoy living unless you work. Unless you do something. I don't do anything. I don't *want* to do anything any more. There isn't anything I can do that won't make me feel embarrassed. Because I can't do simple, good things. I haven't the patience. And I'm too smart. Money is the guiltiest thing in the world. It stinks. Now, don't ever bother me about it again.

TOM. I didn't mean to make you feel bad, Joe.

JOE (*slowly*). Here. Take this gun out in the street and give it to some worthy hold-up man.

LADY. What's he saying?

MAN (*uncrosses legs*). You wanted to visit a honky-tonk. Well, *this* is a honky-tonk. (*To the world*) Married twenty-eight years and she's still looking for adventure.

TOM. How should I know who's a hold-up man?

JOE. Take it away. Give it to somebody.

TOM (*bewildered*). Do I *have* to *give* it to somebody?

JOE. Of course.

TOM. Can't I take it back and get some of our money?

JOE. Don't talk like a business man. Look around and find somebody who appears to be in need of a gun and give it to him. It's a good gun, isn't it?

TOM. The man said it was, but how can I tell who needs a gun?

JOE. Tom, you've seen good people who needed guns, haven't you?

TOM. I don't remember. Joe, I might give it to the wrong kind of guy. He might do something crazy.

JOE. All right. I'll find somebody myself. (TOM *rises*.) Here's some money. Go get me this week's *Life, Liberty, Time,* and six or seven packages of chewing gum.

TOM (*swiftly, in order to remember each item*). *Life, Liberty, Time,* and six or seven packages of chewing gum?

JOE. That's right.

TOM. All that chewing gum? What kind?

JOE. Any kind. Mix 'em up. All kinds.

TOM. Licorice, too?

JOE. Licorice, by all means.

TOM. Juicy Fruit?

JOE. Juicy Fruit.

TOM. Tutti-frutti?

JOE. Is there such a gum?

TOM. I think so.

JOE. All right. Tutti-frutti, too. Get *all* the kinds. Get as many kinds as they're selling.

TOM. *Life, Liberty, Time,* and all the different kinds of gum. (*He begins to go.*)

JOE (*calling after him loudly*). Get some jelly beans too. All the different colors.

TOM. All right, Joe.

JOE. And the longest panatela cigar you can find. Six of them.

TOM. Panatela. I got it.

JOE. Give a news-kid a dollar.

TOM. O.K., Joe.

JOE. Give some old man a dollar.

TOM. O.K., Joe.

JOE. Give them Salvation Army people in the street a couple of dollars and ask them to sing that song that goes—(*He sings loudly*) Let the lower lights be burning, send a gleam across the wave.

TOM (*swiftly*). Let the lower lights be burning, send a gleam across the wave.

JOE. That's it. (*He goes on with the song, very loudly and religiously.*) Some poor, dying, struggling seaman, you may rescue, you may save. (*Halts.*)

TOM. O.K., Joe. I got it. *Life, Liberty, Time,* all the kinds of gum they're selling, jelly beans, six panatela cigars, a dollar for a news-kid, a dollar for an old man, two dollars for the Salvation Army. (*Going*) Let the lower lights be burning, send a gleam across the wave.

JOE. That's it.

LADY. He's absolutely insane.

MAN (*wearily crossing legs*). You asked me to take you to a honky-tonk, instead of to the Mark Hopkins. You're *here* in a honky-tonk. I can't help it if he's crazy. Do you want to go back to where people *aren't* crazy?

LADY. No, not just yet.

MAN. Well, all right then. Don't be telling me every minute that he's crazy.

LADY. You needn't be huffy about it. (MAN *refuses to answer, uncrosses legs. When* JOE *began to sing,* KIT CARSON *turned away from the marble game and listened. While the man and woman are arguing he comes over to Joe's table.*)

KIT CARSON. Presbyterian?

JOE. I attended a Presbyterian Sunday School.

KIT CARSON. Fond of singing?

JOE. On occasion. Have a drink?

KIT CARSON. Thanks.

JOE. Get a glass and sit down. (KIT CARSON *gets a glass from* NICK, *returns to the table, sits down,* JOE *pours him a drink, they touch glasses just as the Salvation Army people begin to fulfill the request. They sip some champagne, and at the proper moment begin to sing the song together, sipping champagne, raising hell with the tune, swinging it, and so on. The* SOCIETY LADY *joins them, and is stopped by her* HUSBAND.) Always was fond of that song. Used to sing it at the top of my voice. Never saved a seaman in my life.

KIT CARSON (*flirting with the* SOCIETY LADY *who loves it*). I saved a seaman once. Well, he wasn't exactly a seaman. He was a darky named Wellington. Heavy-set sort of a fellow. Nice personality, but no friends to speak of. Not until I came along, at any rate. In New Orleans. In the summer of the year 1899. No. Ninety-eight. I was a lot younger of course, and had no mustache, but was regarded by many people as a man of means.

JOE. Know anything about guns?

KIT CARSON (*flirting*). All there is to know. Didn't fight the Ojibways for nothing. Up there in the Lake Takalooca Country, in Michigan. (*Remembering*) Along about in 1881 or two. Fought 'em right up to the shore of the Lake. Made 'em swim for Canada. One

fellow in particular, an Indian named Harry Daisy.

JOE (*opening the box containing the revolver*). What sort of a gun would you say this is? Any good?

KIT CARSON (*at sight of gun, leaping*). Yep. That looks like a pretty nice hunk of shooting iron. That's a six-shooter. Shot a man with a six-shooter once. Got him through the palm of his right hand. Lifted his arm to wave to a friend. Thought it was a bird. Fellow named, I believe, Carroway. Larrimore Carroway.

JOE. Know how to work one of these things? (*He offers* KIT CARSON *the revolver, which is old and enormous.*)

KIT CARSON (*laughing at the absurd question*). Know how to work it? Hand me that little gun, son, and I'll show you all about it. (JOE *hands* KIT *the revolver. Importantly*) Let's see now. This is probably a new kind of six-shooter. After my time. Haven't nicked an Indian in years. I believe this here place is supposed to move out. (*He fools around and gets the barrel out for loading.*) That's it. There it is.

JOE. Look all right?

KIT CARSON. It's a good gun. You've got a good gun there, son. I'll explain it to you. You see these holes? Well, that's where you put the cartridges.

JOE (*taking some cartridges out of the box*). Here. Show me how it's done.

KIT CARSON (*a little impatient*). Well, son, you take 'em one by one and put 'em in the holes, like this. There's one. Two. Three. Four. Five. Six. Then you get the barrel back in place. Then cock it. Then all you got to do is aim and fire.
(*He points the gun at the* LADY *and* GENTLEMAN *who scream and stand up, scaring* KIT CARSON *into paralysis. The gun is loaded, but uncocked.*)

JOE. It's all set?

KIT CARSON. Ready to kill.

JOE. Let me hold it.
(KIT *hands* JOE *the gun. The* LADY *and* GENTLEMAN *watch, in terror.*)

KIT CARSON. Careful, now, son. Don't cock it. Many a man's lost an eye fooling with a loaded gun. Fellow I used to know named Danny Donovan lost a nose. Ruined his whole life. Hold it firm. Squeeze the trigger. Don't snap it. Spoils your aim.

JOE. Thanks. Let's see if I can unload it. (*He begins to unload it.*)

KIT CARSON. Of course you can.
(JOE *unloads the revolver, looks at it very closely, puts the cartridges back into the box.*)

JOE (*looking at gun*). I'm mighty grateful to you. Always wanted to see one of those things close up. Is it really a good one?

KIT CARSON. It's a beaut, son.

JOE (*aims the empty gun at a bottle on the bar*). Bang!

WILLIE (*at the marble game, as the machine groans*). Oh, Boy! (*Loudly, triumphantly*) There you are, Nick. Thought I couldn't do it, hey? *Now,* watch. (*The machine begins to make a special kind of noise. Lights go on and off. Some red, some green. A bell rings loudly six times.*) One. Two. Three. Four. Five. Six. (*An American flag jumps up.* WILLIE *comes to attention. Salutes.*) Oh, boy, what a beautiful country. (*A loud music-box version of the song "America."* JOE, KIT, *and the* LADY *get to their feet. Singing*) My country, 'tis of thee, sweet land of liberty, of thee I sing. (*Everything quiets down. The flag goes back into the machine.* WILLIE *is thrilled, amazed, delighted.* EVERYBODY *has watched the*

performance of the defeated machine from wherever he happened to be when the performance began.*)

WILLIE (*looking aound at everybody, as if they had all been on the side of the machine*). O.K. How's that? I knew I could do it. (*To* NICK) Six nickels. (NICK *hands him six nickels.* WILLIE *goes over to* JOE *and* KIT.) Took me a little while, but I finally did it. It's scientific, really. With a little skill a man can make a modest living beating the marble games. Not that that's what I want to do. I just don't like the idea of anything getting the best of me. A machine or anything else. Myself, I'm the kind of a guy who makes up his mind to do something, and then goes to work and does it. There's no other way a man can be a success at anything. (*Indicating the letter "F" on his sweater*) See that letter? That don't stand for some little-bitty high school somewhere. That stands for *me*. Faroughli. Willie Faroughli. I'm an Assyrian. We've got a civilization six or seven centuries old, I think. Somewhere along in there. Ever hear of Osman? Harold Osman? He's an Assyrian, too. He's got an orchestra down in Fresno. (*He goes to the* LADY *and* GENTLEMAN.) I've never seen you before in my life, but I can tell from the clothes you wear and the company you keep (*graciously indicating the* LADY) that you're a man who looks every problem straight in the eye, and then goes to work and *solves* it. I'm that way myself. Well. (*He smiles beautifully, takes the* GENTLEMAN'S *hand furiously.*) It's been wonderful talking to a nicer type of people for a change. Well. I'll be seeing you. So long. (*He turns, takes two steps, returns to the table. Very politely and seriously*) Good-by, lady. You've got a good man there. Take good care of him. (WILLIE *goes, saluting* JOE *and the world.*)

KIT CARSON (*to* JOE). By God, for a while there I didn't think that young Assyrian was going to do it. That fellow's got something.

(TOM *comes back with the magazines and other stuff.*)

JOE. Get it all?

TOM. Yeah. I had a little trouble finding the jelly beans.

JOE. Let's take a look at them.

TOM. These are the jelly beans. (JOE *puts his hand into the cellophane bag and takes out a handful of the jelly beans, looks at them, smiles, and tosses a couple into his mouth.*)

JOE. Same as ever. Have some. (*He offers the bag to* KIT.)

KIT CARSON (*flirting*). Thanks! I remember the first time I ever ate jelly beans. I was six, or at the most seven. Must have been in (*slowly*) eighteen—seventy-seven. Seven or eight. Baltimore.

JOE. Have some, Tom. (TOM *takes some.*)

TOM. Thanks, Joe.

JOE. Let's have some of that chewing gum. (*He dumps all the packages of gum out of the bag onto the table.*)

KIT CARSON (*flirting*). Me and a boy named Clark. Quinton Clark. Became a Senator.

JOE. Yeah. Tutti-frutti, all right. (*He opens a package and folds all five pieces into his mouth.*) Always wanted to see how many I could chew at one time. Tell you what, Tom. I bet I can chew more at one time than you can.

TOM (*delighted*). All right. (*They both begin to fold gum into their mouths.*)

KIT CARSON. I'll referee. Now, one at a time. How many you got?

JOE. Six.

KIT CARSON. All right. Let Tom catch up with you.

JOE (*while* TOM'S *catching up*). Did you give a dollar to a news-kid?

TOM. Yeah, sure.

JOE. What'd he say?

TOM. Thanks.

JOE. What sort of a kid was he?

TOM. Little, dark kid. I guess he's Italian.

JOE. Did he seem pleased?

TOM. Yeah.

JOE. That's good. Did you give a dollar to an old man?

TOM. Yeah.

JOE. Was he pleased?

TOM. Yeah.

JOE. Good. How many you got in your mouth?

TOM. Six.

JOE. All right. I got six, too. (*Folds one more in his mouth.* TOM *folds one too.*)

KIT CARSON. Seven. Seven each. (*They each fold one more into their mouths, very solemnly, chewing them into the main hunk of gum.*) Eight. Nine. Ten.

JOE (*delighted*). Always wanted to do this. (*He picks up one of the magazines.*) Let's see what's going on in the world. (*He turns the pages and keeps folding gum into his mouth and chewing.*)

KIT CARSON. Eleven. Twelve. (KIT *continues to count while* JOE *and* TOM *continue the contest. In spite of what they are doing, each is very serious.*)

TOM. Joe, what'd you want to move Kitty into the St. Francis Hotel for?

JOE. She's a better woman than any of them tramp society dames that hang around that lobby.

TOM. Yeah, but do you think she'll feel at home up there?

JOE. Maybe not at first, but after a couple of days she'll be all right. A nice big room. A bed for sleeping in. Good clothes. Good food. She'll be all right, Tom.

TOM. I hope so. Don't you think she'll get lonely up there with nobody to talk to?

JOE (*looking at* TOM *sharply, almost with admiration, pleased but severe*). There's nobody *anywhere* for *her* to talk to—except *you*.

TOM (*amazed and delighted*). Me, Joe?

JOE (*while* TOM *and* KIT CARSON *listen carefully,* KIT *with great appreciation*). Yes, you. By the grace of God, you're the other half of that girl. Not the angry woman that swaggers into this waterfront dive and shouts because the world has kicked her around. *Anybody* can have *her*. You belong to the little kid in Ohio who once dreamed of living. Not with her carcass, for *money*, so she can have food and clothes, and pay rent. With *all* of her. I put her in that hotel, so she can have a chance to gather herself together again. She can't do that in the New York Hotel. You saw what happens there. There's nobody anywhere for her to talk to, except you. They all make her talk like a whore. After a while, she'll *believe* them. Then she won't be able to remember. She'll get lonely. Sure. People can get lonely for *misery*, even. I want her to go on being lonely for *you*, so she can come together again the way she was meant to be from the beginning. Loneliness is good for people.

Right now it's the only thing for Kitty. Any more licorice?

TOM (*dazed*). What? Licorice? (*Looking around busily*) I guess we've chewed all the licorice in. We still got Clove, Peppermint, Doublemint, Beechnut, Teaberry, and Juicy Fruit.

JOE. Licorice used to be my favorite. Don't worry about her, Tom, she'll be all right. You really want to marry her, don't you?

TOM (*nodding*). Honest to God, Joe. (*Pathetically*) Only, I haven't got any money.

JOE. Couldn't you be a prize-fighter or something like that?

TOM. Naaaah. I couldn't hit a man if I wasn't sore at him. He'd have to do something that made me hate him.

JOE. You've got to figure out something to do that you won't mind doing very much.

TOM. I wish I could, Joe.

JOE (*thinking deeply, suddenly*). Tom, would you be embarrassed driving a truck?

TOM (*hit by a thunderbolt*). Joe, I never thought of that. I'd like that. Travel. Highways. Little towns. Coffee and hot cakes. Beautiful valleys and mountains and streams and trees and daybreak and sunset.

JOE. There *is* poetry in it, at that.

TOM. Joe, that's just the kind of work I *should* do. Just sit there and travel, and look, and smile, and bust out laughing. Could Kitty go with me, sometimes?

JOE. I don't know. Get me the phone book. Can you drive a truck?

TOM. Joe, you know I can drive a

truck, or any kind of thing with a motor and wheels.

(TOM *takes* JOE *the phone book.* JOE *turns the pages.*)

JOE (*looking*). Here! Here it is. Tuxedo 7900. Here's a nickel. Get me that number.

(TOM *goes to telephone, dials the number.*)

TOM. Hello.

JOE. Ask for Mr. Keith.

TOM (*mouth and language full of gum*). I'd like to talk to Mr. Keith. (*Pause*) Mr. Keith.

JOE. Take that gum out of your mouth for a minute.

(TOM *removes the gum.*)

TOM. Mr. Keith. Yeah. That's right. Hello, Mr. Keith?

JOE. Tell him to hold the line.

TOM. Hold the line, please.

JOE. Give me a hand, Tom. (TOM *helps* JOE *to the telephone. At phone, wad of gum in fingers delicately*) Keith? Joe. Yeah. Fine. Forget it. (*Pause.*) Have you got a place for a good driver? (*Pause.*) I don't think so. (*To* TOM) You haven't got a driver's license, have you?

TOM (*worried*). No. But I can get one, Joe.

JOE (*at phone*). No, but he can get one easy enough. To hell with the union. He'll join later. All right, call him a Vice-President and say he drives for relaxation. Sure. What do you mean? Tonight? I don't know why not. San Diego? All right, let him start driving without a license. What the hell's the difference? Yeah. Sure. Look him over. Yeah. I'll send him right over. Right. (*He hangs up.*) Thanks. (*To telephone.*)

TOM. Am I going to get the job?

JOE. He wants to take a look at you.

TOM. Do I look all right, Joe?

JOE (*looking at him carefully*). Hold up your head. Stick out your chest. How do you feel?

(TOM *does these things.*)

TOM. Fine.

JOE. You *look* fine, too. (JOE *takes his wad of gum out of his mouth and wraps* Liberty *magazine around it.*)

JOE. You win, Tom. Now, look. (*He bites off the tip of a very long panatela cigar, lights it, and hands one to* TOM, *and another to* KIT.) Have yourselves a pleasant smoke. Here. (*He hands two more to* TOM.) Give those slummers one each. (*He indicates the* SOCIETY LADY *and* GENTLEMAN.)

(TOM *goes over and without a word gives a cigar each to the* MAN *and the* LADY.

The MAN *is offended; he smells and tosses aside his cigar. The* WOMAN *looks at her cigar a moment, then puts the cigar in her mouth.*)

MAN. What do you think you're doing?

LADY. Really, dear. I'd like to.

MAN. Oh, this is too much.

LADY. I'd *really,* really like to, dear. (*She laughs, puts the cigar in her mouth. Turns to* KIT. *He spits out tip. She does the same.*)

MAN (*loudly*). The mother of five grown men, and she'll still looking for *romance.* (*Shouts as* KIT *lights her cigar.*) No, I forbid it.

JOE (*shouting*). What's the matter with you? Why don't you leave her alone? What are you always pushing your women around for? (*Almost without a pause*) Now, look, Tom (*The* LADY *puts the lighted cigar in her mouth, and begins to smoke, feeling wonderful.*) Here's ten bucks.

TOM. Ten bucks?

JOE. He may want you to get into a truck and begin driving to San Diego tonight.

TOM. Joe, I got to tell Kitty.

JOE. I'll tell her.

TOM. Joe, take care of her.

JOE. She'll be all right. Stop worrying about her. She's at the St. Francis Hotel. Now, look. Take a cab to Townsend and Fourth. You'll see the big sign. Keith Motor Transport Company. He'll be waiting for you.

TOM. O.K., Joe. (*Trying hard*) Thanks, Joe.

JOE. Don't be silly. Get going.
(TOM *goes.*
LADY *starts puffing on cigar.*
As TOM *goes,* WESLEY *and* HARRY *come in together.*)

NICK. Where the hell have you been? We've got to have some entertainment around here. Can't you see them fine people from uptown? (*He points at the* SOCIETY LADY *and* GENTLEMAN.)

WESLEY. You said to come back at ten for the second show.

NICK. Did I say that?

WESLEY. Yes, sir, Mr. Nick, that's exactly what you said.

HARRY. Was the first show all right?

NICK. That wasn't a show. There was no one here to see it. How can it be a show when no one sees it? People are afraid to come down to the waterfront.

HARRY. Yeah. We were just down to

Pier 27. One of the longshoremen and a cop had a fight and the cop hit him over the head with a blackjack. We saw it happen, didn't we?

WESLEY. Yes, sir, we was standing there looking when it happened.

NICK (*a little worried*). Anything else happen?

WESLEY. They was all talking.

HARRY. A man in a big car came up and said there was going to be a meeting right away and they hoped to satisfy everybody and stop the strike.

WESLEY. Right away. *Tonight.*

NICK. Well, it's about time. Them poor cops are liable to get nervous and—shoot somebody. (*To* HARRY *suddenly*) Come back here. I want you to tend bar for a while. I'm going to take a walk over to the pier.

HARRY. Yes, sir.

NICK (*to the* SOCIETY LADY *and* GENTLEMAN). You society people made up your minds yet?

LADY. Have you champagne?

NICK (*indicating* JOE). What do you think he's pouring out of that bottle, water or something?

LADY. Have you a chill bottle?

NICK. I've got a dozen of them chilled. He's been drinking champagne here all day and all night for a month now.

LADY. May we have a bottle?

NICK. It's six dollars.

LADY. I think we can manage.

MAN. I don't know. I *know* I don't know.
(NICK *takes off his coat and helps*

HARRY *into it.* HARRY *takes a bottle of champagne and two glasses to the* LADY *and the* GENTLEMAN, *dancing, collects six dollars, and goes back behind the bar, dancing.* NICK *gets his coat and hat.*)

NICK (*to* WESLEY). Rattle the keys a little, son. Rattle the keys.

WESLEY. Yes, sir, Mr. Nick. (NICK *is on his way out. The* ARAB *enters.*)

NICK. Hi-ya, *Mahmed.*

ARAB. No foundation.

NICK. All the way down the line. (*He goes.*)
(WESLEY *is at the piano, playing quietly. The* ARAB *swallows a glass of beer, takes out his harmonica, and begins to play.* WESLEY *fits his playing to the* ARAB's.
KITTY DUVAL, *strangely beautiful, in new clothes, comes in. She walks shyly, as if she were embarrassed by the fine clothes, as if she had no right to wear them. The* LADY *and* GENTLEMAN *are very impressed.* HARRY *looks at her with amazement.* JOE *is reading* Time *magazine.* KITTY *goes to his table.* JOE *looks up from the magazine, without the least amazement.*)

JOE. Hello, Kitty.

KITTY. Hello, Joe.

JOE. It's nice seeing you again.

KITTY. I came in a cab.

JOE. You been crying again? (KITTY *can't answer. To* HARRY) Bring a glass. (HARRY *comes over with a glass.* JOE *pours* KITTY *a drink.*)

KITTY. I've got to talk to you.

JOE. Have a drink.

KITTY. I've never been in burlesque. We were just poor.

JOE. Sit down, Kitty.

KITTY (*sits down*). I tried other things.

JOE. Here's to you, Katerina Koranovsky. Here's to you. And Tom.

KITTY (*sorrowfully*). Where *is* Tom?

JOE. He's getting a job tonight driving a truck. He'll be back in a couple of days.

KITTY (*sadly*). I told him I'd marry him.

JOE. He wanted to see you and say good-by.

KITTY. He's too good for me. He's like a little boy. (*Wearily*) I'm— Too many things have happened to me.

JOE. Kitty Duval, you're one of the few truly innocent people I have ever known. He'll be back in a couple of days. Go back to the hotel and wait for him.

KITTY. That's what I mean. I can't stand being alone. I'm no good. I tried very hard. I don't know what it is. I miss— (*She gestures.*)

JOE (*gently*). Do you really want to come back here, Kitty?

KITTY. I don't know. I'm not sure. Everything *smells* different. I don't know how to feel, or what to think. (*Gesturing pathetically*) I know I don't belong there. It's what I've wanted all my life, but it's too *late*. I try to be happy about it, but all I can do is remember everything and cry.

JOE. I don't know what to tell you, Kitty. I didn't mean to hurt you.

KITTY. You haven't hurt me. You're the only person who's ever been good to me. I've never known anybody like you. I'm not sure about love any more, but I know I love you, and I know I love Tom.

JOE. I love you too, Kitty Duval.

KITTY. He'll want babies. I know he will. I know *I* will, too. Of course I will. I can't— (*she shakes her head.*)

JOE. Tom's a baby himself. You'll be very happy together. He wants you to ride with him in the truck. Tom's good for you. You're good for Tom.

KITTY (*like a child*). Do you want me to go back and wait for him?

JOE. I can't *tell* you what to do. I think it would be a good idea, though.

KITTY. I wish I could tell you how it makes me feel to be alone. It's almost worse.

JOE. It might take a whole week, Kitty. (*He looks at her sharply, at the arrival of an idea.*) Didn't you speak of reading a book? A book of poems?

KITTY. I didn't know what I was saying.

JOE (*trying to get up*). Of course you knew. I think you'll like poetry. Wait here a minute, Kitty. I'll go see if I can find some books.

KITTY. All right, Joe.
(*He walks out of the place, trying very hard not to wobble.*
Fog-horn. Music. The NEWSBOY *comes in. Looks for* JOE. *Is broken-hearted because* JOE *is gone.*)

NEWSBOY (*to* SOCIETY GENTLEMAN). Paper?

MAN (*angry*). No.
(*The* NEWSBOY *goes to the* ARAB.)

NEWSBOY. Paper, Mister?

ARAB (*irritated*). No foundation.

NEWSBOY. What?

ARAB (*very angry*). No foundation.
(*The* NEWSBOY *starts out, turns, looks at the* ARAB, *shakes head.*)

NEWSBOY. No foundation? How do you figure?
(BLICK *and* TWO COPS *enter.*)

NEWSBOY (*to* BLICK). Paper, Mister?
(BLICK *pushes him aside. The* NEWSBOY *goes.*)

BLICK (*walking authoritatively about the place, to* HARRY). Where's Nick?

HARRY. He went for a walk.

BLICK. Who are you?

HARRY. Harry.

BLICK (*to the* ARAB *and* WESLEY). Hey, you. Shut up.
(*The* ARAB *stops playing the harmonica,* WESLEY *the piano.*)

BLICK (*studies* KITTY). What's your name, sister?

KITTY (*looking at him*). Kitty Duval. What's it to you? (*Kitty's voice is now like it was at the beginning of the play: tough, independent, bitter and hard.*)

BLICK (*angry*). Don't give me any of your gutter lip. Just answer my questions.

KITTY. You go to hell, you.

BLICK (*coming over, enraged*). Where do you live?

KITTY. The New York Hotel. Room 21.

BLICK. Where do you work?

KITTY. I'm not working just now. I'm looking for work.

BLICK. What kind of work? (KITTY

can't answer.) What kind of work? (KITTY *can't answer. Furiously*) WHAT KIND OF WORK?
(KIT CARSON *comes over.*)

KIT CARSON. You can't talk to a lady that way in *my* presence.
(BLICK *turns and stares at* KIT. *The* COPS *begin to move from the bar.*)

BLICK (*to the* COPS). It's all right, boys. I'll take care of this. (*To* KIT) What'd you say?

KIT CARSON. You got no right to hurt people. Who are *you?*
(BLICK, *without a word, takes* KIT *to the street. Sounds of a blow and a groan.* BLICK *returns, breathing hard.*)

BLICK (*to the* COPS). O.K., boys. You can go now. Take care of him. Put him on his feet and tell him to behave himself from now on. (*To* KITTY *again*) Now answer my question. What kind of work?

KITTY (*quietly*). I'm a whore, you son of a bitch. You know what kind of work I do. And I know what kind you do.

MAN (*shocked and really hurt*). Excuse me, officer, but it seems to me that your attitude—

BLICK. Shut up.

MAN (*quietly*). —is making the poor child say things that are not true.

BLICK. Shut up, I said.

LADY. Well. (*To the* MAN) Are you going to stand for such insolence?

BLICK (*to* MAN, *who is standing*). Are you?

MAN (*taking the* WOMAN's *arm*). I'll get a divorce. I'll start life all over again. (*Pushing the* WOMAN) Come on. Get the hell out of here! (*The* MAN *hurries his* WOMAN *out of the place,* BLICK *watching them go.*)

BLICK (*to* KITTY). Now. Let's begin again, and see that you tell the truth. What's your name?

KITTY. Kitty Duval.

BLICK. Where do you live?

KITTY. Until this evening I lived at the New York Hotel. Room 21. This evening I moved to the St. Francis Hotel.

BLICK. Oh. To the St. Francis Hotel. Nice place. Where do you work?

KITTY. I'm looking for work.

BLICK. What kind of work do you do?

KITTY. I'm an actress.

BLICK. I see. What movies have I seen you in?

KITTY. I've worked in burlesque.

BLICK. You're a liar.
(WESLEY *stands, worried and full of dumb resentment.*)

KITTY (*pathetically, as at the beginning of the play*). It's the truth.

BLICK. What are you doing here?

KITTY. I came to see if I could get a job here.

BLICK. Doing what?

KITTY. Singing—and—dancing.

BLICK. You can't sing or dance. What are you lying for?

KITTY. I can. I sang and danced in burlesque all over the country.

BLICK. You're a liar.

KITTY. I said lines, too.

BLICK. So you danced in burlesque?

KITTY. Yes.

BLICK. All right. Let's see what you did.

KITTY. I can't. There's no music, and I haven't got the right clothes.

BLICK. There's music. (*To* WESLEY) Put a nickel in that phonograph. (WESLEY *can't move.*) Come on. Put a nickel in that phonograph. (WESLEY *does so. To* KITTY) All right. Get up on that stage and do a hot litttle burlesque number. (KITTY *stands. Walks slowly to the stage, but is unable to move.* JOE *comes in, holding three books.*) Get going, now. Let's see you dance the way you did in burlesque, all over the country.
(KITTY *tries to do a burlesque dance. It is beautiful in a tragic way.*)

BLICK. All right, start taking them off! (KITTY *removes her hat and starts to remove her jacket.* JOE *moves closer to the stage, amazed.*)

JOE (*hurrying to* KITTY). Get down from there. (*He takes* KITTY *into his arms. She is crying. To* BLICK) What the hell do you think you're doing!

WESLEY (*like a little boy, very angry*). It's that man, Blick. *He* made her take off her clothes. He beat up the old man, too.
(BLICK *pushes* WESLEY *off, as* TOM *enters.* BLICK *begins beating up* WESLEY.)

TOM. What's the matter, Joe? What's happened?

JOE. Is the truck out there?

TOM. Yeah, but what's happened? Kitty's crying again!

JOE. You driving to San Diego?

TOM. Yeah, Joe. But what's he doing to that poor colored boy?

JOE. Get going. Here's some money. Everything's O.K. (*To* KITTY) Dress in the truck. Take these books.

WESLEY'S VOICE. You can't hurt me. You'll get yours. You wait and see.

TOM. Joe, he's hurting that boy. I'll kill him!

JOE (*pushing* TOM). Get out of here! Get married in San Diego. I'll see you when you get back. (TOM *and* KITTY *go.* NICK *enters and stands at the lower end of the bar.* JOE *takes the revolver out of his pocket. Looks at it.*) I've always wanted to kill somebody, but I never knew who it should be. (*He cocks the revolver, stands real straight, holds it in front of him firmly and walks to the door. He stands a moment watching* BLICK, *aims very carefully, and pulls trigger. There is no shot.* NICK *runs over and grabs the gun, and takes* JOE *aside.*)

NICK. What the hell do you think you're doing?

JOE (*casually, but angry*). That dumb Tom. Buys a six-shooter that won't even shoot once.
(JOE *sits down, dead to the world.* BLICK *comes out, panting for breath.* NICK *looks at him. He speaks slowly.*)

NICK. Blick! I told you to stay out of here! Now get out of here. (*He takes* BLICK *by the collar, tightening his grip as he speaks, and pushing him out.*) If you come back again, I'm going to take you in that room where you've been beating up that colored boy, and I'm going to murder you—slowly—with my hands. Beat it! (*He pushes* BLICK *out. To* HARRY) Go take care of the colored boy.

(HARRY *runs out.*

WILLIE *returns and doesn't sense that anything is changed.* WILLIE *puts another nickel into the machine, but he does so very violently. The consequence of this violence is that the flag comes up again.* WILLIE, *amazed, stands at attention and salutes. The flag goes down. He shakes his head.*)

WILLIE (*thoughtfully*). As far as I'm concerned, this is the *only* country in the world. If you ask me, *nuts* to Europe! (*He is about to push the slide in again when the flag comes up again. Furiously, to* NICK, *while he salutes and stands at attention, pleadingly*) Hey, Nick. This machine is out of order.

NICK (*somberly*). Give it a whack on the side.
(WILLIE *does so. A hell of a whack. The result is the flag comes up and down, and* WILLIE *keeps saluting.*)

WILLIE (*saluting*). Hey, Nick. Something's wrong.
(*The machine quiets down abruptly.* WILLIE *very stealthily slides a new nickel in, and starts a new game. From a distance two pistol shots are heard, each carefully timed.*
NICK *runs out.*
The NEWSBOY *enters, crosses at* JOE's *table, senses something is wrong.*)

NEWSBOY (*softly*). Paper, Mister? (JOE *can't hear him. The* NEWSBOY *backs away, studies* JOE, *wishes he could cheer* JOE *up. Notices the phonograph, goes to it, and puts a coin in it, hoping music will make* JOE *happier. The* NEWSBOY *sits down. Watches* JOE. *The music begins. "The Missouri Waltz."*)
(*The* DRUNKARD *comes in and walks around. Then sits down.* NICK *comes back.*)

NICK (*delighted*). Joe, Blick's dead! Somebody just shot him, and none of the cops are trying to find out who.
(JOE *doesn't hear.* NICK *steps back, studying* JOE.)

NICK (*shouting*). Joe.

JOE (*looking up*). What?

NICK. Blick's dead.

JOE. Blick? Dead? Good! That God damn gun wouldn't go off. I *told* Tom to get a good one.

NICK (*picking up gun and looking at it*). Joe, you wanted to kill that guy! (HARRY *returns.* JOE *puts the gun in his coat pocket.*) I'm going to buy you a bottle of champagne.
(NICK *goes to bar.* JOE *rises, takes hat from rack, puts coat on. The* NEWSBOY *jumps up, helps* JOE *with coat.*)

NICK. What's the matter, Joe?

JOE. Nothing. Nothing.

NICK. How about the champagne?

JOE. Thanks. (*Going*)

NICK. It's not eleven yet. Where you going, Joe?

JOE. I don't know. Nowhere.

NICK. Will I see you tomorrow?

JOE. I don't know. I don't think so.
(KIT CARSON *enters, walks to* JOE. JOE *and* KIT *look at one another knowingly.*)

JOE. Somebody just shot a man. How are you feeling?

KIT. Never felt better in my life. (*Loudly, bragging, but somber*) I shot a man once. In San Francisco. Shot him two times. In 1939, I think it was. In October. Fellow named Blick or Glick or something like that. Couldn't stand the way he talked to ladies. Went up to my room and got my old pearl-handled revolver and waited for him on Pacific Street. Saw him walking and let him have it, two times. Had to throw the beautiful revolver into the Bay.

(HARRY, NICK, *the* ARAB *and the* DRUNKARD *close in around him.*

JOE *searches his pockets, brings out the revolver, puts it in* KIT's *hand, looks at him with great admiration and affection.* JOE *walks slowly to the stairs* *leading to the street, turns and waves.* KIT, *and then one by one everybody else, waves, and the marble game goes into its beautiful American routine again: flag, lights, and music. The play ends.*)

Watch on the Rhine

BY LILLIAN HELLMAN

CHARACTERS

WATCH ON THE RHINE was first produced at the Martin Beck Theatre, New York City, on April 1, 1941, with the following cast:

ANISE	*Eda Heinemann*
JOSEPH	*Frank Wilson*
FANNY FARRELLY	*Lucile Watson*
DAVID FARRELLY	*John Lodge*
MARTHE DE BRANCOVIS	*Helen Trenholme*
TECK DE BRANCOVIS	*George Coulouris*
SARA MÜLLER	*Mady Christians*
JOSHUA MÜLLER	*Peter Fernandez*
BODO MÜLLER	*Eric Roberts*
BABETTE MÜLLER	*Anne Blyth*
KURT MÜLLER	*Paul Lukas*

SCENE

The scene of the play is the living room of the Farrelly country house, about twenty miles from Washington.

The time is late spring, 1940.

ACT ONE: Early on a Wednesday morning.

ACT TWO: Ten days later.

ACT THREE: A half hour later.

Watch on the Rhine

ACT ONE

SCENE: *The living room of the Farrelly house, about twenty miles from Washington, D. C., on a warm spring morning.*

Center stage are large French doors leading to an elevated open terrace. On the terrace are chairs, tables, a large table for dining. Some of this furniture we can see; most of it is on the left side of the terrace, beyond our sight. Left stage is an arched entrance, leading to the oval reception hall. We can see the main staircase as it goes off to the back of the hall. Right stage is a door leading to a library. The Farrelly house was built in the early nineteenth century. It has space, simplicity, style. The living room is large. Up stage right is a piano; down stage left, a couch; down stage right, a couch and chairs; up stage a few smaller chairs. Four or five generations have furnished this room and they have all been people of taste. There are no styles, no periods; the room has never been refurnished. Each careless aristocrat has thrown into the room what he or she liked as a child, what he or she brought home when grown up. Therefore the furniture is of many periods: the desk is English, the couch is Victorian, some of the pictures are modern, some of the ornaments French. The room has too many things in it: vases, clocks, miniatures, boxes, china animals. On the right wall is a large portrait of a big kind-faced man in an evening suit of 1900. On another wall is a large, very ugly landscape. The room is crowded. But it is cool and clean and its fabrics and woods are in soft colors.

AT RISE: ANISE, *a thin Frenchwoman of about sixty, in a dark housekeeper's dress, is standing at a table sorting mail. She takes the mail from a small basket, holds each letter to the light, reads each postal card, then places them in piles. On the terrace,* JOSEPH, *a tall middle-aged Negro butler, wheels a breakfast wagon. As he appears,* FANNY FARRELLY *comes in from the hall. She is a handsome woman of about sixty-three. She has on a fancy, good-looking dressing-gown.*

Left and right are the audience's left and right.

FANNY (*stops to watch* ANISE. *Sees* JOSEPH *moving about on terrace. Calls*). Joseph! (*To* ANISE) Morning.

ANISE (*continues examining mail*). Good morning, Madame.

JOSEPH (*comes to terrace door*). Yes'm?

FANNY. Everybody down?

JOSEPH. No'm. Nobody. I'll get your tea. (*He returns to breakfast wagon on terrace.*)

FANNY. Mr. David isn't down yet? But he knows he is to meet the train.

277

JOSEPH (*comes in from the terrace with the cup of tea*). He's got plenty of time, Miss Fanny. The train ain't in till noon.

FANNY. Breakfast is at nine o'clock in this house and will be until the day after I die. Ring the bell.

JOSEPH. It ain't nine yet, Miss Fanny. It's eight-thirty.

FANNY. Well, put the clocks up to nine and ring the bell.

JOSEPH. Mr. David told me not to ring it any more. He says it's got too mean a ring, that bell. It disturbs folks.

FANNY. That's what it was put there for. I like to disturb folks.

JOSEPH. Yes'm.

FANNY. You slept well, Anise. You were asleep before I could dismantle myself.

ANISE. I woke several times during the night.

FANNY. Did you? Then you were careful not to stop snoring. We must finally get around to rearranging your room. (ANISE *hands her three or four letters.*) Even when you don't snore, it irritates me. (FANNY *opens a letter, begins to read it. After a minute*) What time is it?

ANISE. It is about eight-thirty. Joseph just told you.

FANNY. I didn't hear him. I'm nervous. Naturally. My mail looks dull. (*Reading the letter*) Jenny always tells you a piece of gossip three times, as if it grew fresher with the telling. Did you put flowers in their rooms?

ANISE. Certainly.

FANNY. David ought to get to the station by eleven-thirty.

ANISE (*patiently*). The train does not draw in until ten minutes past noon.

FANNY. But it might come in early. It's been known.

ANISE. Never. Not in the Union Station in Washington, the District of Columbia.

FANNY (*irritably*). But it might. It might. Don't argue with me about everything. What time is it?

ANISE. It's now twenty-seven minutes before nine. It will be impossible to continue telling you the time every three minutes from now until Miss Sara arrives. I think you are having a nervous breakdown. Compose yourself.

FANNY. It's been twenty years. Any mother would be nervous. If your daughter were coming home and you hadn't seen her, and a husband, *and* grandchildren—

ANISE. I do not say that it is wrong to be nervous. I, too, am nervous. I say only that you are.

FANNY. Very well. I heard you. *I* say that I am. (*She goes back to reading her letter. Looks up.*) Jenny's still in California. She's lost her lavallière again. Birdie Chase's daughter is still faire l'amouring with that actor. Tawdry, Jenny says it is. An actor. Fashions in sin change. In my day, it was Englishmen. I don't understand infidelity. If you love a man, then why? If you don't love him, then why stay with him? (*Without turning, she points over her head to Joshua Farrelly's portrait.*) Thank God, I was in love. I thought about Joshua last night. Three grandchildren. He would have liked that. I hope I will. (*Points to other letters*) Anything in anybody else's mail?

ANISE. Advertisements for Mr. David and legal things. For our Count and Countess, there is nothing but what seems an invitation to a lower-class embassy tea and letters asking for bills to get paid.

FANNY. That's every morning. (*Thoughtfully*) In the six weeks the Balkan nobility have been with us, they seem to have run up a great many bills.

ANISE. Yes. I told you that. Then there was a night-letter for Mr. David. (*A very loud, very unpleasant bell begins to ring.*)

FANNY (*through the noise*). Really? From whom?

ANISE. From her. I took it on the telephone, and— (*Bell drowns out her voice.*)

FANNY. Who is "her"? (*Bell becomes very loud.*) Go tell him to stop that noise—

ANISE (*goes toward terrace, calling*). Joseph! Stop that bell. Miss Fanny says to stop it.

JOSEPH (*calls*). Miss Fanny said to start it.

FANNY (*shouts out to him*). I didn't tell you to hang yourself with it.

JOSEPH (*appears on terrace*). I ain't hung. Your breakfast is ready. (*Disappears.*)

FANNY (*to* ANISE). Who is "her"?

ANISE. That Carter woman from Lansing, Michigan.

FANNY. Oh, my. Is she back in Washington again? What did the telegram say?

ANISE. It said the long sickness of her dear Papa had terminated in full recovery.

FANNY. That's too bad.

ANISE. She was returning, and would Mr. David come for dinner a week from Thursday? "Love," it said, "to you and your charming mother." (*To* FANNY) That's you. I think Miss Carter from Lansing, Michigan, was unwise in attending the illness of her Papa.

FANNY. I hope so. Why?

ANISE (*shrugs*). There is much winking of the eyes going on between our Countess and Mr. David.

FANNY (*eagerly*). I know that. Anything new happen?

ANISE (*too innocently*). Happen? I don't know what you mean.

FANNY. You know damn well what I mean.

ANISE. *That?* Oh, no, I don't think that.

JOSEPH (*appears in the door*). The sausage cakes is shrinking.

FANNY (*rises. To* ANISE). I want everybody down here immediately. Is the car ready? (ANISE *nods.*) Did you order a good dinner? (*Shrieks*) David! Oh.
(DAVID FARRELLY, *a pleasant-looking man of thirty-nine, comes in from the entrance hall, almost bumps into* FANNY.)

DAVID. Good morning, everybody.

ANISE (*to* FANNY). Everything is excellent. You have been asking the same questions for a week. You have made the kitchen very nervous.

DAVID (*to* JOSEPH). Why did you ring that air-raid alarm again?

JOSEPH. Ain't me, Mr. David. I don't like no noise. Miss Fanny told me.

FANNY. Good morning, David.

DAVID (*to* JOSEPH). Tell Fred to leave the car. I'll drive to the station.

JOSEPH (*nods*). Yes, sir. (*Exits.*)

DAVID (*to* FANNY, *half amused, half annoyed, as he begins to read his mail*). Mama, I think we'll fix up the chicken-house for you as a playroom. We'll hang the room with bells and you can go into your second childhood in the proper privacy.

FANNY. I find it very interesting. You sleep soundly, you rise at your usual hour—although your sister, whom you haven't seen in years, is waiting at the station—

DAVID. She is not waiting at the station. (*Laughs*) The train does not come in until ten minutes past twelve.

FANNY (*airily*). It's almost that now.

ANISE (*turns to look at her*). Really, Miss Fanny, contain yourself. It is twenty minutes before nine.

DAVID. And I have *not* slept soundly. And I've been up since six o'clock.

FANNY. The Balkans aren't down yet. Where are they?

DAVID. I don't know.

ANISE. There's nothing in your mail, Mr. David. Only the usual advertisements.

DAVID. And for me, that is all that is ever likely to come—here.

ANISE (*haughtily, as she starts toward hall*). I cannot, of course, speak for Miss Fanny. *I* have never opened a letter in my life.

DAVID. I know. You don't have to. For you they fly open.

FANNY (*giggles*). It's true. You're a snooper, Anise. (ANISE *exits.* FANNY *talks as* ANISE *moves out.*) I rather admire it. It shows an interest in life. (*She looks up at Joshua's portrait.*) You know, I've been lying awake most of the night wondering what Papa would have thought about Sara. He'd have been very pleased, wouldn't he? I always find myself wondering what Joshua would have felt.

DAVID. Yes. But maybe it would be just as well if you didn't expect me to be wondering about it, too. I wasn't married to him, Mama. He was just my father.

FANNY. My. You got up on the wrong side of the bed. (*She moves past him. Points to the mail which he is still opening.*) The bills are for our noble guests. Interesting, how many there are every morning. How much longer are they going to be with us?

DAVID (*without looking at her*). I don't know.

FANNY. It's been six weeks. Now that Sara and her family are coming, even this house might be a little crowded— (*He looks up at her. Quickly*) Yes. I know I invited them. I felt sorry for Marthe, and Teck rather amused me. He plays good cribbage, and he tells good jokes. But that's not enough for a lifetime guest. If you've been urging her to stay, I wish you'd stop it. They haven't any money; all right, lend them some—

DAVID. I have been urging them to stay?

FANNY. I'm not so old I don't recognize flirting when I see it.

DAVID. But you're old enough not to be silly.

FANNY. I'm not silly. I'm charming. (MARTHE DE BRANCOVIS, *an attractive woman of thirty-one or thirty-two, enters.*)

MARTHE. Good morning, Fanny. Morning, David.

FANNY. Good morning, Marthe.

DAVID (*warmly*). Good morning.

MARTHE. Fanny, darling, couldn't you persuade yourself to let me have a tray in bed and some cotton for my ears?

DAVID. Certainly not. My father ate breakfast at nine; and whatever my father did . . .

FANNY (*carefully, to* DAVID). There was a night-letter for you from that Carter woman in Lansing, Michigan. She is returning and you are to come to dinner next Thursday. (*As she exits on terrace*) C-A-R-T-E-R. (*Pronounces it carefully*) Lansing, Michigan.

DAVID (*laughs*). I know how to spell Carter, but thank you. (FANNY *exits.* DAVID *looks up at* MARTHE.) Do you understand my mother?

MARTHE. Sometimes.

DAVID. Miss Carter was done for your benefit.

MARTHE (*smiles*). That means she has guessed that I would be jealous. And she has guessed right.

DAVID (*looks at her*). Jealous?

MARTHE. I know I've no right to be, but I am. And Fanny knows it.

DAVID (*carelessly*). Don't pay any attention to Mama. She has a sure instinct for the women I like, and she begins to hammer away early. Marthe— (*Goes to decanter on side-table.*) I'm going to have a drink. I haven't had a drink before breakfast since the day I took my bar examination. (*Pours himself a drink, gulps it down.*) What's it going to be like to stand on a station platform and see your sister after all these years? I'm afraid, I guess.

MARTHE. Why?

DAVID. I don't know. Afraid she won't like me— (*Shrugs.*) We were very fond of each other, but it's been a long time.

MARTHE. I remember Sara. Mama brought me one day when your father was stationed in Paris. I was about six and Sara was about fifteen and you were—

DAVID. You were a pretty little girl.

MARTHE. Do you really remember me? You never told me before.

FANNY (*yelling from the terrace*). David! Come to breakfast.

DAVID (*as if he had not been listening*). You know, I've never met Sara's husband. Mama did. I think the first day Sara met him, in Munich. Mama didn't like the marriage much in those days—and Sara didn't care, and Mama didn't like Sara not caring. Mama cut up about it, bad.

MARTHE. Why?

DAVID. Probably because they didn't let her arrange it. Why does Mama ever act badly? She doesn't remember ten minutes later.

MARTHE. Wasn't Mr. Müller poor?

DAVID. Oh, Mama wouldn't have minded that. If they'd only come home and let her fix their lives for them— (*Smiles.*) But Sarah didn't want it that way.

MARTHE. You'll have a house full of refugees—us and—

DAVID. Are you and Teck refugees? I'm not sure I know what you're refugees from.

MARTHE. From Europe.

DAVID. From what Europe?

MARTHE (*smiles, shrugs*). I don't know. I don't know myself, really. Just Europe. (*Quickly, comes to him.*) Sara will like you. I like you. (*Laughs.*) That doesn't make sense, does it?
(*On her speech,* TECK DE BRANCOVIS *appears in the hall. He is a good-looking man of about forty-five. She stops quickly.*)

TECK (*to* MARTHE *and* DAVID). Good morning.
(*The bell gives an enormous ring.*)

DAVID (*goes to terrace*). Good morning, Teck. For years I've been thinking they were coming for Mama with a net. I'm giving up hope. I may try catching her myself. (*Disappears, calling*) Mama! Stop that noise.

TECK. I wonder if science has a name for women who enjoy noise? (*Goes to table, picks up his mail.*) Many mistaken people, Marthe, seem to have given you many charge accounts.

MARTHE. The Countess de Brancovis. That still does it. It would be nice to be able to pay bills again—

TECK. Do not act as if I refused to pay them. I did not sleep well last night. I was worried. We have eighty-seven dollars in American Express checks. (*Pleasantly, looking at her*) That's all we have, Marthe.

MARTHE (*shrugs*). Maybe something will turn up. It's due.

TECK (*carefully*). David? (*Then, as she turns to look at him*) The other relatives will arrive this morning?

MARTHE. Yes.

TECK (*points to porch*). I think Madame Fanny and Mr. David may grow weary of accents and charity guests. Or is the husband of the sister a rich one?

MARTHE. No. He's poor. He had to leave Germany in '33.

TECK. A Jew?

MARTHE. No. I don't think so.

TECK. Why did he have to leave Germany?

MARTHE (*still reading*). Oh, I don't know, Teck. He's an anti-Nazi.

TECK. A political?

MARTHE. No, I don't think so. He was an engineer. I don't know. I don't know much about him.

TECK. Did you sleep well?

MARTHE. Yes. Why not?

TECK. Money does not worry you?

MARTHE. It worries me very much. But I just lie still now and hope. I'm glad to be here. (*Shrugs.*) Maybe something good will happen. We've come to the end of a road. That's been true for a long time. Things will have to go one way or the other. Maybe they'll go well, for a change.

TECK. I have not come to the end of any road.

MARTHE (*looks at him*). No? I admire you.

TECK. I'm going into Washington tonight. Phili has a poker game every Wednesday evening. He has arranged for me to join it.

MARTHE (*after a pause*). Have you been seeing Phili?

TECK. Once or twice. Why not? Phili and I are old friends. He may be useful. I do not want to stay in this country forever.

MARTHE. You can't leave them alone. Your favorite dream, isn't it, Teck? That they will let you play with them again? I don't think they will, and I don't think you should be seeing Phili, or that you should be seen at the Embassy.

TECK (*smiles*). You have political convictions now?

MARTHE. I don't know what I have. I've never liked Nazis, as you know, and you should have had enough of them. They seem to have had enough of you, God knows. It would be just as well to admit they are smarter than you are and let them alone.

TECK (*looking at her carefully, after a minute*). That is interesting.

MARTHE. What is interesting?

TECK. I think you are trying to say something to me. What is it?

MARTHE. That you ought not to be at the Embassy, and that it's insane to play cards in a game with Von Seitz with eighty-seven dollars in your pocket. I don't think he'd like your not being able to pay up. Suppose you lose?

TECK. I shall try not to lose.

MARTHE. But if you do lose and can't pay, it will be all over Washington in an hour. (*Points to terrace*) They'll find out about it, and we'll be out of here when they do.

TECK. I think I want to be out of here. I find that I do not like the picture of you and our host.

MARTHE (*carefully*). There is no picture, as you put it, to like or dislike.

TECK. Not yet? I am glad to hear that. (*Comes toward her slowly.*) Marthe, you understand that I am not really a fool? You understand that it is unwise to calculate me that way?

MARTHE (*slowly, as if it were an effort*). Yes, I understand that. And I understand that I am getting tired. Just plain tired. The whole thing's too much for me. I've always meant to ask you, since you play on so many sides, why we don't come out any better. I've always wanted to ask you how it happened. (*Sharply*) I'm tired, see? And I just want to sit down. Just to sit down in a chair and stay.

TECK (*carefully*). Here?

MARTHE. I don't know. Any place—

TECK. You have thus arranged it with David?

MARTHE. I've arranged nothing.

TECK. But you are trying, eh? (*He comes close to her.*) I think not. I would not like that. Do not make any arrangements, Marthe. I may not allow you to carry them through. (*Smiles.*) Come to breakfast now. (*He passes her, disappears on the terrace. She stands still and thoughtful. Then she, too, moves to the terrace, disappears.*) (JOSEPH *appears on the terrace, carrying a tray toward the unseen breakfast table. The stage is empty. After a minute, there are sounds of footsteps in the hall.* SARA MÜLLER *appears in the doorway, comes toward the middle of the room as if expecting to find somebody, stops, looks around, begins to smile. Behind her in the doorway, are three children; behind them,* KURT MÜLLER. *They stand waiting, watching* SARA. SARA *is forty-one or forty-two, a good-looking woman, with a well-bred, serious face. She is very badly dressed. Her dress is too long, her shoes were bought a long time ago and have no relation to the dress, and the belt of her dress has become untied and is hanging down. She looks clean and dowdy. As she looks around the room, her face is gay and surprised. Smiling, without turning, absently, she motions to the children and* KURT. *Slowly, the children come in.* BODO MÜLLER, *a boy of nine, comes first. He is carrying coats. Behind him, carrying two cheap valises, is* JOSHUA MÜLLER, *a boy of fourteen. Behind him is* BABETTE MÜLLER, *a pretty little girl of twelve. They are dressed for a much colder climate. They come forward, look at their mother, then move to a couch. Behind them is* KURT MÜLLER, *a large, powerful, German-looking man of about forty-seven. He is carrying a shabby valise and a brief-case. He stands watching* SARA. JOSHUA *puts down the valises, goes to his father, takes the valise from* KURT, *puts it neatly near his, and puts the brief-case near* KURT. BABETTE *goes to* SARA, *takes a package from her, places it near the valise. Then she turns to* BODO, *takes the coats he is carrying, puts them neatly on top of the valises. After a second,* KURT *sits down. As he does so, we see that his movements are slow and careful, as if they are made with effort.*)

BABETTE (*Points to a couch near which they are standing. She has a slight accent*). Is it allowed?

KURT (*Smiles. He has an accent*). Yes. It is allowed.
(BABETTE *and* BODO *sit stiffly on the couch.*)

JOSHUA (*nervously. He has a slight accent*). But we did not sound the bell—

SARA (*idly, as she wanders around the room, her face excited*). The door isn't locked. It never was. Never since I can remember.

BODO (*softly, puzzled*). The entrance of the home is never locked. So.

KURT (*looks at him*). You find it curious to believe there are people who live and do not need to watch, eh, Bodo?

BODO. Yes, Papa.

KURT (*smiles*). You and I.

JOSHUA (*smiles*). It is strange. But it must be good, I think.

KURT. Yes.

SARA. Sit back. Be comfortable. I—I wonder where Mama and David— (*Delighted, sees portrait of Joshua Farrelly, points to it*) And that was my Papa. That was the famous Joshua Farrelly. (*They all look up at it. She wanders around the room.*) My goodness, isn't it a fine room? I'd almost forgotten— (*Picks up a picture from the table.*) And this was my grandmother. (*Very nervously*) Shall I go and say we're here? They'd be having breakfast, I think. Always on the side terrace in nice weather. I don't know. Maybe— (*Picks up another picture.*) "To Joshua and Fanny Farrelly. With admiration. Alfonso, May 7, 1910." I had an ermine boa and a pink coat. I was angry because it was too warm in Madrid to wear it.

BODO. Alfons von Spanien? Der hat immer Bilder von sich verschenkt. Ein schlechtes Zeichen für einen Mann.

JOSHUA. Mama told you it is good manners to speak the language of the country you visit. Therefore, speak in English.

BODO. I said he seemed always to give his photograph. I said that is a bad flag on a man. Grow fat on the poor people and give pictures of the face. (JOSHUA *sits down.*)

SARA. I remember a big party and cakes and a glass of champagne for me. I was ten, I guess— (*Suddenly laughs.*) That was when Mama said the first time a king got shot at, he was a romantic, but the fifth time he was a comedian. And when my father gave his lecture in Madrid, he repeated it— right in Madrid. It was a great scandal. You know, Alfonso was always getting shot at or bombed.

BODO (*shrugs*). Certainement.

JOSHUA. Certainement? As-tu perdu la tête?

BABETTE. Speak in English, please.

KURT (*without turning*). You are a terrorist, Bodo?

BODO (*slowly*). No.

JOSHUA. Then since when has it become *natural* to shoot upon people?

BODO. Do not give me lessons. It is neither right or natural to shoot upon people. I know that.

SARA (*looks at* BABETTE, *thoughtfully*). An ermine boa. A boa is a scarf. I should like to have one for you, Babbie. Once, in Prague, I saw a pretty one. I wanted to buy it for you. But we had to pay our rent. (*Laughs.*) But I almost bought it.

BABETTE. Yes, Mama. Thank you. Tie your sash, Mama.

SARA (*thoughtfully*). Almost twenty years.

BODO. You were born here, Mama?

SARA. Upstairs. And I lived here until I went to live with your father. (*Looks out beyond terrace.*) Your Uncle David and I used to have a garden, behind the terrace. I wonder if it's still there. I like a garden. I've always hoped we'd have a house some day and settle down— (*Stops, nervously, turns to stare at* KURT, *who is looking at her.*) I am talking so foolish. Sentimental. At my age. Gardens and ermine boas. I haven't wanted anything—

KURT (*comes toward her, takes her hand*). Sara. Stop it. This is a fine room. A fine place to be. Everything is so pleasant and full of comfort. This will be a good piano on which to play again. And it is all so clean. I like that. Now, you shall not be a baby. You must enjoy your house, and not be afraid that you hurt me with it. Yes?

BABETTE. Papa, tie Mama's sash, please.

SARA (*shyly smiles at him as he leans down to tie the belt*). Yes, of course. It's strange, that's all. We've never been in a place like this together—

KURT. That does not mean, and should not mean, that we do not remember how to enjoy what comes our way. We are on a holiday.

JOSHUA. A holiday? But for how long? And what plans afterwards?

KURT (*quietly*). We will have plans when the hour arrives to make them. (ANISE *appears from the hall. She starts into the room, stops, bewildered. The* MÜLLERS *have not seen her. Then, as* SARA *turns,* ANISE *speaks. As she speaks, the children rise.*)

ANISE. What? What?

SARA (*softly*). Anise. It's me. It's Sara.

ANISE (*coming forward slowly*). What? (*Then as she approaches* SARA, *she begins to run toward her.*) Miss Sara! Miss Sara! (*They reach each other, both laugh happily.* SARA *kisses* ANISE.) I would have known you. Yes, I would. I would have known— (*Excited, bewildered, nervous, she looks toward* KURT.) How do you do, sir? How do you do? (*Turns toward the children.*) How do you do?

JOSHUA. Thank you, Miss Anise. We are in good health.

SARA (*very happily*). You look the same. I think you look the same. Just the way I've always remembered. (*To the others*) This is the Anise I have told you about. She was here before I was born.

ANISE. But how— Did you just come in? What a way to come home! And after all the plans we've made! But you were to come on the twelve o'clock train, and Mr. David was to meet you—

BABETTE. The twelve o'clock train was

most expensive. We could not have come with that train. We liked the train we came on. It was most luxurious.

ANISE (*very nervously, very rattled*). But Madame Fanny will have a fit. I will call her— She will not be able to contain herself. She—

SARA (*softly*). I wanted a few minutes. I'm nervous about coming home, I guess.

BODO (*conversationally*). You are French, Madame Anise?

ANISE. Yes, I am from the Bas Rhin. (*She looks past* SARA, *and bobs her head idiotically at* KURT.) Sara's husband. That's nice. That is nice.

BODO. Yes. Your accent is from the North. That is fine country. We were in hiding there once.
(BABETTE *quickly pokes him.*)

ANISE. Hiding? You— (*Turns nervously to* KURT.) But here we stand and talk. You have not had your breakfast, sir!

BABETTE (*simply, eagerly*). It would be nice to have breakfast.

ANISE. Yes, of course— I will go and order it.

SARA (*to the children*). What would you like for breakfast?

BABETTE (*surprised*). What would we like? Why, Mama, we will have anything that can be spared. If eggs are not too rare or too expensive—

ANISE (*amazed*). Rare? Why— Oh, I— I must call Miss Fanny now. It is of a necessity. (*Excited, rushing toward terrace, calling*) Miss Fanny. Miss Fanny. (*Back to* SARA) Have you forgotten your Mama's nature? She cannot bear not knowing things. Miss Fanny! What a way to come home! After twenty years and nobody at the station—

FANNY'S VOICE. Don't yell at me. What is the matter with you?

ANISE (*excitedly, as* FANNY *draws near*). She's here. They're here. Miss Sara. She's here, I tell you.
(FANNY *comes up to her, stares at her, then looks slowly around until she sees* SARA.)

SARA (*softly*). Hello, Mama.

FANNY (*after a long pause, softly, coming toward her*). Sara. Sara, darling. You're here. You're really here. (*She reaches her, takes her arms, stares at her, smiles.*) Welcome. Welcome. Welcome to your house. (*Slowly*) You're not young, Sara.

SARA (*smiles*). No, Mama. I'm forty-one.

FANNY (*softly*). Forty-one. Of course. (*Presses her arms again.*) Oh, Sara, I'm— (*Then quickly*) You look more like Papa now. That's good. The years have helped you. (*Turns to look at* KURT.) Welcome to this house, sir.

KURT (*warmly*). Thank you, Madame.

FANNY (*turns to look at* SARA *again, nervously pats her arm. Nods, turns again to stare at* KURT. *She is nervous and chatty*). You are a good-looking man, for a German. I didn't remember you that way. I like a good-looking man. I always have.

KURT (*smiles*). I like a good-looking woman. I always have.

FANNY. Good. That's the way it should be.

BODO (*to* SARA). Ist das Grossmama?

FANNY (*looks down*). Yes. I am your grandmother. Also, I speak German, so do not talk about me. I speak languages very well. But there is no longer anybody to speak with. Anise has half-forgotten her French, which was always bad; and I have nobody with whom to speak my Italian or German or—Sara, it's very good to have you home. I'm chattering away, I—

JOSHUA. Now you have us, Madame. We speak ignorantly, but fluently, in German, French, Italian, Spanish—

KURT. And boastfully in English.

BODO. There is never a need for boasting. If we are to fight for the good of all men, it is to be accepted that we must be among the most advanced.

ANISE. My God.

FANNY (to SARA). Are these your *children?* Or are they dressed up midgets?

SARA (*laughs*). These are my children, Mama. This, Babette. (BABETTE *bows.*) This, Joshua. (JOSHUA *bows.*) This is Bodo. (BODO *bows.*)

FANNY. Joshua was named for Papa. You wrote me. (*Indicates picture of Joshua Farrelly*) You bear a great name, young man.

JOSHUA (*smiles, indicates his father*). My name is Müller.

FANNY (*looks at him, laughs*). Yes. You look a little like your grandfather. (*To* BABETTE) And so do you. You are a nice-looking girl. (*To* BODO) You look like nobody.

BODO (*proudly*). I am not beautiful.

FANNY (*laughs*). Well, Sara, well. Three children. You have done well. (*To* KURT) You, too, sir, of course. Are you quite recovered? Sara wrote that you were in Spain and—

BODO. Did Mama write that Papa was a great hero? He was brave, he was calm, he was expert, he was resourceful, he was—

KURT (*laughs*). My biographer. And as unprejudiced as most of them.

SARA. Where is David? I am so anxious— Has he changed much? Does he . . .

FANNY (*to* ANISE). Don't stand there. Go and get him right away. Go get David. (*As* ANISE *exits*) He's out having breakfast with the titled folk. Do you remember Marthe Randolph? I mean, do you remember Hortie Randolph, her mother, who was my friend? Can you follow what I'm saying? I'm not speaking well today.

SARA (*laughs*). Of course I remember Marthe and Hortie. You and she used to scream at each other.

FANNY. Well, Marthe, her daughter, married Teck de Brancovis. *Count* de Brancovis. He was fancy when she married him. Not so fancy now, I suspect. Although still chic and tired. You know what I mean, the way they are in Europe. Well, they're here.

SARA. What's David like now? I—

FANNY. Like? Like? I don't know. He's a lawyer. You know that. Papa's firm. He's never married. You know that, too—

SARA. Why hasn't he married?

FANNY. Really, I don't know. I don't think he likes his own taste. Which is very discriminating of him. He's had a lot of girls, of course, one more ignorant and silly than the other— (*Goes toward terrace, begins to scream.*) And where is he? David! David!

ANISE'S VOICE. He's coming, Miss Fanny. He's coming. Contain yourself. He was down at the garage getting ready to leave—

FANNY. I don't care where he is. Tell him to come.— David! (*Suddenly points to picture of Joshua*) That's my

JOSHUA. Handsome, eh? We were very much in love. Hard to believe of people nowadays, isn't it?

SARA. Kurt and I love each other.

FANNY. Oh. You do? I daresay. But there are ways and ways of loving.

SARA. How dare you, Mama—

KURT (*laughs*). Ladies, ladies.

SARA (*giggles*). Why, I almost got mad then. You know, I don't think I've been mad since I last saw you.

BODO. My! You and Mama must not get angry. Anger is protest. And so you must direction it to the proper channels and then harness it for the good of other men. That is correct, Papa?

FANNY (*peers down at him*). If you grow up to talk like that, and stay as ugly as you are, you are going to have one of those successful careers on the lecture platform.
(JOSHUA *and* BABETTE *laugh.*)

JOSHUA. Ah. It is a great pleasure to hear Grandma talk with you.

BODO (*to* FANNY, *tenderly*). We will not like each other.
(KURT *has wandered to the piano. Standing, he touches the keys in the first bars of a Mozart Rondo.*)

FANNY. You are wrong. I think we are rather alike; if that is so, let us at least remember to admire each other.
(DAVID *comes running in from the entrance hall. At the door he stops, stares at* SARA.)

DAVID (*to* SARA). Sara. Darling—

SARA (*Wheels, goes running toward him. She moves into his arms. He leans down, kisses her with great affection*). David. David.

DAVID (*softly*). It's been a long, long time. I got to thinking it would never happen. (*He leans down, kisses her hair. After a minute, he smiles, presses her arm.*)

SARA (*excited*). David, I'm excited. Isn't it strange? To be here, to see each other— But I am forgetting. This is my husband. These are my children. Babette, Joshua, Bodo.
(*They all three advance, stand in line to shake hands.*)

BODO (*shaking hand*). How do you do, Uncle David?

DAVID. How do you do, Bodo? (DAVID *shakes hands with* JOSHUA.) Boys can shake hands. But so pretty a girl must be kissed.
(*He kisses* BABETTE. *She smiles, very pleased, and crosses to the side of* SARA.)

BABETTE. Thank you. Fix your hairpin, Mama.
(SARA *shoves back a falling hairpin.*)

DAVID (*crossing to* KURT). I'm happy to meet you, sir, and to have you here.

KURT. Thank you. Sara has told me so much from you. You have a devoted sister.

DAVID (*very pleased*). Have I? Still? That's mighty good to hear.
(ANISE *comes in from the library.*)

ANISE. Your breakfast is coming. Shall I wash the children, Miss Sara?

JOSHUA (*amazed*). Wash us? Do people wash each other?

SARA. No, but the washing is a good idea. Go along now, and hurry. (*All three start for the hall.*) And then we'll all have a fine, big breakfast again.
(*The children exit.*)

FANNY. Again? Don't you usually have a good breakfast?

KURT (*smiles*). No, Madame. Only sometimes.

SARA (*laughs*). Oh, we do all right, usually. (*Very happily, very gaily*) Ah, it's good to be here. (*Puts her arm in* DAVID'S.) We were kids. Now we're all grown up! I've got children, you're a lawyer, and a fine one, I bet—

FANNY. The name of Farrelly on the door didn't, of course, hurt David's career.

DAVID (*smiles*). Sara, you might as well know Mama thinks of me only as a monument to Papa and a not very well-made monument at that. I am not the man Papa was.

SARA (*to* FANNY, *smiles*). How do you know he's not?

FANNY (*carefully*). I beg your pardon. That is the second time you have spoken disrespectfully of your father. (SARA *and* DAVID *laugh.* FANNY *turns to* KURT.) I hope you will like me.

KURT. I hope so.

SARA (*pulls him to the couch, sits down with him*). Now I want to hear about you— (*Looks at him, laughs.*) I'm awfully nervous about seeing you. Are you, about me?

DAVID. Yes. I certainly am.

SARA (*looks around*). I'm like an idiot. I want to see everything right away. The lake, and my old room—and I want to talk and ask questions . . .

KURT (*laughs*). More slow, Sara. It is most difficult to have twenty years in a few minutes.

SARA. Yes, I know, but— Oh, well. Kurt's right. We'll say it all slowly. It's just nice being back. Haven't I fine children?

DAVID. Very fine. You're lucky. I wish I had them.

FANNY. How could you have them? All the women you like are too draughty, if you know what I mean. I'm sure that girl from Lansing, Michigan, would be sterile. Which is as God in his wisdom would have it.

SARA. Oh. So you have a girl?

DAVID. I have no girl. This amuses Mama.

FANNY. He's very attractive to some women. (*To* KURT) Both my children are attractive, whatever else they're not. Don't you think so? (*Points to* DAVID.) He's flirting with our Countess now, Sara. You will see for yourself.

DAVID (*sharply*). You are making nervous jokes this morning, Mama. And they're not very good ones.

FANNY (*gaily*). I tell the truth. If it turns out to be a joke, all the better.

SARA (*affectionately*). Ah, Mama hasn't changed. And that's good, too.

FANNY. Don't mind me, Sara. I, too, am nervous about seeing you. (*To* KURT) You'll like it here. You are an engineer?

KURT. Yes.

FANNY. Do you remember the day we met in München? The day Sara brought you to lunch? I thought you were rather a clod and that Sara would have a miserable life. I think I was wrong. (*To* DAVID) You see? I always admit when I'm wrong.

DAVID. You are a woman who is noble in all things, at all times.

FANNY. Oh, you're mad at me. (*To* KURT) As I say, you'll like it here. I've already made some plans. The new wing will be for you and Sara. The old turkey-house we'll fix up for the children. A nice, new bathroom, and we'll put in their own kitchen, and Anise will move in with them—

SARA. That's kind of you, Mama. But —but—we won't make any plans for a while— (*Very quietly*) A good, long vacation; God knows Kurt needs it—

FANNY. A vacation? You'll be staying here, of course. You don't have to worry about work— Engineers can always get jobs, David says, and he's already begun to inquire—

KURT. I have not worked as an engineer since many years, Madame.

DAVID. Haven't you? I thought—Didn't you work for Dornier?

KURT. Yes. Before '33.

FANNY. But you have worked in other places. A great many other places, I should say. Every letter of Sara's seemed to have a new postmark.

KURT (*smiles*). We move most often.

DAVID. You gave up engineering?

KURT. I gave it up? (*Smiles.*) One could say it that way.

FANNY. What do you do?

SARA. Mama, we—

KURT. It is difficult to explain.

DAVID (*after a slight pause*). If you'd rather not.

FANNY. No, I—I'm trying to find out something. (*To* KURT) May I ask it, sir?

KURT. Let me help you, Madame. You wish to know whether not being an engineer buys adequate breakfasts for my family. It does not. I have no wish to make a mystery of what I have been doing; it is only that it is awkward to place neatly. (*Smiles, motions with his hand.*) It sounds so big: it is so small. I am an Anti-Fascist. And that does not pay well.

FANNY. Do you mind questions?

SARA. Yes.

KURT (*sharply*). Sara. (*To* FANNY) Perhaps I shall not answer them. But I shall try.

FANNY. Are you a radical?

KURT. You would have to tell me what that word means to you, Madame.

FANNY (*after a slight pause*). That is just. Perhaps we all have private definitions. We all are Anti-Fascists, for example—

SARA. Yes. But Kurt works at it.

FANNY. What kind of work?

KURT. Any kind. Anywhere.

FANNY (*sharply*). I will stop asking questions.

SARA (*very sharply*). That would be sensible, Mama.

DAVID. Darling, don't be angry. We've been worried about you, naturally. We knew so little, except that you were having a bad time.

SARA. I didn't have a bad time. We never—

KURT. Do not lie for me, Sara.

SARA. I'm not lying. I didn't have a bad time, the way they mean. I—

FANNY (*slowly*). You had a bad time just trying to live, didn't you? That's obvious, Sara, and foolish to pretend it isn't. Why wouldn't you take money from us? What kind of nonsense—

SARA (*slowly*). We've lived the way we wanted to live. I don't know the language of rooms like this any more. And I don't want to learn it again.

KURT. Do not bristle about it.

SARA. I'm not bristling. (*To* FANNY) I married because I fell in love. You can understand that.

FANNY (*slowly*). Yes.

SARA. For almost twelve years, Kurt went to work every morning and came home every night, and we lived modestly, and happily— (*Sharply*) As happily as people could in a starved Germany that was going to pieces—

KURT. Sara, please. You're angry. I do not like it that way. I will try to find a way to tell you with quickness. Yes. (SARA *turns, looks at him, starts to speak, stops.*) I was born in a town called Fürth. (*Pauses. Looks up, smiles.*) There is a holiday in my town. We call it Kirchweih. It was a gay holiday with games and music and a hot white sausage to eat with the wine. I grow up, I move away—to school, to work—but always I come back for Kirchweih. It is for me, the great day of the year. (*Slowly*) But after the war, that day begins to change. The sausage is made from bad stuff, the peasants come in without shoes, the children are too sick— (*Carefully*) It is bad for my people, those years, but always I have hope. In the festival of August, 1931, more than a year before the storm, I give up that hope. On that day, I see twenty-seven men murdered in a Nazi street fight. I cannot stay by now and watch. My time has come to move. I say with Luther, "Here I stand. I can do nothing else. God help me. Amen."

SARA. It doesn't pay well to fight for what we believe in. But I wanted it the way Kurt wanted it. (*Shrugs.*)

They don't like us in Europe; I guess they never did. So Kurt brought us home. You've always said you wanted us. If you don't, I will understand.

DAVID. Darling, of course we want you—

FANNY (*rises*). I am old. And made of dry cork. And bad-mannered. Please forgive me.

SARA (*goes quickly to* FANNY). Shut up, Mama. We're all acting like fools. I'm glad to be home. That's all I know. So damned glad.

DAVID. And we're damned glad to have you. Come on. Let's walk to the lake. We've made it bigger and planted the island with blackberries— (*She smiles and goes to him. Together they move out the hall entrance.*)

FANNY (*after a silence*). They've always liked each other. We're going to have Zwetschgen-Knoedel for dinner. You like them?

KURT. Indeed.

FANNY. I hope you like decent food.

KURT. I do.

FANNY. That's a good sign in a man.

MARTHE (*coming in from the terrace. Stops in the doorway*). Oh, I'm sorry, Fanny. We were waiting. I didn't want to interrupt the family reunion. I—

FANNY. This is my son-in-law, Herr Müller. The Countess de Brancovis.

KURT AND MARTHE (*together*). How do you do?

MARTHE. And how is Sara, Herr Müller? I haven't seen her since I was a little girl. She probably doesn't remember me at all. (TECK *comes in from the hall. She turns.*) This is my husband, Herr Müller.

KURT. How do you do?

TECK. How do you do, sir? (KURT *bows. They shake hands.*) Would it be impertinent for one European to make welcome another?

KURT (*smiles*). I do not think so. It would be friendly.

BODO (*appears at the hall door*). Papa —(*Sees* TECK *and* MARTHE, *bows.*) Oh, good morning. Miss Anise says you are the Count and Countess. Once before we met a Count and Countess. They had a small room bordering on ours in Copenhagen. They were more older than you, and more poor. We shared with them our newspaper.

MARTHE (*laughs*). It wasn't us, but it might have been. What's your name?

TECK (*laughs*). We hope you will be as kind to us.

BODO. My name is Bodo. It's a strange name. No? (*To* KURT) Papa, this is the house of great wonders. Each has his bed, each has his bathroom. The arrangement of it, that is splendorous.

FANNY (*laughs*). You are a fancy talker, Bodo.

KURT. Oh, yes. In many languages.

BODO (*to* FANNY). Please to correct me when I am wrong. Papa, the plumbing is such as you have never seen. Each implement is placed on the floor, and all are simultaneous in the same room. You will therefore see that being placed most solidly on the floor allows of no rats, rodents or crawlers, and is most sanitary. (*To the others*) Papa

will be most interested. He likes to know how each thing of everything is put together. And he is so fond of being clean—

KURT (*laughs. To* FANNY). I am a hero to my children. It bores everybody but me.

TECK. It is most interesting, Herr Müller. I thought I had a good ear for the accents of your country. But yours is most difficult to place. It is Bayrisch? Or is it—

BODO. That's because Papa has worked in so many—

KURT (*quickly*). German accents are the most difficult to identify. I, myself, when I try, am usually incorrect. It would be particularly difficult with me because I speak other languages. Yours would be Roumanian?

MARTHE (*laughs*). My God, is it that bad?

KURT (*smiles*). I am showing off. I know the Count de Brancovis is Roumanian.

TECK (*heartily*). So? We have met before? I thought so, but I cannot remember—

KURT. No, sir. We have not met before. I read your name in the newspapers.

TECK (*to* KURT). Strange. I was sure I had met you. I was in the Paris Legation for many years, and I thought perhaps—

KURT. Oh, no. If it is possible to believe, I am the exile who is not famous. (*To* FANNY) I have been thinking with pleasure, Madame Fanny, of breakfast on your porch. (*He points to the picture of Joshua Farrelly.*) Your husband once wrote: "I am getting older now and Europe seems far away. Fanny and I will have an early breakfast on the porch and then I shall drive the bays into Washington." (*Remembering*) And then he goes on: "Henry Adams tells me he has been reading Karl Marx. I shall have to tell him my father made me read Marx many years ago and that, since he proposes to exhibit himself to impress me, will spoil Henry's Sunday."

FANNY (*laughs, delighted. Takes* KURT'S *arm*). And so it did. I had forgotten that. I am pleased with you. I shall come and serve your food myself. I had forgotten Joshua ever wrote it. (*They start out of the terrace doors together, followed by* BODO.)

KURT (*as they disappear*). I try to impress you. I learned it last night. (FANNY *laughs. They disappear*.)

TECK (*smiles*). He is a clever man. A quotation from Joshua Farrelly is a sure road to Fanny's heart. Where did you say Herr Müller was from?

MARTHE. Germany.

TECK. I know that. (*Goes to a valise. He leans over, stares at it, looks at the labels, pushes the lock. The lock opens; he closes it. Then he turns and, as he speaks, picks up the brief-case.*) What part of Germany?

MARTHE. I don't know. And I never knew you were an expert on accents.

TECK. I never knew it either. Are you driving into Washington with David this morning?

MARTHE. I was going to. But he may not be going to the office, now that Sara's here. I was to have lunch with Sally Tyne. (TECK *puts down the brief-case.*) What are you doing?

TECK. Wondering why luggage is unlocked and a shabby brief-case is so carefully locked.

MARTHE. You're very curious about Mr. Müller.

TECK. Yes. And I do not know why. Something far away . . . I am curious about a daughter of the Farrelly's who marries a German who has bullet scars on his face and broken bones in his hands.

MARTHE (*sharply*). Has he? There are many of them now, I guess.

TECK. So there are. But this one is in this house. (*He goes to the bell cord, pulls it. She watches him nervously.*)

MARTHE. Is it—is he any business of yours?

TECK. What is my business? Anything might be my business now.

MARTHE. Yes—unfortunately. You might inquire from your friend Von Seitz. They always know their nationals.

TECK (*pleasantly, ignoring the sharpness with which she has spoken*). Oh, yes, I will do that, of course. But I do not like to ask questions without knowing the value of the answers.

MARTHE. Teck. This man is a little German Sara married years ago. I remember Mama talking about it. He was nothing then and he isn't now. They've had a tough enough time already without—

TECK. Have you— Have you been sleeping with David?

MARTHE (*stops, stares at him, then simply*). No. I have not been. And that hasn't been your business for a good many years now.

TECK. You like him?

MARTHE (*nervously*). What's this for, Teck?

TECK. Answer me, please.

MARTHE. I— (*She stops.*)

TECK. Yes? Answer me.

MARTHE. I do like him.

TECK. What does he feel about you?

MARTHE. I don't know.

TECK. But you are trying to find out. You have made any plans with him?

MARTHE. Of course not. I—

TECK. You will try to make him have plans. I have recognized it. Well, we have been together a long— (*JOSEPH enters. TECK stops.*) Joseph, Miss Fanny wishes you to take the baggage upstairs.

JOSEPH. Yes, sir. I was going to. (*He begins to pick up the baggage. MARTHE has turned sharply and is staring at TECK. Then she rises, watches JOSEPH pick up the baggage, turns again to look at TECK.*)

TECK. As I was saying. It is perhaps best that we had this talk.

MARTHE. (*She stops, waits for JOSEPH to move off. He exits, carrying the valises.*) Why did you do that? Why did you tell Joseph that Fanny wanted him to take the baggage upstairs?

TECK. Obviously it is more comfortable to look at baggage behind closed doors.

MARTHE (*very sharply*). What kind of silliness is this now? Leave these people alone— (*As he starts to exit*) I won't let you—

TECK. What? (*As he moves again, she comes after him.*)

MARTHE. I said I won't let you. You are not—

TECK. How many times have you seen me angry? (*MARTHE looks up, startled.*) You will not wish to see another. Run along now and have lunch with something you call Sally Tyne. But do not make plans with David. You will not be able to carry them out. You will go with me, when I am ready to go. You understand. (*He exits during his speech. The last words come as he goes through the door, and as the curtain falls.*)

ACT TWO

SCENE: *The same as Act One, about ten days later. During the act it will begin to grow dark; but the evening is warm and the terrace doors are open.*

AT RISE: SARA *is sitting on the couch, crocheting.* FANNY *and* TECK *are sitting at a small table playing cribbage.* BODO *is sitting near them, at a large table, working on a heating pad. The cord is torn from the bag, the bag is ripped open.* ANISE *sits next to him, anxiously watching him. Outside on the terrace,* JOSHUA *is going through baseball motions, coached by* JOSEPH. *From time to time they move out of sight, reappear, move off again.*

FANNY (*playing a card*). One.

BODO (*after a minute, to* TECK). The arrangement of this heating pad grows more complex.

TECK (*smiles, moves on the cribbage board*). And the more wires you remove, the more complex it will grow.

BODO (*points to bag*). Man has learned to make man comfortable. Yet all cannot have the comforts. (*To* ANISE) How much did this cost you?

ANISE. It cost me ten dollars. And you have made a ruin of it.

BODO. That is not yet completely true. (*To* FANNY) Did I not install for you a twenty-five-cent button-push for your radio?

TECK (*playing a card*). Two and two. (*Moves pegs on the cribbage board.*)

FANNY. Yes, you're quite an installer.

BODO (*to* TECK). As I was wishing to tell you, Count de Brancovis, comfort and plenty exist. Yet all cannot have it. Why?

TECK. I do not know. It has worried many men. Why?

ANISE (*to* BODO). Yes, why?

BODO (*takes a deep breath, raises his finger as if about to lecture*). Why? (*Considers a moment, then deflates himself.*) I am not as yet sure.

ANISE. I thought not.

FANNY (*turns to look at* JOSHUA *and* JOSEPH *on the terrace*). Would you mind doing that dancing some place else?

JOSEPH (*looking in*). Yes'm. That ain't dancing. I'm teaching Josh baseball.

FANNY. Then maybe he'd teach you how to clean the silver.

JOSEPH. I'm a good silver-cleaner, Miss Fanny.

FANNY. But you're getting out of practice.

JOSEPH (*after a moment's thought*). Yes'm. I see what you mean. (*He exits.*)

FANNY (*playing a card*). Three.

JOSHUA. It is my fault. I'm crazy about baseball.

BODO. Baseball players are among the most exploited people in this country. I read about it.

FANNY. You never should have learned to read.

BODO. Their exploited condition is foundationed on the fact that—

JOSHUA (*bored*). All right, all right. I still like baseball.

SARA. Founded, Bodo, not foundationed.

JOSHUA. He does it always. He likes long words. In all languages.

TECK. How many languages do you children speak?

BODO. Oh, we do not really know any very well, except German and English. We speak bad French and —

SARA. And bad Danish and bad Czech.

TECK. You seem to have stayed close to the borders of Germany. Did Herr Müller have hopes, as so many did, that National Socialism would be overthrown on every tomorrow?

SARA. We have not given up that hope. Have you, Count de Brancovis?

TECK. I never had it.

JOSHUA (*pleasantly*). Then it must be most difficult for you to sleep.

TECK. I beg your pardon?

SARA. Schweig doch, Joshua!

FANNY (*to* TECK). Sara told Joshua to shut up. (*Playing a card*) Twelve.

TECK. I have offended you, Mrs. Müller. I am most sorry.

SARA (*pleasantly*). No, sir, you haven't offended me. I just don't like polite political conversations any more.

TECK (*nods*). All of us, in Europe, had too many of them.

SARA. Yes. Too much talk. By this time all of us must know where we are and what we have to do. It's an indulgence to sit in a room and discuss your beliefs as if they were a juicy piece of gossip.

FANNY. You know, Sara, I find it very pleasant that Kurt, considering his history, doesn't make platform speeches. He hasn't tried to convince anybody of anything.

SARA (*smiles*). Why should he, Mama? You are quite old enough to have your own convictions—or Papa's.

FANNY (*turns to look at her*). I am proud to have Papa's convictions.

SARA. Of course. But it might be well to have a few new ones, now and then.

FANNY (*peers over at her*). Are you criticizing me?

SARA (*smiles*). Certainly not.

BABETTE (*Comes running in from the right entrance door. She has on an apron and she is carrying a plate. She goes to* FANNY). Eat it while it's hot, Grandma.
(FANNY *peers down, takes the fork, begins to eat.* ANISE *and* BODO *both rise, move to* FANNY, *inspect the plate.*)

FANNY (*to them*). Go away.

ANISE. It is a potato pancake.

FANNY. And the first good one I've eaten in many, many years. I love a good potato pancake.

BODO. I likewise.

BABETTE. I am making a great number for dinner. Move away, Bodo.

TECK (*playing a card*). Fifteen and two.

ANISE (*who has followed* BODO *back to the chair*). You've ruined it! I shall sue you.

JOSHUA. I told you not to let him touch it.

SARA (*laughs*). I remember you were always saying that, Anise—that you were going to sue. That's very French. I was sick once in Paris, and Babbie stayed up for a whole night and day and finished a dress I was making for a woman on the Rue Jacob. I told her to tell the woman she'd done it—I thought perhaps the woman would give her a candy or something—and anyway, I was very proud of her work. But no. The woman admitted the dress was well done, but said she was going to sue because I hadn't done it myself. Fancy that.

FANNY (*slowly*). You sewed for a living?

SARA. Not a very good one. But Babbie and I made a little something now and then. Didn't we, darling?

FANNY (*sharply*). Really, Sara, were these—these things necessary? Why couldn't you have written?

SARA (*laughs*). You've asked me that a hundred times in the last week.

JOSHUA (*gently*). I think it is only that Grandma feels sorry for us. Grandma has not seen much of the world.

FANNY. Don't you start giving me lectures, Joshua. I'm fond of you. And of you, Babbie. (*To* ANISE) Are there two desserts for dinner? And are they sweet?

ANISE. Yes.

FANNY (*turns to* BODO). I wish I were fond of you.

BODO. You are. (*Happily*) You are very fond of me.

FANNY (*playing a card*). Twenty-five.

BABETTE. This is for you, Grandma. I'm making a bed-jacket. It is nice lace. Papa brought it to me from Spain and I mean for you to have it.

FANNY (*kisses* BABETTE). Thank you, darling. A sequence and three. A pair and five. (*To* TECK, *as they finish the cribbage game*) There. That's two dollars off. I owe you eight-fifty.

TECK. Let us carry it until tomorrow. You shall give it to me as a going-away token.

FANNY (*too pleased*). You're going away?

TECK (*laughs*). Ah, Madame Fanny. Do not sound *that* happy.

FANNY. Did I? That's rude of me. When are you going?

TECK. In a few days, I think. (*Turns to look at* SARA.) We're too many refugees, eh, Mrs. Müller?

SARA (*pleasantly*). Perhaps.

TECK. Will you be leaving, also?

SARA. I beg your pardon?

TECK. I thought perhaps you, too, would be moving on. Herr Müller does not give me the feeling of a man who settles down. Men who have done his work, seldom leave it. Not for a quiet country house.
(*All three children look up.*)

SARA (*very quietly*). What work do you think my husband has done, Count de Brancovis?

TECK. Engineering?

SARA (*slowly*). Yes. Engineering.

FANNY (*very deliberately to* TECK). I

don't know what you're saying. They shall certainly not be leaving—ever. Is that understood, Sara?

SARA. Well, Mama—

FANNY. There are no wells about it. You've come home to see me die and you will wait until I'm ready.

SARA (*laughs*). Really, Mama, that isn't the reason I came home.

FANNY. It's a good enough reason. I shall do a fine death. I intend to be a great deal of trouble to everybody.

ANISE. I daresay.

FANNY. I shall take to my bed early and stay for years. In great pain.

ANISE. I am sure of it. You will duplicate the disgrace of the birth of Miss Sara.

SARA (*laughs*). Was I born in disgrace?

ANISE. It was not your fault. But it was disgusting. Three weeks before you were to come—all was excellent, of course, in so healthy a woman as Madame Fanny—a great dinner was given here and, most unexpectedly, attended by a beautiful lady from England.

FANNY. Do be still. You are dull and fanciful—

ANISE. Mr. Joshua made the great error of waltzing the beauty for two dances, Madame Fanny being unfitted for the waltz and under no circumstances being the most graceful of dancers.

FANNY (*her voice rising*). Are you crazy? I danced magnificently.

ANISE. It is well you thought so. A minute did not elapse between the second of the waltzes and a scream from Madame Fanny. She was in labor. Two hundred people, and if we had left her alone, she would have remained in the ballroom—

FANNY. How you invent! How you invent!

ANISE. Do not call to me that I am a liar. For three weeks you are in the utmost agony—

FANNY. And so I was. I remember it to this day—

ANISE (*to* SARA, *angrily*). Not a pain. Not a single pain. She would lie up there in state, stealing candy from herself. Then, when your Papa would rest himself for a minute at the dinner or with a book, a scream would dismantle the house—it was revolting. (*Spitefully to* FANNY) And now the years have passed and I may disclose to you that Mr. Joshua knew you were going through the play-acting—

FANNY (*rises*). He did not. You are a malicious—

ANISE. Once he said to me, "Anise, it is well that I am in love. This is of a great strain and her Great-uncle Freddie was not right in the head, neither."

FANNY (*screaming*). You will leave this house— You are a liar, a woman of—

SARA. Mama, sit down.

ANISE. I will certainly leave this house. I will—

SARA (*sharply*). Both of you. Sit down. And be still.

ANISE. She has intimated that I lie—

FANNY (*screaming*). Intimated! Is that what I was doing— (ANISE *begins to leave the room.*) All right. I beg your pardon. I apologize. (ANISE *turns.*)

SARA. Both of you. You are acting like children.

BODO. Really, Mama. You insult us.

ANISE. I accept your apology. Seat yourself.
(*They both sit down.*)

FANNY (*after a silence*). I am unloved.

BABETTE. I love you, Grandma.

FANNY. Do you, Babbie?

JOSHUA. And I.

FANNY (*nods very pleased. To* BODO). And you?

BODO. *I* loved you the primary second I saw you.

FANNY. You are a charlatan.

ANISE. As for me, I am fond of all the living creatures. It is true that the children cause me greater work, which in turn more greatly inconveniences the feet. However, I do not complain. I believe in children.

FANNY. Rather like believing in the weather, isn't it? (DAVID *and* KURT *come in from the terrace. Both are in work clothes, their sleeves rolled up.*) Where have you been?

DAVID. Oh, we've been helping Mr. Chabeuf spray the fruit trees.

ANISE. Mr. Chabeuf says that Herr Müller has the makings of a good farmer. From a Frenchman that is a large thing to say.

KURT (*who has looked around the room, looked at* TECK, *strolled over to* BODO). Mr. Chabeuf and I have an excellent time exchanging misinformation. My father was a farmer. I have a wide knowledge of farmer's misinformation.

FANNY. This is good farm land. Perhaps, in time—

DAVID (*laughs*). Mama would give you the place, Kurt, if you guaranteed that your great-grandchildren would die here.

KURT (*smiles*). I would like to so guarantee.

TECK. A farmer. That is very interesting. Abandon your ideals, Herr Müller?

KURT. Ideals? (*Carefully*) Sara, heisst das auf deutsch "Ideale"?

SARA. Yes.

KURT. Is that what I have now? I do not like the word. It gives to me the picture of a small, pale man at a seaside resort. (*To* BODO) What are you doing?

BODO. Preparing an elderly electric pad for Miss Anise. I am confused.

KURT (*wanders toward the piano*). So it seems.

BODO. Something has gone wrong with the principle on which I have been working. It is probably that I will ask your assistance.

KURT (*bows to him*). Thank you. Whenever you are ready. (*Begins to pick out notes with one hand.*)

FANNY. We shall have a little concert tomorrow evening. In honor of Babbie's birthday. (*To* KURT) Kurt, you and I will play "The Clock Symphony." Then Joshua and I will play the duet we've learned, and Babbie will sing. And I shall finish with a Chopin Nocturne.

DAVID (*laughs*). I thought you'd be the last on the program.

TECK. Where is Marthe?

FANNY. She'll be back soon. She went into town to do an errand for me. (*To* DAVID) Did you buy presents for everybody?

DAVID. I did.

SARA (*smiles, to* BABETTE). We always did that here. If somebody had a birthday, we all got presents. Nice, isn't it?

DAVID (*to* ANISE). I shall buy you an electric pad. You will need it.

ANISE. Indeed.

FANNY. Did you buy me a good present?

DAVID. Pretty good. (*Pats* BABETTE's *head.*) The best present goes to Babbie; it's *her* birthday.

FANNY. Jewelry?

DAVID. No, not jewelry.

FANNY. Oh. Not jewelry.

DAVID. Why? Why should you want jewelry? You've got too many bangles now.

FANNY. I didn't say I wanted it. I just asked you.

TECK (*gets up*). It was a natural mistake, David. You see, Mrs. Mellie Sewell told your mother that she had seen you and Marthe in Barstow's. And your mother said you were probably buying her a present, or one for Babbie.

DAVID (*too sharply*). Yes.

TECK (*laughs*). Yes what?

DAVID (*slowly*). Just yes.

FANNY (*too hurriedly*). Mellie gets everything wrong. She's very anxious to meet Marthe because she used to know Francie Cabot, her aunt. Marthe's aunt, I mean, not Mellie's.

SARA (*too hurriedly*). She really came to inspect Kurt and me. But I saw her first. (*She looks anxiously at* DAVID, *who has turned his back on the room and is facing the terrace.*) You were lucky to be out, David.

DAVID. Oh, she calls every Saturday afternoon, to bring Mama all the Washington gossip of the preceding week. She gets it all wrong, you understand, but that doesn't make any difference to either Mama or her. Mama then augments it, wits it up, Papa used to say—

FANNY. Certainly. I sharpen it a little. Mellie has no sense of humor.

DAVID. So Mamma sharpens it a little, and delivers it tomorrow afternoon to old lady Marcy down the road. Old lady Marcy hasn't heard a word in ten years, so she unsharpens it again, and changes the names. By Wednesday afternoon—

TECK (*smiles*). By Wednesday afternoon it will not be you who were in Barstow's, and it will be a large diamond pin with four sapphires delivered to Gaby Deslys.

DAVID (*turns, looks at him*). Exactly.

FANNY (*very nervously*). Francie Cabot, Marthe's aunt, you understand— (*To* KURT) Did you ever know Paul von Seitz, a German?

KURT. I have heard of him.

FANNY (*speaking very rapidly*). Certainly. He was your Ambassador to somewhere, I've forgotten. Well Francie Cabot married him. I could have. Any American, not crippled, whose father had money— He was crazy about me. I was better-looking than Francie. Well, years later when he was your Ambassador—my father was, too, as you probably know—not your Ambassador, of course, ours—but I am talking about Von Seitz.

DAVID (*laughs to* KURT). You can understand how it goes. Old lady Marcy is not entirely to blame.

FANNY. Somebody asked me if I didn't regret not marrying him. I said, "Madame, je le regrette tous les jours et j'en suis heureuse chaque soir." (FANNY *turns to* DAVID.) That means I regret it every day and am happy about it every night. You understand what I meant, by *night*? Styles in wit change so.

DAVID. I understood it, Mama.

JOSHUA. We, too, Grandma.

BABETTE (*approvingly*). It is most witty.

BODO. I do not know that I understood. You will explain to me, Grandma?

SARA. Later.

FANNY (*turns to look at* TECK). You remember the old Paul von Seitz?

TECK (*nods*). He was stationed in Paris when I first was there.

FANNY. Of course. I always forget you were a diplomat.

TECK. It is just as well.

FANNY. There's something insane about a Roumanian diplomat. Pure insane. I knew another one, once. He wanted to marry me, too.

SARA (*laughs*). All of Europe.

FANNY. Not all. Some. Naturally. I was rich, I was witty, my family was of the best. I was handsome, unaffected—

DAVID. And noble and virtuous and kind and elegant and fashionable and simple—it's hard to remember everything you were. I've often thought it must have been boring for Papa to have owned such perfection.

FANNY (*shrieks*). What! Your father bored with me! Not for a second of our life—

DAVID (*laughs*). Oh God, when will I learn?

BODO. Do not shriek, Grandma. It is an unpleasant sound for the ear.

FANNY. Where was I? Oh, yes. What I started out to say was— (*She turns, speaks carefully to* TECK.) Mellie Sewell told me, when you left the room, that she had heard from Louis Chandler's child's governess that you had won quite a bit of money in a poker game with Sam Chandler and some Germans at the Embassy. (KURT, *who has been playing the piano, stops playing very abruptly.* TECK *turns to look at him.*) *That's* how I thought of Von Seitz. His nephew Philip was in on the game.

DAVID (*looks at* TECK). It must have been a big game. Sam Chandler plays in big games.

TECK. Not big enough.

DAVID. Have you known Sam long?

TECK. For years. Every Embassy in Europe knew him.

DAVID (*sharply*). Sam and Nazis must make an unpleasant poker game. (KURT *begins to play a new melody.*)

TECK (*who has not looked away from* KURT). I do not play poker to be amused.

DAVID (*irritably*). What's Sam selling now?

TECK. Bootleg munitions. He always has.

DAVID. You don't mind?

TECK. Mind? I have not thought about it.

FANNY. Well, you ought to think about it. Sam Chandler has always been a scoundrel. All the Chandlers are. They're cousins of mine. Mama used to say they never should have learned to walk on two feet. They would have been more comfortable on four.

TECK. Do you know the young Von Seitz, Herr Müller? He was your military attaché in Spain.

KURT. He was the German government attaché in Spain. I know his name, of course. He is a famous artillery expert. But the side on which I fought was not where he was stationed, Count de Brancovis.

ANISE (BABETTE and JOSHUA *begin to hum the song* KURT *is playing.* SARA *begins to hum*). It is time for the bath and the change of clothes. I will give you five more minutes—

FANNY. What is the song?

TECK. It was a German soldier's song. They sang it as they straggled back in '18. I remember hearing it in Berlin. Were you there then, Herr Müller?

KURT (*the playing and the humming continue*). I was not in Berlin.

TECK. But you were in the war, of course?

KURT. Yes. I was in the war.

FANNY. You didn't think then you'd live to see another war.

KURT. Many of us were afraid we would.

FANNY. What are the words?

SARA. The Germans in Spain, in Kurt's Brigade, wrote new words for the song.

KURT. This was what you heard in Berlin, in 1918. (*Begins to sing in German.*)

"Wir zieh'n Heim, wir zieh'n Heim,
Mancher kommt nicht mit,
Mancher ging verschütt,
Aber Freunde sind wir stets."
   (*In English.*)
"We come home. We come home.
Some of us are gone, and some of us are lost, but we are friends:
Our blood is on the earth together.
Some day. Some day we shall meet again.
Farewell."

(*Stops singing.*) At a quarter before six on the morning of November 7th, 1936, eighteen years later, five hundred Germans walked through the Madrid streets on their way to defend the Manzanares River. We felt good that morning. You know how it is to be good when it is needed to be good? So we had need of new words to say that. I translate with awkwardness, you understand. (*Begins to sing in English.*)

"And so we have met again.
The blood did not have time to dry.
We lived to stand and fight again.
This time we fight for people.
This time the bastards will keep their hands away.
Those who sell the blood of other men, this time,
They keep their hands away.
For us to stand.
For us to fight.
This time, no farewell, no farewell."

(*Music dies out. There is silence for a minute.*) We did not win. (*Looks up, gently.*) It would have been a different world if we had.

SARA. Papa said so years ago. Do you remember, Mama? "For every man who lives without freedom, the rest of us must face the guilt."

FANNY. Yes. "We are liable in the conscience-balance for the tailor in Lodz, the black man in our South, the peasant in—" (*Turns to* TECK. *Unpleasantly*) Your country, I think.

ANISE (*rises*). Come. Baths for everybody. (*To* BODO) Gather the wires. You have wrecked my cure.

BODO. If you would allow me a few minutes more—

ANISE. Come along. I have been duped for long enough. Come Joshua. Babette. Baths.

JOSHUA (*Starts out after* ANISE. BABETTE *begins to gather up her sewing*). My tub is a thing of glory. But I do not like it so prepared for me and so announced by Miss Anise. (*He exits.*)

BODO (*to* ANISE). You are angry about this. I do not blame you with my heart or my head. I admit I have failed. But Papa will repair it, Anise. Will you not, Papa? In a few minutes—

TECK (*to* BODO). Your father is an expert electrician?

BODO. Oh yes, sir.

TECK. And as good with radio—
(BODO *begins to nod*.)

KURT (*sharply*). Count de Brancovis. Make your questions to me, please. Not to my children.
(*The others look up, surprised.*)

TECK (*pleasantly*). Very well, Herr Müller.

ANISE (*as she exits with* BODO). Nobody can fix it. You have made a pudding of it.

BODO (*as he follows her*). Do not worry. In five minutes tonight, you will have a pad far better— (*As* BODO *reaches the door he bumps into* MARTHE *who is carrying large dress boxes*.) Oh. Your pardon. Oh, hello. (*He disappears*.)

MARTHE (*gaily*). Hello. (*To* FANNY) I waited for them. I was afraid they wouldn't deliver this late in the day. (*To* SARA) Come on, Sara. I can't wait to see them.

SARA. What?

MARTHE. Dresses. From Fanny. A tan linen, and a dark green with wonderful buttons, a white net for Babbie, and a suit for you, and play dresses for Babbie, and a dinner dress in gray to wear for Babbie's birthday—gray should be good for you, Sara—all from Savitt's. We sneaked the measurements, Anise and I—

SARA (*she goes toward* FANNY). How nice of you, Mama. How very kind of you. And of you, Marthe, to take so much trouble— (*She leans down, kisses* FANNY.) You're a sweet woman, Mama.

DAVID. That's the first time Mama's ever heard that word. (*He takes the boxes from* MARTHE, *puts them near the staircase*. MARTHE *smiles at him, touches his hand, as* TECK *watches them.*)

FANNY (*giggles*). I have a bottom sweetness, if you understand what I mean.

DAVID. I have been too close to the bottom to see it.

FANNY. That should be witty. I don't know why it isn't.
(BABETTE *goes over to stare at the boxes*.)

SARA. From Savitt's. Extravagant of you. They had such lovely clothes. I remember my coming-out dress— (*Goes to* KURT.) Do you remember the black suit with the braid, and the Milan hat? Not the *first* day we met, but the picnic day? (*He smiles up at her*.) Well, they were from Savitt's. That was over twenty years ago— I've known you a long time. Me, in an evening dress. Now you'll have to take me into Washington. I want to show off. Next week, and we'll dance, maybe— (*Sees that he is not looking at her.*) What's the matter, darling? (*No answer. Slowly he turns to look at her.*) What's the matter, Kurt? (*Takes his arms, very unhappily.*) What have I done? It isn't that dresses have ever mattered to me, it's just that—

KURT. Of course, they have mattered to you. As they should. I do not think of the dress. (*Draws her to him.*) How many years have I loved that face?

SARA (*her face very happy*). So?

KURT. So. (*He leans down, kisses her, as if it were important.*)

SARA (*pleased, unembarrassed*). There are other people here.

MARTHE (*slowly*). And good for us to see.

TECK. Nostalgia?

MARTHE. No. Nostalgia is for something you have known.
(FANNY *coughs.*)

BABETTE (*comes to* FANNY). Grandma, is it allowed to look at my dresses?

FANNY. Of course, child. Run along.

BABETTE (*picks up the boxes, goes toward the hall entrance, stops near* FANNY). I love dresses, I have a great fondness for materials and colors. Thank you, Grandma. (*She runs out of the room.*)
(JOSEPH *appears in the doorway.*)

JOSEPH. There is a long-distance operator with a long-distance call for Mr. Müller. She wants to talk with him on the long-distance phone.

KURT. Oh— Excuse me, please—
(KURT *rises quickly.* SARA *turns sharply to look at him.* TECK *looks up.* KURT

goes quickly out. TECK *watches him go.* SARA *stands staring after him.*)

MARTHE (*laughs*). I feel the same way as Babbie. Come on, Sara. Let's try them on.
(SARA *does not turn.*)

TECK. You also have a new dress?

MARTHE (*looks at him*). Yes. Fanny was kind to me, too.

TECK. You are a very generous woman, Madame Fanny. Did you also give her a sapphire bracelet from Barstow's?

FANNY. I beg your—

DAVID (*slowly*). No. I gave Marthe the bracelet. And I understand that it is not any business of yours.
(FANNY *rises.* SARA *turns.*)

FANNY. Really, David—

DAVID. Be still, Mama.

TECK (*after a second*). Did you tell him that, Marthe?

MARTHE. Yes.

TECK (*looks up at her*). I shall not forgive you for that. (*Looks at* DAVID.) It is a statement which no man likes to hear from another man. You understand that? (*Playfully*) That is the type of thing about which we used to play at duels in Europe.

DAVID (*comes toward him*). We are not so musical comedy here. And you are not in Europe.

TECK. Even if I were, I would not suggest any such action. I would have reasons for not wishing it.

DAVID. It would be well for you not to suggest *any* action. And the reason for *that* is you might get hurt.

TECK (*slowly*). That would not be my reason. (*To* MARTHE) Your affair has gone far enough—

MARTHE (*sharply*). It is not an affair—

TECK. I do not care what it is. The time has come to leave here. Go upstairs and pack your things. (*She does not move.* DAVID *turns toward her.*) Go on, Marthe.

MARTHE (*to* DAVID). I am not going with him. I told you that.

DAVID. I don't want you to go with him.

FANNY (*carefully*). Really, David, aren't you interfering in all this a good deal—

DAVID (*carefully*). Yes, Mama. I am.

TECK (*to* MARTHE). When you are speaking to me, please say what you have to say to me.

MARTHE (*comes to him*). You are trying to frighten me. But you are not going to frighten me any more. I will say it to you: I am not going with you. I am never going with you again.

TECK (*softly*). If you do not fully mean what you say, or if you might change your mind, you are talking unwisely, Marthe.

MARTHE. I know that.

TECK. Shall we talk about it alone?

MARTHE. You can't make me go, can you, Teck?

TECK. No, I can't make you.

MARTHE. Then there's no sense talking about it.

TECK. Are you in love with him?

MARTHE. Yes.

FANNY (*sharply*). Marthe! What is all this?

MARTHE (*sharply*). I'll tell *you* about it in a minute.

DAVID. You don't have to explain anything to anybody.

TECK (*ignores him*). Is he in love with you?

MARTHE. I don't think so. You won't believe it, because you can't believe anything that hasn't got tricks to it, but David hasn't much to do with this. I told you I would leave some day, and I remember where I said it—(*slowly*) —and why I said it.

TECK. I also remember. But I did not believe you. I have not had much to offer you these last years. But if now we had some money and could go back—

MARTHE. No. I don't like you, Teck. I never have.

TECK. And I have always known it.

FANNY (*stiffly*). I think your lack of affections should be discussed with more privacy. Perhaps—

DAVID. Mama—

MARTHE. There is nothing to discuss. Strange. I've talked to myself about this scene for almost fifteen years. I knew a lot of things to say to you and I used to lie awake at night or walk along the street and say them. Now I don't want to. I guess you only want to talk that way, when you're not sure what you can do. When you're sure, then what's the sense of saying it? "This is why and this is why and this—" (*Very happily*) But when you know you can do it, you don't have to say anything; you can just go. And I'm going. There is nothing you can do. I would like you to believe that now.

TECK. Very well, Marthe. I think I made a mistake. I should not have brought you here. I believe you now.

MARTHE (*after a pause, she looks at* DAVID). I'll move into Washington, and—

DAVID. Yes. Later. But I'd like you to stay here for a while, with us, if you wouldn't mind.

SARA. It would be better for you, Marthe—

FANNY. It's very interesting that I am not being consulted about this. (*To* MARTHE) I have nothing against you, Marthe. I am sorry for you, but I don't think—

MARTHE. Thank you, Sara, David. But I'd rather move in now. (*Turns, comes toward* FANNY.) But perhaps I have something against you. Do you remember my wedding?

FANNY. Yes.

MARTHE. Do you remember how pleased Mama was with herself? Brilliant Mama, handsome Mama—everybody thought so, didn't they? A seventeen-year-old daughter, marrying a pretty good title, about to secure herself in a world that Mama liked—she didn't ask me what I liked. And the one time I tried to tell her, she frightened me— (*Looks up.*) Maybe I've always been frightened. All my life.

TECK. Of course.

MARTHE (*to* FANNY, *as if she had not heard* TECK). I remember Mama's face at the wedding—it was *her* wedding, really, not mine.

FANNY (*sharply*). You are very hard on your mother.

MARTHE. Nineteen hundred and twenty-five. No, I'm not hard on her. I only tell the truth. She wanted a life for me, I suppose. It just wasn't the life I wanted for myself. (*Sharply*) And that's what you have tried to do. With your children. In another way. Only Sara got away. And that made you angry—until so many years went by that you forgot.

FANNY. I don't usually mind people saying anything they think, but I find that—

MARTHE. I don't care what you mind or don't mind. I'm in love with your son—

FANNY (*very sharply*). That's unfortunate—

MARTHE. And I'm sick of watching you try to make him into his father. I don't think you even know you do it any more and I don't think he knows it any more, either. And that's what's most dangerous about it.

FANNY (*very angrily*). I don't know what you are talking about.

DAVID. I think you do. (*Smiles.*) You shouldn't mind hearing the truth—and neither should I.

FANNY (*worried, sharply*). David! What does all this nonsense mean? I—

MARTHE (*to* FANNY). Look. That pretty world Mama got me into was a tough world, see? I'm used to trouble. So don't try to interfere with me, because I won't let you. (*She goes to* DAVID.) Let's just have a good time. (*He leans down, takes both her hands, kisses them. Then slowly, she turns away, starts to exit. To* TECK) You will also be going today?

TECK. Yes.

MARTHE. Then let us make sure we go in different directions, and do not meet again. Good-bye, Teck.

TECK. Good-bye, Marthe. You will not believe me, but I tried my best, and I am now most sorry to lose you.

MARTHE. Yes. I believe you. (*She moves out. There is silence for a minute.*)

FANNY. Well, a great many things have been said in the last few minutes.

DAVID (*crosses to bell cord. To* TECK). I will get Joseph to pack for you.

TECK. Thank you. Do not bother. I will ring for him when I am ready. (KURT *comes in from the study door.* SARA *turns, stares at him, waits. He does not look at her.*) It will not take me very long. (*He starts for the door, looking at* KURT.)

SARA. What is it, Kurt?

KURT. It is nothing of importance, darling— (*He looks quickly at* TECK, *who is moving very slowly.*)

SARA. Don't tell me it's nothing. I know the way you look when—

KURT (*sharply*). I said it was of no importance. I must get to California for a few weeks. That is all.

SARA. I—

TECK (*turns*). It is in the afternoon newspaper, Herr Müller. (*Points to paper on table.*) I was waiting to find the proper moment to call it to your attention. (*He moves toward the table, as they all turn to watch him. He picks up the paper, turns it over, begins to read.*) "Zurich, Switzerland: The Zu-

rich papers today reprinted a despatch from the *Berliner Tageblatt*—on the capture of Colonel Max Freidank. Freidank is said—(SARA *begins to move toward him*)—to be the chief of the Anti-Nazi Underground Movement. Colonel Freidank has long been an almost legendary figure. The son of the famous General Freidank, he was a World War officer and a distinguished physicist before the advent of Hitler." That is all.

SARA. Max—

KURT. Be still, Sara.

TECK. They told me of it at the Embassy last night. They also told me that with him, they had taken a man who called himself Ebber, and a man who called himself Triste. They could not find a man called Gotter. (*He starts again toward the door.*) I shall be a lonely man without Marthe. I am also a very poor one. I should like to have ten thousand dollars before I go.

DAVID (*carefully*). You will make no loans in this house.

TECK. I was not speaking of a loan.

FANNY (*carefully*). God made you not only a scoundrel but a fool. That is a dangerous combination.

DAVID (*suddenly leaps toward* TECK). Damn you, you—

KURT (*suddenly pounds on the top of the piano, as* DAVID *almost reaches* TECK). Leave him alone. (*Moves quickly to stop* DAVID.) Leave him alone! *David! Leave him alone!*

DAVID (*angrily to* KURT). Keep out of it. (*Starts toward* TECK *again.*) I'm beginning to see what Marthe meant. Blackmailing with your wife— You—

KURT (*very sharply*). He is not speaking of his wife. Or you. He means me. (*Looks at* TECK.) Is that correct?

(SARA *moves toward* KURT. DAVID *draws back, bewildered.*)

TECK. Good. It was necessary for me to hear you say it. You understand that?

KURT. I understand it.

SARA (*frightened, softly*). Kurt—

DAVID. What is all this about? What the hell are you talking about?

TECK (*sharply for the first time*). Be still. (*To* KURT) At your convenience. Your hands are shaking, Herr Müller.

KURT (*quietly*). My hands were broken: they are bad when I have fear.

TECK. I am sorry. I can understand that. It is not pleasant. (*Motions toward* FANNY *and* DAVID.) Perhaps you would like a little time to— I will go and pack, and be ready to leave. We will all find that more comfortable, I think. You should get yourself a smaller gun, Herr Müller. That pistol you have been carrying is big and awkward.

KURT. You saw the pistol when you examined our bags?

TECK. You knew that?

KURT. Oh, yes. I have the careful eye, through many years of needing it. And then you have not the careful eye. The pistol was lying to the left of a paper package and when you leave, it is to the right of the package.

SARA. Kurt! Do you mean that—

KURT (*sharply*). Please, darling, do not do that.

TECK. It is a German Army Luger?

KURT. Yes.

TECK. Keep it in your pocket, Herr

Müller. You will have no need to use it. And, in any case, I am not afraid of it. You understand that?

KURT (*slowly*). I understand that you are not a man of fears. That is strange to me, because I am a man who has so many fears.

TECK (*laughs, as he exits*). Are you? That is most interesting. (*He exits.*)

DAVID (*softly*). What is this about, Kurt?

KURT. He knows who I am and what I do and what I carry with me.

SARA (*carefully*). What about Max?

KURT. The telephone was from Mexico. Ilse received a cable. Early on the morning of Monday, they caught Ebber and Triste. An hour after they took Max in Berlin. (*She looks up at him, begins to shake her head. He presses her arm.*) Yes. It is hard.

FANNY (*softly*). You said he knew who you were and what you carried with you. I don't understand.

KURT. I am going to tell you: I am a German outlaw. I work with many others in an illegal organization. I have so worked for seven years. I am on what is called a desired list. But I did not know I was worth ten thousand dollars. My price has risen.

DAVID (*slowly*). And what do you carry with you?

KURT. Twenty-three thousand dollars. It has been gathered from the pennies and the nickels of the poor who do not like Fascism, and who believe in the work we do. I came here to bring Sara home and to get the money. I had hopes to rest here for a while, and then—

SARA (*slowly*). And I had hopes someone else would take it back and you would stay with us— (*Shakes her head, then*) Max is not dead?

KURT. No. The left side of his face is dead. (*Softly*) It was a good face.

SARA (*to* FANNY *and* DAVID, *as if she were going to cry*). It was a very good face. He and Kurt—in the old days— (*To* KURT) After so many years. If Max got caught, then nobody's got a chance. Nobody. (*She suddenly sits down.*)

DAVID (*points upstairs*). He wants to sell what he knows to you? Is that right?

KURT. Yes.

FANNY. Wasn't it careless of you to leave twenty-three thousand dollars lying around to be seen?

KURT. No, it was not careless of me. It is in a locked brief-case. I have thus carried money for many years. There seemed no safer place than Sara's home. It was careless of you to have in your house a man who opens baggage and blackmails.

DAVID (*sharply*). Yes. It was very careless.

FANNY. But you said you knew he'd seen it—

KURT. Yes. I knew it the first day we were here. What was I to do about it? He is not a man who steals. This is a safer method. I knew that it would come some other way. I have been waiting to see what the way would be. That is all I could do.

DAVID (*to* FANNY). What's the difference? It's been done. (*To* KURT) If he wants to sell to you, he must have another buyer. Who?

KURT. The Embassy. Von Seitz, I think.

DAVID. You mean he has told Von Seitz about you and—

KURT. No. I do not think he has told him anything. As yet. It would be foolish of him. He has probably only asked most guarded questions.

DAVID. But you're here. You're in this country. They can't do anything to you. They wouldn't be crazy enough to try it. Is your passport all right?

KURT. Not quite.

FANNY. Why not? Why isn't it?

KURT (*wearily, as if he were bored*). Because people like me are not given visas with such ease. And I was in a hurry to bring my wife and my children to safety. (*Sharply*) Madame Fanny, you must come to understand it is no longer the world you once knew.

DAVID. It doesn't matter. You're a political refugee. We don't turn back people like you. People who are in danger. You will give me your passport and tomorrow morning I'll see Barens. We'll tell him the truth— (*Points to the door.*) Tell de Brancovis to go to hell. There's not a damn thing he or anybody else can do.

SARA (*looks up at* KURT, *who is staring at her*). You don't understand, David.

DAVID. There's a great deal I don't understand. But there's nothing to worry about.

SARA. Not much to worry about as long as Kurt is in this house. But he's not going to—

KURT. The Count has made the guess that—

SARA. That you will go back to get Ebber and Triste and Max. Is that right, Kurt? Is that right?

KURT. Yes, darling, I will try. They were taken to Sonnenburg. Guards can be bribed— It has been done once before at Sonnenburg. We will try for it again. I must go back, Sara. I must start.

SARA. Of course, you must go back. I guess I was trying to think it wouldn't come. But— (*To* FANNY *and* DAVID) Kurt's got to go back. He's got to go home. He's got to buy them out. He'll do it, too. You'll see. (*She stops, breathes.*) It's hard enough to get back. Very hard. But if they knew he was coming— They want Kurt bad. Almost as much as they wanted Max— And then there are hundreds of others, too— (*She gets up, comes to him. He holds her, puts his face in her hair. She stands holding him, trying to speak without crying. She puts her face down on his head.*) Don't be scared, darling. You'll get back. You'll see. You've done it before—you'll do it again. Don't be scared. You'll get Max out all right. (*Gasps.*) And then you'll do his work, won't you? That's good. That's fine. You'll do a good job, the way you've always done. (*She is crying very hard. To* FANNY) Kurt doesn't feel well. He was wounded and he gets tired— (*To* KURT) You don't feel well, do you? (*Slowly. She is crying too hard now to be heard clearly.*) Don't be scared, darling. You'll get home. Don't worry, you'll get home. Yes, you will.

ACT THREE

SCENE: *The same. A half hour later.*

AT RISE: FANNY *is sitting in a chair.* KURT *is at the piano, his head resting on one hand. He is playing softly with the other hand.* SARA *is sitting very quietly on the couch.* DAVID *is pacing on the terrace.*

FANNY (*to* DAVID). David, would you stop that pacing, please? (DAVID *comes in.*) And would you stop that one-hand piano playing? Either play, or get up. (KURT *gets up, crosses to the couch, sits.* SARA *looks at him, gets up, crosses to the decanters, begins to make a drink.*)

SARA (*to* DAVID). A drink?

DAVID. What? Yes, please. (*To* KURT) Do you intend to buy your friends out of jail?

KURT. I intend to try.

FANNY. It's all very strange to me. I thought things were so well run that bribery and—

KURT (*smiles*). What a magnificent work Fascists have done in convincing the world that they are men from legends.

DAVID. They have done very well for themselves—unfortunately.

KURT. Yes. But not by themselves. Does it make us all uncomfortable to remember that they came in on the shoulders of the most powerful men in the world? Of course. And so we would prefer to believe they are men from the planets. They are not. Let me reassure you. They are smart, they are sick, and they are cruel. But given men who know what they fight for— (*Shrugs.*) You saw it in Spain. (*Laughs.*) I will console you. A year ago last month, at three o'clock in the morning, Freidank and I, with two elderly pistols, raided the home of the Gestapo chief in Konstanz, got what we wanted and the following morning

Freidank was eating his breakfast three blocks away, and I was over the Swiss border.

FANNY (*slowly*). You are brave men.

KURT. I do not tell you the story to prove we are remarkable, but to prove they are *not*.
(SARA *brings him a drink. Gives one to* DAVID.)

SARA (*softly, touching* KURT'S *shoulder*). Kurt loves Max.

KURT. Always since I came here I have a dream: that he will come in this room some day. How he would like it here, eh, Sara? He loves good food and wine, and you have books— (*Laughs happily.*) He is fifty-nine years of age. And when he was fifty-seven, he carried me on his back, seven miles across the border. I had been hurt— That takes a man, does it not?

FANNY (*to* KURT). You look like a sick man to me.

KURT. No. I'm only tired. I do not like to wait. It will go.

SARA (*sharply*). Oh, it's more than that. This is one of the times you wonder why everything has to go against you.

KURT. Waiting. It is waiting that is bad.

DAVID (*points upstairs*). Damn him! He's doing it deliberately.

KURT. It is then the corruption begins. Once in Spain I waited for two days until the planes would exhaust themselves. I think then why must our side fight always with naked hands. The spirit and the hands. All is against us but ourselves. Sometimes, it was as if you must put up your hands and tear the wings from the planes—and then it is bad.

SARA. You will not think that when the time comes. It will go.

KURT. Of a certainty.

FANNY. But does it have to go on being your hands?

KURT. For each man, his own hands. He has to sleep with them.

DAVID (*uncomfortably, as if he did not like to say it*). That's right. I guess it's the way all of us should feel. But—but you have a family. Isn't there somebody else who hasn't a wife and children—

KURT. Each could have his own excuse. Some love for the first time, some have bullet holes, some have fear of the camps, some are sick, many are getting older. (*Shrugs.*) Each could find a reason. And many find it. My children are not the only children in the world, even to me.

FANNY. That's noble of you, of course. But they are your children, nevertheless. And Sara, she—

SARA. Mama—

KURT (*after a slight pause*). One means always in English to insult with that word noble?

FANNY. Of course not, I—

KURT. It is not noble. It is the way I must live. Good or bad, it is what I am. (*Turns deliberately to look at* FANNY.) And what I am is not what you wanted for your daughter, twenty years ago or now.

FANNY. You are misunderstanding me.

KURT (*smiles*). For our girl, too, we want a safe and happy life. And it is thus I try to make it for her. We each have our way. I do not convert you to mine.

DAVID. You are very certain of your way.

KURT (*smiles*). I seem so to you? Good. (JOSEPH *appears in the hall doorway. He is carrying valises and overcoats.*)

JOSEPH. What'll I do with these, Miss Fanny?

FANNY. They're too large for eating, aren't they? What were you thinking of doing with them?

JOSEPH. I mean, it's Fred's day off.

DAVID. All right. You drive him into town.

JOSEPH. Then who's going to serve at dinner?

FANNY (*impatiently*). Belle can do it alone tonight.

JOSEPH. No she can't. Belle's upstairs packing with Miss Marthe. My, there's quite a lot of departing, ain't there?

FANNY (*very impatiently*). All right, then cook can bring in dinner.

JOSEPH. I wouldn't ask her to do that, if I were you. She's mighty mad: the sink pipe is leaking again. You just better wait for your dinner till I get back from Washington.

FANNY (*shouting*). We are not cripples and we were eating dinner in this house before you arrived to show us how to use the knife and fork. (JOSEPH *laughs.*) Go on. Put his things in the car. I'll ring for you when he's ready.

JOSEPH. You told me the next time you screamed to remind you to ask my pardon.

FANNY. You call that screaming?

JOSEPH. Yes'm.

FANNY. Very well. I ask your pardon. (*Waves him away.*) Go on!

JOSEPH. Yes'm. (*Exits.*)
(TECK *appears in the door. He is carrying his hat and the brief-case we have seen in Act One.* SARA, *seeing the brief-case, looks startled, looks quickly at* KURT. KURT *watches* TECK *as he comes toward him.* TECK *throws his hat on a chair, comes to the table at which* KURT *is sitting, puts the brief-case on the table.* KURT *puts out his hand, puts it on the brief-case, leaves it there.*)

TECK (*smiles at the gesture*). Nothing has been touched, Herr Müller. I brought it from your room, for your convenience.

FANNY (*angrily*). Why didn't you steal it? Since you do not seem to—

TECK. That would have been very foolish of me, Madame Fanny.

KURT. Very.

TECK. I hope I have not kept you waiting too long. I wanted to give you an opportunity to make any explanations—

DAVID (*angrily*). Does your price include listening to this tony conversation?

TECK (*turns to look at him*). My price will rise if I have to spend the next few minutes being interrupted by your temper. I will do my business with Herr Müller. And you will understand, I will take from you no interruptions, no exclamations, no lectures, no opinions of what I am or what I am doing.

KURT (*quietly*). You will not be interrupted.

TECK (*sits down at table with* KURT). I have been curious about you, Herr Müller. Even before you came here. Because Fanny and David either knew very little about you, which was strange, or wouldn't talk about you, which was just as strange. Have you ever had come to you one of those insistent half-memories of some person or some place?

KURT (*quietly, without looking up*). You had such a half-memory of me?

TECK. Not even a memory, but something. The curiosity of one European for another, perhaps.

KURT. A most sharp curiosity. You lost no time examining— (*pats the case*)—this. You are an expert with locks?

TECK. No, indeed. Only when I wish to be.

FANNY (*angrily, to* TECK). I would like you out of this house as quickly as—

TECK (*turns to her*). Madame Fanny, I have just asked Mr. David not to do that. I must now ask you. (*Leans forward to* KURT.) Herr Müller, I got one of the desired lists from Von Seitz, without, of course, revealing anything to him. As you probably know, they are quite easy to get. I simply told him that we refugees move in small circles and I might come across somebody on it. If, however, I have to listen to any more of this from any of you, I shall go immediately to him.

KURT (*to* DAVID *and* FANNY). Please allow the Count to do this in his own way. It will be best.

TECK (*takes a sheet of paper from his pocket*). There are sixty-three names on this list. I read them carefully, I narrow the possibilities and under "G" I find Gotter. (*Begins to read*) "Age, forty to forty-five. About six feet. One hundred seventy pounds. Birthplace unknown to us. Original occupation unknown to us, although he seems to know Munich and Dresden. Schooling unknown to us. Family unknown to us. No known political connections. No known trade-union connections. Many descriptions, few of them in agreement

and none of them of great reliability. Equally unreliable, though often asked for, were Paris, Copenhagen, Brussels police descriptions. Only points on which there is agreement: married to a foreign woman, either American or English; three children; has used name of Gotter, Thomas Bodmer, Karl Francis. Thought to have left Germany in 1933, and to have joined Max Freidank shortly after. Worked closely with Freidank, perhaps directly under his orders. Known to have crossed border in 1934—February, May, June, October. Known to have again crossed border with Max Freidank in 1935—August, twice in October, November, January—"

KURT (*smiles*). The report is unreliable. It would have been impossible for God to have crossed the border that often.

TECK (*looks up, laughs. Then looks back at list*). "In 1934, outlaw radio station announcing itself as Radio European, begins to be heard. Station was located in Düsseldorf: the house of a restaurant waiter was searched, and nothing was found. Radio heard during most of 1934 and 1935. In an attempt to locate it, two probable Communists killed in the tool-house of a farm near Bonn. In three of the broadcasts, Gotter known to have crossed border immediately before and after. Radio again became active in early part of 1936. Active attempt made to locate Freidank. Gotter believed to have then appeared in Spain with Madrid Government army, in one of the German brigades, and to have been a brigade commander under previously used name of Bodmer. Known to have stayed in France the first months of 1938. Again crossed German border some time during week when Hitler's Hamburg radio speech interrupted and went off the air." (*Looks up.*) That was a daring deed, Herr Müller. It caused a great scandal. I remember. It amused me.

KURT. It was not done for that reason.

TECK. "Early in 1939, informer in Konstanz reported Gotter's entry, carrying money which had been exchanged in Paris and Brussels. Following day, home of Konstanz Gestapo chief raided for spy list by two men—" (KURT *turns to look at* FANNY *and* DAVID, *smiles.*) My God, Herr Müller, that job took two good men.

SARA (*angrily*). Even you admire them.

TECK. Even I. Now I conclude a week ago that you are Gotter, Karl Francis—

KURT. Please. Do not describe me to myself again.

TECK. And that you will be traveling home—(*points to brief-case*)—with this. But you seem in no hurry, and so I must wait. Last night when I hear that Freidank has been taken, I guess that you will now be leaving. Not for California. I will tell you free of charge, Herr Müller, that they have got no information from Freidank or the others.

KURT. Thank you. But I was sure they would not. I know all three most well. They will take what will be given them.

TECK (*looks down. Softly*). There is a deep sickness in the German character, Herr Müller. A pain-love, a death-love—

DAVID (*very angrily*). Oh, for God's sake, spare us *your* moral judgments.

FANNY (*very sharply*). Yes. They are sickening. Get on!

KURT. Fanny and David are Americans and they do not understand our world —as yet. (*Turns to* DAVID *and* FANNY.) All Fascists are not of one mind, one stripe. There are those who give the orders, those who carry out the orders, those who watch the orders being car-

ried out. Then there are those who are half in, half hoping to come in. They are made to do the dishes and clean the boots. Frequently they come in high places and wish now only to survive. They came late: some because they did not jump in time, some because they were stupid, some because they were shocked at the crudity of the German evil, and preferred their own evils, and some because they were fastidious men. For those last, we may well some day have pity. They are lost men, their spoils are small, their day is gone. (*To* TECK) Yes?

TECK (*slowly*). Yes. You have the understanding heart. It will get in your way some day.

KURT (*smiles*). I will watch it.

TECK. We are both men in trouble, Herr Müller. The world, ungratefully, seems to like your kind even less than it does mine. (*Leans forward.*) Now. Let us do business. You will not get back if Von Seitz knows you are going.

KURT. You are wrong. Instead of crawling a hundred feet an hour in deep night, I will walk across the border with as little trouble as if I were a boy again on a summer walking trip. There are many men they would like to have. I would be allowed to walk directly to them—until they had all the names and all the addresses. (*Laughs, points his finger at* TECK) Roumanians would pick me up ahead of time. *Germans* would not.

TECK (*smiles*). Still the national pride?

KURT. Why not? For that which is good.

FANNY (*comes over, very angrily, to* TECK). I have not often in my life felt what I feel now. Whatever you are, and however you became it, the picture of a man selling the lives of other men—

TECK. Is very ugly, Madame Fanny. I do not do it without some shame, and therefore I must sink my shame in large money. (*Puts his hand on the brief-case.*) The money is here. For ten thousand, you go back to save your friends, nobody will know that you go, and I will give you my good wishes. (*Slowly, deliberately,* KURT *begins to shake his head.* TECK *waits, then carefully*) What?

KURT. This money is going home with me. It was not given to me to save my life, and I shall not so use it. It is to save the lives and further the work of more than I. It is important to me to carry on that work and to save the lives of three valuable men, and to do that with all speed. But— (*sharply*) Count de Brancovis, the first morning we arrived in this house, my children wanted their breakfast with great haste. That is because the evening before we had been able only to buy milk and buns for them. If I would not touch this money for them, I would not touch it for you. (*Very sharply*) It goes back with me. The way it is. And if it does not get back, it is because I will not get back.
(*There is a long pause.* SARA *gets up, turns away.*)

TECK. Then I do not think you will get back. You are a brave one, Herr Müller, but you will not get back.

KURT (*as if he were very tired*). I will send to you a postal card and tell you about my bravery.

DAVID (*coming toward* KURT). Is it true that if this swine talks, you and the others will be—

SARA (*very softly*). Caught and killed. Of course. If they're lucky enough to get killed quickly. (*Quietly, points to the table*) You should have seen those hands in 1935.

FANNY (*violently, to* DAVID). We'll give

him the money. For God's sake, let's give it to him and get him out of here.

DAVID (*to* SARA). Do you want him to go back?

SARA. Yes. I do.

DAVID. All right. (*Goes to her, lifts her face.*) You're a good girl.

KURT. That is true. Brave and good, my Sara. She is everything. She is handsome and gay and— (*Puts his hand over his eyes.* SARA *turns away.*)

DAVID (*after a second, comes to stand near* TECK). If we give you the money, what is to keep you from selling to Von Seitz?

TECK. I do not like your thinking I would do that. But—

DAVID (*tensely*). Look here. I'm sick of what you'd like or wouldn't like. And I'm sick of your talk. We'll get this over with now, without any more fancy talk from you, or as far as I am concerned, you can get out of here without any money and sell to any buyer you can find. I can't take much more of you at any cost.

TECK (*smiles*). It is your anger which delays us. I was about to say that I understood your fear that I would go to Von Seitz, and I would suggest that you give me a small amount of cash now and a check dated a month from now. In a month, Herr Müller should be nearing home, and he can let you know. And if you should not honor the check because Herr Müller is already in Germany, Von Seitz will pay a little something for a reliable description. I will take my chance on that. You will now say that I could do that in any case—and that is the chance you will take.

DAVID (*looks at* KURT, *who does not look up*). Is a month enough? For you to get back?

KURT (*shrugs*). I do not know.

DAVID (*to* TECK). Two months from to-day. How do you want the cash and how do you want the check?

TECK. *One month from today.* That I will not discuss. One month. Please decide now.

DAVID (*sharply*). All right. (*To* TECK) How do you want it?

TECK. Seventy-five hundred dollars in a check. Twenty-five hundred in cash.

DAVID. I haven't anywhere near that much cash in the house. Leave your address and I'll send it to you in the morning.

TECK (*laughs*). Address? I have no address, and I wish it now. Madame Fanny has cash in her sitting-room safe.

FANNY. Have you investigated that, too?

TECK (*laughs*). No. You once told me you always kept money in the house.

DAVID (*to* FANNY). How much have you got upstairs?

FANNY. I don't know. About fifteen or sixteen hundred.

TECK. Very well. That will do. Make the rest in the check.

DAVID. Get it, Mama, please. (*He starts toward the library door.* FANNY *starts for the hall exit.*)

FANNY (*turns, looks carefully at* TECK). Years ago, I heard somebody say that being Roumanian was not a nationality, but a profession. The years have brought no change.

KURT (*softly*). Being a Roumanian aristocrat is a profession. (FANNY *exits. After her exit, there is*

silence. KURT *does not look up,* SARA *does not move.*)

TECK (*awkwardly*). The new world has left the room. (*Looks up at them.*) I feel less discomfort with you. We are Europeans, born to trouble and understanding it.

KURT. My wife is not a European.

TECK. Almost. (*Points upstairs.*) They are young. The world has gone well for most of them. For us— (*Smiles.*) The three of us—we are like peasants watching the big frost. Work, trouble, ruin,— (*Shrugs.*) But no need to call curses at the frost. There it is, it will be again, always—for us.

SARA (*gets up, moves to the window, looks out*). You mean my husband and I do not have angry words for you. What for? We know how many there are of you. They don't, yet. My mother and brother feel shocked that you are in their house. For us—we have seen you in so many houses.

TECK. I do not say you *want* to understand me, Mrs. Müller. I say only that you do.

SARA. Yes. You are not difficult to understand.

KURT (*slowly gets up, stands stiffly. Then he moves toward the decanter table*). A whiskey?

TECK. No, thank you. (*He turns his head to watch* KURT *move. He turns back.*)

KURT. Sherry?

TECK (*nods*). Thank you, I will.

KURT (*as he pours*). You, too, wish to go back to Europe.

TECK. Yes.

KURT. But they do not much want you. Not since the Budapest oil deal of '31.

TECK. You seem as well informed about me as I am about you.

KURT. That must have been a conference of high comedy, that one. Everybody trying to guess whether Kessler was working for Fritz Thyssen, and what Thyssen *really* wanted—and whether this "National Socialism" was a smart blind of Thyssen's, and where was Wolff—I should like to have seen you and your friends. It is too bad: you guessed an inch off, eh?

TECK. More than an inch.

KURT. And Kessler has a memory? (*Almost playfully*) I do not think Von Seitz would pay you money for a description of a man who has a month to travel. But I think he would pay you in a visa and a cable to Kessler. I think you want a visa almost as much as you want money. Therefore, I conclude you will try for the money here, and the visa from Von Seitz. (*He comes toward the table carrying the sherry glass.*) I cannot get anywhere near Germany in a month and you know it. (*He is about to place the glass on the table.*) I have been bored with this talk of paying you money. If they are willing to try you on this fantasy, I am not. Whatever made you think I would take such a chance? Or *any* chance? You're a gambler. But you should not gamble with your life. (TECK *has turned to stare at him, made a half motion as if to rise. As he does so, and on the words, "gamble with your life," * KURT *drops the glass, hits* TECK *in the face. Struggling,* TECK *makes a violent effort to rise.* KURT *throws himself on* TECK, *knocking him to the floor. As* TECK *falls to the floor,* KURT *hits him on the side of the head. At the fourth blow,* TECK *does not move.* KURT *rises, takes the gun from his pocket, begins to lift* TECK *from the floor. As he does so,* JOSHUA *appears in the hall entrance. He is washed and ready for dinner. As he*

reaches the door, he stops, sees the scene, stands quietly as if he were waiting for orders. KURT *begins to balance* TECK, *to balance himself.* (*To* JOSHUA) Hilf mir. (JOSHUA *comes quickly to* KURT.) Mach die Tür auf! (JOSHUA *runs toward the doors, opens them, stands waiting.*) Bleib da! Mach die Tür zu! (KURT *begins to move out through the terrace. When he is outside the doors,* JOSHUA *closes them quickly, stands looking at his mother.*)

SARA. There's trouble.

JOSHUA. Do not worry. I will go up now. I will pack. In ten minutes all will be ready. I will say nothing. I will get the children ready— (*He starts quickly for the hall, turns for a second to look toward the terrace doors. Then almost with a sob*) This was a nice house.

SARA (*softly*). We're not going this time, darling. There's no need to pack.

JOSHUA (*stares at her, puzzled*). But Papa—

SARA. Go upstairs, Joshua. Take Babbie and Bodo in your room, and close the door. Stay there until I call you. (*He looks at her,* SARA *sits down.*) There's nothing to be frightened of, darling. Papa is all right. (*Then very softly*) Papa is going home.

JOSHUA. To Germany?

SARA. Yes.

JOSHUA. Oh. Alone?

SARA. Alone. (*Very softly*) Don't say anything to the children. He will tell them himself.

JOSHUA. I won't.

SARA (*as he hesitates*). I'm all right. Go upstairs now. (*He moves slowly out, she watches him, he disappears. For a minute she sits quietly. Then she gets up, moves to the terrace doors, stands with her hands pressed against them. Then she crosses, picks up the overturned chair, places it by the table, picks up the glass, puts it on the table. As if without knowing what she is doing, she wipes the table with her hand-kerchief.)*

(FANNY *comes in from hall. After a second,* DAVID *comes in from library. Stops, looks around room.)*

DAVID. Where is he? Upstairs?

SARA. No. They went outside.

FANNY. Outside? They went outside. What are they doing, picking a bouquet together?

SARA (*without turning*). They just went outside.

DAVID (*looks at her*). What's the matter, Sara?
(SARA *shakes her head. Goes to the desk, opens the telephone book, looks at a number, begins to dial the telephone.)*

FANNY. Eleven hundred, eleven hundred and fifty, twelve, twelve-fifty—

DAVID. For God's sake, stop counting that money.

FANNY. All right. I'm nervous. And I don't like to think of giving him too much.

SARA. It's very nice of you and Mama. All that money— (*into the telephone*) Hello. What time is your next plane? Oh. To— South. To El Paso, or— Brownsville. Yes.

DAVID (*to* FANNY). Is Joseph ready?

FANNY. I don't know. I told him I'd call him.

SARA. To Brownsville? Yes. Yes. That's all right. At what time? Yes. No. The ticket will be picked up at the airport.

(DAVID *begins to cross to the bell cord. She looks up.*) No. David. Don't call Joseph. David! Please! (*He draws back, stares at her. Looking at him, she goes on with .the conversation.*) Ritter, R-I-T-T-E-R. From Chicago. Yes. Yes. (*She hangs up, walks away.*)

DAVID. Sara! What's happening? What is all this? (*She does not answer.*) Where is Kurt? What— (*He starts for the terrace door.*)

SARA. David. Don't go out.

FANNY (*rises*). Sara! What's happening—

SARA. For seven years now, day in, day out, men have crossed the German border. They are always in danger. They always may be going in to die. Did you ever see the face of a man who never knows if this day will be the last day? (*Softly*) Don't go out on the terrace, David. Leave Kurt alone.

FANNY (*softly*). Sara! What is—

SARA (*quietly*). For them, it may be torture, and it may be death. Some day, when it's all over, maybe there'll be a few of them left to celebrate. There aren't many of Kurt's age left. He couldn't take a chance on them. They wouldn't have liked it. (*Suddenly, violently*) He'd have had a bad time trying to explain to them that because of this house and this nice town and my mother and my brother, he took chances with their work and with their lives. (*Quietly*) Sit down, Mama. I think it's all over now. (*To* DAVID) There's nothing you can do about it. It's the way it had to be.

DAVID. Sara—

FANNY. Do you mean what I think you — (*Sinks slowly into her chair.*)

SARA (*she turns, looks out toward the the doors. After a pause*). He's going away tonight and he's never coming back any more. (*In a sing-song*) Never, never, never. (*She looks down at her hands, as if she were very interested in them.*) I don't like to be alone at night. I guess everybody in the world's got a time in the day they don't like. Me, it's right before I go to sleep. And now it's going to be for always. All the rest of my life. (*She looks up as* KURT *comes in from the terrace.*) I've told them. There is an eight-thirty plane going as far south as Brownsville. I've made you a reservation. In the name of Ritter.

KURT (*stands looking at her*). Liebe Sara! (*Then he goes to the table at which* FANNY *is sitting. To* FANNY) It is hard for you, eh? (*He pats her hand.*) I am sorry.

FANNY (*without knowing why, she takes her hand away*). Hard? I don't know. I—I don't— I don't know what I want to say.

KURT (*looks at the hand she has touched, then turns to look at* DAVID). Before I come in, I stand and think. I say, I will make Fanny and David understand. I say, how can I? Does one understand a killing? No. To hell with it, I say. I do what must be done. I have long sickened of words when I see the men who live by them. What do you wish to make them understand, I ask myself. Wait. Stand here. Just stand here. What are you thinking? Say it to them just as it comes to you. And this is what came to me. When you kill in a war, it is not so lonely; and I remember a cousin I have not seen for many years; and a melody comes back and I begin to make it with my fingers; a staircase in a house in Bonn years ago; an old dog who used to live in our town; Sara in a hundred places—Shame on us. Thousands of years and we cannot yet make a world. Like a child I am. I have stopped a man's life. (*Points to the place on the couch where he had been sitting opposite* TECK.) I sit here. I listen to him. You will not believe—but I

pray that I will not have to touch him. Then I know I will have to. I know that if I do not, it is only that I pamper myself, and risk the lives of others. I want you from the room. I know what I must do. (*Loudly*) All right. Do I now pretend sorrow? Do I now pretend it is not I who act thus? No. I do it. I have done it. I will do it again. And I will keep my hope that we may make a world in which all men can die in bed. I have a great hate for the violent. They are the sick of the world. (*Softly*) Maybe I am sick now, too.

SARA. You aren't sick. Stop that. It's late. You must go soon.

KURT (*looks up at her*). Maybe all that I have ever wanted is a land that would let me have you. (*Then without looking away from her, he puts out his hands, she touches them.*) I am going to say good-bye now to my children. Then I am going to take your car— (*Motions with his head.*) I will take him with me. After that, it is up to you. Two ways. You can let me go and keep silent. I believe I can hide him and the car. At the end of two days, if they have not been found, you will tell as much of the truth as is safe for you to say. Tell them the last time you saw us we were on our way to Washington. You did not worry at the absence, we might have rested there. Two crazy foreigners fight, one gets killed, you know nothing of the reason. I will have left the gun, there will be no doubt who did the killing. If you will give me those two days, I think I will be far enough away from here. If the car is found before then— (*Shrugs*) I will still try to move with speed. And all that will make you, for yourselves, part of a murder. For the world, I do not think you will be in bad trouble. (*He pauses.*) There is another way. You can call your police. You can tell them the truth. I will not get home. (*To* SARA) I wish to see the children now. (*She goes out into the hall and up the stairs. There is silence.*)

FANNY. What are you thinking, David?

DAVID. I don't know. What are you thinking?

FANNY. Me? Oh, I was thinking about my Joshua. I was thinking that a few months before he died, we were sitting out there. (*Points to terrace.*) He said, "Fanny, the Renaissance American is dying, the Renaissance man is dying." I said what do you mean, although I knew what he meant, I always knew. "A Renaissance man," he said, "is a man who wants to know. He wants to know how fast a bird will fly, how thick is the crust of the earth, what made Iago evil, how to plow a field. He knows there is no dignity to a mountain, if there is no dignity to man. You can't put that in a man, but when it's *really* there, and he will fight for it, put your trust in him."

DAVID (*gets up, smiles, looks at* FANNY). You're a smart woman sometimes. (SARA *enters with* JOSHUA. *To* KURT) Don't worry about things here. My soul doesn't have to be so nice and clean. I'll take care of it. You'll have your two days. And good luck to you.

FANNY. You go with my blessing, too. I like you.
(BODO *enters.*)

SARA. See? I come from good stock. (KURT *looks at* DAVID. *Then he begins to smile. Nods to* DAVID. *Turns, smiles at* FANNY.)

FANNY. Do you like me?

KURT. I like you, Madame, very much.

FANNY. Would you be able to cash that check?

KURT (*laughs.*) Oh, no.

FANNY. Then take the cash. I, too, would like to contribute to your work.

KURT (*slowly*). All right. Thank you.

(*He takes the money from the table, puts it in his pocket.*)

BODO (*to* KURT). You like Grandma? I thought you would, with time. I like her, too. Sometimes she dilates with screaming, but— Dilates is correct?
(BABETTE *enters.* JOSHUA *stands away from the others, looking at his father.* KURT *turns to look at him.*)

JOSHUA. Alles in Ordnung?

KURT. Alles in Ordnung.

BODO. What? What does that mean, all is well?
(*There is an awkward silence.*)

BABETTE (*as if she sensed it*). We are all clean for dinner. But nobody else is clean. And I have on Grandma's dress to me—

FANNY (*very nervously*). Of course. And you look very pretty. You're a pretty little girl, Babbie.

BODO (*looks around the room*). What is the matter? Everybody is acting like such a ninny. I got that word from Grandma.

KURT. Come here. (*They look at him. Then slowly* BABETTE *comes toward him, followed by* BODO. JOSHUA *comes more slowly, to stand at the side of* KURT's *chair.*) We have said many good-byes to each other, eh? We must now say another. (*As they stare at him, he smiles, slowly, as if it were difficult.*) This time, I leave you with good people to whom I believe you also will be good. (*Half playfully*) Would you allow me to give away my share in you, until I come back?

BABETTE (*slowly*). If you would like it.

KURT. Good. To your mother, her share. My share, to Fanny and David. It is all and it is the most I have to give. (*Laughs.*) There. I have made a will, eh? Now. We will not joke. I have something to say to you. It is important for me to say it.

JOSHUA (*softly*). You are talking to us as if we were children.

KURT (*turns to look at him*). Am I, Joshua? I wish you were children. I wish I could say love your mother, do not eat too many sweets, clean your teeth— (*Draws* BODO *to him.*) I cannot say these things. You are not children. I took it all away from you.

BABETTE. We have had a most enjoyable life, Papa.

KURT (*smiles*). You are a gallant little liar. And I thank you for it. I have done something bad today—

FANNY (*shocked, sharply*). Kurt—

SARA. Don't, Mama.
(BODO *and* BABETTE *have looked at* FANNY *and* SARA, *puzzled. Then they have turned again to look at* KURT.)

KURT. It is not to frighten you. In a few days, your mother and David will tell you.

BODO. You could not do a bad thing.

BABETTE (*proudly*). You could not.

KURT (*shakes his head*). Now let us get straight together. The four of us. Do you remember when we read about "Les Misérables"? Do you remember that we talked about it afterwards and Bodo got candy on Mama's bed?

BODO. I remember.

KURT. Well. He stole bread. The world is out of shape we said, when there are hungry men. And until it gets in shape, men will steal and lie and—(*a little more slowly*)—kill. But for whatever reason it is done, and whoever does it —you understand me—it is all bad. I want you to remember that. Whoever does it, is it bad. (*Then very gaily*)

But you will live to see the day when it will not have to be. All over the world, in every place and every town, there are men who are going to make sure it will not have to be. They want what I want: a childhood for every child. For my children, and I for theirs. (*He picks* BODO *up, rises.*) Think of that. It will make you happy. In every town and every village and every mud hut in the world, there is always a man who loves children and who will fight to make a good world for them. And now good-bye. Wait for me. I shall try to come back for you. (*He moves toward the hall, followed by* BABETTE, *and more slowly, by* JOSHUA.) Or you shall come to me. At Hamburg, the boat will come in. It will be a fine, safe land— I will be waiting on the dock. And there will be the three of you and Mama and Fanny and David. And I will have ordered an extra big dinner and we will show them what our Germany can be like— (*He has put* BODO *down. He leans down, presses his face in* BABETTE's *hair. Tenderly, as her mother has done earlier, she touches his hair.*)

JOSHUA. Of course. That is the way it will be. Of course. But—but if you should find yourself delayed— (*very slowly*)—then I will come to you. Mama.

SARA (*she has turned away*). I heard you, Joshua.

KURT (*he kisses* BABETTE). Gute Nacht, Liebling!

BABETTE. Gute Nacht, Papa. Mach's gut!

KURT (*leans to kiss* BODO). Good night, baby.

BODO. Good night, Papa. Mach's gut! (BABETTE *runs up the steps. Slowly* BODO *follows her.*)

KURT (*kisses* JOSHUA). Good night, son.

JOSHUA. Good night, Papa. Mach's gut! (*He begins to climb the steps.* KURT *stands watching them, smiling. When they disappear, he turns to* DAVID.)

KURT. Good-bye, and thank you.

DAVID. Good-bye, and good luck.

KURT (*he moves to* FANNY). Good-bye. I have good children, eh?

FANNY. Yes, you have.
(KURT *kisses her hand.*)

KURT (*slowly, he turns toward* SARA). Men who wish to live have the best chance to live. I wish to live. I wish to live with you.
(*She comes toward him.*)

SARA. For twenty years. It is as much for me today. (*Takes his arms.*) Just once, and for all my life. (*He pulls her toward him.*) Come back for me, darling. If you can. (*Takes brief-case from table and gives it to him.*)

KURT (*simply*). I will try. (*He turns.*) Good-bye, to you all. (*He exits. After a second, there is the sound of a car starting. They sit listening to it. Gradually the noise begins to go off into the distance. A second later,* JOSHUA *appears.*)
JOSHUA. Mama— (*She looks up. He is very tense.*) Bodo cries. Babette looks very queer. I think you should come.

SARA (*gets up, slowly*). I'm coming.

JOSHUA (*to* FANNY *and* DAVID. *Still very tense*). Bodo talks so fancy, we forget sometimes he is a baby. (*He waits for* SARA *to come up to him. When she reaches him, she takes his hand, goes up the steps, disappears.* FANNY *and* DAVID *watch them.*)

FANNY (*after a minute*). Well, here we are shaken out of the magnolias, eh?

DAVID. Yes. So we are.

FANNY. Tomorrow will be a hard day. But we'll have Babbie's birthday dinner. And we'll have music afterwards. You can be the audience. I think you'd better go up to Marthe now. Be as careful as you can. She'd better stay here for a while. I daresay I can stand it.

DAVID (*turns, smiles*). Even your graciousness is ungracious, Mama.

FANNY. I do my best. Well, I think I shall go and talk to Anise. I like Anise best when I don't feel well. (*She begins to move off.*)

DAVID. Mama. (*She turns.*) We are going to be in for trouble. You understand that?

FANNY. I understand it very well. We will manage. You and I. I'm not put together with flour paste. And neither are you— I am happy to learn.

DAVID. Good night, Mama.
(*As she moves out, the curtain falls.*)

The Patriots

BY SIDNEY KINGSLEY

CHARACTERS

THE PATRIOTS was first presented by The Playwrights Company in association with Rowland Stebbins at the National Theatre, New York, on January 29, 1943, with the following cast:

CAPTAIN	*Byron Russell*
THOMAS JEFFERSON	*Raymond Edward Johnson*
PATSY	*Madge Evans*
MARTHA	*Frances Reid*
JAMES MADISON	*Ross Matthew*
ALEXANDER HAMILTON	*House Jameson*
GEORGE WASHINGTON	*Cecil Humphreyes*
SERGEANT	*Victor Southwick*
COLONEL HUMPHREYS	*Francis Compton*
JACOB	*Thomas Dillon*
NED	*George Mitchell*
MAT	*Philip White*
JAMES MONROE	*Judson Laire*
MRS. HAMILTON	*Peg La Centra*
HENRY KNOX	*Henry Mowbray*
BUTLER	*Robert Lance*
MR. FENNO	*Ronald Alexander*
JUPITER	*Juano Hernandez*
MRS. CONRAD	*Leslie Bingham*
FRONTIERSMAN	*John Stephen*
THOMAS JEFFERSON RANDOLPH	*Billy Nevard*
ANNE RANDOLPH	*Hope Lange*
GEORGE WASHINGTON LAFAYETTE	*Jack Lloyd*

SCENES

The Patriots

1790. A section of the deck of a schooner. A star-lit night, wind in the sails, rushing water, the creak of tackle.

A middle-aged man and a girl lean on the ship's rail and gaze out over the ocean: JEFFERSON *and his daughter,* PATSY. *He is tall and thin, his face too sensitive, a gentleness almost womanish written on it. He has dispensed with the wig of the period. His hair, ruffled by the winds, is reddish, streaked with gray. The girl is in her late teens, vibrant, lithe, handsome. Above them a helmsman, in shadow, steers the ship.*

The CAPTAIN *approaches them.*

CAPTAIN. Evening, sir.

JEFFERSON. Good evening, Captain.

PATSY. Are we nearing land, Captain?

CAPTAIN. If we hold to our course. Gittin' impatient?
(PATSY *laughs.*)

JEFFERSON. Tell me, does the voyage home always take forever?

CAPTAIN. Longer'n that, sometime. (*Looks at the sky.*) May blow up a bit, sir. Better think a goin' below.
(*He salutes, goes off.* PATSY *and* JEFFERSON *stare out over the ocean.*)

PATSY. I wonder will the house be the way I remember it.

JEFFERSON. Not as large, perhaps. You were only a little lady when we left.

PATSY. How long ago that seems!

JEFFERSON. Doesn't it?

PATSY. It's odd. Now that we're coming home again, all those years in Paris suddenly seem so unreal, don't they, Papa?

JEFFERSON. Yes.
(*She sighs.* JEFFERSON *looks at her, smiles.*)

PATSY. Are we going to New York first?

JEFFERSON (*shakes his head*). Direct to Monticello.

PATSY. I thought you might want to see President Washington at once.

JEFFERSON. We'll go home first and arrange your wedding.

PATSY. Won't the President be waiting your answer?

JEFFERSON. Not particularly—no.
(*Pause*)

PATSY. Papa?

JEFFERSON. Yes, dear?

PATSY. I've been wondering.

JEFFERSON. What?

PATSY. Do you think we should put it off? My wedding?

JEFFERSON. Put it off?

PATSY. If you accept the President's offer, you'll have to live in New York. You'll be alone for the first time in your life. You'll be utterly miserable. I know you too well.

JEFFERSON. But I have no intention of accepting.

PATSY. You haven't?

JEFFERSON. He's given me the option of refusal. And I certainly mean to take advantage of it.

PATSY (*vastly relieved*). Why didn't you tell me?

JEFFERSON. It never occurred to me. (*Pause*) You see, dearest, I discovered a long time ago that Nature didn't make me for public office. I accepted the French post only because—at the time—your mother's death had left me so blank. . . . I fancied a change of scene would . . . (*He breaks off.*)

PATSY. I know, Father. (*A long pause as they both stare into space*) Strange out there.

JEFFERSON. Time and space seem to disappear.

PATSY. I wish she were waiting for us at home.

JEFFERSON. Your mother?

PATSY. Yes. I never think of Monticello without thinking of her. She used to love to tell me about *your* wedding night.

JEFFERSON. Did she?

PATSY. In the garden cottage, midst such a clutter of your drawings and your books and your inventions, you could hardly move about.

JEFFERSON (*smiles*). That's right.

PATSY. And how you lit a fire, and found half a bottle of wine a workman had left behind some books. And mother played the pianoforte and you your violin, and you sang old songs. (*The wind rises.* JEFFERSON *draws his cloak tighter.*)

JEFFERSON. It is blowing up a bit. Excuse me. (*He starts off.*)

PATSY. Where are you going?

JEFFERSON. I want to take a look at your sister.

PATSY. She's asleep, Father.

JEFFERSON. She'll have kicked off her blanket. She might catch a chill. We don't want her coming home with the sniffles. (*He goes off.*)

PATSY (*calls after him*). Father!

JEFFERSON (*off*). Yes?

PATSY. I'll go. You wait here.

JEFFERSON. All right, dear. (*Re-enters.*)

PATSY. I'll be right back.
(PATSY *goes.* JEFFERSON *stares off toward the horizon. The hypnotic surge of the water. . . . The moonlight fades until he and the ship become a single silhouette in the night. Soft music dimly heard. . . . Slowly, dancing as if on the ocean, the exterior of an enchanting house materializes.* Monticello! *Snow is falling and has piled deep around it.*)
(*Laughter is heard offstage.* TOM JEFFERSON, *a young man, and* MARTHA, *a young woman, radiantly beautiful, appear, shaking the snow off their cloaks.*)

MARTHA. Was there ever such a wedding night? I declare, Tom Jefferson, those last few miles the horses fairly flew through the snow.

JEFFERSON (*points to the house*). There it is, Martha.
(MARTHA *turns, gasps.*)

MARTHA. Oh, Tom!

JEFFERSON. You like it?

MARTHA. I never dreamed it would . . . You really designed this, yourself?

JEFFERSON. For you, Martha. (*Takes her hand.*)

MARTHA. It's incredibly lovely.

JEFFERSON. Your hand is like ice. Come!

MARTHA. No! I want to stand here and look at it a minute more. Please!

JEFFERSON. It'll be ready for us to move into by April. Till then we'll use the garden cottage. (*Apologetically*) It's only one room.

MARTHA (*laughs*). Like a couple of dormice. We won't stir till Spring. (*Looks about, enchanted. Points offstage.*) Your Blue Ridge Mountains are out there?

JEFFERSON (*nods*). There's one peak, Martha, the sun tips with pure gold. And from here Nature spreads a magic carpet below—rocks, rivers, mountains, forests . . .

MARTHA. I can't wait for morning.

JEFFERSON. When stormy weather's brewing, you can look down into her workshop and see her fabricating clouds and hail and snow and lightning —at your feet.

MARTHA. Tom, dearest?

JEFFERSON. Yes, Martha?

MARTHA. I can't tell you what you've done for me.

JEFFERSON. What I've done for you?

MARTHA. Before I met you, circumstances and the intolerance of little men had begun to make me lose faith. The earth had begun to shrink. Living had become something quite unimportant. Then, the night we met, after the gay chatter, when you began to talk gravely, I suddenly fell in love, not only with you. I fell in love with the possibilities of the whole race of man. (*She stops short. He is gazing at her, laughing.*) Now, what are *you* laughing at, Mr. Jefferson?

JEFFERSON. If I live to be a thousand and close my eyes—this is the way I'll see you, my love. With snow on your face and your eyes shining!

MARTHA. Oh, Tom, I'm only trying to say I'm happy.

JEFFERSON. Are you?

MARTHA. And I want to be bussed. (*He kisses her tenderly.*)

JEFFERSON.
"When we dwell on the lips of the lass
    we adore,
Not a pleasure in nature is missing.
May his soul be in Heaven
He deserved it, I'm sure,
Who was first the inventor of kissing."
(*She laughs. They embrace.*)

MARTHA. Will you love me so forever, Tom?

JEFFERSON. Forever and ever—and ever . . . (*She shivers.*) You shivered? You are cold.
(*The light begins to fade.*)

MARTHA. A bit!

JEFFERSON. Come, Mrs. Jefferson. (*He sweeps her up in his arms.*) We'll light a fire that will warm you to the end of time! (*He carries her off. Suddenly the roar of a rising wind. Men's voices far off.*)

CAPTAIN'S VOICE (*offstage*). Port quarter!
(*Monticello fades and vanishes.* CAPTAIN *enters, approaches the dreaming silhouette of* JEFFERSON.)

CAPTAIN. Runnin' into a patch of ugly weather. Better go below, sir. (*The sudden roar of wind. The wheel spins.*) Watch the helm, Higgins! Bring the wind on the port quarter!
(VOICE *offstage:* "Aye, sir." *Many voices offstage. Exit* CAPTAIN. *The babble of men's voices raised in argument.*)
(*Another vision appears in space. Young* JEFFERSON, *seated at a desk, a manuscript before him. As the voices are heard, he looks from one antagonist to another.*)

FIRST VOICE. Georgia votes nay.

SECOND VOICE. This document is a mass of glittering generalities.

THIRD VOICE. Carolina votes nay. I move to strike out the clause condemning the slave traffic. It has no place here. Georgia and Carolina object.

FOURTH VOICE. Motion to strike out clause condemning the slave traffic. Hands! For? (JEFFERSON *looks about, dismayed, counting the votes.*) Against? (JEFFERSON *raises his hand.*) Motion carried. You will please strike out that clause.
(JEFFERSON *bitterly scratches out the offending clause.*)

REID'S VOICE. That second sentence. Don't like it.

JEFFERSON. But this is the heart of it, man. Are we going to have to creep up on liberty, inch by inch?

VOICE. Where does this lead? No wonder we're driving all our men of property into the arms of the loyalists.

JEFFERSON. I was asked to write the declaration and I wrote it. I haven't tried to be original. This is a simple expression of the American mind. Our people want this.

REID'S VOICE. From a legalistic viewpoint . . .

JEFFERSON. The men who migrated to America, who built it with their sweat and blood were laborers, not lawyers.

REID'S VOICE. Plague on't, boy! You want some precedent. Where can you show me anything like this in history?

JEFFERSON. Where in history do we see anything like this new world or the man of this new world? Where have we ever seen a land so marked by destiny to build a new free society based on the rights of man? Precedent? Let's make precedent! Better to set a good example, than follow a bad one.

REID'S VOICE. Are you aware, sir, of the consequences?

JEFFERSON (*controls his emotion, rises, steps from behind the desk, appeals to the assembly*). There is not a man in the whole empire who wished conciliation more than I. But, by the God that made me, I would have sooner ceased to exist than yield my freedom. And, in this, I know I speak for America. I am sorry to find a bloody campaign is decided on. But, since it is forced on us, we must drub the enemy and drub him soundly. We must teach the sceptered tyrant we are not brutes to kiss the hand that scourges us. But this is not enough. We are now deciding everlastingly our future and the future of our innocent posterity. Our people have already been fighting a year—for what? (*He picks up the document.*) For this. Let us give it to them—in writing—now.

Now is the time to buttress the liberty we're fighting for. It can't be too strongly emphasized! *Now,* while men are bleeding and dying. Tomorrow they may grow tired and careless, and a new despot may find in the old laws an instrument to rob their liberty again. Now is the time to build a free society. Now! Not later.

REID'S VOICE. I'll debate this point all day.

JEFFERSON (*fiercely*). No member of this Congress is more eager than I to settle the business on hand and go home. My wife is ill and bearing me a child, and while I stay here she's doing all my work at home. I'm half mad with anxiety, but I'll stay on all summer, if necessary, to fight for this one sentence.
(*Pause*)

REID'S VOICE. Well—er—Read it again. Let's examine it again!

JEFFERSON (*sits. Reads from the document, his voice rich with deep emotion*). We hold these truths to be self-evident: that all men are created equal; that they are endowed by their Creator with certain inalienable rights; that among these are life, liberty, and the pursuit of happiness; that to secure these rights, governments are instituted among men, deriving their just powers from the consent of the governed.
(*The Liberty Bell begins to peal. Young* JEFFERSON's *face is transfigured by an almost sacred light, which grows brighter, then fades and vanishes. Total darkness obscures even the shadowy ship and the dreaming silhouette of* JEFFERSON. *In the darkness the Liberty Bell peals louder and louder, then fades off—Soft, sweet, ghostly music. . . . The image of* MARTHA *appears, smiling sadly. The dreamer on the ship becomes visible again. He reaches out his hand.*)

JEFFERSON (*murmurs*). Forgive me,

Martha! It was such a price to ask of you. Forgive me! I wanted a happy world—for us; and, reaching for it, I lost you. (*The ghost of* MARTHA *smiles sadly and shakes her head.*) Oh, my darling, in every picture I ever painted of the future you were the foreground. Without you, there's no picture. There's . . .

PATSY'S VOICE (*off*). Father!
(*The ghost of* MARTHA *reaches out her hand, then fades and vanishes.* PATSY *appears.*)

PATSY. Father! (*The light comes on slowly. The ship again.* PATSY *is at his side.*) Maria's all right, Father.

JEFFERSON. Hm?

PATSY. She's sound asleep—Maria.

JEFFERSON. Oh! Good. Did she kick off the blanket?

PATSY. Yes, but I tucked her in again. Tight.

JEFFERSON. Good.

PATSY. You were so deep in meditation. What were you thinking?

JEFFERSON. Oh—nothing, dear. Just thinking.
(*From above, the watch suddenly cries out,* "Land ho!" *The cry is repeated below. From above,* "Two points to the starboard! Land ho!")

PATSY. Father! There it is! Do you see?

JEFFERSON. No. Where, Patsy? Where?

PATSY. That light! There!

JEFFERSON (*peering off, his face working with emotion*). Yes, yes, it's land! It's America, Patsy.

PATSY. We're home, again.

ACT ONE

SCENE I

SCENE: *New York, Spring 1790. The MacComb mansion on lower Broadway, the Presidential residence.* PRESIDENT WASHINGTON, *tight-lipped and grave, is listening to scholarly, prematurely wizened* JAMES MADISON *and* ALEXANDER HAMILTON, *a short, handsome, young man of flashing personality and proud carriage.* COLONEL HUMPHREYS, *foppish and affected, stands by, his face a mirror reflecting Hamilton's lightning changes of mood.*

MADISON (*vehemently*). If Colonel Hamilton's treasury bill is re-introduced, Congress will kill it again.

HAMILTON (*dryly*). Mr. Madison, I am tempted to seize your Congress by their separate heads and knock them together into a collective jelly.

MADISON. What would that achieve?

HAMILTON. Unity! Of some kind.

MADISON. Yes, but what kind? That's the question.

HAMILTON. You cry, "Speculation!" That's not the issue at all, and you know it.

MADISON. I know nothing of the sort. On the contrary.

HAMILTON. You deny your South is afraid the North will profit a little more?

MADISON. And will they? Will they?

HAMILTON. That's beside the point. Yes, they will. What of it? (*He turns to* WASHINGTON, *pleading.*) The crying need of this infant government *now* is confidence in its financial policy.

MADISON. Exactly. And is this the way to achieve it?

HAMILTON. Question? Can the wise and learned Congressman from Virginia propose any better plan?

MADISON. Colonel Hamilton! Personalities are not the . . .

WASHINGTON. Gentlemen! Gentlemen! Thank you, Mr. Madison, for your views. Of course it is not in this office to interfere with the people's legislature.

MADISON. Thank you!

HAMILTON. But, Mr. President! You . . .

WASHINGTON. Congress must decide the merits of your bill.

MADISON. Good day, Mr. President. (*Bows to* HAMILTON, *who is almost bursting with fury.*) Colonel Hamilton.

HAMILTON. My congratulations! You've won a noble victory over unity and honor. (MADISON *smiles, shakes his head, goes.* HAMILTON *turns to* WASHINGTON.) I warn you, sir . . .

WASHINGTON. Slow, Colonel. Slow but sure. That must be our political maxim.

HAMILTON. I'm afraid I may have to resign.

WASHINGTON. Now, my boy!

HAMILTON. I can't build a treasury out of thin air.

WASHINGTON. I know, my boy. I know. (*He hands* HAMILTON *some papers.*) Check these figures for me. (*He ruffles some other documents.*) These we'll go over this evening. Mrs. Washington is expecting you and your lady.

HAMILTON. Mrs. Hamilton is confined to bed.

WASHINGTON. She is? Anything wrong?

HAMILTON. On the contrary.

WASHINGTON. Another?

HAMILTON. On the way.

WASHINGTON. By God! You little men! My congratulations.

HAMILTON (*laughs*). Thank you, sir. I'll check these, now. Is there anything else?

WASHINGTON. No. (HAMILTON *turns to go. A sergeant enters.*)

SERGEANT. His Excellency's Ambassador to the Court of France, Mr. Jefferson!

WASHINGTON. Oh! Good! Show him in.

SERGEANT. Yes, sir. (SERGEANT *exits.* HAMILTON *wheels around.*)

HAMILTON. Mr. Jefferson in New York?

HUMPHREYS. He arrived last night. (HAMILTON *glares at him.* HUMPHREYS *whines.*) I thought you knew, Alec. . . . I . . .

HAMILTON (*suddenly very excited, to the President*). Providence is with us. Mr. Jefferson could easily persuade the South to vote for my treasury bill. I have never met him, so if you'd speak to him . . .

WASHINGTON. I can't do that.

HAMILTON. Why not?

WASHINGTON (*groans*). Again? Must we go over the ground again, and again, and again, and again, and again?

HAMILTON. It seems nothing but a catastrophe will make any impression. (*Sweetly*) But I am optimistic. I expect very shortly we will see a colossal catastrophe. (*He smiles ironically, bows, and goes.* COLONEL HUMPHREYS *follows.* WASHINGTON *stares after him, a shadow of a smile on his grim face.* JEFFERSON *enters.*)

JEFFERSON. General Washington!

WASHINGTON (*rises*). Mr. Jefferson! Welcome home. Let me look at you. (*The two men study each other.*) Six years!

JEFFERSON. Six. A long time.

WASHINGTON (*sighs*). Yes. How was Patsy's wedding?

JEFFERSON. Beautiful. (*He hands* WASHINGTON *some parcels.*) For Mrs. Washington. For you.

WASHINGTON. Oh! You shouldn't have. (*Goes to his desk, picks up a knife, slits the seals of the parcels and opens them.*)

HUMPHREYS (*entering*). Jefferson, *mon vieux!*

JEFFERSON. Billy Humphreys! How are you?

HUMPHREYS. *Assez bien! Assez bien! Et notre charmante Paris? Comment va-t-elle?*

JEFFERSON. Changed. Everybody in Paris now talks politics. And you know how the French love to talk.

HUMPHREYS. Ha! (*Laughs—a high, affected cackle.*) *Et la chere reine? Et le roi?* How are they? (*Daintily pinches some snuff into his nostrils.*)

JEFFERSON. The King hunts one half the day, drinks the other half.

HUMPHREYS (*slyly*). La! La!

JEFFERSON. The Queen weeps, but sins on.

HUMPHREYS. Ho, ho! *Mechante* . . .

WASHINGTON (*opens his package, takes out some lily bulbs*). By God! Lily bulbs!

JEFFERSON. The loveliest species I've ever seen. Magnificent flower. Found them in the south of France.

WASHINGTON. And rice seed.

JEFFERSON. Italy!

WASHINGTON. Beautiful grain.

JEFFERSON. Look at the size!

WASHINGTON. Mm. Beautiful! Sit here! (*Moves a chair for him.*)

JEFFERSON. Thank you. (*Sits.*)

WASHINGTON (*crosses to a cabinet, takes out decanter and glasses, pours wine*). And you found Virginia?

JEFFERSON. Ah!

WASHINGTON. Mm!

JEFFERSON. Yes!

WASHINGTON. Crops?

JEFFERSON. Rye's splendid. Wheat's good. It's going to be an excellent harvest.

WASHINGTON (*sighs*). So I hear.

JEFFERSON. Of course, my own lands are almost ruined.

WASHINGTON. These damnable overseers! Ignorant. Careless. (*Hands him a glass of wine.*)

JEFFERSON. Mine complained the rabbits always ate the outside row of cabbages.

WASHINGTON. Humph! What'd you tell him?

JEFFERSON. Told him to remove the outside row.

WASHINGTON (*laughs*). Good! (*He draws up a chair and sits close to* JEFFERSON.)

HUMPHREYS. Your Excellency, I believe you have an appointment. . . .

WASHINGTON (*dismisses* HUMPHREYS *with a gesture*). All right, Colonel Humphreys, later.

HUMPHREYS. *Monsieur l'Ambassadeur!* Your Excellency! (*He makes several exaggerated bows and backs off.*)

JEFFERSON (*stares after* HUMPHREYS, *amused*). Tell me, don't the little boys in the street run after him? (WASHINGTON *looks after* HUMPHREYS, *turns to* JEFFERSON, *nods gravely.* JEFFERSON *laughs. They raise their glasses.*)

WASHINGTON. The Republic! (*They drink.* JEFFERSON *sips the wine appreciatively, holds it up to examine the color.*) Recognize it? (JEFFERSON *nods.*) Excellent Madeira!

JEFFERSON. Patsy and I shopped all over Paris for it.

WASHINGTON. Mr. Adams is very pleased with the wines you sent him. But—er—(*he looks gravely at* JEFFERSON) his daughter is disappointed in the purchase you made for her.

JEFFERSON. Mrs. Smith? Now, what did she . . . ? The Paris corset? (WASHINGTON *nods*.) It didn't fit?

WASHINGTON. No! (*He gestures with his hands, indicating the outlines of an ample bosom*.)

JEFFERSON. Oh, what a tragedy!

WASHINGTON. It's very pretty, too. Mrs. Adams showed it to Mrs. Washington. Pink ribbons. The ladies are heartbroken.

JEFFERSON. They mustn't despair. Tell Mrs. Smith to put it aside. After all, there are ebbs as well as flows in this world. When the mountain didn't go to Mohamet, Mohamet went to the mountain.

WASHINGTON (*smiles, drains his glass, puts in on the sideboard*). So Lafayette is trying to establish a republic in France?

JEFFERSON. Slowly, by constitutional reform. In my rooms in Paris he drew up the first bill of rights for France. The people are all looking to our experiment. It's a heart-warming thought that in working out the pattern of our own happiness, we are inadvertently working for oppressed people everywhere. There's a great danger there, though. I toured France, incognito. Visited the peasants in their hovels. The poverty and ignorance! Appalling! If they should ever lose Lafayette . . . (*Shakes his head, finishes his drink*.)

WASHINGTON. Anarchy?

JEFFERSON. Yes.

WASHINGTON (*sighs heavily*). Yes.

JEFFERSON (*studying him*). Mr. President, you look tired.

WASHINGTON (*rising*). I'm not accustomed to this indoor life. I need activity.

JEFFERSON. Long walks. The best exercise.

WASHINGTON. It's not permitted. The dignity of the State forbids it, I'm told. When we lived on Cherry Street, I couldn't go down the street without a parade. But I can tell you since we moved here to Broadway, it's a Godsend. Now, occasionally, I can steal out that door to the back yard, across the meadow and down to the river.

JEFFERSON. What do you do down at the river?

WASHINGTON. Go fishing.

JEFFERSON. Ah!

WASHINGTON (*rises, fetches a dish of biscuits*). I've had two attacks of illness this year. I doubt if I'd survive a third. Oh, well, tomorrow or twenty years from now, we are all in the hands of a Good Providence. Try one of these biscuits.

JEFFERSON. Thank you.

WASHINGTON (*goes to his desk*). I'm organizing the ministers of the various departments into a cabinet to advise me. As our Secretary of State, you're . . .

JEFFERSON. General Washington.

WASHINGTON. Mm?

JEFFERSON. In your letter you did give me the option of refusal.

WASHINGTON. You can't mean to refuse?

JEFFERSON. I must.

WASHINGTON. Why?

JEFFERSON. I've been away so long. I know none of the duties of this office. I may bungle it. I have forebodings.

WASHINGTON. We're all groping. This will be a government of accommodation.

JEFFERSON (*shakes his head*). I'm sorry. I want you to understand. Whatever spice of political ambition I may have had as a young man has long since evaporated. (*He rises, places the half-nibbled biscuit on a dish.*) I believe every man should serve his turn. I think I've done my share. Now I want to go home. I must complete my house. Twenty years it's waited. Patsy and her husband have come to stay with me at Monticello. The truth of the matter is, I've lived with my children so long, I've come to depend on their affection and comfort.

WASHINGTON. Tom, have you ever thought of marrying again?

JEFFERSON. No.

WASHINGTON. She was a wonderful woman, your Martha.

JEFFERSON. Yes. (*Pause*) When I came home—she was in every room. (*Pause*) I've learned one thing. For me there's no peace anywhere else in the world but Monticello. You understand why I must refuse your offer?
(HUMPHREYS *enters.*)

HUMPHREYS. Excuse me, sire.

WASHINGTON. Yes, Humphreys?

HUMPHREYS. The theatre box and guard of honor are arranged.

WASHINGTON (*dryly*). Good.

HUMPHREYS. And I've discovered the Ambassador of the Sultan of Turkey is going to be present.

WASHINGTON (*with a notable lack of enthusiasm*). Mm, mm.

HUMPHREYS. A suggestion, Excellency?

WASHINGTON. Yes?

HUMPHREYS. Wouldn't it be advisable to return to six horses on the coach?

WASHINGTON. I thought we compromised on four.

HUMPHREYS. When I was at the court of Louis . . .

WASHINGTON (*slowly, making a great effort to contain his impatience*). Colonel Humphreys, I recognize the importance of these forms to the dignity of a state, particularly one so young as ours. Understand, I know nothing of these matters. I've never been to the courts of Europe. I'm just an old soldier. I leave the ceremonies in your hands. (*The impatience wears thin and he growls.*) But it seems to me four horses and that canary coach with the pink and gilt angels will be enough to impress even the Ambassador of the Sultan of Turkey.

HUMPHREYS. But, sire . . .

WASHINGTON. Four will do—that's final. (*He ruffles some papers, frowns.*) On second thought, I won't be free to go to the theatre tonight. Cancel it!

HUMPHREYS. Sire, if I may . . .

WASHINGTON (*rises, thundering*). Don't sire me! How many times must I tell you? By the Eternal! I am not a King! I am the elected head of our people. This is a republic. Can you get that through your skull? (*He controls himself. Wearily*) All right! Go!

HUMPHREYS. Very well, Mr. President. (*He goes.* WASHINGTON *sighs heavily.*)

WASHINGTON. I was offered the crown.

JEFFERSON. The crown!

WASHINGTON. Twice. (*Pause*) I don't want to be a king, Tom. (*He crosses* to the cabinet, takes up a pipe, fills it with tobacco from a jug.)

JEFFERSON. I know you don't, Mr. President.

WASHINGTON. You've no idea. (*He touches a taper to the flame of a burning candle.*) Every eye is on this office. A number of our people suspect me. As God is my judge, I would rather live and die on my farm than be emperor of the world. (*He lights his pipe, puffing angrily.*)

JEFFERSON (*pause*). I know. And yet—since I've been back—particularly here in New York—I find alarming yearnings. Our fashionable folk appear to be looking wishfully for a king and a court of our own.

WASHINGTON. Yes. I suppose so. (*He sighs, exhales a huge puff of smoke, extinguishes the taper.*) On the other hand, there is the equal danger of anarchy. We came close to it while you were away! (*He puffs nervously at his pipe.*) We walk between those two pitfalls. Our people don't take to discipline. But, without it—we shall be lost. We've yet to see how large a dose of freedom men can be trusted with. Tom, from the earliest days in Virginia, you were close to them, you seemed always to understand them. In this office I find myself far removed from direct contact with them. I need your agency. I need their faith in you. This is the last great experiment for promoting human happiness. I need the hand that wrote, "All men are created equal." I can't let you go home yet! I need you here.
(*A long pause.* JEFFERSON *turns to the desk, pours back the rice-seed he has been fondling, turns to* WASHINGTON.)

JEFFERSON. It's for you to marshal us as you see fit.

WASHINGTON (*goes to him, grips his shoulder*). Good!

JEFFERSON. It's a great honor. I hope I can be worthy of it.
(HUMPHREYS *enters.*)

HUMPHREYS. Mr. President?

WASHINGTON. I don't wish to be disturbed. . . .

HUMPHREYS. His Excellency, the Minister of Spain is arrived to pay his respects. It had already been arranged, sir. Just the courtesies!

WASHINGTON. All right. (*Sighs. Beckons to the reception room.*) I'll see him. (*To* JEFFERSON) You'll excuse me? It will be a few minutes. There are some journals.

JEFFERSON (*holds up his portfolio*). I have my tariff reports to study.
(WASHINGTON, *escorted by* HUMPHREYS, *goes up corridor.* HAMILTON *drifts into the room, some papers in his hand. The two men look at each other.*)

HAMILTON. You're Jefferson?

JEFFERSON. Yes.

HAMILTON. I'm Hamilton.

JEFFERSON. The Hamilton?

HAMILTON (*bows*). Alexander.

JEFFERSON. Your servant.

HAMILTON. Yours.

JEFFERSON. I read your Federalist papers while I was in France. Brilliant! You've given me a great deal of pleasure.

HAMILTON. Thank you. (HAMILTON *looks at his papers, groans, shakes his head, throws the papers on the President's desk.*)

JEFFERSON. Troubles?

HAMILTON (*groans again*). God! Yes. You have a pleasant voyage home?

JEFFERSON. It seemed forever.

HAMILTON (*smiles*). Of course. (*He arranges papers on desk.*) Have you accepted the Secretary of State?

JEFFERSON. Yes.

HAMILTON. My congratulations. We must work in concert.

JEFFERSON. I'm such a stranger here, I shall lean on you.

HAMILTON. No, I'm afraid—it's—I who need your help. (*Suddenly agitated, emotional*) Mr. Jefferson, it's enough to make any man who loves America want to cry. Forgive me! I really shouldn't burden you with this. It's a matter of my own department.

JEFFERSON. If I can be of any assistance . . . ?

HAMILTON. It's often been remarked that it's given to this country here to prove once and for all whether men can govern themselves by reason, or whether they must forever rely on the accident of tyranny. An interesting thought, Mr. Jefferson.

JEFFERSON. God, yes. We live in an era perhaps the most important in all history.

HAMILTON. An interesting thought! An awful thought! For, if it is true, then we dare not fail.

JEFFERSON. No.

HAMILTON. But we are failing. The machinery is already breaking down. (*He snaps his fingers.*) We haven't that much foreign credit. The paper money issued by the States is worthless. We are in financial chaos. (*He paces to and fro.*) The galling part is I have a remedy at hand. The solution is so simple. A nation's credit, like a merchant's, depends on paying its promissory notes in full. I propose to pay a hundred cents on the dollar for all the paper money issued by the States. Our credit would be restored instantaneously.

JEFFERSON (*worried*). Mr. Madison spoke to me very briefly of your bill last night. It seems there's been some speculation in this paper, and he fears . . .

HAMILTON. Madison! I loved that man. I thought so high of that man. I swear I wouldn't have taken this office—except I counted on his support. And now, he's turned against me.

JEFFERSON. Mr. Madison has a good opinion of your talents. But this speculation . . .

HAMILTON. I don't want his good opinion. I want his support. Will you use your influence?

JEFFERSON. You understand I've been away six years. I've gotten out of touch here. I'll need time to study the facts.

HAMILTON. There is no time.

JEFFERSON. Well, three or four weeks.

HAMILTON. Three or four . . . ? For God's sake, man, can't you understand what I'm trying to tell you? The North is about to secede!

JEFFERSON. Secede?

HAMILTON. Hasn't the President told you?

JEFFERSON. No.

HAMILTON. Unless my bill is passed there is every prospect the Union will dissolve.

JEFFERSON. I'm aware there's a great deal of tension here, but . . .

HAMILTON. Walk in on a session of Congress tomorrow.

JEFFERSON. I see evils on both sides. (*A long pause*) However, it seems to me —if the Union is at stake—reasonable men sitting about a table discussing this coolly should arrive at some compromise. (*He comes to a sudden decision.*) Have dinner with me tomorrow night?

HAMILTON. Delighted.

JEFFERSON. I'll invite a friend or two.

HAMILTON. Mr. Madison?

JEFFERSON. I can't promise anything. He's bitterly opposed to your plan.

HAMILTON. I have a way to sweeten the pill. The cost of living in New York has become so unreasonable there's talk of moving the capital.

JEFFERSON. Yes.

HAMILTON. It's already been promised temporarily to Philadelphia. Give me my bill and I can promise Madison the nation's capital will go to the South. Permanently. I was born in the West Indies—I have no local preference. However, for the sake of the Great Man, I'd like to see it go to Virginia.

JEFFERSON (*pause*). Well, I'll bring you together, and sit at the table to see you don't shoot each other.

HAMILTON (*laughs*). Fair enough.

JEFFERSON (*takes out his fan-shaped notebook, jots down the appointment*). You see, Colonel Hamilton, we must never permit ourselves to despair of the republic.

HAMILTON. My dear Jefferson, if I haven't despaired of this republic till now, it's because of my nature, not my judgment. (JEFFERSON *laughs.*) Your address?

JEFFERSON. Twenty-three Maiden Lane.

HAMILTON. Twenty-three Maiden Lane. At seven?

JEFFERSON. Make it seven-thirty. (WASHINGTON *enters.*)

WASHINGTON. You two gentlemen have met?

HAMILTON. Yes. What impression did the Spanish Ambassador leave with you?

WASHINGTON. Like all the rest. They regard us as a contemptuous joke.

HAMILTON. Well . . . (*looks at* JEFFERSON, *smiles*) we shan't despair. Seven-thirty? (*He bows to* WASHINGTON.) Excellency. (*He goes.*)

JEFFERSON. Remarkable young man.

WASHINGTON. They call him the Little Lion.

JEFFERSON. Little Lion! I can see it. (*Picks up his portfolio.*) Shall I review my report on the French Tariff situation?

WASHINGTON. Yes, yes, do.

JEFFERSON. Just before I left France, I had conversations with Monsieur Neckar on the matter of fishing rights. During the last year, some 23,000 francs . . . (WASHINGTON *heaves a huge sigh.* JEFFERSON *looks up. The* PRESIDENT *is staring out the window.*) Nice day out, isn't it?

WASHINGTON (*distracted, turns*). Hm? Oh, yes—yes.

JEFFERSON (*grins*). Have you a fishing pole for me?

WASHINGTON (*looks at* JEFFERSON, *goes to a closet, takes out two fishing poles*). How'd you know? (*Hands one to* JEFFERSON.) You don't mind, now?

JEFFERSON (*laughs*). I can't think of a better way to discuss the affairs of a republic.
(WASHINGTON *removes his jacket, takes an old one from the closet, calls gruffly:*)

WASHINGTON. Sergeant! (JEFFERSON *helps him on with the jacket.*) Sergeant!
(SERGEANT *enters.*)

SERGEANT. Yes, sir?

WASHINGTON. I'm not to be disturbed. By anyone. I'm in conference with my Secretary of State.

SERGEANT (*knowingly*). Yes, sir. (*Exits.*)

WASHINGTON (*whispers to* JEFFERSON). If Humphreys caught me in these clothes, I'd never hear the end. (WASHINGTON *removes his wig, sets it on a stand, claps on a disreputable battered old hat, picks up his pole and some documents, opens the door, starts out, sees someone off, draws back, signaling* JEFFERSON *to wait.*) One of the servants.

JEFFERSON. Don't they approve of democracy?

WASHINGTON (*looks at* JEFFERSON, *shakes his head sadly*). No! (*He peers out again. The coast is clear, now. He signals* JEFFERSON *to follow him.*) Come! (*stealthily, they exit.*)

SCENE II

SCENE: *The smithy of an inn in New York. Through the large open door a glimpse of the courtyard of the inn.* JACOB, *the smith, is hammering out a horseshoe.* MAT, *his apprentice, is pumping the bellows. Burst of laughter and men's voices from the inn courtyard.* POTBOY *crosses doorway clutching several foaming tankards.*

JACOB. Pump her, Mat!
(*His hammer comes down with a clang.* MAT *pumps the bellows. The fire glows.* NED THE POTBOY *enters.*)

POTBOY. Colonel Hamilton wants his horse saddled right off.

JACOB. He in a hurry?
(*Clang*)

POTBOY. Yep.

JACOB. Leavin' his party? So soon?

POTBOY. Yep.

MAT. Why, they ain't hardly started a-belchin' yet.

JACOB. Fire's gettin' cold, Mat.

MAT. I'm a-pumpin'!

POTBOY. Wants her saddled right off, he said.

MAT. We heard you.

POTBOY (*irritably*). I'm only tellin' yuh what . . .

MAT (*sharply*). Awright.

JACOB. Here! Kinda techy, you two, today. Ain't you?
(*Pause. He looks at them both, shakes his head, hammers away at the horseshoe.*)

POTBOY (*apologetically*). Standin' by, listenin' to that Tory talk out there! Gets me mad.

JACOB. Git the saddle on, Mat!

MAT. Awright. (*Fetches saddle.*)

POTBOY. Braggin' about the millions they made in paper money! I keep thinkin' of my sister.

MAT. And me! Don't fergit me! Three hundred dollars—whish!—right out-a me pocket. (*Laughter off. He spits.*)

POTBOY. Know what one was a-sayin'? President ain't a good title for the head of the United States. Ain't got enough distingay.

MAT. French words!

POTBOY. 'At's what he said. There are presidents of cricket clubs and fire companies, he said.

MAT. What the plague do they want? Royal Highness?

POTBOY. Yep. That's it. (*JACOB looks up, a frown on his face.*)

JACOB. You mean that?

POTBOY. 'At's what they said.

MAT. Fer cripes sake! (*He goes. Just outside the door he greets newcomers, "Good afternoon, sir." JEFFERSON's voice: "Afternoon, Mat." JEFFERSON enters with MONROE and MADISON.*)

JEFFERSON (*to MADISON*). You tell my children they're to write me more often, will you, Jemmy?

MADISON. I'll do that.

JEFFERSON. I want to hear about everything at Monticello from Patsy to Grizzle.

MONROE. Who's Grizzle?

JEFFERSON. Our pet pig. (*MONROE and MADISON laugh.*)

JACOB. Afternoon, Mr. Jefferson!

JEFFERSON. How are you today, Jacob?

JACOB. Middlin'. I forged them fittin's you ordered. They're right over there on that tool bench.

JEFFERSON. Fine.

MONROE. Smith, my horse is limpin' on the off-front foot.

JACOB. Picked up a pebble?

MONROE. May have.

JEFFERSON. Looks to me as if she's sprung a shoe, James.

MONROE. Think so?

JACOB. Find out fer yuh in a minute.

MADISON. Give my nag a good going over too, will you, smith? I'm off on a long journey.

JACOB. Where to, Mr. Madison?

MADISON. Home.

JEFFERSON (*sits on a keg examining the fittings*). Virginia.

JACOB. Oh! Nice weather.

MADISON. Ideal.

JEFFERSON. The lilacs'll be in full bloom and the golden willows and the almond trees.

JACOB. Not so early.

JEFFERSON. Oh, yes. In Virginia.

JACOB. That so? (*A burst of laughter, offstage*)

MADISON. A festive board out there!

JACOB. Some a Colonel Hamilton's friends givin' him a party.

MONROE. Celebrating the passage of his bill, I suppose.

JACOB. Yep. (*He goes off.*)

MONROE (*bitterly*). Yes.

JEFFERSON. Now, James.

MONROE. Well, plague on it, Mr. Jefferson!

MADISON. I have to agree with Mr. Jefferson. *Ad necessitatus rei.*

MONROE. No matter how many fine Latin names you call it—"a pig is a pig."

MADISON. This was the lesser of two evils.

MONROE. You honestly think so?

MADISON (*without conviction*). I do. Yes.

MONROE. And you, Mr. Jefferson?

JEFFERSON (*doubtfully.*) I don't know. I—hope so. I'm . . .
(*Laughter offstage.* MONROE *growls in disgust.* JEFFERSON *looks up at him, smiles wryly at* MADISON, *picks up the fittings* JACOB *has forged for him, examines them.*)

MONROE. You've seen the newspapers, of course?

JEFFERSON. Yes, I've seen them.

MAT (*enters. To* MADISON). Wants a feedin', your mare does. She's askin' for it.

MADISON. All right. Some oats, please. (MAT *pours some oats in a bag.*)

MAT. Senator Monroe?

MONROE (*looks at his watch*). Yes. It's her dinnertime

MAT. Mr. Jefferson?

JEFFERSON (*rises*). I just fed my horse, Mat, thank you. A couple of carrots, though. So he doesn't feel neglected.

MAT (*laughs*). Got some in the kitchen. (*Hands* MADISON *and* MONROE *bags of oats.* MADISON *exits with bag of oats.* MAT *exits.* JACOB *enters, holding a horseshoe in his nippers.*)

JACOB. Sprung it, awright.

MONROE. Did, hm? Shoe her at once, will you, smith?

JACOB. Yes, sir.
(MONROE *exits with bag of oats.* JACOB *puts the horseshoe in the furnace and proceeds to pump the bellows.* JEFFERSON *examines the metal fittings* JACOB *has forged for him.*)

JEFFERSON. You've done an excellent job on these.

JACOB. They awright?

JEFFERSON. Good. You know your craft!

JACOB. Ought to. Twenty years a-doin' it. (JEFFERSON *places some of the metal bits together.*) Makin' another one of your inventions, are you?

JEFFERSON. A "convenience."

JACOB. What is it this time?

JEFFERSON (*crosses to Jacob*). A sort of closet on pulleys that will come up from the kitchen to the dining room—carry the food hot and the wine cold right in, without people running up and down stairs.

JACOB. Now, say, that's a purty good invention.

JEFFERSON. You think so?

JACOB. Told my wife about the collapsible buggy top you invented. Kinda useful idea, she said. But this'll catch her fancy. What do you call this here invention?

JEFFERSON (*smiles*). A "dumbwaiter."

JACOB. Dumbwaiter? (*He puzzles it out.*) Oh, yeah! (*Gets it.*) Oh, yeah! (*Roars with laughter.*) A dumbwaiter. Purty good. (JACOB, *chuckling, extracts a horseshoe from the fire and begins to shape it on the anvil.*)

JEFFERSON. Jacob!

JACOB (*intent on his work*). Yes?

JEFFERSON. I need your advice.

JACOB. What about?

JEFFERSON. This money bill we've just passed.

JACOB. Oh! (*Looks up for a moment.*)

JEFFERSON. What do you think of it?

JACOB. Don't like it much.

JEFFERSON. You don't?

JACOB. Nope. (*Frowns, hammers the shoe.*)

JEFFERSON. Because of the speculators?

JACOB. Yep.

JEFFERSON. I see. Still, it's done the country considerable good?

JACOB. Mebbe.

JEFFERSON. What do your friends think of it, generally?

JACOB. Don't like it much.

JEFFERSON. I see.
(POTBOY *pokes in his head.*)

NED. Saddled yet? He's waitin'!

JACOB. Tell Mr. Jefferson, Ned. He's askin' about the money bill.

NED. A blood-suckin' swindle, Mr. Jefferson. (*He is suddenly all aflame.*) Look at my sister! Her husband was killed at the battle of Saratoga. Left her two little ones and some paper money they paid him. She's been savin' that for years. Two months ago the speculators told her it would be years more before she got anything on it, if ever. Got her to sell it for forty dollars. Six hundred dollars' worth! 'N they got Jacob's savin's.
(MAT *enters.*)

JEFFERSON. They did?

JACOB. Nine hundred.

NED. From the Revolution. His pay.

JACOB. That ain't what we fit the Revolution fer.

JEFFERSON (*rises, restlessly*). No.

MAT. I tell you it's gettin' time we . . .
(HAMILTON *enters.*)

HAMILTON. Is my horse ready, Jacob? Mr. Jefferson! I thought I saw you in the courtyard. I've some very good reports for you.
(NED *exits.*)

JEFFERSON. Splendid.

JACOB. Mat?

MAT. She's ready. (*Exits.*)

JACOB. Your horse is ready, Colonel Hamilton.

HAMILTON. Thank you! Fine day, Jacob!

JACOB (*grunts*). Yep. (*Exits.*)

HAMILTON (*to* JEFFERSON). A little soured this morning, isn't he? Liver?

JEFFERSON (*shakes his head*). Speculators.

HAMILTON. Jacob? (JEFFERSON *nods*.) A shame.

JEFFERSON. And Mat. And the potboy.

HAMILTON. Why didn't they hold on to their paper?

JEFFERSON. Apparently they did. For almost seven years.

HAMILTON. Tch! Too bad. They should have had more faith in their government.

JEFFERSON. They had no way of knowing the bill was about to redeem that paper. I'm very disturbed by this.

HAMILTON. You are?

JEFFERSON. Very, Apparently a handful of speculators, many of them in high places, have taken advantage of their knowledge of the bill to feather their own nests.

HAMILTON. Oh, now! Don't paint it worse than it is.

JEFFERSON. There's a good deal of bitter talk.

HAMILTON. Idle gossip!

JEFFERSON. Hardly.

HAMILTON. The treasury can't ask every man who submits a paper note how he came by it. At least in this way these people received something.

JEFFERSON. There must have been a means to avert this speculation.

HAMILTON. Look here—I don't quite understand your attitude. (*Burst of laughter, offstage*) If we want to de-velop this country we've got to create great personal fortunes. Those men out there are building manufactories and industry. They're building America!

JEFFERSON. Good. Let's encourage them! But not at the expense of the people!

HAMILTON. You and Madison! The people whisper—you tremble.
(MONROE *and* MADISON *enter, stand silently listening.*)

JEFFERSON. That's as it should be, isn't it?

HAMILTON. I am determined this country's happiness shall be established on a firm basis. I think its only hope now lies in a moneyed aristocracy to protect it from the indiscretions of the people.

JEFFERSON. I see. And this bill is to lay the foundation for such an aristocracy?

HAMILTON. Exactly.

JEFFERSON. I wasn't aware of that. You said nothing of that to me. I must be quite honest with you. I regret that I have been made a party to your bill.

HAMILTON. Made? Made, you say? You've been in politics twenty-one years. Don't play the innocent with me! Are you dissatisfied with your bargain? Is that it?

JEFFERSON. Bargain?

HAMILTON. The capital of the nation is going to *your* state—not mine.

JEFFERSON. Oh, for God's sake!

HAMILTON. Frankly, these alarms smell of hypocrisy. One minute you say you know nothing of Treasury matters; the next you set yourself up as an authority.

MONROE. What do you suppose, Colonel? Shall we scrap the Constitution at once?

HAMILTON (*Turns, sees* MONROE *and* MADISON, *murmurs, in disgust*). The Constitution!

JEFFERSON. You supported it.

HAMILTON (*flaring*). I had no choice. I couldn't stand by and see the country go down in convulsions and anarchy. (*Pause. He controls himself.*) I must confess it's my opinion this government won't last five years. However, since we've undertaken this experiment, I'm for giving it a fair trial. But, be certain of this: while it lasts it will be an aristocratic republic. If any man wants a democracy, let him proceed to the confines of some other government. Good day, gentlemen. (*He goes.*)

JEFFERSON (*to* MONROE). My apologies. I was wrong. (*To* MADISON) Forgive me, Jemmy. I shouldn't have asked you to compromise.

MADISON. Tom, we can't escape it. He's trying to administer the Constitution into something it was never intended to be.

MONROE. I have a statement from a man who swears that Hamilton gave him money out of the public treasury to speculate with.

JEFFERSON. That I don't believe.

MONROE. There are also some letters in Hamilton's hand.

JEFFERSON. Don't believe it! He's personally honest. I'll vouch for that.

MONROE. Will you at least confront him with these letters? Ask him to explain them?

JEFFERSON. I can't.

MONROE. Why not?

JEFFERSON. Oh, for God's sake, James!

MONROE. You fight fire with fire.

JEFFERSON. I'm no salamander. Fire's not my element.

MONROE. His bill has made the fortunes of half the prominent men in the Federalist Party. It's a ring he's put through their nose. And it's clear enough, God knows, where he intends to lead them. You can't allow that. You've got to fight him. You've got to wrest the leadership of the Federalist Party away from him!

JEFFERSON (*a surge of revulsion*). If there's one thing makes me sick to death—it's the whole spirit of party politics. James, if the only way I could enter heaven was on the back of a political party, I'd rather burn in purgatory.
(JACOB *appears in the doorway, adjusting saddle.*)

JACOB. Your horse is ready, Mr. Jefferson.

JEFFERSON (*looks at him, pauses*). Oh, thank you, Jacob.

JACOB. Ready your horses, gentlemen?

MADISON. Yes, please.
(JACOB *exits.*)

JEFFERSON (*staring after Jacob, his voice harsh and lifeless*). You're wrong about the letters, James. For the rest, his bill has values. But it's hurt our people. Through it, he's created a corrupt squadron. Naturally, if he does try to pervert the Constitution, I shall oppose him. But I must do it in my own way. I'm not a brawler; I'm not a politician. (*Crosses to* MADISON.) Say howdya to all my neighbors for me. (MADISON *nods.*) The matter I spoke to you of . . . ? (*Hands a paper to* MADISON.)

MADISON (*nods*). I'll tend to this first thing on my arrival.

JEFFERSON. Thanks, Jemmy.

MADISON. I know how important it is to you.

JEFFERSON. Very. Pleasant journey, Jemmy. Hurry back. (*To* MONROE, *gently*) A game of chess tonight? (MONROE *nods.* JEFFERSON *goes.*)

MONROE (*looking after him*). Blast it! This isn't the Jefferson we knew.

MADISON. No.

MONROE. The country's red hot. It's being shaped, *now*. What does it need to wake him again?

MADISON. The tears Christ wept before the tomb of Lazarus.

MONROE. You talk of Tom as if he were dead.

MADISON (*holds up the paper Jefferson gave him*). He asked me to order a new stone for Martha's grave. (*Unfolds paper.*) Do you understand Greek?

MONROE. No. Translate it!

MADISON (*translates*). Roughly . . .
"If in the shades below,
The fires of friends and lovers cease to glow,

Yet mine, mine alone
Will burn on through death, itself."

MONROE. After nine years?

MADISON. After nine years!
(JACOB *and* MAT *enter, go to hearth.*)

JACOB. Horses ready!

MONROE. Thank you, Jacob.
(NED *enters.* MADISON *and* MONROE *exit.*)

NED (*raging as he tears off his apron*). I'll be damned if I'll serve on them any more! Know what they're saying now? Dukes and Lords we oughta have!

MAT. Dukes and Lords?

NED. Ay! The blood-suckin' swindlers!

JACOB. Pump her, Mat! Pump her!

MAT. What do they want to do? Make serfs outa us?

NED. Is that what we fought Lexington and Bunker Hill for? Is this the freedom my brother and my sister's husband died for? Where's your goddamn revolution now?

JACOB (*between his teeth, grimly*). Pump her, Mat! Come on, pump her! (MAT *pumps. The forge glows, highlighting the taut and angry faces.* JACOB *hammers the hot iron with mighty, ringing blows.*)

ACT TWO

SCENE I

SCENE: HAMILTON's *home. Candlelight.* HAMILTON, HUMPHREYS *and* KNOX *are having coffee.* MRS. HAMILTON *is pouring coffee.* HAMILTON *is opening a package of cigars.*

MRS. HAMILTON (*seated on sofa*). When I think of Louis and Marie in jail!

HUMPHREYS. I haven't slept a wink since the palace fell. Dreadful! Did you read Fenno's piece in the *Gazette* today?

MRS. HAMILTON. I never miss Fenno. Brilliant, wasn't it?

HUMPHREYS. *Un chef-d'œuvre!*

MRS. HAMILTON. Veritable!

KNOX. The situation seems to be growing worse, too. What do you think, Alec, of this French Republic?

HAMILTON. Dangerous. Highly dangerous. I'm particularly disturbed by the effect it may have on some of our inflammables. (*He places the cigars on a tray.*)

HUMPHREYS. You certainly lashed Mr. Jefferson on that score! *Ma foi!* Gave it to him. But proper!

MRS. HAMILTON (*to* KNOX). Sugar?

KNOX. Please.

MRS. HAMILTON. Mr. Jefferson isn't really one of these filthy Democrats?

HAMILTON. I'm afraid so, my dear.

MRS. HAMILTON. Does he *really believe*

every man is as good as every other man?

HAMILTON. Even better.
(*They laugh.* HUMPHREYS *applauds.*)

MRS. HAMILTON. Cream?

KNOX. Please.

HAMILTON. And our people seem so convinced of it. They can't wait to cut each other's throats. (*Offers cigars to* KNOX.) Try one of these.

KNOX. Yes. You saw it so clearly during the war. In the army.

HAMILTON. Army? (*He offers cigars to* HUMPHREYS). Colonel Humphreys?

HUMPHREYS (*takes a cigar, examines it apprehensively*). So this is one of these new "cigars"?

HAMILTON (*crosses to table, sets down cigars, lights a taper*). From the Spanish Islands. . . . Army? It was no army, it was a mob. Only one man held it together. (*He holds the lighted taper to* KNOX's *cigar.*)

KNOX. The Chief. (*Lights his cigar with huge puffs.*)

HAMILTON (*nods*). Washington. (*Lights* HUMPHREYS' *cigar.*)

KNOX (*examines his cigar*). Very interesting leaf.

HUMPHREYS (*puffing away*). Mm! Good! Good!

HAMILTON (*to* KNOX). I hope you like them, Henry. I've ordered a packet for you.

KNOX. Why, thank you, Alec.

HAMILTON. Not at all. (*Selects and lights a cigar for himself.*)

KNOX. Yes. The Chief made an army out of a rabble, all right. There's no doubt of that.

HAMILTON. Ah! But to accomplish it, even he had to resort to the gallows and the lash. As with an army, so with a nation. You need one strong man.

KNOX. The Chief's getting old, though.

HAMILTON. Exactly. Sometimes I lay awake nights wondering how we can ever hold this country together, when he's gone.

KNOX. Personally, I think it's his character alone that does it. I wouldn't give a penny for the Constitution without him.

HAMILTON (*sits*). Well, it's real value is as a stepping-stone. (*Purring over his cigar*) Wonderful flavor?

KNOX. Mm!

HUMPHREYS (*wryly*). A bit strongish. (*They laugh. He disposes of his cigar in tray beside chair.*) I agree with Alec. A monarchy would have been our best salvation.

MRS. HAMILTON. Only today I was talking to some of the ladies of our court on this subject. You go out in the streets. It's frightening. We're all agreed, the time is ripening for us to have a *real* king.

BUTLER (*entering*). Senator Monroe is calling, sir.

HAMILTON. Monroe? What's he want? (*Rises*) Show him in.

BUTLER. Yes, sir. (BUTLER *exits.*)

HUMPHREYS (*rises*). Now, there's a country bumpkin! James Monroe. *Pas d'élégance!*

KNOX. He's a good soldier! Fought in almost every important battle of the war.

HAMILTON. The soul of a clerk, though. I can't abide that.

HUMPHREYS. He was, you know. He was a clerk in Jefferson's law office ten years ago.

HAMILTON. Still is, as far as I'm concerned. (*They laugh.*) I'll wager ten to one he's here on some errand for Mr. Jefferson! Mark! You'll see! (BUTLER *enters.*)

BUTLER. Colonel Monroe.

MONROE (*enters, bows*). Gentlemen! Colonel Hamilton. (KNOX *rises, bows briefly, and sits again.*)

HAMILTON. Colonel Monroe. This in an unexpected pleasure. You've met my lady.

MONROE. Mrs. Hamilton (*He bows.*) I was reluctant to intrude on you in your home.

HAMILTON (*crosses to pick up tray of cigars*). Quite all right.

MONROE. However, I've been trying to make an appointment with you at your office for several weeks.

HAMILTON (*crosses to* MONROE, *offers him cigars*). My office has been so busy. . . . The new taxes. Cigar?

MONROE. No, thanks.

HAMILTON. From the Spanish Islands.

MONROE. No, thanks. I should like to speak with you alone, if I may.

MRS. HAMILTON. My dear, it sounds ominous.

KNOX (*rises*). Well—er . . .

HUMPHREYS. I have an engagement with my wig-maker.

HAMILTON (*restrains them*). No. Stay, gentlemen. Pray. (*To* MONROE) What's on your mind?

MONROE (*grimly*). I said alone.

HAMILTON (*curbs his annoyance, smiles*). I'm sorry. I've had an exhausting day. I refuse to discuss business now. I'll see you at my office. Tomorrow at four-thirty, if you wish.

MONROE. I'm seeing the President at four.

HAMILTON. Next week, perhaps.

MONROE. I'm seeing him on a matter that concerns you.

HAMILTON. Me? Indeed! Well, I wish you luck. You're sure you won't have one of these cigars—to smoke on the way?

MONROE. No, thanks.

HAMILTON. You'll excuse us, I'm sure. (*To* BUTLER, *who is waiting at the door*) Chandler!

BUTLER (*steps forward*). Yes, sir.

MONROE. Very well. I have some papers I intend to submit to the President. I wanted to give you a chance to explain.

HAMILTON. Give me a chance to . . . ? I don't like your tone. I don't like it at all.

MONROE. I think you should be informed. There have been charges leveled against you.

HAMILTON. What charges?

MONROE. Of appropriating treasury funds.

HAMILTON. What! (*Moves toward* MONROE.) You dare to come into my house and accuse me of . . . ?

MONROE. *I'm* not accusing you. I'm inquiring into the facts.

HAMILTON. General Knox, will you act as my second?

KNOX. Your servant.

HAMILTON. Sir, you will name your friend to this gentleman. They can arrange weapons, time, and place. Good night.

MONROE. I'll be very happy to oblige you.

HAMILTON (*to* SERVANT). Show him out.

MONROE (*takes some letters out of his pocket*). But I must first demand you explain these letters. . . .

HAMILTON (*raging—moves down, facing* MONROE). Any man who dares call me thief . . .

MONROE. To Mr. Reynolds.

HAMILTON (*stops short*). Reynolds?

MONROE. Yes.

HAMILTON. I see. May I . . . ? (*He puts out his hand.* MONROE *gives him one of the letters. He glances at it, returns it.*)

MONROE. Is that your writing?

HAMILTON. It is. This puts the matter on a different footing. I have no objection to a fair inquiry. And I think you are entitled to a frank answer.

KNOX. We'll go, Alec. (KNOX *starts to go,* HAMILTON *restrains him.*)

HAMILTON. I want you as a witness to this.

KNOX. Of course.

HAMILTON (*to* MONROE). If you will be at my office tomorrow evening, I . . .

MONROE (*stubbornly*). I'm seeing the President at *four*.

HAMILTON. In the morning, then. It happens, fortunately, I can supply you with all the letters and documents in this instance.

MONROE. Mr. Reynolds charges you gave him money from the public treasuries to speculate with in your behalf.

HAMILTON. Where is Mr. Reynolds now?

MONROE. I've no idea.

HAMILTON. He's in jail. Subornation of perjury in a fraud case. You take the word of such a character?

MONROE. Did you give him this money?

HAMILTON. I did. But it was my own.

MONROE. And why did you give money to such a character?
(*A long pause*)

HAMILTON. He was blackmailing me.

MRS. HAMILTON. Alec!

MONROE. What for?

HAMILTON. A personal matter which has nothing to do with the treasury. I'll prove that to your full satisfaction.

MONROE. Under any circumstances, I shall ask for an accounting to Congress.

HAMILTON. As a Senator that is your privilege. And I shall oblige you. I will invite all America to look into the window of my breast and judge the purity of my political motives. Not one penny of the public funds have I ever touched. I would sooner pluck out my eye by the roots.
(MONROE *remains stonily unmoved.* HAMILTON's *smile becomes cynical.*)

MONROE. At your office. Tomorrow at ten.

HAMILTON. Ten will do.

MONROE. If it's as you say, the matter will, of course, be kept confidential.

HAMILTON (*ironically*). Yes, I'm sure it will. (MONROE *bows, turns to go.*) Tell him for me, Colonel Monroe, it would have been more manly, at least, to have come here, himself.

MONROE. Who are you referring to?

HAMILTON. Who sent you, Colonel Monroe?

MONROE. No one sent me, Colonel Hamilton.

HAMILTON. No one?

MONROE. No one! (MONROE *goes.*)

HUMPHREYS. *Quelle folie!*

HAMILTON. Henry! Humphreys! Will you gentlemen . . . ?

KNOX. Of course, Alec. We were just leaving. If there's anything we can do? Anything at all, call on us. All your friends will be at your disposal.

HAMILTON. Thank you. It's not as serious as that, believe me.

HUMPHREYS. Ridiculous, of course. A bagatelle! When I was at the court, there was such an incident. . . .

KNOX. Come, Humphreys!

HUMPHREYS. Hm? Oh, yes, yes! (*Bows.*) Your servant, my lady. (*To* HAMILTON) *Votre cher ami*, Colonel.

KNOX. Mrs. Hamilton! Alec! (*They go.*)

HAMILTON. Betsy, I tried to spare you this.

MRS. HAMILTON (*rises*). We'll go to father. He'll help you, darling. I know he will. You mustn't worry.

HAMILTON. It's not a question of money. Good God, Betsy, do *you* think I'm an embezzler?

MRS. HAMILTON. I only know you're in trouble and I want to help you.

HAMILTON. Thank you, my dear. Thank you. (*He kisses her.*) You've been a wonderful wife, Betsy. Far better than I deserve.

MRS. HAMILTON. What was this man blackmailing you for? What have you done, Alec?

HAMILTON. I've been very foolish, Betsy.

MRS. HAMILTON. Please, Alec. Tell me!

HAMILTON. When I wooed you, do you remember I said I wanted a wife who would love God but hate a saint?

MRS. HAMILTON. Don't jest with me now, Alec.

HAMILTON. I'm not.

MRS. HAMILTON. What was this man blackmailing you for?

HAMILTON. Philandering with his wife.

MRS. HAMILTON. Oh! I see. (*Turns away—sits, controlling herself.*) Who is she? Do I know her?

HAMILTON. No. It was a game they were playing together. She and her husband. He suddenly appeared one night, claimed I'd ruined his life, and threatened to inform you, unless I gave him a thousand dollars. He's been bleeding me dry ever since. Now, he's gotten himself in jail, and wants me to use my influence to release him. I refused. This is his revenge. (*Contritely*) Forgive me, dearest. I would do anything . . . (*He sits beside her.*)

MRS. HAMILTON. Let's not discuss that, Alec. The question is, what shall we do now to clear you?

HAMILTON. My accounts will do that, Betsy. Congress will clear me.

MRS. HAMILTON. Oh! (*Pause*) Good, then. (*She turns to* HAMILTON.) Why didn't you tell me this before?

HAMILTON. I didn't want to hurt you.

MRS. HAMILTON (*suddenly rises, moves away*). Then I wish to Heaven you hadn't told me at all.

HAMILTON (*rises*). I'm forced to it, Betsy. Jefferson obviously wants to destroy my position as leader of the party. As long as these letters in his hands go unexplained—by insinuation, he could undermine belief in my honesty. I must be prepared to *publish* the facts, if necessary. (*He goes to her, takes her arm.*) Betsy . . .

MRS. HAMILTON (*drawing arm away*). Please, Alec!

HAMILTON. You understand, don't you?

MRS. HAMILTON. Oh, yes.

HAMILTON. Believe me, I love you.

MRS. HAMILTON (*her indignation explodes with an icy blast*). And slept with a harlot! Don't insult me, Alec! You never loved me.

HAMILTON. Why did I marry you?

MRS. HAMILTON. Was it because my father was General Schuyler?

HAMILTON (*flaring*). And I the illegitimate son of a Scotch peddler? I married you for your wealth and your position! Is that what you believe?

MRS. HAMILTON (*wearily*). I don't know what to believe.
(BUTLER *enters.*)

BUTLER. Excuse me, sir. Mr. Fenno calling on you, sir.

HAMILTON. Tell him to go away!

MRS. HAMILTON. Show him in, Chandler. (*The* BUTLER *hesitates.*) Show him in!

BUTLER. Yes, Ma'am. (*Exits.*)

HAMILTON. Betsy, I want to talk this out with you.

MRS. HAMILTON (*presses her fingers to her temples*). I don't care to discuss this any more.

HAMILTON (*takes her by shoulders*). Listen to me, Betsy! You must listen . . .

MRS. HAMILTON. Alec, please! (*She draws away from him.*) I don't care to hear any more, now. I'm—tired.
(*As she turns and goes, her handkerchief falls to the floor. He stares after her a moment, sees the handkerchief, picks it up.*)

BUTLER. Mr. Fenno.
(*Enter* MR. FENNO, *a dandified gentleman; at the moment, however, he is in a lather of perspiration.*)

FENNO. My dear Alec. I had to rush here and tell you. We have just received some shocking news. I—I'm trembling so, I can hardly talk. (*The* BUTLER *exits.*)

HAMILTON (*turning to* FENNO, *wearily*). What is it, Fenno?

FENNO. The King and Queen of France have been executed.

HAMILTON. They've . . . ?

FENNO. Guillotined.

HAMILTON. Monstrous!

FENNO (*sinks into a chair, mops his forehead with his kerchief*). The mobs in France are utterly out of hand. Burning, looting, killing. A blood bath! Unbelievable, isn't it? Simply unbelievable!

HAMILTON. I was afraid of this.

FENNO. Worse. I've heard ugly rumors here. I passed a house yesterday, and I heard a group of men down in the cellar, singing "Ça Ira"! Rufus King told me he'd heard open threats against us. Even against General Washington.

HAMILTON. I've no doubt of it.

FENNO. I fear this is going to spread like the smallpox.

HAMILTON. Yes. And who've we to thank? Jefferson! Jefferson!

FENNO. Oh, no, I don't think he would dare . . .

HAMILTON (*pacing furiously*). I tell you, yes! The man's a lunatic. He's been encouraging our people to all sorts of wild illusions. Bill of rights! Freedom! Liberty! License! Anarchy! This is the fruit of his disordered imagination. That man will stop at nothing to achieve chaos. But there'll be no more of him here! I promise you. I will see to it. (*Looks at* BETSY's *handkerchief, smooths it, a note of savage* | *heartbreak in his voice.*) There's no longer any room in this country—in this world, for both me and that—fanatic!

SCENE II

SCENE: *The wild strains of "Ça Ira." As the music fades away, the harsh, discordant voices of a crowd chanting it are heard.*

Philadelphia. 1793. Evening.

A room in a house rented by JEFFERSON. *A mist hangs outside the window. Under the window, on the table, a row of potted plants. On a large table in the center of the room, books and papers piled high; a vise, some tools, a machine in process of construction. A kettle of water on a Franklin stove. The noise of the crowd in the street faintly heard.*

JEFFERSON *enters, hat in hand. He goes to the window, looks out. The sound of the crowd fades. He strikes flint and tinder and lights an oil lamp. Its light only serves to reveal the cheerlessness of the room. He extracts a journal from his pocket, sits, studying it, frowning.*

JUPITER, *his body servant, enters. A Negro with a good, intelligent face.*

JUPITER. Evenin', Mister Tom!

JEFFERSON. Good evening, Jupiter.

JUPITER (*goes about lighting the lamps*). You come in so quiet. Didn't hardly hear you. We have a busy day, Mister Tom?

JEFFERSON. Mm, hm.

JUPITER. Supper's ready soon as you say.

JEFFERSON. I'm not very hungry, Jupiter.

JUPITER. But yuh got to tuck sumpin' in yuh.

JEFFERSON. Later, perhaps. (*With an exclamation of disgust,* JEFFERSON *rises, throws the newspaper on the chair.* JUPITER *looks up, surprised at this unusual outburst.* JEFFERSON *walks over to the potted plants, examines them.* JUPITER *picks up the newspaper, looks at it quizzically, places it on the table.*

JEFFERSON *examines the potted plants, nips off a few dead leaves.*)

JUPITER (*wheedles*). Good supper. We got basted puddin' an' chicken.

JEFFERSON (*shakes his head*). Thanks. (*Picks up a little watering pot near by and waters the plants.*)

JUPITER. You just come fum one a dem cabinet meetin's?

JEFFERSON (*nods, smiles*). Yes!

JUPITER. Mm, mm! (*Nods knowingly.*) Funny weather outside. Sticky! That yeller fog hanging all over Philadelphia. I heard today ten white folk died o' the fever.

JEFFERSON. More than that.

JUPITER. Don't like it none. (*Turns to go.* JEFFERSON *notices* JUPITER's *hand is roughly bandaged with a blood-stained handkerchief.*)

JEFFERSON. What's happened to your hand?

JUPITER. Oh, it's nothin'.

JEFFERSON. Let me look at it! Come here. (*He removes the bandage.*) A nasty gash. Sit over here! (*JUPITER sits. JEFFERSON goes to the stove, pours some water into a cup, selects a bottle of wine and cruet of oil from the cupboard.*) How did you do that, Jupiter?

JUPITER. When I do my marketin' this afternoon, Mister Tom.
(*JEFFERSON sets the cup, the wine and the oil on the table, opens a drawer, and takes out some cloth. He opens JUPITER's hand, examines it.*)

JEFFERSON. This is going to sting a bit. (*Tears cloth into strips.*)

JUPITER. That's all right, Mister Tom.

JEFFERSON (*dips the cloth in the water and starts to clean the wound. He soaks the cloth with wine, dabs the wound. JUPITER winces*). Hurt you? (*JUPITER stoically shakes his head.*) How did you do this?

JUPITER. Down outside Bainbridge Market. Just as I came out.

JEFFERSON. Yes?

JUPITER. Three men was talkin'. "Mr. Jefferson's a devil," they say. Colonel Hamilton tell dem you gonna bring the French Revolution here. Murder everybody. I don't like that. I told them that ain't true. "Ain't you Jefferson's nigger?" they say. They say they was gonna kill me. One of 'em tried to hit me on the head with a stick. I put my hand up. The stick had a nail in it.

JEFFERSON. Oh, Jupiter! Haven't you learned yet?

JUPITER. They talk bad about you. What I'm gonna do?

JEFFERSON. When an angry bull stands in your path, what do you do?

JUPITER. What I do?

JEFFERSON. A man of sense doesn't dispute the road with such an animal. He walks around it. (*He smiles. JUPITER laughs and nods.*)

JUPITER. Yeah, I guess so.

JEFFERSON. What happened then, Jupiter?

JUPITER. Then a crowd came down the street, yellin'! Dey's a lot a crowds in de street, Mister Tom.

JEFFERSON. I know.

JUPITER. De men see dat crowd. Dey get scared an' run away. Mister Tom—dem crowds in de street—dey're talkin' wild. Yellin' "Kill de aristocrats! Break dere windows! Burn dere houses!" Singin' French songs.

JEFFERSON (*he bandages the hand*). Hurt? Too tight?

JUPITER (*shakes his head*). Dey talkin' bad about President Washington.

JEFFERSON. Washington?

JUPITER. Yes, Mister Tom. (*JEFFERSON frowns as he bandages the hand.*) Dat get me all mixed up. I know he fight for liberty. I remind me you tell me General Washington try to free my people.

JEFFERSON. That's right. He did.

JUPITER. I remind me, how you try, Mister Tom. I like to see my little Sarah free some day. An' I remind me how you say we gotta some day open all that land in the Northwest and ain't gonna be no slaves there. An' how we gotta git my people education, an' we gotta git 'em land, an' tools.

JEFFERSON. Some day, Jupiter. It's written in the book of fate. Your people will be free.

JUPITER. Mister Tom. Dat crowd. Git me mixed up. Git me all mixed up. I don't like it. Dey jus' gonna make trouble.

JEFFERSON. I'm afraid you're right, Jupiter. You see, the men who beat you—they're Monarchists. They want a king here. The others—the crowd—they're mixed up. It's what's happening in France now. It's gone wild. (*Finishes bandaging* JUPITER's *hand.*) How's that feel?

JUPITER. Fine, Mister Tom. (*He tries his hand.*) Fine.

JEFFERSON. Don't use that hand for a while.

JUPITER. No, Mister Tom. (*The bell tinkles.*)

JEFFERSON. The door-pull! (JUPITER *goes to answer it.* JEFFERSON *picks up the wine, returns it to cupboard.*)

JUPITER (*appears in the doorway, excited and laughing*). Mister Tom! Looka here! Look who's here. (PATSY *enters.*)

PATSY. Father!

JEFFERSON. Patsy? Darling. (*They rush to each other and embrace.*)

PATSY. Oh, Father. It's so good to see you.

JEFFERSON. My dearest. What in the world . . . ?

PATSY. I wanted to surprise you.

JEFFERSON. It's a wonderful surprise. Jupiter, kill the fatted calf! Two for supper.

JUPITER. It's chicken. (*They laugh.*)

JEFFERSON. Kill it, anyway.

JUPITER (*laughs*). He got his appetite back! Looka his face. You shore good medicine, Mrs. Patsy.

JEFFERSON. Where's your trunk?

PATSY. The coachman left it outside.

JUPITER. I get it right away. (*Starts off.*)

JEFFERSON. I'll fetch it, Jupiter. Your hand is . . .

JUPITER (*holds up his good hand*). That's all right, Mister Tom. I kin manage.

PATSY (*goes to* JUPITER). Your wife sends you her love, Jupiter. And Sarah.

JUPITER (*stops, and turns*). Dey all right?

PATSY (*nods*). I've brought you some presents they made for you.

JUPITER. Thanks, Mrs. Patsy! It's sure good to have you here, Mrs. Patsy! (*He exits.*)

JEFFERSON. How's little Jeff, and my sweet Anne, and Maria? And Mr. Randolph? Here! Give me your cloak. (JEFFERSON *takes her cloak, places it on a chair.*)

PATSY. Jeff has two new teeth.

JEFFERSON. Two? Wonderful!

PATSY. He's beginning to talk. Anne's growing so. You'd hardly recognize her.

JEFFERSON. Does she still remember me, Patsy?

PATSY. Of course. She's always playing that game you taught her—I love my love with an A. She's forever chattering about you. "Where's grandpapa? When's grandpapa coming home? What presents is grandpapa going to bring me?"

JEFFERSON (*chuckles*). Mm, hm!

PATSY. Maria sends love, squeezes and kisses. We both adored the hats and veils.

JEFFERSON. Did they fit?

PATSY. Perfectly. And the cloaks were beautiful.

JEFFERSON. The style was all right?

PATSY. Oh, yes.

JEFFERSON. And how's your good husband?

PATSY. Mr. Randolph's well, working hard. Doing the best he can with the overseer. . . . Is it always so close in Philadelphia?

JEFFERSON. This is very bad weather. A contagious fever's broken out here.

PATSY (*looks about*). So this is where you live?

JEFFERSON. Do you like my quarters?

PATSY. A little gloomy, isn't it?

JEFFERSON (*laughs*). You must be exhausted. A glass of sherry?

PATSY. I'd love it. (JEFFERSON *crosses to wine cabinet.*) Father! Coming here —the coach had to stop. There was such a crowd of people up the street.

JEFFERSON. The French Ambassador's been haranguing them lately. There have been some disorders. This epidemic of fever here seems to bring a moral contagion with it. (*He selects several bottles, holds them up.*) Dry or sweet?

PATSY. Dry, please. (*She toys with a mechanical device on the table.*) What's this? Another "convenience" of yours?

JEFFERSON. That's a copying machine. Very handy. It makes duplicate copies of letters. I'll show you how it works.

PATSY (*laughs*). Oh, Father. You and your inventions! Sometimes I . . . (*Her eye is caught by the journal on the table. She stops laughing, frowns, picks it up, reads it. Her face sets in anger.*)

JEFFERSON (*pouring sherry*). Has Maria learned to baste a pudding yet? In her last letter she said Aunt Eppes was teaching her . . .

PATSY. Father!

JEFFERSON. Hm? (*Turns, sees her with the newspaper.*) Oh! You don't want to read that! (*Crosses to take it from her.*)

PATSY. Oh, my God!

JEFFERSON. Now don't get upset, dear!

PATSY. What sort of a newspaper is this?

JEFFERSON. The "court" journal. The snobs nibble it for breakfast. Here, drink your sherry.

PATSY. I'd heard what they were doing to you here, but this is worse than I could have possibly imagined.

JEFFERSON. It's very flattering. Especially that bit about the harem! A harem! At my age! Pretty good. . . .

PATSY. I don't see any humor in it! You'll answer these charges?

JEFFERSON. Answer one lie, they print twenty new ones.

PATSY. Then what are you going to do?

JEFFERSON. Let's ignore it, dear, hm?

PATSY. Who wrote it? Who's Pacificus?

JEFFERSON. I don't know. It's a pseudo-nym.

PATSY (*Pause. She looks at him, almost in tears; finally, very bitterly*). You must enjoy being the Secretary of State very much to put up with such abuse.

JEFFERSON. It's my job, dear.

PATSY. Job? (*Rises, walks to the window, agitated.*) Father?

JEFFERSON. Yes, dear?

PATSY. Don't you think you've sacrificed enough?

JEFFERSON. I haven't suffered anything.

PATSY. You haven't?

JEFFERSON. No.
(*Pause*)

PATSY. A few weeks ago I found a pamphlet Mother had written during the Revolution to the Women of Virginia on the necessity for them (*bitterly*) to make sacrifices to help win the war. I remember Mother so ill she could hardly walk, doing ten men's work at home. I remember, after she died, sitting on the cold floor outside your door, listening to you sob till I thought you, too, must die. I remember hearing you cry out, you'd sacrificed her to the Revolution.

JEFFERSON (*sinks into a chair*). Patsy.

PATSY. The morning and afternoon of your life you sacrificed. Wasn't that enough?

JEFFERSON. Patsy, dear! Please!

PATSY. No. If you won't think of your-self, what of us? A child of twelve and a baby of four, torn from our home, from all we loved, taken to a foreign land, seeing you only on occasion, longing always for home and security and . . . Why? For what? Is there no end . . . ?

JEFFERSON. Patsy, I beg of you!

PATSY. Don't you owe anything to yourself? Don't you owe anything to us? I tell you, Father, everything at home is going to pieces. If you don't come back soon, there'll be nothing left. Nothing!

JEFFERSON (*rises, in agony*). Patsy! Will you, for God's sake, stop!

PATSY (*crosses to him, overcome with remorse*). Father! Oh, Father, I didn't mean to . . .

JEFFERSON (*takes her in his arms*). I know. I know.

PATSY. Forgive me.

JEFFERSON. Of course.

PATSY. I've been so confused and un-happy. I had to come and talk it out with you.

JEFFERSON. Of course you did. I should have been very hurt if you hadn't.

PATSY. It's the business of running Monticello and the farms. We try! Lord knows we try! But Mr. Randolph has no talent for it. And his failure makes him irritable. And I worry so. I'm afraid you may lose everything you own.

JEFFERSON. I see, my dear. I see. (*He strokes her hair.*) I haven't been alto-gether insensible to this. It's weighed on me very heavily, the trouble I put your good husband to.

PATSY. I shouldn't have said anything.

I know what your work here means to you.

JEFFERSON (*a sudden surge of bitterness*). I have never loathed anything as much in my life. You've no idea, Patsy, of the rank and malignant hatreds here. Politics destroy the happiness of every being in this city! I'm surrounded here by hate and lies. Lately I've seen men who once called themselves my friends go so far as to cross the street to avoid tipping their hats to me.

PATSY. You of all people! Why?

JEFFERSON. There are a gang of king-jobbers here who are bent on changing our principle of government—by force, if necessary. Since Mr. Madison and Mr. Monroe have left, I'm alone against them. I can't contend with them, Patsy.

PATSY. What of the President?

JEFFERSON. Only his strength and his stubborn purity oppose them. But he's old, and he's sick. (*Sits*) I work from morning till night. They undo everything. This isn't spending one's life here. It's getting rid of it.

PATSY. Oh, my poor father! (PATSY *goes to him, kneels at his feet. He draws out a locket hanging around his neck.*)

JEFFERSON. Do you know, dear, my only pleasure? For an hour or so every evening I sit and dream of Monticello. I find myself more and more turning to the past and to those I loved first. Your mother . . . (*He opens the locket, studies it.*) She was a beautiful person, Patsy. She loved you all so dearly. (*Closes the locket.*) You're right, Patsy. If I hadn't neglected my duties at home during the war, she would have been alive today. It's true. I sacrificed your mother to the Revolution. And now I'm doing the same to you. Dar-ling, your happiness is more important to me than my life. And, like a fool, I've been jeopardizing it. For the privilege of being (*rises, picks up the newspaper.*) called in the public prints "lecher, liar, thief, hypocrite!" (*He throws down the newspaper.*) But no more! You mustn't worry, dearest. Everything's going to be all right. I promise you. I'm tending to my own from now on. (*Grim-faced, he takes down a portable writing-desk from the mantlepiece, sits, places it on his lap, opens it, extracts paper and pen, and begins to write furiously.*) Patsy!

PATSY. Yes.

JEFFERSON. Will you ring for Jupiter? The bell-pull's there. (PATSY *pulls the cord. A tinkle is heard, offstage.*) I have a job for you tomorrow.

PATSY. Good. What is it?

JEFFERSON (*as he writes*). I want you to help me select what furniture and articles suit Monticello, and pack and ship them to Richmond.

PATSY. To Richmond?

JEFFERSON. I'll be busy here the next few weeks, but we'd better get them off at once while the shipping lanes are still seaworthy. (*He sands the letter, blows it, reads it a moment.* JUPITER *enters.*)

JUPITER. Yes, Mister Tom?

JEFFERSON. You know where the President's home is?

JUPITER. Yes.

JEFFERSON. Please deliver this letter there at once.

JUPITER. After supper?

JEFFERSON (*rises*). No, now, Jupiter.

JUPITER. My supper's gonna get spoiled.

JEFFERSON. At once, Jupiter. (*To* PATSY) We're going home, together. To stay, Patsy. I'm resigning. (*He places the open portable desk on the table.*)

JUPITER. You goin' home, Mister Tom?

PATSY. Yes, Jupiter.
(JUPITER *stares at* JEFFERSON.)

JUPITER. Mister Tom goin' home . . . ?

PATSY. Oh! I'm so happy, Father, I . . . (*The faint noise of a crowd outside.* PATSY *breaks off, listens. The noise grows.*)

JEFFERSON. The crowd again. (*He crosses to the window and looks out.*) This is good fuel for the Federalists! (*The chanting of the mob suddenly becomes loud and ominous.*)

PATSY. What are they chanting?

JEFFERSON. I can't make it out. (*The chanted words: "Down with . . ."* *become distinguishable.*)

PATSY. Down with—who?

JEFFERSON (*as the last word becomes clearly "Washington"*). Washington? Wash——! (*He and* PATSY *look at each other. A moment of shocked silence*) He's all that stands between them and their enemies. (*Pause*) Patsy! When all our names are sponged from the records, his will burn brighter, wherever men fight for freedom. (*Irritably, to* JUPITER *who is standing there as if rooted to the spot.*) All right, Jupiter. Run along! What are you waiting for? JUPITER *goes.* PATSY *looks at* JEFFERSON *questioningly.*) No, darling. It isn't going to make any difference. If our people won't deserve their liberty, no one can save it for them. I'm going home. (*He picks up the portable desk, slams it shut, and places it back on the mantle.*)

SCENE III

SCENE: *The same, a few days later. Most of the furnishings are now gone, leaving noticeably naked areas in the room. There are several bundles of books, etc., on the floor.* PATSY *is wrapping pictures and the more fragile articles in several layers of cloth, and packing them carefully in a barrel.* JEFFERSON, *sitting at his desk, is writing furiously, disposing rapidly of a great mass of documents piled before him. Clouds of smoke hang over the room, fed by several braziers.*

JUPITER *enters, his face sick with apprehension. He picks up a bundle of books, starts to take them out. The ominous rumbling of a cart is heard outside.* PATSY, JEFFERSON *and* JUPITER *straighten up, listening.*

JUPITER. De death cart! (*He goes to the window.*) It's piled full, Mister Tom . . . (*He crosses to the braziers.*) Dis yellow fever everywhere! White folks droppin' like flies, Mister Tom! (*He pours some nitre into the braziers. Fresh ribbons of smoke spiral up.*)

JEFFERSON (*to* PATSY). You hear that? (PATSY *stubbornly continues her wrapping.*)

JUPITER. I never seen nuttin' like dis.

JEFFERSON. Jupiter! Take Mrs. Randolph at once to Germantown.

PATSY. I shan't go.
(*The door-pull tinkles.* JUPITER *goes to answer it.*)

JEFFERSON. Patsy! I'll pick you up there

in a few days, and then we'll go on home together.

PATSY. I shan't leave you here alone.

JEFFERSON. I have work to finish.

PATSY. Then I'll stay, too.

JEFFERSON. You're a stubborn child.

PATSY. I come by it honestly.
(*Enter* JUPITER *and* HAMILTON.)

JUPITER. Mister Tom, you have a visitor.

JEFFERSON (*rises*). Colonel Hamilton.

HAMILTON. Has the President arrived yet?
(JUPITER *exits.*)

JEFFERSON. Not yet. My daughter, Mrs. Randolph. Colonel Hamilton.
(PATSY *curtsies.* HAMILTON *bows.*)

HAMILTON. He asked me to meet him here. I'll wait in my carriage.

JEFFERSON. You're welcome to sit here.

HAMILTON. Thank you!

PATSY. Excuse me, Father! Colonel Hamilton! (*She curtsies, goes.*)

HAMILTON. There's a fellow lying on the sidewalk dead of the plague. (JEFFERSON *goes to the window.*) Not a pleasant sight. I sent my driver to fetch the death cart.

JEFFERSON. A bad business!

HAMILTON. Getting worse by the minute. (*Looks about.*) You moving?

JEFFERSON. Yes. You'll have to pardon our appearance. (*Sits, picks up his pen.*) Excuse me! I . . . (*Indicates his work.*)

HAMILTON. Quite all right. Please! Don't let me disturb you.
(JEFFERSON *goes back to his writing.*)

JEFFERSON. The President should have left the city immediately.

HAMILTON. You may be sure I ordered him out. The great man's a stubborn warrior, though. Can't budge him. Never could. (JEFFERSON *concentrates on his writing.* HAMILTON *glances at several magazines on table near his chair, selects one with great, surprise, glances toward* JEFFERSON *with uplifted brows, then, smiling mischievously.*) *The Gazette?*
(JEFFERSON *looks up from his work, searches* HAMILTON *with a cold glance, murmurs dryly.*)

JEFFERSON. Yes.

HAMILTON. I notice an article referring to you. Have you read it?

JEFFERSON (*stops writing, looks up*). I have. (*There is a pause. He goes back to his writing.*)

HAMILTON (*smiles, enjoying the game immensely*). Well-phrased.

JEFFERSON. Brilliantly. And thoroughly untrue, Colonel Hamilton. Thoroughly.

HAMILTON. Oh, come now, Mr. Jefferson—you do well with the ladies?

JEFFERSON (*writes on*). So I see in *The Gazette.*

HAMILTON. When I read this article I . . .

JEFFERSON. Read it? It's commonly supposed, Mr. Hamilton, that you wrote it.

HAMILTON. It's written by some person called— (*peers at journal mockingly*) Pa—ci—fi—cus.

JEFFERSON (*savoring the irony, smiles wryly*). Pacificus. Peaceful! A proper pen name. Colonel Hamilton, almost since our first cabinet meeting—you and I have been thrown at each other like cocks in a pit. The cock fight is over. Peaceful will soon have the cabinet to himself.

HAMILTON. How is that?

JEFFERSON. Hasn't the President informed you?

HAMILTON. No.

JEFFERSON. I've resigned.

HAMILTON. Oh! I'm sorry to hear that.

JEFFERSON. I'm not. I'm very happy, Colonel.

HAMILTON (*rises, moves to window*). In that event I rejoice with you.

JEFFERSON. Colonel Hamilton, you're going to your home in the country, now, to wait out the plague?

HAMILTON. Yes.

JEFFERSON. I, too, will be gone in a few days. We may never see each other again. (*Crosses to mantel; places portable writing-desk on it.*)

HAMILTON. Quite probably we won't.

JEFFERSON. I should like to ask you as man to man, without rancour or warmth— (*he picks up the newspaper*) is this fitting to the dignity of a Minister of State?

HAMILTON (*bitterly*). Was it fitting the dignity of your high office to send your henchmen prying into my private life?

JEFFERSON. I never did that.

HAMILTON. You thought I would keep silent did you? You thought sooner than risk my personal happiness I'd let you call me thief? Well! You see what you've done? Congress has cleared my public name, and I'm all the stronger for it! I didn't run away! However, in your case, I think it wise for you to go home and sit on your mountain-top. The philosophic experiment is over. Your Democracy is finished.

JEFFERSON. You really think that?

HAMILTON. I know it. I knew it six years ago. (*The bell-pull tinkles.*) My God, aren't the omens clear enough, even to a Utopian? What do you think of your people now? Your fellow dreamer, Lafayette, in irons, rotting in a German jail, his only refuge from the very ones he sought to free. At that he's lucky. If he hadn't escaped in time, even now his head would be lying in the basket, his blood flowing in the gutters, running into a river of the noblest blood of France—for your drunken swine, the people, to swill in. I tell you—it nauseates me to the very heart. And now, the same rioting mobs here, and next the same terror!

JUPITER (*enters*). General Washington.

WASHINGTON (*enters*). Gentlemen! (*He is getting very old. His face is tired and bewildered, but a bulwark of grim, stubborn determination. JUPITER exits.*)

JEFFERSON. Mr. President. (*Moves to WASHINGTON; takes his hat and stick.*)

HAMILTON. No asafoetida pad? (*Produces a spare pad and hands it to the PRESIDENT.*) In these times, Mr. President, we can't afford to lose you. I beg of you!

WASHINGTON. Very well. (*Accepts pad.*) Thank you! (*Sits down heavily, silent for a moment, as he broods, all the while tapping the arm of the chair as if it were a drum. The death cart outside rumbles by.*) More than two thousand dead already. This plague is worse than a hundred battles of cannon. (*Sighs, taps.*)

HAMILTON. You should have left the city immediately, sir.

WASHINGTON. I think I almost prefer to be in my grave than in the present situation. (*Taps, sighs heavily. A long pause*) What does it mean? (*Silence; taps*) Incredible. Aren't men fit to be free? Is that the answer? Have you spoken to the French minister?

JEFFERSON. Yes. One can't reason with him. He's a lunatic! I've demanded his recall.

WASHINGTON. They're all lunatics. Lafayette fleeing for his life? Lafayette? And here now, mobs rioting! What does this mean? (*Pause*) We must do what we can to help Lafayette.

JEFFERSON. I've already despatched a letter to Ambassador Morris, urging him to make every solicitation in his power.

WASHINGTON. I don't know if it'll help. I doubt it. (WASHINGTON *nervously picks up* The Gazette, *glances quickly at* JEFFERSON. *To* HAMILTON, *with a touch of sternness*) Do you mind waiting below? I should like to talk with you.

HAMILTON (*glances a bit guiltily at* JEFFERSON, *then smiles ironically*). I'll wait in your carriage. (WASHINGTON *nods.*) Your servant, Mr. Jefferson.

JEFFERSON. Mr. Hamilton.
(HAMILTON *goes.*)

WASHINGTON. I shall have to speak to him again. He's very difficult. He's always been that way, though. Once, during the war, when he was my aide, he kept me waiting two hours. When I rebuked him, he resigned. Sulked like a little boy. (*Softens, with evident love of* HAMILTON.) Finally I gave him what he wanted—a command in the field. He was a very good soldier. Led his troops in the first assault on Yorktown. He's an invaluable man. Why can't you two work together?

JEFFERSON. Our principles are as separate as the poles.

WASHINGTON. Coalesce them!

JEFFERSON. It can't be done.

WASHINGTON. Let me be the mediator.

JEFFERSON. You've tried before.

WASHINGTON. Let me try again.

JEFFERSON. It's no use. Believe me. Neither of us could honestly sacrifice his belief to the other.

WASHINGTON (*sighs, taps*). Well, I'm ordered back home. Any messages to Albemarle County?

JEFFERSON (*sits next to* WASHINGTON). My best regards to Mr. Madison. And you might look at my new threshing machine. If it interests you, the millwright's in Richmond now. He'd be very happy for any new commissions. You get eight bushels of wheat an hour out of two horses.

WASHINGTON. Hm! I'll certainly examine it.

JEFFERSON. Tell Madison next spring we'll be planting our gardens together.

WASHINGTON. No, Tom. I'm afraid you won't.

JEFFERSON. Why not?

WASHINGTON (*rises. Takes out a paper, lays it on desk*). Your resignation. I can't accept it.

JEFFERSON (*rises*). I'm sorry, Mr. President. You'll have to.

WASHINGTON. Where can I find anyone to replace you?

JEFFERSON. I don't flatter myself on that score. I've failed.

WASHINGTON. Let me be the judge of that.

JEFFERSON. I've spent twenty-four years in public life. I'm worn down with labors that I know are as fruitless to you as they are vexatious to me. My personal affairs have been abandoned too long. They are in utter chaos. I must turn to them and my family.

WASHINGTON. And the good esteem of your fellowmen?

JEFFERSON (moves away). There was a time when that was of higher value to me than anything in the world. Now I prefer tranquillity. Here, for everything I hate, you ask me to give up everything I love. I'm sorry, no! I want a little peace in my lifetime.

WASHINGTON. I know. I know. I'm sick, Tom, and I'm getting old, and I catch myself dreaming of the Potomac and Mount Vernon (He almost shouts.) Don't you think I hate this, too? Don't you think I yearn for the peace of my own farm? Don't you think all this—all this . . . (Controls himself. There is a long silence. He murmurs.) Peace in our life? Where . . . ? (His memories turn back as he searches for the phrase.) Oh, yes. . . . Paine wrote it. Was it in The Crisis? "These are the times that try men's souls. The summer soldier and the sunshine patriot will in this crisis shrink . . ." (JEFFERSON sinks into a chair; unwittingly, the PRESIDENT has dealt him a stunning blow.) How that brings back the picture! As if it were yesterday. My men starved, naked, bleeding. I read Paine's essay. You know, it lent me new strength. I had it read to my men through trumpets. Nailed it on trees for them to read. It helped them. Gave them sore-needed courage. Do you remember the passage on the Tory innkeeper who was opposed to the war because . . . (he finds the phrase he's been searching for.) that's it— "He wanted peace in his lifetime?" And Paine looked down at the innkeeper's

children crawling on the floor and thought, "Were this Tory a man, he would say: If there must be conflict with tyranny, let it come in my time. Let there be peace and freedom in my children's time." Yes. That's the answer, I suppose. The only answer. (Suddenly, desperately, he grips JEFFERSON's arm.) Tom! The fabric is crumbling. Our Republic is dying. We must bolster it, somehow—some way. (Fiercely, a grim, stubborn, warrior fighting a ghost. He pounds the table.) It must have a chance. It will, I say. It will, it will, it will! I'll defend its right to a chance with the last drop of my blood. (The fierceness vanishes. Again he becomes a tired, sick, old man.) You'll stay on a few days more? Till I find someone else?

JEFFERSON. Yes.

WASHINGTON. Good! You see, I'm like a man about to be hanged. Even a few days' reprieve makes me rejoice. (Sighs heavily, starts to go, turns.) I wouldn't stay here. Take your papers, go to the country. You can work there. (Bows.) Mr. Jefferson.

JEFFERSON (rises). Mr. President. (WASHINGTON goes. Outside, the death cart rumbles by. JEFFERSON, torn and tortured, drops back into his chair. JUPITER enters, pours more nitre into the braziers. PATSY enters, holding up a music box.)

PATSY. Father! Look! I found this little music box inside. May I . . . Father! You're not ill?

JEFFERSON. No, Patsy.

PATSY. You look so pale. Are you sure, Papa?

JEFFERSON. Yes, dear.

PATSY. Can I get you something? A drink of water?

JEFFERSON. No, dear. I'm all right.
(*Pause.* JUPITER *exits.*)

PATSY. May I take this home to Anne?

JEFFERSON. Yes, dear.
(*She turns a knob. The music box plays a tinkling melody.*)

PATSY. Anne will love it. Can't you just see her face?

JEFFERSON. Mm.
(*Pause.*)

PATSY. Did the President accept your resignation?

JEFFERSON. Yes.

PATSY. I spoke to him in the hallway. He looks so old, doesn't he? (JEFFERSON *nods.* PATSY *shuts off the music box.*) Oh, Father, please! Please don't torment yourself so!

JEFFERSON (*rises*). He's a dying man, Patsy. He's dying. And, when he's gone, they'll take the reins. And that'll be the end, Patsy. That'll be the end of the Republic.

PATSY. Perhaps we weren't ready for it, Father.

JEFFERSON (*moves about, restlessly*). If not here and now, where then? Where will men ever have such a chance again? This was my dream, Patsy! From my earliest youth.

PATSY. You've done your best, Father.

JEFFERSON. Not good enough, apparently. Summer soldier. (*Pause*) It was seventeen years ago, *here in Philadelphia,* I wrote the Declaration of Independence. That's how I dreamed of America, Patsy. A beacon for all mankind. (*Pause*) Patsy! It's not our people who've failed us. It's we who've failed them. Yes. I see that now.

(*Paces about the room.*) These fermentations are a healthy sign. Our people are groping. They're jealous of their rights? Good! They want a larger share in their government. Most of them today haven't even the privilege of voting. It would take so little education to make them understand these disorders are not to their advantage. That's where we've failed them, Patsy. It's not enough to create the form of a Republic. We must *make* it work. We must see that our people get the right to vote. We must educate them to use it and be worthy of it. We must give them free schools, and universities and a liberal press. Only an enlightened people can really be free. Till now, the genius of the common people has been buried in the rubbish heap. We must rescue that! I'm convinced of it! We must make war on ignorance and poverty. We must go into the streets and the squares and the smithies. . . .

JUPITER (*entering*). Mister Tom.
(HAMILTON *appears in the doorway.*)

HAMILTON. I beg your pardon. I didn't mean to . . .
(JEFFERSON *faces* HAMILTON. JUPITER *exits.*)

JEFFERSON. It's quite all right. Come in!

HAMILTON. The President asked me to speak to you. He's greatly distressed.

JEFFERSON. Yes, I know he is.

HAMILTON. He asked me to make an effort to coalesce our differences. There's no reason why we shouldn't.

JEFFERSON. You think we can?

HAMILTON. If you will only stop regarding the Constitution as something handed down from Mount Sinai.

JEFFERSON. I see.

HAMILTON. If we're to work together, you'll . . .

JEFFERSON. We're not!

HAMILTON. Oh!

JEFFERSON. We are natural enemies.

HAMILTON. Well, I offered peace.

JEFFERSON. The wolves offered the sheep peace.

HAMILTON. You don't flatter me!

JEFFERSON. It is not an American art.

HAMILTON. I am an American by choice, not by accident.

JEFFERSON. Yet you bring here a lie bred out of the vices and crimes of the old world.

HAMILTON. Lie?

JEFFERSON. The lie that the masses of men are born with saddles on their backs, and a chosen few booted and spurred to ride them legitimately, by the grace of God.

HAMILTON. It's laughable! You, born to wealth and land and slaves, driveling about the common people!

JEFFERSON. Search your own birth, Mr. Hamilton, and you'll . . .

HAMILTON. Don't say it! (*Trembling with rage*) I must warn you.

JEFFERSON. Say what? That you as a boy were poor? That you came to this country and it gave you honor and wealth? I believe every boy in this land must have that opportunity.

HAMILTON. Why do you think I want the country strong?

JEFFERSON. It can only be strong if its people govern it.

HAMILTON. You think the peasants on my farm can make it strong?

JEFFERSON. There are no peasants in America.

HAMILTON. Words! What do I care for them! Call them yeomen! Call them what you will! Men cannot rule themselves.

JEFFERSON. Can they then rule others? Have we found angels in the forms of kings and dictators to rule them?

HAMILTON. I've made my last gesture. Go! Run back to your hill! From here on, I promise you, you will never again dare raise your head in this party.

JEFFERSON. I hate party. But if that's the only way I can fight you—then I'll create another party. I'll create a people's party.

HAMILTON. Now it comes out. You want two parties! You want blood to flow! At heart you, too, are a Jacobin murderer.

JEFFERSON. That's another lie you believe because you wish to believe it. It gives you the excuse you need to draw your sword! I'm sick to death of your silencing every liberal tongue by calling "Jacobin murderer."

HAMILTON. Well, aren't you? Confess it!

JEFFERSON. Go on! Wave the raw head and the bloody bones! Invent your scares and plots! We were asleep after the first labors, and you tangled us and tied us, but we have only to awake and rise and snap off your Lilliputian cords.

HAMILTON. Very well. Let it be a fight, then. But make it a good one. And, when you stir up the mobs, remember —we who really own America are quite prepared to take it back for ourselves, from your great beast, "The People."

JEFFERSON. And I tell you, when once our people have the government securely in their hands, they will be strong as a giant. They will sooner allow the heart to be torn out of their bodies than their freedom to be wrested from them by a Caesar!

HAMILTON (*bows*). Good day, Mr. Jefferson.

JEFFERSON. Good day, Colonel Hamilton. (HAMILTON *exits*. JEFFERSON *turns to* PATSY.) Patsy, this is a fight that may take the rest of my life. . . .

PATSY. Yes.

JEFFERSON. But I have to! I hate it, but I have to, Patsy. I want Anne and Jeff and their children to grow up in a free republic. I have to, Patsy.

PATSY. Of course you do. (*Rises. Crosses to* JEFFERSON.) Of course you do, Father. (*She takes his hand impulsively, kisses it.*)

ACT THREE

SCENE I

SCENE: *The new city of Washington, 1801.* JEFFERSON's *rooms in Conrad's Boarding House.*

JEFFERSON *seated at his desk, writing. His grandchildren, a little boy and a girl, playing on the floor at his feet.* PATSY *seated, crocheting. Outside, in the hallway, the excited babble of many voices.* JUPITER *is placing a tray on the desk. Prominently set on the mantel is a marble bust of Washington. A knock at the door.* PATSY *starts up.* JUPITER *turns to the door.*

PATSY. I'll take it, Jupiter.
(*She hurries to the door, opens it. A* MESSENGER *hands her a message. A crowd of boarders surrounds him, asking questions.*)

MESSENGER. Twenty-seventh ballot just come up.

PATSY. Thank you. (*The crowd assails her with questions.*) In a minute. (*She hands the message to her father.* JEFFERSON *reads it, while she waits anxiously.* JEFFERSON *crumples it, throws it away, smiles, shakes his head.*)

JEFFERSON. The same.

PATSY. Oh, dear! (*She goes to the door.*) No. I'm sorry. Congress is still deadlocked.
(*The crowd in the hallway becomes persistent.*)

FIRST MAN. We heard Mr. Burr lost a vote to your father.

PATSY. That's not true, as far as I know.

MESSENGER (*shakes his head*). No. I told them. (*To others*) I told you. (*He goes.*)

SECOND MAN. We elected Mr. Jefferson to be President. What's Congress fiddling around for, anyway? What are they up to, Mrs. Randolph?

THIRD MAN. Is it true the Feds are going to try and just make one of their own men President?

PATSY. I can't say. . . .
(*Suddenly a high-pitched voice is heard and a little lady comes pushing through the crowd. She is* MRS. CONRAD, *the proprietress of the boarding house.*)

MRS. CONRAD. In the parlor, please! All my boarders. Downstairs! In the parlor! You'll get the returns there as soon as you will up here. Now, stop a pesting

Mr. Jefferson! Give a man a little privacy, will you? Downstairs in the parlor! (*She enters, apologetically, in a whisper*) Everybody's so worked up, you know.

PATSY. It's all in the family.

MRS. CONRAD. Well, I can't have the other boarders disturbing your father at a time like this.

PATSY. Thank you.
(*A husky voice is heard singing "Outa my way." "One side!" The boarders are tumbled aside. A man in frontier outfit, armed to the teeth, appears in door.*)

FRONTIERSMAN. Tom Jefferson here?

PATSY. What is it?

FRONTIERSMAN. Message from Governor Monroe of Virginia.

JEFFERSON. Here!

FRONTIERSMAN. You're Tom Jefferson?

JEFFERSON. Yes.

FRONTIERSMAN (*hands him message*). Governor Monroe said to deliver it to you personal.

JEFFERSON. Thank you! (*Opens it. Reads it.*) Sit down.

FRONTIERSMAN. Don't mind astandin'. Rid my horse hard all a way from Richmond. She's got a mean jog. Governor's waitin' on your answer.

JEFFERSON. No answer, yet.

FRONTIERSMAN. Nothing settled yet on the election?

JEFFERSON. No. You'd better stand by.

FRONTIERSMAN. Yep.

JEFFERSON. Mrs. Conrad, will you see this gentleman gets something warm to eat? Jupiter, will you saddle a fresh horse?

JUPITER. Yes, Mr. Tom. (*Exits.*)

MRS. CONRAD. I'll tend to it right away, Mr. Jefferson. (*Goes to door, calls*) Nathan!

VOICE (*offstage*). Yes, Mrs. Conrad.

MRS. CONRAD. Fix up some vittles right off!

PATSY. Perhaps you'd like a drink?

FRONTIERSMAN. Why, thank you, Ma'am. Now that's a Christian thought. (PATSY *smiles, fetches brandy bottle.* MRS. CONRAD *returns.*)

BOY. Gramp! Play with me.

PATSY (*pouring drink*). Jeff, Grandpapa's busy.

BOY. Come on, Gramp . . .

JEFFERSON. Later, Jeff. I've a new game to teach you.

BOY. A new one?

JEFFERSON. A good one.

BOY. Is it like riding a horse to market?

GIRL. Oh, goody, Grandpapa! Shall I get the broom?

PATSY (*hands drink to the Frontiersman*). Children! Go inside.

JEFFERSON. No, no. They don't disturb me. I want them here.
(PATSY *beckons the children away from the desk, seats them in the corner by her side.*)

FRONTIERSMAN (*tosses down the drink*). Hm! That washes the dust down!
(*A knock at the door.* PATSY *hurries to*

it. MADISON *is there. Crowded behind him in the hall is the group of boarders. They are asking him questions.* MR. MADISON *is saying, "That's the latest balloting. I've just come from the Capitol.")*

MADISON (*enters, worn, breathless, almost crumbling with fatigue*). I've just come from the House of Representatives. I had to push my way here. The streets are jammed with people. I've never seen so many human beings.

JEFFERSON. Jemmy, you look like a dead one.

MADISON (*sits and groans*). I am. The twenty-seventh ballot came up.

JEFFERSON. We just got the message.

MADISON. You should see Congress! What a spectacle! They fall asleep in their chairs, on their feet. Red-eyed, haggard!

JEFFERSON. Mr. Nicholson's fever any better?

MADISON. Worse. He's resting in a committee-room. He has about enough strength to sign his ballot.

JEFFERSON. Who's attending him?

MADISON. His wife's by his side, giving him medicine and water.

JEFFERSON. He should be removed to a hospital.

MADISON. He won't budge. Insists he'll vote for you till he dies. I doubt whether he'll survive another night. (JEFFERSON *shakes his head.*) Tom, there's an ugly rumor going around. The crowds are getting angry.

JEFFERSON. Yes, I know. May be more than a rumor, I'm afraid. (*He hands* MADISON *a communication.*)

MADISON. Gad! How's this going to end?

MRS. CONRAD. I been talkin' to my husband, Mrs. Randolph, and we both decided the whole way of votin' now just ain't right.

MADISON. Agreed. Agreed.

MRS. CONRAD. Take my husband. He wanted your father for President, Mr. Burr for Vice-President. Well, he should be allowed to put that down on the ballot instead of just the two names and lettin' Congress decide. Stands to reason, don't it? See what happens? We beat the Federalists, and then the old Congress, most of 'em Feds themselves, don't know who to pick. Deadlocked six days now. They might like as not go on being deadlocked four years, and we'll have no President at all. Now, I say, it's deliberate. Everybody's sayin' that!

JEFFERSON. They are?

MRS. CONRAD. Stands to reason. (*She nods vigorously and scurries off, having said her piece.*)

MADISON. We should have foreseen this difficulty. We certainly bungled the electoral system.

FRONTIERSMAN. Constitution's gotta be changed so a man can put down who he wants for President.

JEFFERSON. Well, it can be amended. That's the great virtue of the Constitution. It can grow.

MADISON. If we ever have the chance to amend it. I'm worried sick by this, Tom.
(A YOUNG MAN *appears in the doorway.*)

YOUNG MAN. Does Monsieur Jefferson live here?

MRS. CONRAD (*appears*). In the parlor! Down in the parlor!

PATSY. It's all right, Mrs. Conrad.

MRS. CONRAD. Oh, excuse me. I thought he was one a my boarders. (*She goes.*)

YOUNG MAN. Monsieur Jefferson?

JEFFERSON. Yes, young man.

YOUNG MAN. You do not remember me? Twelve years ago, Paris?

JEFFERSON. You're . . . ? Of course, you're Lafayette's boy.

YOUNG MAN (*nods*). Your servant.

JEFFERSON. I was expecting you. I'd heard you were in America. You remember Patsy? (*To* PATSY) George Washington Lafayette.

PATSY. Of course.
(LAFAYETTE *bows and* PATSY *curtsies*.)

LAFAYETTE. She has not changed one little bit. Only more beautiful, if possible.

PATSY (*laughs*). He's Lafayette's son, all right.

JEFFERSON. He has the gift. And these are my grandchildren.

PATSY (*proudly*). My daughter, Miss Anne Randolph.

ANNE (*curtsies*). Monsieur Lafayette.

LAFAYETTE (*bows*). Miss Randolph.

PATSY. Monsieur George Washington Lafayette . . . (*Brings the little boy forward.*) My son . . . (*Proudly*) Thomas Jefferson Randolph.
(*The little boy makes a deep bow.* LAFAYETTE *smiles at* JEFFERSON, *who beams.*)

JEFFERSON. My friend, Mr. Madison.

LAFAYETTE. The father of your immortal Constitution? (*Bows.*) My veneration!

MADISON (*drily*). Immortal? It's running a high fever now. The next few days, the next few hours, may tell whether it's going to live at all, or die in hemorrhage. (*To* JEFFERSON) Tom! I'm as nervous as a cat. I haven't slept a wink in three nights.

JEFFERSON. Lie down inside.

MADISON. No, no.

JEFFERSON. Go on! Patsy, make up the bed for Jemmy.

MADISON. No! I couldn't. Please! Just let me sit here. (*Sits.*)

JEFFERSON (*moves chair for Lafayette*). We're passing through a terrible storm here.

LAFAYETTE (*sits*). I am sorry to come in the midst of all this, but as soon as I arrive I hurry to you.

JEFFERSON (*to* LAFAYETTE). Tell me! How is your father?

LAFAYETTE. He is out of prison now.

JEFFERSON. I'd heard. I haven't written him because things here, too, have been so bad these last years, my letter would never have reached him. (*Pause.*) How does he look?

LAFAYETTE. Six years in prison.

JEFFERSON. They didn't break his spirit?

LAFAYETTE. That they will never break.

JEFFERSON. No.

LAFAYETTE. He asked me to explain he dare not write. Bonaparte watches him. He is only free on—a string.

JEFFERSON (*sighs*). I had hoped at first Bonaparte would value the real glory of a Washington as compared to that of a Caesar. (*He glances at bust of* WASHINGTON.)

LAFAYETTE (*follows his glance*). When we heard he died, my father wept like a child.
(*Pause.*)

JEFFERSON. A great man fell that day. America now must walk alone.

LAFAYETTE. Here—forgive me. This isn't the America I expected. This is like when Bonaparte came to us.

JEFFERSON. There is an ominous note in this dissension. You've sensed it. Our own little Bonaparte may step in with his comrades at arms and force salvation on us in his way.

LAFAYETTE (*rises*). That must not be. This is the message my father asked me to deliver. Tell Jefferson, he says to me, tell him the eyes of all suffering humanity are looking to America. It is their last hope on earth.
(*A knock at the door.* JEFFERSON *opens the door. A* COURIER *stands there.*)

COURIER. Mr. Jefferson?

JEFFERSON. Yes?

COURIER. Message!

JEFFERSON. Thank you! (COURIER *goes.* JEFFERSON *takes message, opens it, reads it, becomes grave.*)

MADISON (*rises*). What is it, Tom?

JEFFERSON. A group of the Federalists are meeting tonight.

MADISON. To set aside the election?

JEFFERSON. Possibly. (*Hands the message to* MADISON. MADISON *reads it, groans.*)

FRONTIERSMAN. Like hell they will! Nobody's gonna take my Republic from me.

JEFFERSON (*to the* FRONTIERSMAN). That's right, my friend. (*He crosses to his desk, picks up the letter he has been writing, folds it.*) I'm afraid there's no time for that meal now. Will you see if your horse is ready?

FRONTIERSMAN. Yep. (*Goes.*)

JEFFERSON (*seals letter. To* PATSY). I think you had better plan on going home.

PATSY. Very well, Father.

JEFFERSON. I don't know how long this will keep up. I don't know how it will end.
(FRONTIERSMAN *returns.*)

FRONTIERSMAN. Horse is saddled and out front.

JEFFERSON (*hands letter to him*). To Governor Monroe, with my compliments.

FRONTIERSMAN. Yes, sir.

JEFFERSON. Give your horse the spur!

FRONTIERSMAN. Ride him like the wind, Mr. Jefferson. No fear! (*He goes.*)

PATSY. When do you want us to leave?

JEFFERSON. Now. (*Looks at his watch.*) After dinner.

PATSY. So soon?

JEFFERSON. Please.

PATSY. There's going to be serious trouble?

JEFFERSON. I don't know, Patsy.

PATSY. General Hamilton? Again? Is there no end to that man's malevolence?

LAFAYETTE. Hamilton? (*He looks about at a loss.*) But, during the war, he was my father's friend, too. My father often speaks of him.

PATSY. People changed here after the war, Monsieur Lafayette. The real revolution has been fought in the last six years.

MADISON. And our people have won, Monsieur Lafayette. Through the ballot they've taken the government into their own hands. But now the Federalists intend to drag everything down with them, rather than admit defeat. (*There is a knock at the door.*)

PATSY. They've turned President Adams completely against my father—one of his oldest friends!

LAFAYETTE. This shocks me. I cannot believe it.

PATSY. Do you know *why* he didn't write your father all these years? He couldn't! They opened his mail! They twisted phrases he used in his letters, and printed them against him. (*The knock is repeated.*)

JEFFERSON. These are things, Patsy, that are best forgotten.

PATSY. Father, there are men in the streets with guns. They're expecting Hamilton and his troops. They say there'll be shooting. (*The doors open.* HAMILTON *stands there. A long, stunned silence.*)

HAMILTON. Mr. Jefferson.

JEFFERSON. General Hamilton.

PATSY. You dare . . . !

JEFFERSON. Pat! Go inside, please.

PATSY. Yes, Father. Come, children! (*She steers the children off.*)

JEFFERSON. General Hamilton, Monsieur George Washington Lafayette.

HAMILTON. Lafayette? You're his son?

LAFAYETTE. Yes.

HAMILTON. Of course. I knew your father well. He was my friend.

LAFAYETTE. He often speaks of you. He was yours.

MADISON (*picks up his hat and starts to leave*). Gentlemen!

LAFAYETTE. I go with you, if I may.

MADISON. Come along.

JEFFERSON. You'll dine with us? (LAFAYETTE *nods.* JEFFERSON *looks at his watch.*) In twenty-three minutes.

LAFAYETTE. Twenty-three.

JEFFERSON. On the dot. Mrs. Conrad runs her boarding house along democratic lines. The early birds get the choice cuts. (LAFAYETTE *smiles, turns to* HAMILTON, *bows.*)

LAFAYETTE. Monsieur Hamilton. (HAMILTON *bows.* LAFAYETTE *goes.* JEFFERSON *and* HAMILTON *survey each other.*)

JEFFERSON. What can I do for you, General Hamilton?

HAMILTON. Nothing! But I can do something for you. I'm not going to equivocate, Mr. Jefferson. My sentiments toward you are unchanged. I still despise you and everything you represent.

JEFFERSON (*moves to desk. Indicates a chair*). Chair, General?

HAMILTON. Is that understood?

JEFFERSON. I think pretty widely. (*Points to chair.*) Chair?

HAMILTON (*sits*). Thank you. (*Pause. They survey each other*) You've grown leaner.

JEFFERSON. And you stouter.

HAMILTON. Not at all. It's this waist-coat . . . A few pounds, perhaps. (*Pause.* HAMILTON *glances out the window.*) So this is your city of Washington. A mud hole.

JEFFERSON. A few trees and some sidewalks and it will do.

HAMILTON. The first day we met this was born.

JEFFERSON. Yes.

HAMILTON. You remember?

JEFFERSON. Oh, yes.

HAMILTON. The Presidential Mansion appears not bad.

JEFFERSON. Not bad.

HAMILTON. Large enough.

JEFFERSON. Large enough for two emperors and a rajah.

HAMILTON. Who's it to be—Aaron Burr or you?

JEFFERSON. Congress will decide.

HAMILTON (*rises*). I have some friends in that body. I can influence this decision for or against you, I believe.

JEFFERSON. I'm certain of that.

HAMILTON. Certain? I'm not. You'd be astonished, Mr. Jefferson, at the number of gentlemen who, no matter what I counsel, would vote for the devil himself in preference to you.

JEFFERSON. Yes. That's quite probable.

HAMILTON. Not that I approve of it. I don't. I deplore it. In the matter of the public good, men must consult their reason, not their passions. I believe I can swing Congress over to you, *if you* accede to certain conditions.

JEFFERSON. I see.

HAMILTON (*moves to desk*). One: I want your solemn assurance that you will continue all my friends in the offices they now fill. Two: I want . . .

JEFFERSON (*smiles, shakes his head*). I'm sorry.

HAMILTON. You refuse?

JEFFERSON. This time no bargains. I appreciate your motives . . .

HAMILTON (*in a rage, shouting*). Bargains? What puny channels your mind runs in!

JEFFERSON. No need to shout, General.

HAMILTON (*pacing furiously*). I'll raise the roof if I please.

JEFFERSON (*nods toward the next room*). My grandchildren . . .

HAMILTON. Excuse me.

JEFFERSON. This is like old times, General.

HAMILTON. Do you realize how dangerous this situation has become?

JEFFERSON. Yes.

HAMILTON. I came here to compromise. I hoped to avert the more drastic alternative. But the years have made you even more pig-headed, if possible. I might have spared myself this trouble.

JEFFERSON. I couldn't enter the Presidency with my hands tied.

HAMILTON. Don't concern yourself. You won't enter it at all! My friends are meeting tonight. You oblige them to act to set aside this election altogether and choose their own man.

JEFFERSON (*grimly*). They would be smashing the Constitution.

HAMILTON. Stretching it!

JEFFERSON (*rises*). Smashing it, I say. (HAMILTON *shrugs his shoulders, turns to go.*) Have you seen the crowds about the Capitol Building?

HAMILTON. A pistol-shot and they'd disperse.

JEFFERSON. Don't deceive yourself! Our people will not be *"put aside."* (*Hands him a letter.*) From Maryland. Fifteen hundred men met last night. Resolved: If anyone dares usurp the Presidency, they will come here in a body and assassinate him. (*He picks up several letters.*) From Governor McKean of Pennsylvania . . . From Governor Monroe of Virginia. Their militia are ready to march at a moment's notice. If you put aside this election tonight, tomorrow morning there will be blood in the streets.

HAMILTON. I am an old soldier, Mr. Jefferson. If you give us no alternative . . .

JEFFERSON. But you have an alternative. End this deadlock at once! Use your influence with your friends. I shall use mine. Make Aaron Burr President.

HAMILTON. Aren't you being whimsical?

JEFFERSON. No. I should honestly prefer that.

HAMILTON. So you want Aaron Burr to be President?

JEFFERSON. He's a superior man, energetic, sharp, believes in our people.

HAMILTON. God! You're gullible! I know the man. He despises your Democracy more than I. Yet he has chimed in with all its absurdities. Why? Because he is cunning, and audacious, and absolutely without morality—possessed of only one principle, to get power by any means and keep it by all.

JEFFERSON. That's an opinion.

HAMILTON. That's a fact. He has said it to me to my face. A dozen times.

JEFFERSON. He has sworn the contrary to me.

HAMILTON. Burr has been bankrupt for years. Yet he spent vast sums of money on this campaign. Where do they come from?

JEFFERSON. I don't know.

HAMILTON. What do you think has been the sole topic of conversation at his dinner table? To whom are the toasts drunk? Can you guess?

JEFFERSON. No.

HAMILTON. The man who supplies his funds, the man with whose agents he is in daily conference.

JEFFERSON. What man?

HAMILTON. Bonaparte.

JEFFERSON. Bonaparte? I can hardly . . .

HAMILTON (*extracts some documents from his pocket and places them on the desk*). Proofs, if you wish them. Burr is the Cataline of America. He'll dare anything. You may as well think to bind a giant by cobwebs as his ambition by promises. Once President, he'd destroy all our institutions. Usurp for himself complete and permanent power. Make himself dictator.

JEFFERSON. I know you have no faith in them, but do you think the American people would stand idly by?

HAMILTON. No, I have no faith in them. But they'd fight. I grant you that. There'd be bloody civil war! And that's all Bonaparte would need. He would swoop down on us—(*Slams his fist on the desk.*) Like that! (*Long pause. JEFFERSON picks up the "proofs," studies them.*) Now you know my motive. I'm afraid, I'm profoundly afraid for the happiness of this country. (HAMILTON *examines the bust of* WASHINGTON.) Currachi?

JEFFERSON (*looks up from the "proofs"*). Yes.

HAMILTON. Excellent! I've commissioned him to sculp one of the Great Man for me. (JEFFERSON *looks up, sighs.*) Well? (JEFFERSON *lays down the papers. He is tired and confused.*) You've been duped, my friend.

JEFFERSON (*smiles feebly*). I suspected only you.

HAMILTON. Of what?

JEFFERSON. Planning to be our Bonaparte.

HAMILTON. When Washington died, I could have. Why didn't I?

JEFFERSON. Why?

HAMILTON. Burr asked me that question. Contemptuously. This may be difficult for you, but try to grasp it. I happen to love this country, too. I have fought for it in field and council. Above every small selfish personal desire, I want to see it peaceful and prosperous and strong. (*Triumphant*) Well? Will you meet my terms? (*Pause.*)

JEFFERSON (*miserably*). I can't.

HAMILTON (*moves to desk*). My conscience is clear. I know how to proceed.

JEFFERSON. If you do this, it can only lead to the very thing you condemn.

HAMILTON (*reaches for papers*). Perhaps. Perhaps that is the only hope for us in a world of Bonapartes and Burrs.

JEFFERSON. Then what will we have gained?

HAMILTON. Good day, Mr. Jefferson. (*Goes to the door.*)

JEFFERSON (*rising*). I warn you, there will be bloodshed tomorrow.

HAMILTON. Oh, no, there won't. You see, I'm counting on you. You will prevent it.

JEFFERSON (*with sudden new-born fierceness*). You're wrong, my friend.

HAMILTON (*pauses, turns*). You'd condone it?

JEFFERSON (*crosses to* HAMILTON). I'd be part of it.

HAMILTON. You?

JEFFERSON (*growls*). I.

HAMILTON (*returns, looks at him, surprised*). You really mean it.

JEFFERSON. By the God that made me, I mean it. I'd open my veins and yours in a second.

HAMILTON. You amaze me.

JEFFERSON. Why? Isn't the blood of

patriots and tyrants the natural manure for liberty?

HAMILTON. You've become a tough old man.

JEFFERSON. Who made me tough?

HAMILTON (*laughs ironically*). Then I haven't lived in vain.

JEFFERSON. That's right. (HAMILTON *is staring at* JEFFERSON.) Listen to me, Hamilton!

HAMILTON. This is a strange . . .

JEFFERSON. Listen to me! I know you love this country. But you have never understood it. You're afraid of Bonaparte? Well, there's no need to be. Bonaparte will die and his tyrannies will die, and we will be living, and we will be free. You're afraid of Burr? If Burr tries any quixotic adventures, he will smash himself against the rocks of our people. You see, this is the mistake you have always made. You have never properly estimated the character of the American people. You still don't understand them. At this moment. (*There is a long silence.*)

HAMILTON. I confess it. I don't. (*Sits.*)

JEFFERSON (*standing over him. Gently*). This is not the way, Hamilton. Believe me. If you really love this country, this isn't the way. Our people who fought the revolution from a pure love of liberty, who made every sacrifice and met every danger, did not expend their blood and substance to change this master for that. (*His voice grows strong.*) But to take their freedom in their own hands so that never again would the corrupt will of one man oppress them. You'll not make these people hold their breath at the caprice, or submit to the rods and the hatchet of a dictator. You cannot fix fear in their hearts, or make fear their principle of government. I know them. I place my faith in them. I have no fears for their ultimate victory.

HAMILTON (*wavering*). I wish I had such faith. (*Shakes his head.*) I don't know. I frankly don't know. I find *myself lost here.* Day by day, I am becoming more foreign to this land.

JEFFERSON. Yet you helped build it.

HAMILTON. There is a tide here that sweeps men to the fashioning of some strange destiny, even against their will. I never believed in this—and yet, as you say, I helped build it. Every inch of it. (*Pause. He rises.*) And still, I must admit it has worked better than I thought. If it could survive—if . . .

JEFFERSON. It can. And it will. This tide is irresistible. You cannot hold it back. This is the rising flood of man's long lost freedom. Try as you will, you cannot stop it. You may deflect it for a moment. But in the end you will lose. Try the old way of tyranny and usurpation and you *must* lose. Bonapartes may retard the epoch of man's deliverance, they may bathe the world in rivers of blood yet to flow, and still, still, in the end, they will fall back exhausted in their own blood, leaving mankind to liberty and self-government. No, General Hamilton, this way you lose. Believe me. (*He crosses to his desk, crisp and final.*) I shall not compromise, General Hamilton. You do whatever you choose. I cannot compromise on this.

HAMILTON (*holds out his hand. It is shaky*). Since the fever took me, I can't hit the side of a barn with a pistol. Burr is cool as a snake, and one of the best shots in America. I've fought him for five years now. If I cross him in *this*—he will challenge me. I have no doubt of that. I am a dead man already. But at least you are honest. I shall urge my friends to break the deadlock. You will be President. Your victory is complete.

JEFFERSON. There is no personal victory in this for me. I didn't *want* this for myself. I still don't. If it will give you any satisfaction, my own affairs have been neglected so long . . . In another office, with time to mend them, I might

have saved myself from bankruptcy. As President, I am certain to lose everything I possess, including Monticello, where my wife and four of my children lie. Where all the dreams of my youth lie. No matter! I thank you—for a glorious misery.

(HAMILTON *bows, goes.* JEFFERSON *turns, stares at the statue of* WASHINGTON.)

SCENE II

SCENE: *The interior of the Senate Chamber.*
JEFFERSON, *hand raised, is taking the oath of office from* CHIEF JUSTICE MARSHALL.

JEFFERSON. I do solemnly swear that I will faithfully execute the office of President of the United States, and will, to the best of my ability, preserve, protect, and defend the Constitution of the United States.

(JUSTICE MARSHALL *waves* JEFFERSON *to assembled audience. Nervously, hesitantly,* JEFFERSON *steps forward to the audience, looks about. His glance rests on* PATSY, *standing proudly with* ANNE *and* JEFF. PATSY *smiles and nods.* JEFFERSON *faintly smiles. He turns to the audience, begins to speak in a voice hesitant and uncertain.*)

JEFFERSON. Friends and fellow citizens: Called upon to undertake the duties of the first executive of our country, I will avail myself of the presence of that portion of my fellow citizens which is here assembled to express my grateful thanks for the favor with which they have been pleased to look upon me. A rising nation spread over a wide and fruitful land, advancing rapidly to destinies beyond the reach of mortal eye— when I contemplate these transcendent objects and see the honor, the happiness and the hopes of this beloved country committed to the issue of this day, I— I shrink before the magnitude of the undertaking. Utterly, indeed, should I

despair if not for the presence of many whom I see here. To you, then, I look for that guidance and support which may enable us to steer with safety the vessel in which we are all embarked amid the conflicting elements of a troubled world.

This is the sum of good government. Equal and exact justice to all men, of whatever state or persuasion, a jealous care of the right of election, absolute acquiescence to the decisions of the majority, the vital principle of republics, from which is no appeal but to *force,* the vital principle and parent of despotism . . . Freedom of religion, freedom of press, freedom of person, and trial by juries impartially selected. These form the bright constellation which has gone before us and which has guided us in an age of revolution and reformation. The wisdom of our sages, and the blood of our heroes have attained them for us. They are the creed of our political faith, the touchstone of our public servants. Should we wander from them in moments of error or alarm, let us hasten to retrace our steps and to regain this road which alone leads to peace, liberty and safety. During the present throes and convulsions of the ancient world, during these agonizing spasms of blood and slaughter abroad, it was not strange that the agitation of the billows should reach even this distant and peaceful shore. That this should be more felt and feared by some than by others. I know, indeed, that some honest men fear that a republic cannot be strong, that this government is not strong enough. But would the honest patriot in the full tide of successful experiment, abandon a government which has so far kept us free and firm, on the theoretic fear that it may possibly want energy to preserve itself? I trust not. I believe this, on the contrary, the only government where every man would fly to the standard and meet invasions of the public order as his own personal concern. I believe this the strongest government on earth. I believe, indeed, I know, this government is the world's best hope . . .